From the New Deal to the War on Schools

DANIEL S. MOAK

From the New Deal to the War on Schools

Race, Inequality, and the Rise of the Punitive Education State

The University of North Carolina Press *Chapel Hill*

This book was published with the assistance of the Anniversary Fund of the University of North Carolina Press.

Set in Arno Pro by Westchester Publishing Services
Manufactured in the United States of America

The University of North Carolina Press has been a member of the
Green Press Initiative since 2003.

Library of Congress Cataloging-in-Publication Data
Names: Moak, Daniel S., author.
Title: From the New Deal to the war on schools : race, inequality, and the rise of
 the punitive education state / Daniel S. Moak.
Description: Chapel Hill : University of North Carolina Press, [2022] |
 Includes bibliographical references and index.
Identifiers: LCCN 2021054798 | ISBN 9781469668192 (cloth) |
 ISBN 9781469668208 (paperback) | ISBN 9781469668215 (ebook)
Subjects: LCSH: Education—United States—History—20th century. | Racism
 in education—United States—History—20th century. | Discrimination in
 education—United States—History—20th century. | United States—Social
 policy—20th century.
Classification: LCC LA209 .M58 2022 | DDC 370.973—dc23/eng/20211116
LC record available at https://lccn.loc.gov/2021054798

Cover illustration: Broken pencil by Mark S. Moak.

To my first teachers, my parents,
Mark Moak and Rhett Moak
and the many other teachers
who made this book possible

Contents

Acknowledgments

I first became fully aware of the deeply political nature of education in 2002 during my junior year of high school. The teachers of School District 2 in Billings, Montana, after years of languishing wages and rising insurance costs, and in the face of the new threat of No Child Left Behind, went on strike for the first time in twenty-seven years. For three weeks, they demonstrated the power of collective action as they articulated demands that centered the value of education as a public good. Shortly before Thanksgiving, their efforts resulted in substantial victories. That moment, and the discussion with teachers that followed, was a turning point for me. For this, and for the tireless efforts of all of the teachers throughout my time in the public school system, I am forever grateful to the teachers of the Billings Public Schools.

I was fortunate enough to have brilliant mentors throughout my time in higher education. The earliest germs of this project were developed in Melissa Buis Michaux's transformational classroom at Willamette University, and I still hear the voices of David Gutterman and Sally Markowitz in my mind when I write. Rogers Smith and Sigal Ben-Porath have offered extensive feedback and mentorship for the last ten years. Marie Gottschalk, my mentor since my first day of graduate school, has never stopped providing support and insight. Her patience, perspective-shifting teaching, and committed scholarship are testaments to what academia can be at its best. Throughout many seminar courses, one-on-one meetings, and after-work drinks, Adolph Reed has profoundly shaped my view of the world. His friendship throughout this process has made a difficult road much more enjoyable, and his dedication to fighting for working people provides a source of continuous inspiration.

Throughout my time in graduate school at the University of Pennsylvania, I was fortunate enough to meet and become friends with incredibly gifted scholars and outstanding human beings. Their influence is present throughout this book. Thank you to Emmerich Davies, Joshua Darr, Chelsea Schafer, Ian Hartshorn, Joanna Wuest, Carly Regina, Danielle Hanley, Anthony Grasso, Evan Perkowski, Laura Silver, Chris Brown, Allison Evans, David Bateman, and Tim Weaver.

For providing an intellectual home and encouragement, I want to thank the faculty and staff of the African American Studies Department at Ohio

University. Gary Holcomb, Akil Houston, Bayyinah Jeffries, Robin Dearmon Muhammad, and Patricia Gunn have been steadfast in their support, especially when times have been tough.

My Ohio University colleagues from outside my department have been critical for finishing the project. Nicole Kaufmann, Haley Duschinski, Yeong-Hyun Kim, Larry Hayman, Jennifer Fredette, Lauren Elliot-Dorans, and Kathleen Sullivan provided guidance and encouragement at critical parts of the process. I am particularly indebted to Kirstine Taylor, Susan Burgess, Kate Leeman, Laura Black, Ted Welser, Marina Baldisserra Pachetti, and Yoichi Ishida—the Mystic Monday squad—who offered support and love when I needed it most.

No person had greater influence on this project than Sarah Cate. She has read every word of every iteration of this book, for which I am both sorry and incredibly grateful. Her critical eye and profound intellect has made this project better and her wisdom, selflessness, and humor has made my life better.

I am so grateful for the people at the University of North Carolina (UNC) Press. Brandon Proia, my editor, has been a joy to work with. This book could not have happened without his careful feedback and encouragement. I would also like to thank series editors Rhonda Williams and Heather Ann Thompson for their support. Thank you also to the staff of UNC Press, and to the anonymous reviewers.

I am particularly thankful for the committed public servants at the Krassel Fire Office on the Payette National Forest. Their support of fire lookouts is unrivaled, and I am incredibly proud to work with them. And thank you to Williams Peak—which provided support by way of long walks, unmatched views, and huckleberries.

My parents, Mark and Rhett Moak, were the first to teach me that the value of education extended beyond some abstract future financial reward. Their skills in the classroom and their life-changing impact on their students inevitably inspired me to attempt to follow in their footsteps. Their tireless support, encouragement, and love made this endeavor possible. I will never be able to thank them enough. My sisters, Leah and Ellen, have been my first, fiercest, and most frequent intellectual challengers on matters big and small. The ability to run ideas by their two brilliant minds has been invaluable, and their humor has kept me laughing—and humble—for over three decades. Huck has been a loyal and constant companion throughout this process and has reminded me that walks are an essential part of the creative process. For teaching me to struggle for a better world, you all have my thanks and my love.

Abbreviations Used in the Text

AFT	American Federation of Teachers
ATA	American Teachers Association
BRL	Behavioral Research Laboratories
CEA	Council of Economic Advisors
CIO	Congress of Industrial Organizations
CORE	Congress of Racial Equality
CPUSA	Communist Party of the United States of America
CRC	Civil Rights Congress
CSPP	Center for the Study of Public Policy
CTU	Chicago Teachers Union
DAR	Daughters of the American Revolution
DHEW	Department of Health, Education, and Welfare
ESEA	Elementary and Secondary Education Act
ESSA	Every Student Succeeds Act
HUAC	House Un-American Activities Committee
JNE	*Journal of Negro Education*
MARC	Metropolitan Applied Research Center
NAACP	National Association for the Advancement of Colored People
NCLB	No Child Left Behind
NEA	National Education Association
NLRA	National Labor Relations Act
NNC	National Negro Congress
NSSFNS	National Scholarship Service and Fund for Negro Students
NUL	National Urban League
OEO	Office of Economic Opportunity
RTT	Race to the Top

SNCC   Student Nonviolent Coordinating Committee
UN   United Nations
USOE   U.S. Office of Education
WTU   Washington Teachers' Union

From the New Deal to the War on Schools

The Politics of the Federal Education State

Faith in Education and the Turn toward Punitiveness

On July 23, 2010, Washington, D.C.'s chancellor of education Michelle Rhee fired 241 teachers in a single day. In addition to roughly 5 percent of the total teachers in the district, sixty-one other district employees lost their jobs, including librarians, counselors, and custodians.[1] The mass layoff was just the latest evidence of the expansive nature of the aggressive education reform occurring in Washington, D.C.—and throughout the nation.

Rhee had quickly commenced restructuring public education in the nation's capital after being appointed to the newly created position of chancellor in 2007. Backed by millions of dollars from the nonprofit foundations of some of the nation's most prominent billionaires, including $25 million from the Walton Foundation, Rhee went to war with the D.C. teachers' union.[2] In her short three-and-a-half-year tenure, Rhee closed or reconstituted dozens of traditional public schools, pushed for the expansion of charter schools, and tied the pay of teachers, principals, and even janitors to student test scores. The effects were dramatic. Rhee fired or dismissed approximately 1,000 educators during her time as chancellor, and by the end of her tenure, only half of the teachers and principals that had been there when she started were still in the district.[3]

Politicians and media outlets from across the political spectrum praised Rhee's harsh reforms as necessary to save an education system whose failure to serve America's children had reached the point of crisis. In the 2008 presidential campaign, Barack Obama and John McCain argued about whose education vision was more in line with Rhee's, and *Time* magazine published an issue with Rhee on the cover with a broom next to the headline "How to Fix America's Schools."[4] President Obama maintained this commitment to education reform after being elected, and the Obama administration devoted more than a billion dollars to the promotion of "performance-based" reforms like those pursued by Rhee in D.C.[5] Cities and states across the country rushed to replicate versions of the reforms pursued in Washington, D.C. In Philadelphia, an unelected school reform commission voted to close twenty-three neighborhood schools over intense community opposition, disrupting the education of well over 10,000 of the city's students.[6] In Louisiana, Republican governor Bobby Jindal signed sweeping education legislation that reduced tenure protection for schoolteachers, made it easier to establish charter schools, and expanded the state's voucher program.[7] After being elected mayor of Chicago, President Obama's former chief of staff, Democrat Rahm Emanuel, pursued his own school reform efforts, which culminated in the largest intentional mass closure of public schools in the nation's history.[8]

Remarkably, the faith in these policies remains widespread even in the face of mounting evidence of negative educational consequences, particularly for the poor and communities of color. Teachers across the country have seen their working conditions and job security deteriorate—and thousands more have been fired—with teachers of color often bearing the brunt of these changes.[9] In Washington, D.C., as the district continues to shut down schools with low test scores, the scramble to find new academic homes with little connection to friends or neighborhoods is an increasingly common part of everyday life for parents and schoolchildren.[10] As hundreds of millions of dollars in federal funds flowed into charter schools that were shut down due to mismanagement or never even opened, tens of thousands of students in the greater Washington, D.C., area were being denied hot lunches due to student lunch debt.[11] While politicians and reformers continue to point to Rhee's D.C. education reforms as the model for the country, the district was investigated by the FBI, the U.S. Department of Education, and the D.C. Office of the Inspector General for a number of scandals, including a massive manipulation of the high school graduation rate.[12] Despite this evidence, less than two weeks after his 2016 victory, President-elect Donald Trump met with—and effusively praised—Michelle Rhee as he was considering her for the position of secretary of education.[13] Although President Trump ultimately chose conservative activist Betsy Devos, the new secretary of education was Rhee's ideological ally—and as chairperson of the school voucher advocacy group American Federation for Children had lavished praise and an award on Rhee for her reform agenda.[14] After touring several states supporting legislation aimed at eliminating collective bargaining rights, expanding charter schools and vouchers, and improving teacher quality, Rhee eventually moved to Sacramento where she now serves as the chair of the board for a charter school chain that she owns with her husband.[15]

The reforms pushed by Michelle Rhee and others are just the latest consequences of political decisions and developments that occurred more than fifty years ago. A policy landscape that prescribes intensive standardized testing for students and ties the fate of public schools and teachers to these scores is not simply the result of the choices of the latest wave of "innovative" policy actors. Rather, the widespread adoption of these policies is the result of decades of ideological and institutional changes that have shaped Americans' understanding of the purpose and value of education. A full explanation of why policy makers across the country have embraced decidedly punitive education policies requires an examination of the remarkable debates and developments in how we conceptualize the sources of inequality, poverty, and the ideal democratic society.

From the New Deal to the War on Schools tells the story of why K–12 education is dominated by punitive policies aimed at schools, teachers, and students. Through tracing the ideological conflicts, the shifting coalitions, and the surprising construction of the federal education state since the mid-twentieth century, this book explains how we came to believe that education can solve seemingly intractable problems, and why this belief pushes us toward policies that punish teachers and schools when education fails to repair deeper problems. Through analyzing the origins of today's punitive education landscape, this book seeks to offer a clear analysis of how we got here in the hopes of providing a foundation for an alternative vision for the future.

Liberal Incorporation and the Punitive Federal Education State

Since the 1960s, the belief that education holds the key to individual success, social mobility, and racial equality has driven the construction of an expansive and increasingly punitive federal education state committed to addressing broad social problems through the public education system. This faith in education that drives both increased federal funding and increased expectations is the hallmark of the liberal incorporationist education order. Established during the Great Society, this order is *liberal* in its commitment to extend to all the liberal democratic ideal of equality of opportunity through education, backed by a robust commitment of the federal government. The order is *incorporationist* in its goal of bringing all citizens, particularly racial minorities and other disadvantaged groups, into the broader existing economic and social structures. For racial minorities, incorporation implied integration and educational opportunity in order to ensure the ability to compete on equitable terms with their white counterparts. Incorporation requires the elimination of arbitrary barriers to success—like race—and adjusting individuals to succeed in the established societal structures. Importantly, incorporation suggests that the broader existing economic and social structure will remain intact. Although alternative visions of education that centered the need for worker solidarity, teacher activism, and reconstruction of the economic order had enjoyed popularity during the New Deal era, since the 1960s the commitment to liberal incorporation has been the lodestar of the dominant educational order.[16]

The passage of the Elementary and Secondary Education Act (ESEA) in 1965 represented a critical juncture in the building of the federal education state and helped usher in this new educational order. The liberal incorporationist consensus that education was the most effective means of addressing the issue of unemployment and poverty created a powerful coalition in Congress to push for federal involvement in elementary and secondary education. The interpretation of poverty and unemployment as largely attributable to individual deficiencies in skill or culture drove the compensatory approach of ESEA, in which funds were targeted toward the disadvantaged poor.[17] The focus on disadvantaged students through compensatory aid was a significant shift, as federal lawmakers had tried—and failed—to pass general education aid for all students since the late 1800s.

Federal policy makers built an education order in which faith in education as a solution to poverty, unemployment, and racial disparities led to the development of an increasingly punitive education state. Those on the left concerned with inequality, unemployment, and the status of racial minorities— but ultimately unwilling to fundamentally challenge the economic system— looked to education as the most effective way to solve these problems. By adopting an understanding of these problems as best addressed at the individual rather than the structural level, these actors turned to education as an alternative to more direct economic redistribution or federal intervention in the labor market.

In the years following 1965, this educational order justified an expansive federal commitment in the realm of education. It also led to demands that schools be held accountable for addressing poverty, unemployment, and racial inequality. These lofty expectations meant that funding was attached to increasingly harsh measures to ensure accountability. Teachers who fail to raise test scores face loss of pay and firing; students who fail to meet sufficient scores on standardized exit exams face denial of high school diplomas; and schools that fail to achieve testing benchmarks face transformation into a charter school, privatization, or closure.

The educational commitments established during the Great Society continue to drive education policies. The term *punitive* when describing education is most often associated with suspensions, expulsions, and the relationship between schools and the justice system—all of which are significant features of the current landscape. However, I also want to draw attention to the relationship of *punitive governmentality* that has increasingly targeted schools, teachers, and students.[18] As the federal government has expanded its authority in the realm of education, it has embraced policies that seek to regulate actions within the education system through the threat of disciplinary action if actors fail to enact its normatively desired goals. The liberal incorporationist education order has not only changed policies but also shifted the ways in which policy makers and the public understand the purpose and problems of education. As policy makers increasingly embraced the idea that schools could solve myriad social problems, they also embraced punitive policies such as closing neighborhood schools, firing teachers, attacking tenure protections, and privatizing "low-performing" schools when these social problems continued. The punitive governmentality of the liberal incorporationist order is one where schools and teachers are given impossible tasks and then punished for failing to achieve them.

The reality is that schools could not—and cannot—counter the major drivers of poverty, unemployment, and inequality. Greater federal education funding could do little to address the effects of automation or deindustrialization. Demanding higher standards and more standardized tests does little to alter the reality of a labor market where wages and union power have been steadily hollowed out over the last fifty years. Although changes in the labor market are beyond the schools' control, policy makers embraced education as a panacea for the deficiencies of the broader political economy. The resilience of the liberal incorporationist faith in education has positioned schools as both savior and scapegoat, facilitated the rise of punitive accountability policies, and pushed alternative redistributive political economic approaches into the background.

Rethinking the Origins of the Federal Education State

As politicians from across the country and across the political spectrum have enthusiastically embraced punitive accountability education reforms, the distinctly negative consequences of these reforms on students, teachers, and the public education system more broadly have come into clear focus. Researchers have found evidence that the high-stakes tests and punitive turnaround strategies for failing schools such as transformation into charters, merit pay for teachers, privatization, and school closure required by No Child Left Behind (NCLB) and Race to the Top (RTT) have had numerous and severe unintended consequences. In the classroom, studies have suggested that these reforms have narrowed the curriculum,[19] caused teachers to focus on border-line or "bubble" students most likely to increase their test scores,[20] led to deceitful reclassification or expulsion of low-performing students as a means of raising test averages,[21] increased teacher turnover and decreased teacher satisfaction,[22] and increased student dropout rates.[23] Scholars have also found that these negative consequences disproportionally affect the poor, students of color, and urban communities.[24] These outcomes and their inequitable distribution have led to serious concerns that the current educational policy landscape is hobbling the democratic responsiveness and purpose of public education.[25]

As evidence of the negative consequences of recent educational reforms has become widespread, scholars from several disciplines have sought to explain the origins of these policies. While some scholars suggest that the ideological roots for current reforms stretch back the late 1970s,[26] education professor Ann Winfield reflects a broad consensus in claiming, "the historical dividing line that marks the starting point for the present era, few would argue, is the election of Ronald Reagan."[27] According to these accounts, the "conservative restoration" brought to power a broad coalition of groups opposed to egalitarian Great Society education policy. This coalition composed of religious conservatives seeking greater funding for religious schools and a greater religious emphasis in the public classroom,[28] neoconservatives concerned about declining test scores and a decaying national culture,[29] and neoliberal and corporate interests seeking to introduce market forces in public education are pointed to as the progenitors of the current constellation of punitive education policies.[30]

Several existing accounts point to the inflammatory 1983 *Nation at Risk* report and the 1988 ESEA reauthorization as critical moments in the reorientation of the federal education state.[31] As fears of a loss of national standing and decreased social mobility drove public dissatisfaction with public education, this coalition successfully pushed for reforms that centered on holding schools accountable. The changes initiated by the political right were solidified in the 1990s as members of the Democratic Party recognized the need to adjust their stance as Republican efforts gained traction with voters. This shift accelerated as it became clear that many of the educational policies advocated by the Republican Party appealed to many racial minority and urban families, constituencies that were traditionally Democratic.[32] Since the passage of the NCLB in 2001, Democrats and Republicans have been united in pressing for market-based reforms as a means of improving education. This bipartisan consensus on the appropriate role and policies of the modern federal education state is positioned as having its foundations in the "watershed of a new economic and political world order" ushered in by the Reagan Revolution.[33] Scholarship from the fields of political science and education points to the 1980s as a moment of a paradigm shift in education, when excellence replaced equity as the guiding principle of the federal education state, ushering in policies designed to raise the educational achievement of all students through clear standards, accountability, and standardized testing.[34]

However, this book illuminates the fact that demands for accountability were coupled with policies like sanctions and annual testing in the original construction of the federal education state in 1965. In this earlier era, the most vocal supporters of accountability policies in federal education came predominantly from the political left and civil rights advocates. To fully grasp the ideological and institutional precursors to the current moment requires an understanding of how the cleavages and battles of the 1930s through the 1950s resulted in the construction of a federal education state centered on holding schools responsible for solving poverty, racial disparity, and unemployment. Accountability politics and policies were firmly established in the federal education state well before the 1980s. Pointing to the 1980s as the origins of this movement masks the considerable ideological continuity between the 1960s and 1980s in federal education policy.[35] The accountability turn in education policy emerged from the ideological battles of the 1930s through the 1950s and was firmly institutionalized in the Great Society expansion of the federal education state.

This account adds to a growing literature that argues that the political compromises and state-building efforts of the New Deal and Great Society eras were critical to facilitating the neoliberal turn in social policy.[36] Scholars have demonstrated how the ideological and state-building activity of the mid-twentieth century stunted redistributive welfare policies, laid the foundation for punitive approaches to social problems, and shaped the direction of social policy for decades.[37] As these accounts suggest, an examination of ideological debates of the 1930s through the 1950s and the state-building activities of the Great Society is key in understanding the origins of the education policies that characterize the current era.

In surveying the deeper origins of current policies and institutions, scholars have argued that the role of race looms large in explaining the peculiarities of the American social welfare state. This scholarship, which focuses on the ways in which race has shaped the institutional structure of the welfare state, suggests the need for close attention to the role of race in the development of the federal education state.[38] In addition to shaping the institutional structure of the welfare state, scholars from a wide array of disciplines have shown how racial ideology has shaped the political demands and agendas of individuals and coalitions, particularly those of Black Americans.[39] Tracing the important political and policy consequences of developments in racial ideology points to the need for an examination of the role of race in structuring the ideological contours of the educational order. Close attention to the ideological and institutional consequences of race in American political development helps illuminate why certain ideologies, coalitions, and institutions gained prominence and how they continue to shape the educational landscape.

One of the most striking aspects of the education state is the ideological continuity guiding its development for the last fifty years. An examination of the ideas that shaped, and continue to shape, the institutional development of the federal education state is a critical component in understanding the educational order.[40] The shifting ideological understanding of what school could and should do is critical in explaining the institutional development of the federal education state—and the current educational landscape. Focusing on the history of these different educational visions allows us to uncover the ways in which these ideas helped construct coalitions and shaped the way the public and policy makers interpreted social problems and the purpose of education. Investigating the individuals, coalitions, and institutions enlisted in supporting one vision of education over another helps explains why some visions win and others lose out—and how the winning vision drove institutional development. The work of uncovering the foundation of the current federal education order—dominated by holding schools, teachers, and students accountable through increasingly punitive means—is critical to fighting against its many harmful effects.

Historical Conflicts and the Origins of Punitive Education Policies

My account begins with the debate over the purpose of education during the Great Depression. The three chapters in part I trace the rise and fall of the economic transformational coalition and its replacement with a coalition committed to an educational system that did not radically challenge existing economic structures. Relying on a comprehensive review of some of the most influential professional education journals between 1932 and 1970 (*The Social Frontier, Frontiers of Democracy,* and *The Journal of Negro Education*) and the papers of key thinkers (including George Counts, Edward Thorndike, Thurgood Marshall, and Bayard Rustin), I show that throughout the

1930s and into the 1940s a powerful alliance of educational progressives and civil rights activists advocated for an educational pedagogy centered on transforming the existing social structures, with the aim of greater equality through economic redistribution. These educational progressives stressed the need to ground education policy and aims in a strong commitment to economic equality as a critical aspect of democratic citizenship.

The development of this economic egalitarian coalition fostered the growth of a counter movement of racial liberals and scientific efficiency educators seeking a fairer and more effective education system within the existing economic framework. These groups ultimately formed a broad coalition united by a commitment to equality of educational opportunity in a free market economic system, or what I term a *liberal incorporationist ideology*. Significantly, the purpose of education that emerged from the battles of this time period was strongly connected to human capital and culture of poverty theory. Liberal incorporationists advocated for equality of opportunity for all races within the existing economic structure and pushed for the development of standardized testing as a means of guiding education policy and holding educators accountable.

Chapter 1 follows a group of progressive educators known as the social reconstructionists who began to articulate a vision of education and the public school system as the handmaiden of economic transformation in the early 1930s. Led by George Counts and his best-selling 1932 pamphlet *Dare the Schools Build a New Social Order?*,[41] the social reconstructionists were highly critical of the excessive individualism, exploitation, and widespread poverty that characterized the existing economic order. With John Dewey and Harold Rugg, among others, this group included many of the most prominent education leaders of the era. The social reconstructionists advocated for a new educational approach in which teachers in the public schools would be the vanguard of social transformation away from an exploitative economic system.

As the social reconstructionists were pushing for changes to the economic structure in the 1930s and early 1940s, a number of Black intellectuals were urging civil rights groups to shift their focus to an economic analysis of the problems facing Black people in the United States. Some of the most influential Black leaders of the era, including Ralph Bunche, A. Phillip Randolph, and Doxey Wilkerson, were part of this group. These authors cautioned that the existing strategic course had placed too much emphasis on the racial aspect of problems like poverty and unemployment. They pushed for an analysis that placed the origins of these problems squarely as a result of an exploitative economic system. This group was committed to a vision of economic democracy, in which the education system would educate students on the importance of interracial class consciousness, the necessity of unionization, and the need for government-supported full employment.

These economic progressive visions of education's purpose were some of the most prominent views expressed throughout the 1930s and into the early 1940s. Both the social reconstructionists and economic democrats offered an understanding of education that stressed the need to ground education policy and aims in a strong commitment to economic equality as a critical aspect of democratic citizenship. Ultimately, since these groups traced the responsibility for unemployment, poverty, and racial inequality to the economic system, any educational program that hoped to address these problems would have to take aim at the economic system itself.

Despite their prevalence, these economic analyses always sat uneasily with many on the political left who were less comfortable directly challenging the economic system. Throughout the 1930s, 1940s, and 1950s, a fierce debate played out among those on the left over how far to push the challenge to the existing economic order. Within the progressive education movement, the social reconstructionist position competed with the position offered by the scientific efficiency progressives. Although both fell under the broad banner of the progressive education movement, they differed considerably in respect to their end goals and pedagogy. Scientific efficiency progressives were committed to developing the educational tools that would most efficiently aid the adjustment of the individual into the existing economic and social structures. These educators pushed for the implementation of educational tools like intelligence and achievement testing, student tracking, and vocational training to aid in the creation of a meritocratic society. Importantly, the scientific efficiency progressives saw the appropriate role of education as facilitating the entrance of students into the existing economic and social structure. Chapter 1 maps the political and policy cleavages between the social reconstructionist educational coalition grounded in a critique of the economic system and a counter coalition of scientific efficiency progressives committed to introducing scientific educational methods in order to aid the adjustment of individuals into the labor market.

As chapter 2 demonstrates, a similar divide characterized thinking about Black education, as several prominent Black intellectuals who were uncomfortable with the more radical claims of the economic democrats called instead for a program of racial democracy.[42] This group sought fair incorporation into the existing order, or for Black people to be treated "like everyone else," rather than broad transformation of the economy.[43] Instead of capitalism, these authors identified racial prejudice and cultural problems among lower-class Black people as foundational to disparate levels of Black poverty, unemployment, and other social inequalities.[44] The educational perspective of these racial democrats was focused on preparing Black students for fair competition with their white counterparts through programs aimed at combating white prejudice, facilitating cultural assimilation, and ensuring the equitable provision of educational opportunity. These scholars saw public education as one of the most effective means of addressing the most pressing problems facing the Black community including poverty, unemployment, and racial inequality.

Chapter 3 traces a number of important political developments in the 1940s and 1950s that help explain why the racial democracy and scientific efficiency visions of education became dominant. The shifting international context at the end of World War II meant that the federal government was particularly concerned about domestic racial politics. Facing the need to appeal to a number of non-white nations, the federal government increasingly embraced integration and racial democracy as a means of demonstrating the appeal of the U.S. economic and political system.[45] At the same time, federal courts became increasingly sympathetic to challenges to Jim Crow under the Equal Protection Clause. In the critical 1954 *Brown* case, the U.S. Supreme Court based its decision on the psychological (rather than material) harm that segregation posed to Black children, an argument that emerged from scholars committed to racial democracy. The judiciary's increasing willingness to accept equal protection arguments strengthened the hand of racial democrats.[46]

Another critical factor in the demise of the economic coalition was the brutal political repression of many of the most vocal supporters of social reconstruction and economic democracy during the Second Red Scare. As several scholars have noted, the loyalty investigations of the 1940s and 1950s had a chilling effect on individuals and coalitions on the political left.[47] The investigation of prominent intellectuals on the left like George Counts, Harold Rugg, and Doxey Wilkerson by state and national government officials had serious consequences for the ability of economic progressives to maintain social networks or organize politically. Indeed, under the threat of loyalty investigations, many openly rejected or substantially modified their earlier positions. Finally, the shifting macroeconomic position of federal policy makers in the 1940s created an environment that was much more amenable to the vision of education put forth by the scientific efficiency progressives and racial democrats. Moving away from a firm commitment to full employment, policy actors increasingly supported a "commercial Keynesianism" that privileged concerns about inflation and pursued tax cuts as the most effective means of economic management. Unlike their New Deal predecessors who argued unemployment was in large part the result of fundamental flaws in a market economy, commercial Keynesians shifted explanatory focus to the individual, arguing that unemployment was largely the result of marginal workers failing to keep up with skill demands of the changing labor market.[48]

Changes in the international context, court doctrines, political repression, and macroeconomic policy beliefs created a political situation in which the collective understanding of the purpose of the public education system shifted away from the economic progressive understandings that dominated the 1930s and 1940s. These political developments created the conditions that led to the establishment of a liberal incorporationist order in education. A broad coalition united by a commitment to providing equality of educational opportunity in a free market economic system supported this new liberal incorporationist education order. Racial democrats, pushing for fair incorporation into the existing economic and social structures, argued that such a commitment was necessary to address the undemocratic relegation of Black people to inferior status simply because of skin color. Scientific efficiency progressives, commercial Keynesians, and conservative economists backed this commitment to equitable educational opportunity as the most efficient way of ensuring individual success in the labor market and of effectively using national human resources. They positioned education as the best policy tool available to address the problems of poverty, unemployment, and racial disparity. Additionally, by the 1960s, as it became clear that the liberal incorporationist ideology was better able to accommodate the changing political environment, many prominent supporters of economic democracy shifted their positions to align more closely with that of liberal incorporation.[49] The education policy proposals that emerged were committed to facilitating incorporation into the existing economic and social structures, rather than challenging them.

Importantly, as part II of the book demonstrates, this understanding of education guided the construction of the federal education state. Covering the period between 1960 and 1980, the chapters in part II examine how the ideological understanding of education that emerged from prior debates structured the institutions of the new federal education state, with a particular focus on the role of federal policy makers and the 1965 ESEA and its subsequent amendments. The evidence for these chapters comes from the congressional record, presidential papers, and oral histories of the Kennedy, Johnson, and Nixon administrations.

The interpretation of poverty, unemployment, and racial disparity as attributable to individual deficiencies in skill or culture helped build a coalition of policy makers committed to addressing these problems through an expansive federal education state. The turn toward education coincided with a growing reluctance from Democratic lawmakers to use federal power to intervene in the national economy for redistributive purposes. This political context, coupled with the decisive ideological victory of the liberal incorporationist coalition described in part I, meant that much of the programmatic structure that emerged from the ESEA established a liberal incorporationist pedagogy and understanding of public education's purpose. Rather than stressing the need for economic reform, Great Society liberals shifted toward a narrower vision of equality that focused on the provision of equitable opportunity as sufficient for democratic legitimacy.

The liberal incorporationist framing of education as a solution to poverty, racial disparity, and unemployment provided a powerful vehicle for the establishment of the first major federal intervention in the realm of primary and secondary education policy, the 1965 ESEA. Indeed, it was this ideological framing that proved especially effective at neutralizing and overcoming much of the long-standing legislative opposition to an expansive federal role in education. Chapter 4 traces how the liberal incorporationist understanding of education both provided the justification for the ESEA and shaped the particular education policies that emerged. In his message to Congress urging passage of the ESEA, President Lyndon Johnson underlined its importance by arguing, "with education, instead of being condemned to poverty and idleness, young Americans can learn the skills to find a job and provide for a family."[50] This interpretation of the origins of poverty, unemployment, and racial disparity drove the institutional structure of the ESEA, which was centered on providing compensatory funds for schools with high numbers of disadvantaged students. The decision to invest heavily in education was a clear indication of the move away from more directly interventionist approaches to address these problems as policy makers sought to attack the hypothesized individual causes of poverty and unemployment rather than pursue broad macroeconomic solutions such as a commitment to full employment, public sector job creation, and strongly redistributive taxation.

Passage of the ESEA represented institutionalization at the federal level of the liberal incorporationist ideology that had emerged from earlier debates over the purpose of education. The institutionalization of this ideology marks a significant moment for the development of accountability policies in education. As Democrats backed off earlier commitments to full employment and strong federal intervention in the economy, the understanding of education as the central mechanism for overcoming poverty and unemployment also drove many policy makers and scholars to criticize public schools and teachers as responsible for these problems and to demand strict accountability for federal funds distributed by the ESEA. Senator Robert Kennedy (D-NY), U.S. Commissioner of Education Francis Keppel, psychologist Kenneth Clark, and other liberal incorporationists led the charge in the 1960s for extensive evaluation and reporting requirements and pointed to standardized tests as the best means of evaluating program success.[51] The belief that the equalization of educational opportunity would help eliminate poverty, unemployment, and racial disparities drove these educational policies.

Chapter 5 focuses on how building the ESEA on liberal incorporationist terms has framed and structured subsequent developments. As federal investment in education failed to show the lofty results predicted by the liberal incorporationists, federal policies grew increasingly punitive. Early reports indicating educational programs targeted toward the poor had little to no effect on educational outcomes prompted swift reaction from congressional actors. Disappointed policy makers passed a number of amendments in the 1960s and 1970s that increased evaluation and reporting requirements for ESEA programs and strengthened the reliance on standardized achievement tests as the best evaluation metric. Additionally, these amendments mandated strict sanctions against states and school systems that failed to meet expectations and increased funds for the enforcement activity of federal agencies in charge of oversight.

Beyond strengthening reporting and sanction efforts, the federal government began to fund experiments in education policies designed to punish schools for failing to solve social problems in the late 1960s and early 1970s. As prominent academics, activists, and large nonprofit foundations grew frustrated at evidence that suggested federal dollars had failed to improve test scores or reduce racial achievement gaps, they began to press for greater accountability for teachers and alternatives to traditional public schools. The liberal incorporationist coalition pushed the federal government to fund a number of early experiments in punitive accountability policies including strict standardized testing requirements, vouchers, merit-based teacher pay, and privatized alternatives to the public school system. Significantly, it was liberals that were the earliest and most ardent supporters in promoting these policies designed to punish schools for their perceived failures. As the liberal incorporationists kept the faith in education despite disappointing evidence, they increasingly blamed the public schools and teachers within them for the continued existence of poverty and racial inequality.

Establishing education as the solution to poverty, unemployment, and racial disparity ensured continued dissatisfaction with public education and drove punitive reforms. The concluding chapter briefly traces the convergence of the political parties from the mid-1980s through 2020 around a federal education state designed to hold schools accountable for social problems. Recent reauthorizations of the ESEA and other federal efforts indicate the resilience of liberal incorporationist understanding about the purpose and problems of education. Public education is seen as broken and the federal government is viewed as the most effective driver of badly needed reforms. Policies like high-stakes standardized tests, merit-based teacher pay, mass closings of schools deemed underperforming, and the expansion of charter and private options in schooling have become bipartisan solutions to a system in crisis. The result is a firmly entrenched federal education state committed to the use of these punitive accountability policies, with particularly pernicious consequences for the most disadvantaged.

Revisiting the founding of the federal education state clarifies that the turn to market incentives and punitive education policies is not a break from the liberal incorporationist education order. In fact, these reforms are the result of a constant source of tension embedded within the liberal incorporationist order. The vision of education as a solution to a number of social problems means that the continued existence of these problems spurred continuous calls for education reform. Harsh accountability policies are driven by the belief that if schools are effective in raising test scores and reducing racial disparities on these achievement metrics, it will ultimately lead to a reduction in poverty, unemployment, and racial inequality. And as earlier, the willingness to fund an increasingly punitive education state corresponds with a rejection of interventionist macroeconomic policies to address these problems more directly. The growth of privatization, high-stakes testing, and mass firings of public schoolteachers do not represent a challenge to the liberal incorporationist order established during the Great Society but are rather an increasingly destructive extension of the institutional and ideological commitments it established.

Despite the durability of the liberal incorporationist order, recent years have also shown evidence of resistance. Teachers in concert with parents and students have openly and in some cases aggressively pushed back against some of the most punitive education policies. In the last decade, teachers have been powerful agents of political change, winning greater school funding, stopping cuts to Medicaid, and even extracting wage increases for workers outside the education sector.[52] These victories indicate the potential significance of education and schools as a part of the broader struggle for justice and equality. The fight for an alternative vision of education must be undertaken with an understanding of how we got here and a clear notion of what schools can—and cannot—do, in order to break with the destructive policies of the past.

Part I

From Political Economy to Equal Opportunity

The Struggle over Ideas, 1932–1965

CHAPTER ONE

To Reconstruct or Adjust?

The Battle within the Progressive
Education Movement, 1920s–1940s

In July 2010, just two years after the start of the Great Recession that devastated the lives of millions of Americans and helped launch him into the presidency, President Barack Obama walked up to a lectern to address the Centennial Conference of the National Urban League. The destruction of the Great Recession was still roiling the nation, 8.7 million would lose their jobs, the unemployment rate topped 10%, 10 million people lost their homes, and one in seven Americans was living below the poverty line.[1] As President Obama was greeted joyfully by the crowd in Washington, D.C., he told the audience he wanted to focus on "an issue I believe will largely determine not only African American success, but the success of our nation in the 21st century."[2] The issue was reforming the education system. Indeed, according to the president, "education is an economic issue—if not 'the' economic issue of our time."[3] After lamenting that the existing education system had produced racial achievement gaps and students ill prepared for the labor market, and placed American in an inferior position to international competitors—the president pressed for more and better testing, workforce training, and greater accountability for schools and teachers. As the Great Recession was exposing the horrors of years of neoliberal economic policies, the president excoriated the educational—not the economic—status quo, proclaiming "this status quo is morally inexcusable, it's economically indefensible, and all of us are going to have to roll up our sleeves to change it."[4]

This speech by President Obama is indicative of the current consensus that the education system is in crisis, and that educational reforms are key to solving myriad social problems. Both major political parties and important interest groups have voiced concerns about the quality of schooling, the effectiveness of teachers, the difficulty of curriculum, the need for more accountability, and the comparative effectiveness of the public education system in the United States. Underlying this diagnosis of school deficiency is a remarkable consensus about the purpose of the education system. Elites from across the political spectrum promote the idea that the public education system should be focused on imparting skills that offer *individuals* the potential for future success within the existing social and economic order.

From the political right, this view of education is defended as the most efficient way of ensuring that individual earnings are tied to the skills the individual brings to marketplace and that there is a steady supply of skilled
workers for the labor market, and as the best means of preserving the nation's
international preeminence.[5] The political left embraces this understanding
out of a belief that an education system ordered on these principles provides
the best means of economic mobility for the meritorious and offers a path to
success even for individuals from traditionally disadvantaged groups.[6]

What is striking about this vision of the purpose and function of education in American society is its narrowness. The role of education is reduced
to developing and then efficiently and equally distributing the opportunity
for individuals to compete in the existing social and economic order. If these
educational conditions are met, subsequent inequalities that arise are viewed
as essentially justified. Absent from this vision of education is any notion that
it is possible or desirable for the public education system to challenge the existing structural order, which guarantees that even equitable educational opportunity ultimately results in inequality.[7] In short, the current educational
consensus has no broader social vision for challenging the extreme inequities
that can result from a capitalist economic system.

An examination of the past indicates that liberal incorporationist vision
has deep—but not uncontested—roots in American political thought. This
chapter returns to another era of economic turmoil, the Great Depression, to
trace a significant division within the progressive education movement from
the 1920s to the 1940s—the division between the social efficiency progressives and the social reconstructionists.[8] As progressives, social efficiency progressives and social reconstructionists agreed broadly that dramatic changes
were needed in educational practice in order to prepare students for participation in a democratic society; however, the two groups differed significantly
about the appropriate educational methods, the role of teachers, the relationship between education and political economy, and the requirements of democracy.[9] Broadly, the central cleavage between the two groups was that,
whereas the scientific efficiency progressives believed that education should
help adjust the individual for success in the existing economic status quo, the
social reconstructionists argued that the schools should help prepare students to fundamentally change the social order.[10]

The focus of this chapter and the one that follows is on the particular
debates between the key individuals and organizations within progressive
groups that preceded the founding of the federal education state. The attention to ideas—and which ideas emerged ascendant—clarifies which visions

helped stitch together the coalition that was ultimately successful in passing the most significant federal expansion in the realm of education policy.[11] Furthermore, focusing on the debate with progressive education reveals the tight connection between education and political economy. As the Great Depression opened a space for radical reimaging of the economic and educational possibilities, educational visions that called for fundamental changes to the economic structures of the United States proved much less able to accommodate the political and material moment when this crisis faded.

The chapter begins by outlining the core ideological commitments and the educational program of the social efficiency progressives through an examination of the writings of some of the most important members of this coalition. This group dominated the progressive educational landscape for much of the early decades of the twentieth century. However, the stock market crash of 1929 and the extended economic hardship of the Great Depression gave rise to a rival group of progressives, the social reconstructionists—who held surprising influence throughout the 1930s. These two groups vigorously competed for the soul of public education, as they offered distinct, and often contradictory, policy prescriptions for the education system. These educational disagreements mapped onto broader political disagreements between the two groups over fairness of a capitalist economy, the requirements of equality, and support of New Deal policies. Although neither group was completely able to implement their vision, social efficiency progressives proved much more successful in imprinting substantial portions of their methodological and ideological program on American education. Indeed, the consequences of these victories by the social efficiency progressives continue to reverberate throughout the education system today.

The Social Efficiency Progressives

In the early decades of the twentieth century, the Progressive Era brought a growing national faith that methods and knowledge of the sciences could be harnessed to address national concerns such as the growth of large corporations and corruption in government. A group of individuals who held similar hope for the promise of science in guiding best practices in the organization and methods of teaching dominated the national conversation in education during the first half of the twentieth century. Broadly known as the progressive education movement, these social scientists and educators advocated for a sharp departure from the traditional curricula and methods of teaching, pushing for new approaches that were better suited to address current national problems and needs.

Spurred by the rapid changes brought by industrialization, urbanization, and demographic change in the early twentieth century, the progressive education movement was also a reaction to educational conservatives. Associated with organizations such as the American Legion and Daughters of the American Revolution, educational conservatives argued that the central purpose of schools was to maintain both traditional education practice and social mores. These conservatives argued that teachers should be authorities that focused on delivering and instilling the traditional values of patriotism, religion, culture, and economics to students.[12] Educational progressives viewed the traditional approach as an overly rigid system that failed to take the needs of the child into account. Progressives argued that the significant societal changes demanded revolutionary educational change and pushed for a child-centered pedagogy that drew from scientific approaches in order to discover best educational practices.[13]

United by their faith in science and their rejection of traditional educational methods, the progressive education movement had a powerful and continuing effect on the ideas and methods of the nation's education system. However, the broad label of progressive education masks substantial and significant differences within this group. As educational historian David Labaree has noted, "the progressive education movement in the United States was not a single entity, but a cluster of overlapping and competing tendencies."[14] The beginning of the twentieth century brought the emergence of a powerful coalition of progressive academics and educators—the social efficiency progressives. This group of progressive educators pressed for dramatic educational reforms, arguing that children and society more broadly could best be served by creating a more rational and systemic approach to education. Many of the coalition's most prominent members, including Edward L. Thorndike, Henry H. Goddard, Charles H. Judd, and Robert M. Yerkes, came from the newly emerging academic field of psychology. Education was also emerging as an academic field and as a separate department in many universities, and influential early members of the field such as John Franklin Bobbitt, Ellwood P. Cubberley, David Snedden, and Charles Prosser were also social efficiency progressives.

Although this coalition was certainly not uniform in their ideological outlook, it was united by several common commitments and beliefs about needed educational reforms. Focused on the need to make the schools more efficient and more reflective of the needs of society, social efficiency progressives proposed a number of reforms to school governance, organization, and teaching methods, including tracking, intelligence testing, standardized achievement testing, routinized teaching methods, and vocational education. This educational vision was accompanied by a belief that all children were not equal in intelligence or potential value to society, and efficiency therefore demanded that children of different intelligence be treated differently. This group of progressives advocated turning away from the rote formalism of existing pedagogy that involved teaching students of all abilities the same thing and the tendency to focus on college preparation in high school with methods that were scientifically proven to be effective and were more appropriate for each student's ability and future station in life. The educational vision and ideological commitments of the social efficiency progressives dominated the landscape of the early progressive education movement.

One of the core commitments that united social efficiency progressives was a desire to introduce the principles of industrial management into the public school system. Largely inspired by Frederick W. Taylor's writings about effective industrial management, social efficiency advocates sought to adapt the management principles outlined by Taylor to the day-to-day operation of the school.[15] For this group of progressives, the implementation of industrial management methods such as routinization, constant evaluation, differentiation, and efficiency provided promising avenues of reforming the education system. The desire to introduce scientific management techniques spawned dramatic reform proposals that touched nearly every aspect of schooling, including administrative organization, the curricula, and the act of teaching itself.

John Franklin Bobbitt was one of the staunchest and most influential advocates of introducing the logic of industrial management into the schools' scientific management. A longtime professor of school administration at the University of Chicago, Bobbitt also served briefly as assistant schools superintendent of Los Angeles and Toledo.[16] Bobbitt was one of the most enthusiastic proponents of extending the methods of business management into the schools, a position he outlined early in his career for the 1913 *Yearbook of the National Society for the Science of Education*. In the extensive piece, entitled "The Supervision of City Schools: Some General Principles of Management Applied to the Problems of City-School Systems," Bobbitt argued that since "education is a shaping process as much as the manufacture of steel rails," it made sense to apply the scientific management techniques used in business to the realm of education.[17] Extending the metaphor of the school as a business, Bobbitt's educational approach described school administrators as supervisors, the teachers as workers on the line, and the students as the educational products, and put forth a number of management principles designed to maximize efficiency in education. In this new educational system envisioned by Bobbitt and others, "'social efficiency' is to become the chief watchword and the chief aim."[18]

The most pressing task in applying scientific management techniques to the school was to develop standards in order to rationalize and routinize the educational process. The usefulness of standards was largely a function of the ability to make different aspects of the educational process comparable, and social efficiency progressives argued that the most effective standards would involve reducing the educational process to easily quantifiable and comparable metrics. Bobbitt argued that each academic subject should have a set of concrete standards that outlined the expectations of what students should know by the time of the completion of each grade.[19] Bobbitt's faith in the ability to quantify and measure all aspects of the educational process was reflected by Edward Thorndike—a fellow social efficiency progressive and professor at Columbia's Teachers College—who argued that "whatever exists, exists in some amount."[20] Standards were the foundation of the scientific management program, as they allowed for the evaluation of which teaching methods were most effective as well as the personal evaluation of students, teachers, and principals.

Significantly, for Bobbitt, the setting of these standards was not the role of the teachers or others within the education system. Rather, the educational standards should be set by the needs of the broader community, and the demands of the labor market in particular. Bobbitt's belief that "it is the need of the world affairs that determines the standard specifications for the educational product" led him to privilege the input of business and corporate leaders in the creation of education standards.[21] Bobbitt argued that "the commercial world can best say what it needs" and called for the "business world.... [to] state in specific terms the kinds of educational product that it desires in the workers that come to it."[22] By informing the schools about the labor needs of industry, Bobbitt hoped to use educational standards to help schools shape and prepare students for their position in the labor market.

The view that schools were central to facilitating entry into the labor market meant that social efficiency progressives argued that one function of a rationalized school system was to sort students into different categories based on ability and future vocation. Bobbitt advocated for differentiation of standards based on the "native ability" of students and envisioned three separate tracks of educational standards based on the results of an intelligence test.[23] Significantly, Bobbitt claimed that differentiation of standards allowed for schools to begin the process of preparing students for the vocational task and social role for which their intelligence best suited them. As Bobbitt argued, "differentiation of standards on the basis of native ability is closely related to the differentiation of standards according to vocational and social destiny."[24] Differentiation would allow for the development of different standards and curricula for different groups of students, which would ultimately smooth the transition of each group of students into their appropriate place in the labor market.[25]

The commitment to different educational tracks based on intelligence scores was a central aspect of the social efficiency progressive movement. Edward Thorndike echoed Bobbitt in calling for the differentiation of educational standards and resources on the basis of intelligence, arguing "it certainly is not reasonable that the intellectually ablest 5 per cent of boys should be kept in school to an age only four months beyond that to which the least able are kept" and that "increased resources should be used to aid young men and women whom nature and nurture have chosen to profit from schooling."[26] The differentiation of standards was framed as a means of rationally distributing educational resources. This differentiation of educational standards also supported subsequent social and class differentiation, framing the unequal distribution of educational resources and opportunities as a rational extension of meritocracy.

The creation of standards was also meant to help define the role of teachers in the classroom and to determine the most effective teaching methods. In applying the methods of scientific management in business to the classroom, Bobbitt conceptualized the teacher as an assembly-line worker whose "task is to turn out a product of definite sort in the shape of developed abilities within the pupils."[27] According to Bobbitt, "the burden of finding the best methods is too large and too complicated to be laid on the shoulders of the teachers"; instead, the "doctrine of scientific management" required that teaching methods should be determined by school administrators.[28] For the teacher, the implementation of scientific management techniques would mean the substantial loss of professional autonomy. The social efficiency progressives believed that the freedom of teachers in the classroom had to be curtailed, as it implied variation from methods that had been shown to be effective. The goal was a standardized approach in all classrooms, as Bobbitt argued, "after experimentation and statistical comparisons have shown the methods that are best, then *these methods must be used* by the teachers."[29] The methods proposed by social efficiency progressives removed teachers as the authorities in education, replacing them with administrators who evaluated which methods were most effective. The role of the teacher was to be reduced to little more than that of a technician implementing methods determined by others to help students reach the standards set for each grade and subject.[30]

Finally, in addition to rationally distributing educational opportunities and defining the appropriate role of the teacher, social efficiency progressives valued the ability of educational standards to aid in accountability. Once clear standards had been set and effective methods determined, there could be no excuse for failing to produce the desired educational product. Although the development of standards held the possibility of accountability for principals and administrators, it was clear that social efficiency progressives were most interested in evaluating the performance of teachers. Bobbitt claimed that the current system of promotion and salary tied to length of service was irrational and argued that it should be replaced by one in which teacher appointment, promotion, and salary were all tied to their ability to get their students to reach the appropriate educational standards.[31] Furthermore, according to Bobbitt, the implementation of standards would provide supervisors with "incontestable evidence of inefficiency against the weak teacher who cannot or who refuses to improve. And the present day difficulty of removing such a teacher from the service, transferring her, or retiring her, will be instantly overcome."[32] As on the efficiently managed shop floor, the implementation of scientific management techniques in the schools would aid supervisors in the identification and termination of inefficient workers. Bobbitt argued that accountability in education required more or less constant testing of the students and extensive record keeping, just as it did in the business world.[33]

Bobbitt was one of the earliest and most vocal advocates of the introduction of scientific management techniques, but he certainly was not alone. The desire to implement scientific reforms that would increase the efficiency of the educational system was shared by many other prominent social efficiency reformers, including Edward Thorndike, David Snedden, Charles Judd, and Henry Goddard.[34] Ellwood Cubberley, a well-known and early leader in the emerging field of educational administration, offered a nearly identical assessment as that of Bobbitt in 1916, writing: "Our schools are, in a sense, factories in which the raw products (children) are to be shaped and fashioned into products to meet the various demands of life. The specifications for manufacturing come from the demands of twentieth-century civilization, and it is the business of the school to build its pupils according to the specification laid down. This demands good tools, specialized machinery, continuous measurement of production to see if it is according to specifications, the elimination of waste in manufacture, and a large variety in the output."[35] The faith that reforms that had revolutionized the factory floor could also help revolutionize social institutions motivated many of the progressive efforts of the day. This faith also was a significant factor in the expansion of one of the most consequential educational reforms to emerge from this era: widespread standardized testing.

Testing

The desire to introduce scientific management techniques into the schools was a primary driver of increased demand for the development and implementation of standardized tests in education. Social efficiency progressives argued that efficiency demanded the use of standardized tests to determine both the appropriate educational track for students and also to evaluate the success of schools in meeting newly developed standards. As a result, educational psychologists devoted substantial time and resources to developing intelligence tests meant to differentiate students by inborn intelligence, and also achievement tests meant to evaluate the progress students had made toward meeting newly developed standards. These tests would be the central tools in the attempt to reorganize the schools in the most socially efficient manner, allowing for appropriate distribution of educational resources, determination of the best educational methods, and increased accountability.

Although widespread standardized testing of intelligence and achievement in education had long been the goal of the social efficiency progressives, this position gained broader support after World War I. As the United States entered the conflict, the military turned to scientific management techniques as a means of efficiently dealing with the dramatic increase in the scale of operations and number of soldiers for which it was now responsible. The army hired a number of the nation's most prominent psychologists, including Edward Thorndike, Henry Goddard, Lewis Terman, and Robert Yerkes, to help implement new methods of dealing with the massive increase in manpower. Seizing the opportunity, Yerkes led a team of psychologists that developed and deployed an intelligence test in 1917 and 1918. The forty-minute test given to groups of new recruits was designed to help military authorities quickly and efficiently identify those candidates who were intelligent enough to be officers, as well as identify those who were unfit for service due to low intelligence. As a greater number of soldiers were tested, the psychologists developed intelligence guidelines for increasingly specific army vocations. Ultimately, throughout the war, more than 1.75 million soldiers took intelligence tests. The adoption of intelligence as a category that influenced placement was a radical development for the military, which had never considered intelligence or mental capacity a meaningful qualification prior to World War I. By the end of World War I, the U.S. military had fully embraced psychological methods and intelligence tests.[36]

The widespread use of intelligence tests in the war effort helped legitimize and popularize the concept of intelligence and its potential use for guiding social institutions. By 1920 Henry Goddard, a prominent psychologist and the first person to translate the Binet intelligence test into English, asserted that in the wake of "this army experience it is no longer possible for anyone to deny the validity of mental tests."[37] After the war, social efficiency progressives quickly turned their attention back to the schools and attempted to implement a similar program in education. In their postwar assessment of the army intelligence tests, Robert Yerkes and Clarence Yoakum, two of the individuals intimately involved in developing the tests, advocated for the introduction of intelligence tests in schools. In discussing the practical applications of testing after the end of the war, the two psychologists proposed "that children should be classified in accordance with mental ability either as they enter school or shortly thereafter and that mental ability should thereafter be taken into account in connection with their educational treatment."[38] Much like their function in the military, social efficiency progressives hoped that the tests would be used to sort children into their appropriate track, and eventually the vocation most suited to their intelligence level.

In 1919, the General Education Board, a philanthropic organization funded by John D. Rockefeller, provided $25,000 for the development of tests designed to measure the intelligence of children in elementary schools. The group of psychologists that comprised the committee in charge of developing the standards was made up of many of the same individuals who had developed army intelligence tests, including Lewis M. Terman, Edward L. Thorndike, and Robert M. Yerkes. Yerkes had served as chairman in the military effort and also served as chairman of the new effort to develop intelligence tests for elementary school students. The committee developed two different tests, and by 1920 had secured an agreement from the World Book Company to publish and distribute the new tests under the title of "National Intelligence Tests."[39]

According to social efficiency progressives it was not only tests of intelligence that would prove useful in education: achievement tests were also critical to ensuring an efficiently run educational system. Edward Thorndike, the educational psychologist who had been in charge of examining the accuracy of the intelligence tests during the war, pressed for the extension of both intelligence and achievement testing in education, arguing, "education is one form of human engineering and will profit by measurements of human nature *and* achievement, as mechanical and electrical engineering have profited by using the foot-pound, calories, volt, and ampere."[40] Similarly, Henry Goddard advocated for the introduction of an initial intelligence test to sort students into appropriate educational tracks, to be followed by frequent testing of achievement throughout the educational career of the student. The ultimate goal was "not only to give each student a mental rating but to discover by proper tests the special abilities of various students with an idea to guiding them in their choice of work or profession."[41] The faith that social efficiency progressives placed in the ability of tests to accurately determine intelligence and measure educational achievements meant that this group proselytized for the extension of testing throughout the educational process.

The enthusiasm for testing was largely motivated by the desire to increase the efficiency of the schools. The psychologists advocating for intelligence and achievement tests fundamentally agreed with Bobbitt's prescription for school reform and viewed the extension of testing as a necessary aspect of bringing scientific management to the education system. Goddard argued that "a knowledge of the intelligence level and a conscious effort to fit every man to his work in accordance with his intelligence level, is the surest way of promoting social efficiency."[42] The introduction of testing would allow for the sorting and assignment of students to the most appropriate educational track for their intelligence level and for tailoring the educational program to their future place in the labor market as determined by the mental capacity of the student. The social efficiency progressives believed that this reform would represent a substantially more efficient school system, as it avoided wasting educational resources on those with low intelligence and allowed for greater educational investment in the highly intelligent students who would be most likely to benefit.[43] Edward Thorndike captured the centrality of testing to the social efficiency progressive educational vision in a 1920 *Harper's* essay, where he argued "exact and complete knowledge about the correlations of mental traits will be of enormous importance for the utilization of man-power by schools, churches, employers, and the state. When we have such exact knowledge, we shall be able to make up a bill of specifications of the sort of intellect and character required for a certain job, select men efficiently instead of haphazard, and train them according to their individual needs instead of indiscriminately."[44] The legitimacy granted to the psychologists after their perceived success in World War I meant that these recommendations carried substantial weight. By the 1920–1921 school year, more than one million schoolchildren had been given general intelligence tests, and more than two million achievement tests had been administered in several different school subjects.[45]

The desire of social efficiency progressives to increase testing in the education system was motivated to a substantial degree by the belief that intelligence was a fundamentally fixed and heritable individual quality. Social efficiency progressives such as Thorndike and Goddard were some of the most prominent national proponents of the theory that intelligence was a trait passed down from parents to children. This genetic theory positioned intelligence as a static trait of individuals, meaning that there was little that social institutions could do to alter this inherited individual trait. Many of the educational reform proposals of social efficiency progressives, including differentiated curriculum and standards, the routinization of teaching, and greater focus on vocational education, were motivated by their understanding of the nature of intelligence as a fixed genetic trait.

The belief in the heritability of intelligence meant that social efficiency progressives had a particular interest in the family background of students. Henry Goddard pushed for teachers to collect information on the intelligence of students' relatives, arguing "could we but know the ancestral tendency of all children in our public schools, we would have one very helpful guide toward the direction in which the child's mind could be most easily and successfully developed."[46] For Goddard, if a student's family background contained a number of low-intelligence or "feebleminded" individuals, it was a good indication that the student was likely also of low intelligence given that intelligence was a genetic trait. Thorndike traced the differences in intelligence levels to the "enormous amount of variation in the nature of fertilized ova which are the original nature of men."[47] This belief that intelligence was heritable also provided the foundation for the belief that there were identifiable intelligence differences between sexes, social class, and, in particular, racial groups. Pointing to the fields of psychology and anthropology, Thorndike asserted that there was ample evidence that "there are inborn differences between human strains" when it came to intelligence.[48] In a 1946 article outlining his belief that intelligence was correlated to racial groups, Thorndike compared racial groups to different breeds of cows, arguing, "Jersey cows, Guernseys, Holsteins, Herefords, etc. are distinguishable as Norwegians, South Italians, Bantu Negroes, and Japanese are. Cows can be ranked on value scales for production of milk and butterfat, for production of meat, for resistance to disease, etc., as men can be ranked for intellect, character, skill, and other qualities serviceable for human welfare."[49] Given the social efficiency progressives' contention that educational resources should be distributed on the basis of intelligence, the belief in racial differences in intelligence necessarily implied racial difference in educational resources.

In addition to the assertion that intelligence was inherited, the social efficiency progressives also argued that it was essentially an unalterable individual trait, much like hair color. Thorndike also believed that the inborn trait of intelligence was correlated with a number of other socially desirable and hereditary traits, asserting that "in human nature good traits go together. To him that hath a superior intellect is given also on the average a superior character; the quick boy is also in the long run more accurate; the able boy is also more industrious."[50] For the social efficiency progressives, the measurement of intelligence in schoolchildren could then be used as a proxy for a number of desirable traits and, ultimately, future success.

The identification of intelligence as a static trait possessed by the individual meant that it could be a particularly useful tool in efficiently organizing the education system. As Thorndike wrote, "an individual's intelligence compared with that of other individuals of his age is within limits, a stable, permanent characteristic of him. It can be at least roughly measured and the measurement used to prophesy and direct his career."[51] Social efficiency progressives argued that because intelligence was a unchangeable trait within the individual and was highly correlated with other desirable qualities and the likelihood of future success, individual intelligence was a particularly useful tool in engineering an efficient education system. If an individual's intelligence was fixed at birth, then the assignment of an individual to a particular educational track on the basis of an intelligence test made sense from a scientific management perspective. The differing distributions of inborn intelligence required different educational curricula and experiences for different levels of individual intelligence.[52]

The belief in the fixed nature of intelligence also implied that there was little that teachers, schools, or the educational system more broadly could do to change the social destiny of the individual student. This understanding justified existing inequalities in wealth and power as largely the natural result of differences in intelligence. Goddard argued that failure to grasp the unchangeable nature of intelligence had resulted in dangerous public acceptance "of the sophistry 'that education and environment will offset the handicap of heredity.'"[53] The belief that intelligence was hereditary meant that the educational vision of social efficiency progressives was one in which the transformative power of education was necessarily limited. In his discussion of the racial differences of intelligence, Thorndike reflected on his belief in the limited ability of education to change fundamental aspects of heredity, claiming, "if large random samplings of North Europeans and Central Africans . . . were given identical opportunities from birth and fully tested at age twenty, there would be substantial differences in ability to manage ideas and symbols in favor of the North Europeans."[54] The educational implications of this belief were clearly anti-egalitarian, as equality in education would mean an inefficient distribution of educational resources. Instead of treating every student the same, Thorndike argued that it was important to recognize "the differences between the genes of races," and that "education should be informed about the raw material with which it operates."[55] Similarly, Goddard pressed for educational reforms that acknowledged "all children are not of equal value" and pushed for a distribution of educational resources based on the principle that "each child has a value to society in proportion to his degree of intelligence."[56] Focusing more educational resources and opportunities on the most intelligent was efficient because those with low intelligence could not benefit from increased educational opportunities. Failure to tailor educational opportunities on the basis of intelligence also harmed the most intelligent, as they were forced to learn at the slower pace of their less intelligent peers. Social efficiency progressives therefore advocated for a distribution of educational resources and differentiated educational tracks that reflected the distribution of intelligence.[57]

Political Commitments

The ideological positions of the social efficiency progressives that motivated their educational reform proposals, including the heritability of desirable traits and the drive to implement scientific management techniques, also structured their broader political beliefs and positions. The consequences of these beliefs became particularly clear in the wake of the market crash of 1929 and subsequent New Deal policies. Although the individuals in this group were broadly progressive, many were openly hostile to the reforms pursued by the New Deal coalition and by their more radical colleagues in the progressive education movement. The ideological commitment of the social efficiency progressives caused many of them to portray broad political and economic reforms as irresponsible, undemocratic, and inefficient.

The belief in the wide variation of fixed levels of intelligence shaped the social efficiency progressives' understanding of democracy. Although Henry Goddard acknowledged that "the essential point of democracy is that every citizen shall have a chance to say whom he thinks is the best," he also believed that only those with high levels of intelligence were suited to lead.[58] For Goddard, the "perfect Government" was an "Aristocracy in Democracy," where the most intelligent were elected to lead.[59] A knowledge of varied intelligence levels was central to democracy, as "a perfect democracy is only to be realized when it is based upon an absolute knowledge of mental levels and the organ-ization of the social body on that basis."[60] Thorndike offered a similar under-standing of democracy, noting that "the argument for democracy is not that it gives power to all men without distinction, but that it gives greater freedom for ability and character to attain power."[61] For Thorndike, the fact that "the abler persons in the world . . . are more clean, decent, just, and kind" made them ideal leaders. Thorndike openly advocated for leadership on the basis of intelligence, arguing, "it seems entirely sage to predict that the world will get better treatment by trusting its fortunes to its 95- or 99-percentile intelli-gences than it would get by itself."[62]

Social efficiency progressives justified this elitist vision of democracy on the utilitarian grounds that giving greater resources and the reins of power to the most intelligent would ultimately result in greater social benefit than a more egalitarian distribution of power. This position also provided substan-tial justification for the status quo, and the extreme inequities in income and power that characterized the 1920s. Thorndike viewed these inequities as arising from "natural processes which give power to the men of ability to gain it and keep it" and argued that these inequities were fundamentally moral because "such men are, by and large, of superior intelligence, and conse-quently of somewhat superior justice and good-will."[63] By justifying existing power disparities as both natural and desirable, the social efficiency progres-sive ideology was essentially a ruling-class ideology.[64]

The Great Depression, and the widespread economic chaos and unem-ployment that resulted, provided a fundamental challenge to the faith in the ruling class. The federal elections of 1932 ushered in unified control of the Congress and the presidency under the Democratic Party, as the Republi-cans lost more than one hundred seats in the House of Representatives and twelve seats in the Senate, and lost the presidency in a landslide. The newly elected Congress rushed to enact the dramatic economic reforms of Presi-dent Franklin D. Roosevelt. These reforms, and much of the New Deal policy agenda, were based in part on significant distrust of the business and financial elites, who were believed to bear substantial culpability for the catastrophic consequences of the Great Depression. The market crash of 1929 and the sub-sequent New Deal policies substantially shifted power from private business to the federal government, and laws such as the National Labor Relations Act shifted power from management to workers. Weighing in on this new politi-cal climate, many social efficiency progressives were skeptical of New Deal policies that pushed for greater equality in industrial relations and in eco-nomic distribution of resources.

Henry Goddard had been explicit in his criticism of a left politics centered on economic redistribution well before the market crash. In 1920, he claimed that those advocating for economic redistribution and greater incomes for laborers were fundamentally misguided because they failed to take into account the differences in levels of intelligence. Goddard criticized the idea that laborers and workmen needed the same kinds of housing, luxuries, and incomes as their more intelligent fellow citizens. According to Goddard, individuals with different levels of intelligence required different economic resources to be content. Furthermore, Goddard claimed that even if society were to give more resources and higher wages to those with low intelligence, the end result would be the same since this group had foolish spending habits and an inability to save and plan ahead. Goddard argued that these facts fundamentally undercut the arguments of those advocating for better housing, better incomes, and more opportunities for the poor. As Goddard rhetorically asked, "How can there be such a thing as social equality with this wide range of mental capacity?"[65] In the aftermath of the market crash of 1929, Goddard remained hostile to redistributive politics and sought to blame those with low intelligence for the negative consequences of the Great Depression. In a 1931 address commemorating the anniversary of the Vineland laboratory, where he had helped Yerkes and others develop the army intelligence tests, Goddard stated, "the very serious problems that are confronting us right now in unemployment and the consequent poverty and starvation are to a very large degree due to the fact that the great mass of these people have not had the intelligence and foresight to save some of their earnings, when they had employment at good wages, in anticipation of just such difficulties as they are now facing."[66] Although the market crash and prolonged depression had caused many in the United States to rethink their faith in business leaders and question the fairness of a loosely regulated capitalist economy, Goddard remained convinced of the fundamental efficiency of organizing social institutions along the lines of intelligence.

Goddard was not alone in his continued adherence to scientific efficiency and hereditarian ideological commitments in the starkly changed political environment. In a 1936 article, Edward Thorndike directly criticized the "desire to have many or all men equal" that he believed served as the foundation of many of the recent New Deal reforms, claiming that "equality is a false and useless God."[67] Thorndike argued that the push for equality was both against the tendencies of human nature and inefficient. Rather than focusing on equalizing material wealth, Thorndike asserted that "it is better to expend the time and energy in increasing goods than in equalizing them."[68] Thorndike still claimed that the best means of improving human welfare and increasing the overall wealth of the country was to give favorable opportunities and more resources to the most intelligent "rather than to distribute them equally."[69] Even as much of the country was calling for greater equality in economic distribution in the face of the prolonged hardship of the Great Depression, social efficiency progressives continued to advocate for strongly differentiated opportunities and outcomes distributed on the basis of intelligence.

The Emerging Social Reconstructionist Alternative

The shifting political context of the Great Depression caused many academics, policy makers, and educators to question the core ideological commitments of the social efficiency progressives. The social efficiency progressives maintained their allegiance to their pre-1929 educational programs even as the Great Depression spurred the rise of a new coalition of progressive educators. While still progressive in their opposition to the rigidity and formalism of traditional schooling methods, this new group of educators had core ideological differences with the social efficiency progressives and rejected much of their educational proposals. This new coalition of social reconstructionists was highly critical of the excessive competitiveness and individualism that they believed characterized American life and the education system. In stark contrast with the social efficiency progressives, the social reconstructionists rejected educational tracking, were suspicious of standardized testing, and argued that teachers should have the central role in leading the transformation of social and economic institutions that the Great Depression had exposed as fundamentally unfair. Throughout the 1930s, the social efficiency progressives and social reconstructionists offered starkly different visions of a path forward for the progressive education movement.

With unemployment hovering around 20 percent, the national income at half of what it had been three years earlier, and an outbreak of violent incidents between police and desperate men with no means to support themselves or their families, 1932 was one of the most tumultuous years in the nation's history. Franklin Roosevelt's decisive victory against an incumbent president provided a good indication of the widespread disillusionment in the existing political order, and a hunger for extensive political change to drag the country out of depths of the Great Depression and to ensure that such an event could never happen again. The dissatisfaction with the status quo was soon extended to the public education system, as educational professionals began to take a critical look at the role of the public education system in society. In the wake of the extreme conditions, some academics began to express frustration over "feelings of impotence against the depressed conditions that threatened the children's health, school budgets and even their own jobs."[70] It was in this context that George Counts, a professor at the Teachers College, launched the social reconstructionist movement in education in a series of speeches before several national meetings of the nation's most prominent educators in February 1932. The speeches, later published as *Dare the School Build a New Social Order?*, offered both a critique and a path forward for progressive educators seeking dramatic reform in the context of the Great Depression.

In his speeches, Counts offered deep criticism of the existing social, political, and economic structures. Spelling out the existing contradictions of a system in which "dire poverty walks hand in hand with the most extravagant living the world has ever known" and "an abundance of goods of all kinds is coupled with privation, misery and even starvation,"[71] Counts laid the blame squarely at the feet of the "ideal of rugged individualism . . . used to justify a system which exploits pitilessly and without thought of the morrow."[72] Educators, specifically, were condemned for the role of the school in the current crisis, as Counts claimed existing schools were organized around preparing students to fit into and embrace the problematic existing social orders. This had led to an educational philosophy that made success "an individual rather than a social goal, driv[ing] every one of us into an insane competition with his neighbors."[73] This critique ultimately indicted the existing form of capitalism and "its deification of the principle of selfishness,"[74] leading Counts to proclaim "if democracy is to survive in the United States, it must abandon its individualistic affiliations in the sphere of economics."[75]

In the extreme volatility of the early 1930s, Counts sensed a moment of great possibility. With the times "literally crying for a new vision of American destiny," Counts argued that the "teaching profession, or at least its progressive elements, should eagerly grasp the opportunity which the fates have placed in their hands."[76] If teachers "could increase sufficiently their stock of courage, intelligence, and vision, [they] might become a social force of some magnitude."[77] Counts called teachers to "make certain that every Progressive school will use whatever power it may possess in opposing and checking the forces of social conservatism and reaction,"[78] and instead "become centers for the building, and not merely for the contemplation, of our civilization. . . . We should . . . give to our children a vision of the possibilities which lie ahead and endeavor to enlist their loyalties and enthusiasms in the realization of the vision."[79] For Counts, this involved the active cultivation of "democratic sentiments" in schoolchildren as a means to bring about desirable social reconstruction.

This represented a major challenge to the social efficiency progressive positions. Counts's proposals of greater teacher autonomy in the direction of the classroom ran directly counter to the routinized and standardized role that scientific management techniques demanded in order to ensure efficiency. Furthermore, his argument for the teacher-led development of educational content as a means of combating social conservatism was directly in conflict with the fundamental belief of social efficiency progressives that educational standards and curriculum content should largely come from the business leaders who best understood the skill demands of the labor market. Counts's critique of the social order was fundamentally also a critique of a social efficiency progressive education system designed to differentiate children and prepare them for life in an extremely inequitable social system.

For Counts, the social efficiency progressive position was untenable. In a speech given at the annual convention of the Progressive Education Association in Baltimore in 1932, Counts addressed this directly, telling the audience, "If an educational movement, or any other movement, calls itself progressive, it must have orientation; it must possess direction."[80] Counts charged that by maintaining silence in the classroom on major political issues, progressives were complicit in the creation of a system that favored the upper middle class. Clearly aware that the progressive education movement had been wary of the label of "indoctrination," Counts nonetheless told the audience that "neutrality with respect to the great issues that agitate society, while perhaps theoretically possible, is practically tantamount to giving support to the forces of conservatism."[81] This critique was especially stinging considering both the audience and the dire circumstances of the economic calamity facing most Americans.

Counts offered a clear path forward for educators and politicians concerned about what type of social reform to pursue in the wake of the Great Depression. Noting that "there can be no good individual apart from some conception of the *good* society; and the good society ... must be fashioned by the hand and brain of man,"[82] Counts issued a clear call to teachers to "deliberately reach for power and then make the most of their conquest"[83] and argued that "the school must shape attitudes, develop tastes, and even impose ideas."[84] The vision put forth was one in which a clear vision of social good (and one quite distinct from the "rugged individualism" of a capitalist economy) was the guiding educational principle, with teachers taking a leading role in the development of a new social order through the schools. Education was to be the midwife of social transformation.

Building the Social Reconstructionist Coalition

The challenge issued by Counts soon drew other prominent educational figures to join the call for teachers to usher in a new social order. William H. Kilpatrick, who at the time was perhaps the nation's second most famous progressive educator (behind only his mentor, John Dewey), soon joined the cause with the publication of *Education and the Social Crisis*. At the time of publication, Kilpatrick, also on the faculty of the Teachers College, was well known for his development of the popular "project method" of teaching, the establishment of the National Conference on Educational Method, and for founding the *Journal of Educational Method*.[85] Like Counts, Kilpatrick criticized the extreme individualism that the schools were currently emphasizing and called for the teaching of cooperative attitudes to schoolchildren instead. Like Counts, Kilpatrick's critique was couched in a broader critique of the existing economic order, and he called for a new order based on social control of economic institutions. For Kilpatrick, teachers would be vital as leaders of a coalition seeking broader social reform.

Another colleague of Counts at the Teachers College, Harold Rugg, soon joined to call for more socially conscious schooling. Rugg was another high-profile educator, with widespread name recognition. In addition to his professorship, Rugg was the director of research at the progressive Lincoln School in New York City, and in 1929 had written a series of textbooks called *Man and His Changing Society*, in which the social purpose of schooling was central. The series was quite successful, selling 1,317,960 books and 2,687,000 workbooks between 1929 and 1939.[86] In December 1932, Rugg clearly indicated his embrace of Counts with an article in *Progressive Education* entitled "Social Reconstruction Through Education," in which he forcefully claimed "nothing less than thoroughgoing social reconstruction is demanded, and there is no institution known to the mind of man that can compass that problem except education."[87] Rugg echoed the call by Counts for teachers to engage in the problems of the day, and construct an educational program centered on the problems of the current social situation. Rugg argued that in the current era, this would mean a new educational program in which youth "will be brought to see how the concept of *laissez-faire* in the marriage of politics and economics has produced enormous inequalities in wealth and social income . . . the disastrous imperialistic exploitation of agrarian and non-militarized peoples, and . . . mad international rivalries and world war."[88] The ultimate goal was the reconstruction of a society no longer based on the "doctrine of individual success through competition," but rather one in which students would have a "strong loyalty for the brotherland of all men on the earth."[89] The open embrace by another prominent educator (and an educator with one of the most widely used textbooks of the era) suggests the breadth of influence of the social reconstructionist idea.

Individual professors were not the only ones that showed interest in the social reconstructionist position. The National Education Association (NEA), at the time the largest and most powerful education group in the nation, also suggested that it was sympathetic to this new approach to education in the early 1930s. In his 1932 report to the association's annual meeting, Fred J. Kelly, the president of the NEA's Committee on Social Economic Goals for America, issued a call strikingly similar to that of Counts. After acknowledging *Dare the Schools Build a New Social Order?*, the report called on the NEA to take the lead in transforming the social order. In a remarkable passage for an organization that had traditionally been quite timid in embracing controversial political positions, the report stated, "The NEA is saying, and I hope saying more or less militantly, that a social order can be built in which a social collapse such as the present one, will be impossible. They are saying further that the educators of America propose to assume major responsibility for building such a social order."[90]

The records of the annual meeting of the NEA throughout the 1930s provide evidence that the ideas of the social reconstructionists were taken seriously and that many in the organization supported this mission for the association. The proceedings of the 1933 annual meeting are littered with favorable references to Counts, Kilpatrick, and Rugg. In a speech before the general session entitled "Applying Ethics to Economics," Robert Moore, the secretary of the Illinois state association, argued that the breakdown in the economic system offered both a challenge and an opportunity to teachers. With specific reference to Harold Rugg and William Kilpatrick, Moore excoriated "rugged individualism" and proclaimed that "the public mind must be informed of the evils of the present system of economics."[91] Moore claimed that "such diffusion is in part the work of teachers, since they are teachers and molders of the minds of youth. Teachers must have a real understanding of the wrongs in recent economic practices" and "a burning zeal to correct them."[92]

In another speech before the general session on the issue of "Teacher Training for the New Age," H. L. Donovan, the president of Eastern Kentucky State Teachers College, noted that he "thoroughly agree[d] with Dr. George Counts" on the issue of the role of the teacher in ushering a new age.[93] Donovan then called for a new teachers' education that stressed the knowledge of social and political programs and that would produce teachers who were "active, aggressive, competent, and effective participants in society" and who were willing to engage in politics and run for political office.[94] The annual conventions also served as a means for some of the most prominent social reconstructionists to address the NEA directly, as Kilpatrick did in his 1935 speech that reiterated key positions from *Education and the Social Crisis*. Kilpatrick told the assembly that "the effecting of the desired social-economic changes will have to be a matter of decades, so that education ... can and must be a significant factor in the process."[95] The attention given to these ideas about the active role of teachers in reforming education to help reform society further demonstrates the penetration of social reconstructionist ideology into the most mainstream educational organizations.

The American Historical Association (AHA) was another source of support for the social reconstructionist position. Noting the importance of social studies curriculum for "the life, the institutions, the thought, the aspirations, and the far-reaching policies of the nation in its world setting," the AHA undertook a multiyear study on how schools should arrange the social studies curricula.[96] The conclusion of the study, published in 1934, offered an analysis of how schools should teach social studies based on "the conclusion that, in the United States as in other countries, the age of individualism and *laissez faire* in economy and government is closing and that a new age of collectivism is emerging."[97] In an echo of Counts's thoughts on the impossibility of neutrality in education, the report noted, "Education *always* expresses some social philosophy, either large or small, involves some choices with respect to social and individual action and well-being, and rests upon some moral conception."[98] The report found that current educational orientation emphasized "the traditional ideas and values of economic individualism" and warned that failure to adjust would "intensify the conflicts, contradictions, maladjustments, and perils of the transition" that it saw as inevitable.[99] Given the failure of the capitalist economy in its existing form, the report stated: "the great purpose of the American public school ... is to prepare the younger generation for life in a highly complex industrial society ... that is in rapid transition from an economy based on individual enterprise and competition for private gain to an economy essentially co-operative and integrated in character and dependent for efficient operation and careful planning on co-ordination of production and consumption."[100] The report's findings and recommendations were directly in line with those proposed by Counts two years prior. Teachers were to abandon attempts at neutrality, and the schools were to prepare students for the new social order. The AHA report provided unqualified support of the social reconstructionist vision for public education.[101]

The position initially advocated by George Counts had quickly gained support from a variety of sources. Equally striking given the fairly radical nature of the claims, their deviation from previous progressive positions, and the stature of the individuals making the case was the very limited criticism that the social reconstructionist position faced. Although there were a few journalists who questioned some of the assumptions about the viability and appropriateness of this position, the response to the increasing popularity from the vast majority of scholars and educators was either silence or support.[102] In the early 1930s, the position outlined by Counts was supported by a broad coalition of educators and social scientists as a feasible and desirable path forward in reforming the public education system.

The Social Frontier

As the individual efforts of prominent scholars brought significant attention, a group of professors and graduate students centered in the Teachers College decided to establish a regular journal to provide a unified voice for the social reconstructionist position. After George Counts agreed to serve as the editor, the founding members spent much of 1934 securing funding, working out organizational structure, and gathering material for the new journal, which was to be called the *Social Frontier*. The inaugural issue of the new journal was published in October 1934, and the journal found immediate support, with more than 2,000 subscriptions for the first edition.[103]

William Kilpatrick, who served as the chairman of the board of directors, boldly laid out the vision of the journal, noting "education has an important, even strategic, role to play in the reconstruction of American society," and that the organizers' goal was to make "the *Social Frontier* a prime medium for the development of a constructive social consciousness among educational workers."[104] The initial edition attempted to unify the strands of progressivism from a variety of academic sources, a tactic that would remain a strength of the journal throughout its existence. The journal contained articles by prominent intellectuals from various academic fields including historian Charles Beard, economist Harold Laski, philosopher Sidney Hook, psychologist Goodwin Watson, and sociologist Henry Fairchild.[105] All seriously engaged the challenge of the opening editorial to actively shape a new educational frontier, recognizing that reform would "either make easy or difficult the transfer of the democratic ideal from individual to social foundations."[106]

The first issue of the journal was also notable for its clear statement of support from John Dewey, the most renowned and respected educational scholar of the era. In what was to be the first of many articles for the *Social Frontier*,

Dewey offered a full-throated defense of the social reconstructionist vision.[107] Hitting the familiar criticisms of "rugged individualism"[108] and the essential conservatism of teachers attempting to remain neutral,[109] Dewey noted that there was a clear means through which teachers, and the system of education more broadly, could lead a transformation of the existing societal structures. According to Dewey, the public education system should be reformed around a purpose of "laying the *basis*, intellectual and moral, for a new social order," which he hoped would "arouse a new spirit in the teaching profession and to give direction to radically changed effort."[110] Dewey continued to reiterate his support throughout his association with the journal, with his considerable prestige and influence offering a prominent boost to the social reconstructionist vision.[111]

The pages of the *Social Frontier* also provide a good indication of the popularity of the social reconstructionist position. The journal often reprinted newspaper editorials and letters of support received from educators across the country, including a glowing review from the *New York Times*, whose editorial board raved: "That men of such high professional knowledge and strong patriotic purpose should undertake this venture will at any rate lead to a fresh appraisement of educational values in the face of the changing order and make against the lethargy into which fixed systems are so apt to lead. . . . It is a good thing for society to have such educational leaders out on the frontiers, ever in search for the better."[112] The first several issues indicate broader support from the education community, including professors of education, professional groups, and prominently placed educational bureaucrats.[113] The positive reception of the *Social Frontier* and the social reconstructionist vision for education would not last. The very popularity and the seriousness with which the education community seemed to take the charge for social reconstruction of the social, economic, and political institutions prompted vociferous opposition from both conservative groups and the social efficiency progressives.

Progressive Divisions

The division between the social reconstructionists and the social efficiency progressives represented a significant split within the broader progressive education movement. Throughout the 1930s and into the early 1940s, these two groups articulated distinct visions of progressive education reform. The varying, and in some instances opposing, educational programs of the two coalitions flowed from their fundamentally distinct understandings of the purpose of education and its relation to the broader social and economic structures.

The social efficiency progressives understood the role of education to be the efficient integration of students into the existing social and economic landscape. This belief resulted in an educational program that focused on detecting the most efficient means of organizing the education system around this goal. Furthermore, the belief that children were unequal in intelligence meant that an efficiently organized education system required differentiation, with educational resources and opportunities distributed on the basis of these inequalities. This set of beliefs about the purpose of education and human nature led to the advocacy of a particular set of educational policies, including educational tracking, widespread use of intelligence and standardized achievement tests, and increased emphasis on vocational education.

The social reconstructionists viewed the role of the education system as primarily one of helping to bring about desired social transformation. This coalition critiqued existing economic and social institutions as fundamentally unfair, arguing that they favored a small class of wealthy individuals at the expense of the masses. For the social reconstructionists, the existing educational system and the proposals of the social efficiency progressives were part of the problematic social order because it was organized largely to reproduce and justify existing economic and social arrangements. The appropriate role of teachers and the education system more broadly was to prepare students to change these unfair social arrangements, rather than to prepare them for roles in the existing landscape. This belief about the purpose of education resulted in proposals for classroom instruction focused on social problems of the community, economic literacy, project-based learning in a common classroom, and the inducement of economic class mentality.[114] Social reconstructionists pushed for significant teacher autonomy and academic freedom in developing their preferred methods in the classroom and advocating for social reforms outside of it.[115]

Significantly, these groups understood their visions to be in conflict with one another. Much of the motivation behind the organization of the social reconstructionist coalition was in response to what they viewed as the deficiencies in the social efficiency progressive vision. The editorial board of the *Social Frontier* criticized social efficiency progressives as "apostles of merely transmissive education," stating that they "would have schools contribute to nothing but repetition of what society already is or is doing."[116] Given the dramatic events and prolonged economic suffering of the Great Depression, the social reconstructionists argued that reducing schools to "a mere tool . . .

that is applied to social material as instruments for molding, stamping, and welding are lied to steel in a factory" was a deeply problematic educational vision that promised to reproduce an unfair social order.[117]

The social efficiency progressives were similarly critical of the educational vision of the social reconstructionists. One of the most vocal critics of the social reconstructionists was Charles H. Judd, a professor and educational psychologist at the University of Chicago who also worked as the director of the education program of the National Youth Administration. In a number of articles throughout the 1930s, Judd characterized the social reconstructionists as "extremists" who were "repelled by logic."[118] Judd criticized the unwillingness of this group to make use of the important educational methods found to be effective through experimentation and "scientific instruments of evaluation."[119] Judd was publicly critical of prominent social reconstructionists such as Charles Beard and, in particular, George Counts. Judd accused Counts of being "blinded by the present-day shadow of unemployment which darkens the world," and of reducing the role of teachers to nothing other than "correct[ing] the evils of capitalism and industrialism."[120] According to Judd, in their zeal to move past the "formalism of certain types of logical arrangements, they have discarded all organization."[121] For Judd and other social efficiency progressives, the failure of the social reconstructionists to understand that "the cure for industrial chaos is intelligent *adaptation of individuals to the conditions* which surround them" had resulted in an educational program that was unwise and unsound.[122]

Throughout the 1930s, one of the central and most pressing cleavages between the two groups of educators remained over whether schools should adjust individuals to the demands of the social order, or whether they should play a role in transforming these fundamentally unfair social institutional arrangements. The consequences of the differing perspectives were particularly clear when it came to the relationship between the labor market and the classroom. In a 1940 coauthored article entitled "Occupational Adjustment of Young Adults," Judd reiterated the social efficiency progressive commitment to organize schools around the demands of the labor market. Judd suggested that part of the unemployment problem could be traced to the fact that the high school still tended to train students for college and professional life, despite the fact that the vast majority would end up performing jobs that required substantially different skill sets.[123] Judd and other social efficiency progressives argued that the education system needed to better reflect the skill demands of the available jobs and to design curriculum tracks that better reflected the students' social destiny.[124] For social efficiency progressives, inefficiently organized schools resulted in the overproduction of students with professional training, which ultimately contributed to their unemployment when they could not find a job in the oversaturated job market.

At the time that Judd was making his argument for efficient organization as a means of addressing unemployment, William Carr, the director of research for the NEA, articulated a very different understanding of the relationship between school and the labor market. At the time, Carr and the NEA were staunch advocates for many of the educational reforms proposed by the social reconstructionists. Carr was called to appear before a congressional hearing on the "Concentration of Economic Power" and was asked about the mismatch of students receiving professional training and the number that actually went on to work in white collar professional jobs. In his testimony, Carr argued that the fact that there were so many students on the college and professional track rather than the vocational track was primarily due to student demand. According to Carr, students preferred these courses because they understood them as the path to jobs that promised higher wages and more prestige.[125] Rather than adjust the curriculum and force students into particular courses based on intelligence or achievement, Carr suggested that economic reforms could be used to change the preferences of students in the classroom. Referencing the high numbers of students choosing to pursue professional rather than vocational education, Carr told the committee, "I can imagine, for instance, that if I could take a group of high school students and tell them, 'If you will go into domestic service you can look forward to $25 a week,' that situation . . . would not exist, in quite as great a degree, at least."[126] Carr's suggestion reflected the broader social reconstructionist perspective of the need to adjust institutional and economic arrangements outside the walls of the schoolhouse to better serve students. As prominent historian and *Social Frontier* contributor Harold Laski noted, "those who seek any serious adaptation of our educational system must work for the transformation of our economic system as the necessary condition of their success."[127] This was a clear point of disagreement between the social reconstructionists and social efficiency progressives.

The differences in the educational vision of the two groups of progressive educators also reflected fundamentally different understandings of the requirements of democratic governance. The social reconstructionists emphasized the need for introducing a spirit of cooperation and respect for fellow students in the classroom as a necessary reform to the antidemocratic competitiveness and excessive individualism of the existing social order. This implied the need for a common and egalitarian classroom where students of all backgrounds and abilities learned together. Additionally, social reconstructionists stressed the need for schools to provide economic literacy on the consequences of various economic arrangements, because "unless the average citizen is the final arbiter of economic issues, democracy is functioning poorly."[128]

For the social efficiency progressives, democracy required differentiation. The social efficiency progressives argued that because children by their nature had differing levels of intelligence, merit, or talent a truly democratic educational system would take this into account when developing an educational system. As Henry Goddard argued, "if democracy means equal opportunity for all . . . then special classes are required; for no child has an equal opportunity in any class where he is forced to mark time because the majority are slower than he."[129] The hope was that educational differentiation in the schools would better prepare those individuals that were best suited for leadership. For the social efficiency progressives, differentiation of educational opportunity and social power on the basis of intelligence represented a rational and beneficial organization of a democratic nation.

THESE TWO VISIONS of progressive education competed for the soul of the education system throughout the 1930s and into the 1940s. As will be discussed in chapter 3, when the extreme economic instability and policy experimentation of the New Deal era gave way to a more conservative era of World War II and the subsequent Cold War, the changed political context proved particularly unfavorable to the political and educational programs of the social reconstructionists. Given how much the social reconstructionist position was dependent on commitment to broader social transformation, once the political support for dramatic economic transformation subsided, the energy behind the social reconstructionist educational vision also faded. For social reconstructionists, schools could train and create the conditions necessary for change, but they could not directly change the political economic system. That was a multigenerational project dependent on students taking the values they learned in schools and changing those systems after leaving. As the commitment to this broader transformation waned, so did the influence of the social reconstructionist vision. Although social efficiency progressives also faced challenges in the post–World War II context, ultimately their educational vision and policy proposals were much better positioned to accommodate the demands of the more conservative political era.[130]

Although both the social efficiency progressives and social reconstructionists fell under the progressive banner, their fundamentally conflicting understandings of the appropriate relationship between education and the broader economic system resulted in starkly different educational visions. As historian of education Ellen Lagemann has noted, "one cannot understand the history of education in the United States during the twentieth century unless one realizes that Edward L. Thorndike won and John Dewey lost."[131] The tendencies to view education as central to the economic success of the individual and the nation, to press for more and better testing tied to national standards, and to measure teacher performance on the basis of tests all have roots in the social efficiency progressive program. The social efficiency victory was not total—few today suggest heredity is critical for shaping education policy—but substantial ideological and methodological aspects of the social efficiency program are still evident in educational discussions today, as indicated by President Obama's speech that opened this chapter.

The social efficiency advocacy that the education system be rationalized in order to most effectively distribute educational opportunity on the basis of merit hinged significantly on how one determined merit and worth—ideas that were deeply intertwined with racial ideology in the early twentieth century. To fully appreciate the contours of the modern education policy landscape and the liberal incorporationist order requires an understanding of the racial politics and Black educational thought that also shaped their formation. Chapter 2 turns to an exploration of the cleavages that divided Black political organizations—which in many ways were quite similar to those dividing the progressive education community—and the consequences for education policy.

CHAPTER TWO

The Achievement of Civil Rights within the Status Quo

Race and Class in Black Political Visions, 1930s–1950s

In the midst of the Great Depression, dramatically different Black educational visions vied for prominence. Ralph Bunche, a professor of political science at Howard University and the eventual first Black president of the American Political Science Association, criticized what he viewed as the dangerous orientation of the education system around fulfilling the demands of the capitalist class. Arguing that "we are living in an economy of capitalism and our educational system consistently harmonizes with the dominant capitalistic pattern," Bunche lamented the fact that "students are infected with the spirit of competition, in harmony with the dominant motif of American business," which hindered working-class solidarity and political advancement.[1] For Bunche, "the proper approach to [the] particular problem of the education of the Negroes . . . must embrace a clear understanding of the relation of the Negro to the American political and economic structure."[2] Although Bunche openly questioned the emphasis on education as a tool of liberation, he argued that, to the extent that there should be "Negro education," it should be alongside white people in similar economic conditions and focused on building awareness and solidarity among the working class—as he put it, "the sort of education which will actually equip them to fight the terrific battles which must be waged in order that they may win economic and political justice."[3]

Howard Hale Long—one of the most prominent Black educators in the country, serving as the assistant superintendent in charge of education research of the Washington, D.C., school system from 1925 to 1948—reflected a starkly different educational vision. Long argued for an educational approach that focused on preparing Black students for the competitive job market and changing backward behavior in order to ensure the advancement of Black people as a group. Indeed, to the extent that a properly designed education system encouraged the union of better-off Black students, Long suggested that education could have positive euthenic *and* eugenic effects.[4] Long argued that education was central to Black political advancement, noting that "there will be accelerated improvement in well-being in so far as it depends upon increased education and increased culture."[5] Contrary to Bunche, Long suggested that competition and efficiency should be integral aspects of Black education and suggested that the "Negro educator should stress the ideal of social efficiency as an indispensable asset in competitive society and the fact that excuses will not suffice."[6] Whereas Bunche argued that education should facilitate challenges to the capitalist economy, Long argued that education should ensure Black cultural and economic integration into the existing class and social structure.[7]

As several scholars have noted, the linkage between education and freedom has meant that education has frequently occupied a prominent place in Black political activity and thought. Scholars have provided extensive coverage of the development of Black education in the antebellum,[8] reconstruction,[9] and postbellum eras[10]—highlighting how the close connection between schooling, citizenship, and economic power has converged to make education a central terrain of political struggle.[11] As the political and material conditions drove education to the center of the agenda, the quotes above reveal that the 1930s were a time of significant disagreement over what counted as liberation, equality, and democracy. And as the quotes from Bunche and Long demonstrate, how one answered these questions had a significant impact on how they understood the purpose and pedagogy that should guide the education of Black students.

The 1930s through the 1950s represent some of the most tumultuous and significant years in Black politics in America. As Risa Goluboff has noted, the popular and scholarly focus on the politics of this era has often emphasized the fight against segregation in transportation, education, and private accommodations as the dominant priorities of Black politics. This view is often accompanied by a triumphalist interpretation of the political victories of this era, culminating in the 1954 Supreme Court decision in *Brown v. Board of Education* that set the stage for the subsequent achievements of the Civil Rights Movement in the 1960s.[12] However, there were also critical and substantial divisions within Black politics that drove starkly different education visions and approaches to education policy.

The central cleavage in Black political thought during these years involved debates over the compatibility of capitalism with democracy, equality, and Black political advancement. I describe the dueling visions as *economic democracy* versus *racial democracy*.[13] Economic democrats argued that racial subordination was fundamentally a problem of the exploitative economic system and advocated prioritizing solutions such as interracial labor organization, economic redistribution, and public job creation as the most effective ways to address the subordinate position of Black Americans. The pedagogical approach of the economic democrats thus included teaching students about the problematic aspects of existing social and economic institutions and encouraged an educational program that promoted class solidarity, educated workers, and unionization.

Alternatively, racial democrats interpreted the primary problem facing Black people as arbitrary exclusion on the basis of skin color. They were committed to the goal of fair incorporation into the existing economic and social order. Racial democrats placed great faith in the ability of equality of educational opportunity to facilitate the fair incorporation of Black students into the economic order and thus pushed for an educational program that privileged combating segregated schools, combating racial prejudice, and ensuring equitable opportunity.[14] Importantly, the two groups disagreed vehemently over the fundamental compatibility of the existing economic institutions with democracy and over the ability of education to address racial subordination in the absence of broader economic reform.

The competing political and educational visions of economic democrats and racial democrats are the subject of this chapter. Although the division within Black education thought during this time period looked similar to broader debates among progressive educators—as Long's affinity for eugenics and the use of the phrase "social efficiency" makes clear—the debates were also distinctive in that these scholars directly address the relationship between education and the position of Black people in the United States. The chapter begins by describing the fundamental political commitments that distinguished these two coalitions. The most significant distinction between these two groups was the disagreement over whether to pursue racial incorporation into the existing social and economic order or to fundamentally challenge and change this order. After identifying the broad political visions of these groups, the chapter then turns to an examination of how these visions guided the differing educational programs promoted by the two coalitions. As in the case of the progressive education movement, examining the divisions within Black politics during this era is critical for understanding why education policy took the shape it did. The reverberations of the fierce debates about the purpose of education and the vision of democracy, as well as the eventual dominance of the racial democracy position, continues to shape the educational landscape today.

The Problems with Democracy

The clearest indication of the disagreements over the appropriate direction for Black politics, and the implications for education policy, come from articles in the *Journal of Negro Education* (*JNE*). The debates that raged in the pages of the *JNE* in part reflected earlier intellectual debates over the purpose of education from the Progressive Era described in chapter 1; however, they were also distinct in their focus on education for Black children. In the early 1930s, there were substantial disagreements over whether to pursue integration in education. Indeed, several authors argued against strong efforts at integration that they saw as unlikely to be achieved[15] and instead advocated embracing segregation as an opportunity to control the education of Black students.[16] As Ralph Bunche noted, in 1935 these voices came from across the political spectrum, with Marcus Garvey and the "back to Africa" movement on the same side as adherents to the "economic separatism" ideas of Booker T. Washington in expressing doubts about the efficacy and desirability of pursuing integration.[17] Others like Congregationalist minister Buell Gallagher advocated embracing segregation in order to build Black schools aimed at reconstructing broader societal institutions, eventually including segregation.[18] Perhaps the most prominent scholar to question the pursuit of integration in the 1930s was W. E. B. Du Bois. Although Du Bois clearly felt that "mixed schools" would be preferable in a perfect world, given the degree of white opposition, the efforts of Black people would be better spent in improving the schools that Black children attended. Indeed, he noted several benefits of segregated schools, arguing "when our schools are separate, the control of the teaching force, the expenditure of money, the choice of textbooks, the discipline and other administrative matters of this sort ought, also, to come into our hands, and be incessantly demanded and guarded."[19] Although the push for desegregation had it skeptics within the Black political community, by the 1930s, it was clear that a majority of Black activists and organizations were firmly in support of pursuing integration.

The push for integration drew support from a broad coalition from across the political spectrum. The editors of the *JNE*, *Opportunity: A Journal of Negro Life*,[20] and the *Journal of Negro History* all endorsed integration as an appropriate political goal. Du Bois's support of a planned segregated economy led the National Association for the Advancement of Colored People (NAACP) to openly repudiate his view, which resulted in his resignation in 1934 as editor of *Crisis*, the NAACP's flagship publication.[21] The journals published the most prominent Black intellectuals, who in large part also advocated the pursuit of integration in education. The NAACP, which had been founded in part as an explicit repudiation of the accommodationism of Booker T. Washington and whose founding platform included a commitment to the elimination of segregation, was already pursuing a legal strategy aimed at integration by the mid-1930s.[22] Even the normally cautious National Urban League (NUL) actively joined the push for integration during the mid-1930s.[23] The opposition to segregation was supported by a variety of other political organizations on the left as well, including the Workers Party, the Socialist Party, and the Communist Party.[24]

Importantly, the broad coalition supporting a project of desegregation consisted of groups with substantial ideological disagreements over pedagogy, the role of education in society, and the political path forward for Black people in the United States. Although the dimensions of disagreement were many, the most consequential division that emerges from an analysis of the early discussions within this community was whether to pursue a political program centered on economic or on racial democracy. The economic democracy position pointed to broad economic inequality resulting from an economic system that concentrated wealth in the hands of the few at the expense of the majority of workers.[25] This ideology suggested a vision of reform that focused on confronting a capitalist political economy to redress inequality.[26] The support for integration from this view stemmed from a broader commitment to extending democracy to economic life in general. The racial democracy framework identified the failure of the United States to fully extend civil and political rights to Black people as a fundamental flaw in American democracy. Advocates of racial democracy argued that until all citizens were guaranteed equal access to the social and economic opportunities offered by the free market, the United States had failed to live up to its democratic ideals. Programmatically, racial democracy ideology privileged securing individual equality of opportunity within the existing political and economic order, and as such the elimination of segregation was central to this political project.

Broadly, those subscribing to the racial democracy position identified segregation as a violation of the ethos of equality of opportunity. Inequities in education were considered especially pernicious as they ultimately put Black students at a disadvantage in the labor market and led to a host of other arbitrary disparities between white and Black citizens. Ideally, the schools should offer an equitable chance for Black and white students to succeed or fail, ensuring that those of equal merit had the same footing when leaving the public education system. Given the understanding that the races did not differ when it came to intelligence, any disparity in educational outcome could be considered a failure of the education system to provide equal opportunity. The central concern with equitable outcomes for those of equal merit led to a natural focus on metrics of comparison of inputs and outputs between white and

Black schools and students, including school funding, intelligence tests, achievement tests, and teacher quality.[27] Pedagogically, this meant a focus on determining the best methods of eliminating differential educational outcomes between similar white and Black students as well as testing to ensure that racial outcomes were indeed substantially similar.

Those committed to an economic democratic vision tended to view segregation as symptomatic of the types of inequities and exploitation that resulted from a relatively unrestrained capitalist economic system. This meant that the fight against segregation was not necessarily primary in the ordering of political grievances but was rather connected to a larger program of broad economic demands such as higher and equal wages, fair employment, political enfranchisement, and fostering interracial class solidarity. Inequities in education were not necessarily more problematic than inequities elsewhere, a reality reflected by the fact that in general economic democrats focused much less on the specifics of educational policy and organization. However, schools could serve as important sites in which to foster worker solidarity and much of the pedagogical practices that were advocated tended to stress the importance of grounding education in the problems of the community and connecting these problems to the existing economic order. There was substantial criticism of the excessively individualistic and competitive ethos of the existing school system and suspicion of the value of standardized educational programs and tests.

The fact that these two ideological programs were both united in the fight against integration throughout the 1930s and into the mid-1940s masked important differences in the end goals of groups within the Black popular front coalition. The writings of central figures and the educational programs of Black political organizations during this period reveal the starkly divergent understandings of the purpose of education and appropriate pedagogical approaches. These differences, although at times submerged during the fight for integration, would return to the surface later in the century in ways that shape educational policy and politics in significant ways.

Economic Democracy

An examination of the pages of the journals focused on Black education demonstrates that throughout the 1930s and into the mid-1940s, the center of gravity in Black political thought was grounded in a commitment to economic democracy that was strongly critical of the existing economic order.[28] Many advocating the economic democracy position had deep ties with unions and left political parties. This group also included several of the most prominent Black academics and government employees. Writing in the wake of the Great Depression and during the height of the New Deal, these authors identified exploitation under the existing economic order as the central problem facing Black people in the United States. The economic democracy position gained traction in Black political thought at a time when radical critiques of the existing economic order were more broadly popular in the midst and aftermath of the Great Depression.

For the economic democrats, a political program centered on organizing the Black masses as workers provided the clearest means of confronting the existing economic order. While individual economic democrats differed on many particular policy prescriptions and end goals, they were united by their belief in the fundamentally economic nature of the problems facing Black people in the United States. This was an important unifying commitment and distinguished this group from the other dominant strand of Black intellectual thought, which sought to center Black politics on racial solidarity. In 1936, just one year after he had helped found the National Negro Congress, John P. Davis wrote, "There can be little doubt that the inequalities experienced by the Negro masses under the New Deal stem from economic and not racial causes."[29] This clear identification of the primacy of the economic over the racial was echoed by former school superintendent E. E. Lewis in the *JNE*'s 1939 yearbook devoted to the position of Black people in the social order. Lewis argued that when comparing the importance of racial and economic elements in the problems facing Black people, "one is led inevitably to the conclusion that the economic rather than the racial factor is fundamental."[30]

Many economic democrats were focused on the economic system as not only a problem for Black people but as a challenge to the democratic ideal more generally. The existence of broad economic inequality was interpreted as evidence of an unjust economic order that concentrated wealth and power in the hands of the affluent few at the expense of the vast majority of workers. Those who were able to unfairly accumulate wealth and power had an outsized voice in the political process, which they used to rig the system further in their favor. Ralph Bunche, one of the most prominent Black intellectuals of the era, argued that democracy had never truly been extended to Black people or the working class as "modern democracy . . . was early put out to work in support of those ruling middle-class interests of capitalistic society which fathered it."[31] Unsurprisingly, Black people had faired particularly poorly under this system that consistently favored the interest of the largely white middle and upper classes. From this standpoint, improving democracy would require significant changes to the existing political economy. Economic democrats had fundamental differences with other Black political thinkers over the question of the desirability of racial inclusion in the economic status quo as an end goal.

Identifying the economic causes as the primary source of problems facing Black Americans suggested a significantly different agenda than identifying racism as the central problem. Pivotal to the political program of the economic democrats was the unionization of the Black working class.[32] Ralph Bunche, a professor of political science at Howard University, clearly articulated the central vision of many in this group in 1939. Bunche advocated for a program that "place[d] less emphasis on race and more on economics and broad political and economic forces."[33] This political program would "avoid dependence on professional Negro leaders" and instead turn to labor leaders, and "devote its full energy toward the incorporation of Negro workers in labor unions, and would carry on incessant educational propaganda among both black and white workers toward this end."[34] George L. P. Weaver, the director of the civil rights committee of the Congress of Industrial Organizations (CIO), echoed many of Bunche's sentiments. Weaver stressed the importance of economic solidarity over racial solidarity, arguing, "We must not only consider the raising of the black worker to a position of equality, but must also consider raising the standards of all workers" and suggested that an "enlightened labor movement more and more considers this a workers' problem, instead of a Negro problem."[35] This stance was repeated by Willard Townsend, the first Black man elected to the board of the CIO, who noted, "Since I firmly believe that economic security is a forerunner of social and political impartiality, it would follow that the Negro must look to organized labor for economic security . . . the so-called racial problem is a workers' problem and must be solved by the organizations and education of workers."[36]

Beyond the call to unionize, full employment was the most common policy proposal that united those pushing the economic democracy view. The focus on full employment was driven not only by the belief that it would materially benefit Black people given their disproportionate share among the unemployed, but that the widespread availability of work would alleviate one of the main drivers of racial tension. George L. P. Weaver noted that full employment would strike at the heart of "racialism" among white and Black people alike, which he understood to be founded on "the fear of job insecurity and competition."[37] Throughout the *JNE*, the belief that problems between the races were primarily driven by job scarcity and economic competition was a common refrain from the economic democracy camp.[38]

The economic democrats saw advancement on the employment and unionization fronts as critical democratic advancements. A. Phillip Randolph framed the fight for organizing workers, higher wages, and better hours as essential to "the larger objective of industrial and political democracy."[39] For Mary Foley Grossman, vice president of the Philadelphia American Federation of Teachers (AFT), a strong public education system was critical for protection against "economic rulers" that "distrust democracy" and sought to "legalize and perpetuate their class oppression."[40] Lucy Randolph Mason, one of the CIO's most active organizers in the South, pushed for cooperation between industry, government, and labor to protect unionization rights and achieve full employment since "economic democracy and political democracy are inseparable—the one cannot be realized without the other."[41] Sociologist Oliver Cox, who advocated a more openly confrontational approach to capitalism, suggested that "the greater the development of democracy, the greater limitations upon capitalist freedom."[42] Like Mason, Cox interpreted the push for full employment as "simply another attempt of workers and their leaders to push democracy another step forward."[43] For the economic democrats, the push for unionization and full employment were central to rectifying key defects of modern democracy.

Those pressing for economic democracy argued not just for centrality of the economic structure as the appropriate focal point for political contestation but forcefully asserted the danger of pursuing a political project aimed only at racial incorporation into existing institutions. The economic democrats contended that the arguments emerging from racial democrats incorrectly placed the blame for the status of Black people on individual beliefs and racial prejudice rather than on the broader political economy. This logic led racial democrats to a political program centered on "the achievement of civil rights within the status quo"[44] and calls for an agenda aimed at eliminating the misconceptions of racial difference that were viewed as the foundation of racial prejudice. For the economic democrats like Cox, this was a fundamental misunderstanding that obscured the fact that "the exploitative act comes first; the prejudice follows."[45] Former school administrator E. E. Lewis noted that "raising the Negro to the white man's present level would mean at best the elimination of narrow margins,"[46] a point echoed by Cox who argued that such a politics sought "to eliminate only the racial aspects of the exploitative system."[47]

Several authors pointed out that racial democracy was a class-inflected position that was "essentially an appeal to the consciousness of the ruling class."[48] The sharpest critiques on this front were frequently aimed at the

NAACP. Ralph Bunche noted "the N.A.A.C.P. has elected to fight for civil liberties rather than for labor unity; it has never reached the masses of Negroes, and remains strictly Negro middle-class, Negro-*intelligentsia*, in its leadership and appeal."[49] Ernest Neal of the Tuskegee Institute noted that the preoccupation with challenging segregation in universities, restaurants, hotels, and public transportation was evidence of the class bias of the NAACP's agenda, since only those relatively well off in the Black community would be able to afford such luxuries if segregation were defeated.[50] Emmett Dorsey, the head of the Political Science Department at Howard University, argued that the NAACP was incapable of developing a broadly progressive "economic program because such a program must necessarily stress labor solidarity and fundamental social relations reform," a position that was "incompatible with the Association's middle class and thoroughly racial philosophy."[51]

Beyond simply failing to reflect the concerns of the vast majority of poor Black people, several articles in the *JNE* pointed out that the NAACP was actively hostile to some of the central efforts of the economic democrats. Ernest Rice McKinney, a journalist and labor organizer who helped found an NAACP chapter at Oberlin while in college, concluded that "the day is rapidly passing and has almost passed in which such groups as the N.A.A.C.P. and the National Negro Business League can play any progressive role at all for the black worker."[52] As labor leader A. Phillip Randolph argued, efforts to unionize Black workers had "suffered greatly and been incalculably hindered" by conservative Black leaders who were "simply opposed to organized labor for the same reason that Mellon or Morgan is opposed to it."[53]

These articles reveal the central tension between the economic and racial democracy ideologies. The economic democrats' belief that economic exploitation was the foundation of Black oppression meant that any broad political strategy aimed at improving the position of Black people would include structural reforms to the existing economic order. Importantly, there was significant disagreement as to what these reforms would be. For many, this meant replacing capitalism with an alternative economic system like socialism. Others thought that reforms could be made within a capitalist system that would sufficiently address the problems of the working class. Despite these differences, these views were united in identifying economic reforms as central to improving the position of Black people. Such a commitment was not intrinsic to the racial democracy position. The racial democrats' belief that the status of Black people was due to the denial of equal civil rights and liberties as well as racial prejudice resulted in a political commitment first and foremost to equalizing opportunities within the existing order.[54] Although several racial democrats also supported the economic reforms advocated by the economic democrats, many others openly opposed them.

Racial Democracy

The main alternative to economic democracy was racial democracy. Mainline civil rights organizations, such as the NAACP and the NUL, as well as many prominent Black professionals and businessmen, were the most prominent proponents of this position. Less radical than the economic democracy ideology, the racial democracy framework identified the failure to extend political and civil rights to Black people as the fundamental flaw of American democracy and the most pressing political grievance. The racial democracy ideology proved much more capable of adapting to the changing political context as the populist fever of the New Deal era gave way to a more conservative economic and international political outlook in the postwar era.

The political program of this group was primarily based on fair access and incorporation into the existing social and economic structures of white America. Although the articulation of goals occasionally differed between individuals and organizations, racial democrats were united by a belief that the fundamental problems facing Black people in the United States could ultimately be traced back to the color line. Their critiques of U.S. social and economic institutions were primarily based on the fact that they unfairly excluded Black people. This differed from the economic democracy framework, which tended to point to the unfair treatment of Black people as a symptom of institutions that were fundamentally unfair for all Americans. Adopting the racial democracy framework resulted in a politics that took race as the primary analytical tool when determining the justness of societal arrangements. Since these groups broadly rejected the notion of biological racial difference or inferiority, any disparity that correlated with race was prima facie evidence of an unjust societal arrangement requiring redress. Programmatically, racial democracy ideology privileged securing individual equality of opportunity within the existing political and economic order. As a result, the elimination of segregation was central to this political project.

The racial democracy framework existed alongside the economic democracy framework in the pages of the *JNE*. Dillard professor of history Lawrence Reddick offers an emblematic summary of the political end goals of racial democrats, arguing: "he (the negro) wants the elimination of the 'race' differential from the social order. He wants to be treated 'like everybody else.' . . . for the

Negro, as *Negro*, the end-purpose of his 'struggle' is to wipe out every distinction on the basis of 'color.' This is the long-time goal."[55] The desire to "be treated like everybody else" was a common refrain and underlined that the primary goal was incorporation into, rather than transformation of, the existing social and economic institutions. Like those in the economic democracy camp, racial democrats were concerned about the economic condition of Black people, but they had a different notion of economic equality. Founder and longtime editor of the *JNE* Charles H. Thompson articulated the problem facing Black people as "Negro workers . . . being denied *economic* equality—equal opportunity for employment and promotion without regard to race."[56]

The notion of "equal opportunity" was fundamental to the racial democracy position and was often used as a means of distinguishing it from the more radical calls for economic redistribution and institutional restructuring emanating from economic democrats. A. D. Beittel, the president of Talladega College, made this distinction quite clear, arguing, "the American ideal does not demand that all be reduced to a dead level of mediocrity, but it does insist on a fundamental equality of opportunity."[57] The former vice president and provost of the University of California, Berkeley, Monroe Deustch, echoed Beittel in a speech marking the opening of the NAACP chapter at the university, claiming: "That is the word 'Equality of opportunity'; all anyone of us has right to ask is 'a fair chance,' and that means the open door to education, the opportunity to do the work for which he is fitted, such promotion as his abilities warrant (not limited by any form of discrimination). . . . *In the race of life you have a right to toe the same mark as all others. You ask nothing more— no one of us can ask more.*"[58] The racial democracy framework did not reject economic differentiation or disparity, but it strongly objected to the arbitrary barriers, like segregation or discrimination, that rigged the game in favor of one group over another. In fact, in attacking discrimination based on race, racial democrats often actively supported discrimination on the basis of what they perceived to be an nonarbitrary dimensions, such as academic merit. For example, F. D. Patterson, director of the Phelps-Stokes Fund and president of the United Negro Fund, called for high academic standards for entrance to college, arguing that "the aristocracy of such institutions must be an aristocracy not of wealth but of talent."[59] The notion of educational "equality of opportunity" was critical in articulating the political program of racial democracy. The focus on ensuring that white and Black people were given a fair and equal shot meant that disparities that did not correlate neatly along race lines, such as *intragroup* economic inequality, faded to the back of the political agenda.

This ordering of political grievances was evident in one of the biggest differences between the racial and economic democracy positions; their diverging views on the importance of material differences between individuals. For the economic democrats the existence of broad economic inequality, regardless of racial distribution, was evidence of a fundamental problem. The same was not true of the racial democrats; indeed, many strenuously objected to the overarching emphasis some of their colleagues placed on material differences. Howard Hale Long, who held a Ph.D. in psychology from Harvard University and served as an associate superintendent of the Washington, D.C., public school system from 1925 through 1948, claimed: "If we succeed in diverting some of the excess emphasis upon the material aspects of the Negro's struggle for survival to the subtler problem of the enduring and determining psycho-physical sets towards himself and the world about him, our efforts will have been more than repaid."[60] This view appears in part attributable to the fact that many in the racial democracy camp were fundamentally less radical on the economic front than their economic counterparts, a distinction that would be sharpened by the 1940s.

The tendency of the racial democracy advocates to focus on nonmaterial foundations of racial inequality was also reflected in their focus on the psychological basis of racial prejudice and attitudes. In part reflecting the burgeoning number of studies from social science disciplines such as psychology and sociology, racial democrats identified irrational attitudes and stereotypes about Black people as foundations of racial inequality and the Jim Crow system. In addition to being irrational, racial democrats warned that racial prejudice caused psychological damage to those who faced segregation.[61] The embrace of the idea that prejudice and attitudes were causal factors in maintaining racial inequality meant that racial democrats embraced the idea that changing attitudes held the potential to pave the way for the full inclusion of Black people into the economic and social order. As sociologist Mary Ellen Goodman argued in the *JNE*, "If we were to educate really intensively and extensively for human relations, from beginning to end of [the] school experience, there might in two generations [be] rather little awareness of race in our society and few problems arising from it."[62] As racial democrats embraced and developed programs to change attitudes and prejudice, such as "intergroup relations" and "interracial education," they portrayed these efforts as essentially apolitical programs to correct misinformation.[63]

This understanding of the origins and significance of racial prejudice was profoundly different than that found among economic democrats. As Oliver Cox argued, "the exploitative act comes first; the prejudice follows," and prejudiced "belief is an empty, harmless, illusion, like beliefs in werewolves or fairies, without the exploitative interest with which it is impregnated."[64] Sociologist William Brown was particularly critical of approaches like intergroup education, arguing that race prejudice "is not going to be appreciably weakened by preachments or by mere assaults upon the stupid misconceptions current among whites about Negroes. Such approaches and programs attack the symptoms and manifestations of race prejudice, rather than its associated factors. *Any realistic program will take into account the economic foundations of race prejudice.*"[65] It was this economic interpretation of racial prejudice that led economic democrats like CIO board member Willard Townsend to advocate for a political program aimed at full employment, since it would both advance the material interest of Black people and lead "to the removal of the white worker's fear of him as an economic rival."[66] For Cox and others in the economic democracy vein, this focus on prejudice and belief was a dangerous political move because it fed the mysticism that beliefs were "prime movers," which turned attention away from the intense political fight needed to improve the status of Black people, which was the only way to effectively address prejudice.[67]

For many racial democrats, a key part of changing the prejudices held by white people involved changing Black behavior that contributed to these prejudices. These efforts were driven by the belief that the particular shortcomings of Black family and culture were central mechanisms in keeping Black people in a subordinate position. Howard University sociologist E. Franklin Frazier argued that Black "family disorganization probably has been the most important social problem that has retarded the development of the Negro since his emancipation,"[68] claiming that because it "has failed in its function as a socializing agency, it has handicapped the children in their relations to the institutions in the community."[69] Any broad political agenda that hoped to fully integrate Black people into American society would thus have to address perceived deficiencies in the Black family that harmed Black children and spurred white prejudice. As a result, racial democrats argued that programs geared toward educating and changing Black behavior were a key to advancing racial equality.[70] These programs were often specifically geared to lower-class Black people, whose family "subculture" was considered particularly problematic.[71] Indeed, several authors were careful to distinguish that many of the behavioral problems that resulted in low standards of living for Black people and stimulated white prejudice were specific to lower-class Black subculture.[72] Significantly, since racial democrats like psychologist Herman Canady suggested "a psychologically good home or a highly stimulating situation can be set up at any economic level," this was a political program that stressed primarily attitudinal changes over structural ones.[73]

The tendency of the racial democracy advocates to focus on the standards and behavior of the Black family or Black culture was roundly criticized by those in the economic democracy camp. The most central critique from this angle was directed at the failure to examine the economic foundations of the supposed poor standards and home life of Black people. Cox summarized what many in the economic democracy camp saw as a fundamental flaw in racial ideology vision, noting, "both race prejudice and Negro standards are consistently dependent variables. They are both produced by the calculated economic interests of the Southern oligarchy. Both prejudice and the Negro's status are dependent functions of the latter interest."[74] For Cox and other economic democrats, the "deficiencies" of Black life and culture and racial prejudice that racial democrats focused on were both fundamentally the result of exploitative economic interests.

In addition to attitudes and behavior, racial democrats also looked toward the underdeveloped skills of the Black workforce as an explanatory factor for the social and economic position of Black people. Although racial democrats recognized that prejudice may keep some employers from hiring Black workers, many also argued that Black underemployment stemmed from the fact that white workers were typically better skilled. Indeed, many racial democrats viewed the poor skills of Black people as a *greater* barrier in the workplace than racial prejudice. As prominent NUL leader T. Arnold Hill argued, there was "some evidence that indicates a preference for proficiency that *overrides* race prejudice."[75] Hill and others argued that in an era of rapid technological advance in changing labor market demands, concentrating on improving the skills of Black employees could be a particularly effective means of racial advancement.[76] The focus on upgrading the skills of Black workers so that they could compete more fairly with white workers was an indication that racial democrats were largely comfortable with the free market economy and the inequitable distribution of goods, so long as the inequity was not the result of some arbitrary factor like race.[77]

While acknowledging that racial discrimination and segregation were problems, the focus on training highly skilled workers as a way to potentially overcome these barriers was essentially an affirmation of the potential fairness of the market in distributing jobs and wages. This was a fundamental difference with those advocating an economic democracy approach, many of whom explicitly critiqued the exploitative nature of the market. For the economic democrats, the distribution of employment and wages was fundamentally the result of a political contestation between labor and management rather than the just reward for an individual's marketable skills. Apart from the focus on racial prejudice, racial democrats were generally loath to place the blame for Black unemployment and poor wages on the operation of the broader labor market, looking instead to strategies to increase the competitiveness of Black people as a means of uplift.

Like the economic democrats, the racial democrats argued for their political agenda as a move toward perfecting democracy. Claiming that the social sciences had shown that intellectual capabilities were normally distributed in the human population and did not correlate with race, W. Hardin Hughes argued in the *JNE* that "Equality, not of achievement as measured materially but of opportunity, is a basic principle of democracy."[78] A foundational problem with segregation and discrimination for the racial democracy viewpoint was that it created a situation in which competition between white and Black workers was not fundamentally free and fair. For the racial democrats, inequality that resulted from unfair competition was a violation of the liberal democratic ideal.[79]

Given this articulation of the problems facing American democracy and Black Americans specifically, many in the racial democracy camp equated democracy with a capitalist economic system. In a 1941 *JNE* article, Charles Johnson proclaimed, "Political democracy has been associated with the economic system of capitalism and the repudiation of free capitalism, when it has occurred, has been accompanied by the repudiation of democracy as we know it. Our present national concern for the preservation of democracy is bound up in considerable measure with our concern for the preservation of our economic system, which is the basis of our present living standards and our hopes for the future."[80] Although the virtues of a capitalist economy and its essential connection to democracy were increasingly stressed as the Cold War intensified, the ideological outlines of the racial democracy position were present well before the onset of the Cold War.[81] While the economic democrats viewed the economic system as perpetuating an undemocratic concentration of wealth and power, racial democrats were most concerned with the fact that the concentration of wealth was exclusively reserved for white citizens. Whereas economic democrats called for class solidarity to press for common political interests, racial democrats like Howard Hale Long asserted, "the Negro group must maintain a diversity of interests. Only sterility is likely to result from too much solidarity. Let Negros be found in the ranks of all social and economic movements."[82] Ultimately, for racial democrats, until all citizens were guaranteed equal access to the social and economic opportunities offered by the free market, the United States had failed to live up to its democratic ideals.

Distinctions in Educational Purpose and Pedagogy

The division between racial and economic democrats on the source of Black inequality and broader political goals drove distinctly different educational programs. Although both groups coalesced around an anti-segregation position by the 1950s, this common opposition to desegregation obscured educational visions that were frequently in conflict about the purpose of education. The two groups differed about classroom practices, the function of education, and the overall importance of education to racial equality.

Education held a particularly prominent place in the political program of racial democracy. Racial democrats coalesced around an understanding of education's purpose that emphasized its ability to facilitate the fair incorporation of Black people into the broader social and economic institutions that had largely been reserved for white Americans. Racial democrats argued that Black children had long suffered from inferior education. This inequality of educational opportunity was seen as the foundation for a host of subsequent racially disparate outcomes. Furthermore, racial democrats were committed to the belief that racial stereotypes and prejudice could be attacked with a proper educational program. The faith in the potential for education to broadly improve the material, political, and interpersonal situation of Black people was foundational to the racial democracy vision. This particular vision of the purpose of education in turn drove the racial democrats to advocate for a specific set of educational programs and pedagogical approaches to achieve their objectives. The racial democrats' faith that education was pivotal to incorporation ultimately translated to support for specific classroom strategies such as interracial education to undermine prejudice, adjustment education to ensure that the students were equipped with the skills necessary to compete in the labor market, and eventually a muscular testing requirement to ensure the equitable provision of education.

On the other hand, economic democrats were advocating for the radical redistribution of wealth and moving away from a market economy. For economic democrats, the value in education was its ability to help individuals understand the economic basis of social problems as well as the ability to promote the solidarity necessary to challenge the existing economic order. Fundamentally, whereas racial democrats sought an educational program designed with an aim to better prepare Black students for a fair shot within the existing economic structures, for economic democrats, the value of education was in its ability to lay the foundations for changing those same economic structures. Although education was a central aspect of the racial democratic agenda, education was of much less programmatic importance in the broader political strategy of the economic democrats.

The differences in approaches of the two groups is clear when considering some of the specific educational programs proposed in the 1940s and 1950s. Economic and racial democrats disagreed on the value and importance of intercultural education, adjustment education, and standardized testing for improving the economic and political situation of Black Americans. These disagreements over the purpose of education and specific pedagogical approaches ultimately reflected the profoundly different political commitments of the two groups.

One of the most significant educational programs that emerged from Black educators and social scientists in the 1940s was the push for interracial education.[83] This movement was based on the understanding that inaccurate beliefs and uncorrected racial stereotypes led to racial prejudice and discrimination, which ultimately propped up segregation. Interracial education, according to schoolteacher and frequent *JNE* contributor Rose Zeligs, was "the instruction in knowledge, interest, respect and mutual appreciation of different cultures" with the goal to "make children conscious of the process by which they get and keep their prejudices, and to eliminate weird and grotesque concepts and stereotypes."[84] This educational strategy found broad support from several teacher, religious, philanthropic, and civil rights organizations. Although both racial democrats and economic democrats supported versions of interracial education, the content and expectations of their respective programs were substantially different.

For racial democrats, the interracial education movement was an attempt to attack the attitudes they believed were the foundation of racial discrimination. Although white attitudes were the primary target, intercultural education was also viewed as a means of addressing the low self-esteem of Black youths due to their own exposure to these stereotypes. Through providing information that rectified negative stereotypes about Black people, those advocating for interracial education hoped to correct and eventually eliminate beliefs they thought held up the regime of racial discrimination and segregation.

For many, the interracial education movement fit particularly well with the racial democratic ideal. In 1944, the *JNE* devoted its entire annual yearbook to "Education for Racial Understanding," an educational strategy that was gaining traction among racial liberals. Around the same time, the New York

City–based Bureau for Intercultural Education began to publish a series of manuals and short books that sought to guide public schoolteachers in best practices.[85] By the 1940s, with several nationally prominent educators on the board of directors and with a climate that was increasingly amenable to intercultural education programs, the bureau began to publish a series that focused more specifically on race.[86] Entitled *Problems of Race and Culture in American Education*, the series reflected many of the discussions present in the *JNE* and there was substantial crossover between the two. Hortense Powdermaker and Ina Corrine Brown, both contributors to the *JNE*, wrote books for the series and several authors that were active in the *JNE* served on the board or as advisors to the bureau, including William Kilpatrick, Alain Locke, Allison Davis, Theodore Brameld, and Charles Johnson.[87]

Significantly, many saw interracial education as an alternative to an economic approach to addressing racial inequality. As the report from the Second National Conference on Intergroup Relations noted, this was an agenda that called for an "approach free from dependence upon cliches," such as a class analysis. The focus was instead on developing "knowledge of the dynamics of intergroup relations and conflicts . . . not explained by any one isolated factor such as the economic."[88] This vision of interracial education fit well with the racial democracy framework, specifying the ultimate "ends to be achieved—complete and unqualified integration of all minorities into the total American community."[89] For many proponents of interracial education, and the racial democracy framework more broadly, achievement of integration and full incorporation into American society did not require fundamental transformation of economic and social structures. Integration could be achieved through education to eliminate prejudice. Proper education could reduce white prejudice, which would inevitably lead to an improvement in Black societal standing.[90]

In his introduction to the *JNE* yearbook, Martin Jenkins, professor of education at Howard University, provided a comprehensive outline of the contours and purpose of an interracial education program, and why such a program was seen as necessary. Identifying the primary problem facing Black people as the denial of the "right to equal opportunity for participation in the economic, political and social organization" of the United States, Jenkins noted that the purpose of the yearbook was to investigate how education could bridge the divide between the ideal of equality of opportunity and the reality of widespread prejudice and segregation.[91] Arguing that "education, the deliberate use of words and symbols, can be effective in modifying racial attitudes," he pushed for a program of interracial education, which he understood as "any organized and consciously designed program which has as its primary aim the improvement (i.e. changing in a favorable direction) of attitudes concerning subordinate racial groups in our society."[92] A well-designed interracial education program could be a particularly effective tool in improving racial relations, and for Jenkins, "the most desirable programs are those which have as their goal the *unqualified assimilation* of Negroes into American life."[93] The promise that interracial education could eventually undermine prejudice and pave the way for full racial incorporation into American life meant that it had particular appeal to racial democrats.

The concept of interracial education extended beyond the formal primary and secondary classroom. The *JNE* yearbook carried articles that examined existing programs and their potential for changing attitudes of adults, focusing especially on those in religious organizations,[94] interracial organizations,[95] Black organizations,[96] philanthropic foundations,[97] labor organizations,[98] the mass media,[99] and government agencies.[100] While it was recognized that efforts that targeted the racial attitudes of adults were worthwhile, it was broadly understood that interracial education could be especially effective for children.[101] Racial democrats understood that public primary and secondary schools were critical sites if interracial education efforts were to succeed.

The *JNE* featured several articles that described the particulars of what an interracial education strategy would include. Anthropologist Hortense Powdermaker offered specific advice for how to attack race prejudice in the classroom. First and foremost in Powdermaker's program (and central to most interracial education programs) was the "wide-spread popularization of the scientific facts of race and the anthropological concept that difference does not necessarily connote superiority."[102] The elimination of the idea of biological racial difference, particularly in terms of intelligence, was a central part of the interracial education movement.[103] This meant exposing students to research that demonstrated that there were no innate differences between races.

Apart from challenging the notion of inherent racial difference, interracial education advocates pushed for changes in the curriculum to include discussion of the positive contributions of non-majority groups. In his 1944 *JNE* yearbook article, Roy Wilkins noted that the majority of textbooks either completely ignored the role of minorities or actively promoted ideas of white racial superiority.[104] For Wilkins and others, this was particularly problematic for Black children, as the lack of exposure to "great men" of their race ultimately meant "they cannot function in a democracy without the self-respect which comes from a knowledge of the intrinsic worth of their own people."[105] The calls for changed textbook and interracial education were amplified as psychologists increasingly focused on the damage to the Black child's personality associated with segregated education and racist textbooks.[106] This idea of harm inflicted on the Black personality by inequitable and segregated education would become a major plank in the NAACP's legal fight against segregation. Interracial education advocates were focused on both white prejudice and the psychological damage that such prejudice posed to Black students.[107]

In her 1944 manual *Probing Our Prejudices*, Powdermaker offered several other activities that could be useful in exposing the problems of prejudice, including assigning students to give a variety of reports focusing on race in other countries, the historical use of prejudice against religious and racial groups, and the prejudice of the Nazi regime, all with the aim of "exploding the myth of racial superiority."[108] Powdermaker and other interracial education advocates called for the broad incorporation of social scientific research into school curricula and attention to the achievements of minorities in the hopes that this would begin to break down the misguided and irrational idea of racial superiority.[109]

In addition to the factual focus, interracial education advocates sought to tap into the emotional responses of students to break down racial stereotypes. In the first manual published in the Intercultural Education Bureau's *Problems of Race and Culture in American Education* series, William Vickery and Stewart Cole advised that "teachers should plan experiences for their pupils which will affect their emotional reactions toward those of a different race."[110] The authors suggested a variety of techniques that might be useful in achieving the desired reactions, including hearing speakers of different races, exposing students to art and music of minority groups, and field trips to minority neighborhoods.[111] Such activities were premised on the hope that they would "enable youngsters of the dominant group to identify themselves more humanely with their classmates."[112] For the vast majority of interracial education advocates, this also naturally meant a commitment to racial integration in the classroom, as direct exposure to students of different races was especially powerful in helping make emotional connections across race lines. In fact, as historian Leah Gordon has noted, the rise in the focus on racial prejudice as a problem correlated with the disappearance of critiques of integration from the pages of the *JNE*.[113]

Interracial educational advocates also pressed for the use of attitudinal tests to determine the existing prejudices of the students. One of the most popular of these tests, known as the Social Distance Scale, asked students to self-report their willingness to interact with members of different races and cultures in a variety of different contexts including friendship, the workplace, in the neighborhood, and marriage.[114] Powdermaker claimed that this test could be useful in forcing students to confront their own prejudices and suggested that teachers host "truth parties" in the classroom where students would tell the class their prejudices and how they thought they had acquired them.[115] In a reflection of the ultimate aims of this kind of interracial education, Vickery and Cole argued that these attitude tests were particularly useful tools in evaluating the success of a particular interracial program. The authors suggested that the test should be administered both before and after students had been exposed to a particular interracial education program, arguing that movement toward less prejudiced responses indicated success.[116] For the vast majority of interracial education advocates, attitudinal shifts were the end goal.

Importantly, in conjunction with factual and emotional strategies, interracial education experts were vocal about the need to make use of "American values," especially a commitment to equality of opportunity, to stress the inconsistency between racial prejudice and the "American Creed."[117] Powdermaker noted "the inconsistencies between the prejudiced attitudes to Negroes and our values should be made very clear."[118] She pushed for teachers to have students focus on the tension between the foundational documents like the Bill of Rights and the current treatment of minorities in the United States.[119] Vickery and Cole stressed the need for "a unit on the ideals of equal opportunity in education,"[120] with particular attention to how denial of equal opportunity "threatens American democracy by keeping part of the population ignorant, unequipped for work, and incapable of self-improvement."[121] In Ina Corinne Brown's manual for the Bureau of Intercultural Education, *Race Relations in a Democracy*, Brown was careful to point out the pivotal place of education for economic, political, and civic equality, arguing that "equality of educational opportunity underlies all the others."[122]

Consistent with the racial democracy position, the interracial education advocates were careful to suggest that value of equality of educational opportunity was important because it helped ensure that academic merit or talent rather than race would be the critical factor in social position. Vickery and Cole suggested teaching students this as early as kindergarten, noting that teachers should stress "How everybody is rewarded according to his ability, talent, and good manners—no special favors accorded to the socially elite or to any particular racial, religious, nationality, or socio-economic group."[123] Powdermaker echoed this sentiment, praising the ability of equality of opportunity to create a society in which a "man could get rich through his own ability and effort and rise from the class into which he had been born."[124] Like the broader racial democracy position, the dominant version of interracial education articulated in the 1940s was consistent with the idea of social and economic inequality as long as such inequality was based on a "neutral" category like academic talent rather than an arbitrary category like race, ethnicity, or nationality.

The calls for interracial education programs did not exclusively come from racial democrats. Several authors in the economic democracy camp attempted to articulate a version of interracial education in the pages of the *JNE*. In his article in the 1944 yearbook, J. Max Bond, an administrator at the Tuskegee Institute, argued for the importance of education for the elimination of racial misunderstanding. However, Bond was careful to connect the existence of this racial misunderstanding to the economic forces of capitalism. He suggested that the most promising form of interracial education could be found in the educational programs of the labor movement.[125] Criticizing "our highly individualized, competitive, capitalistic society,"[126] Bond asserted that the labor movement's promotion of education "center[ed] around job and wage discriminations, housing, health, collective bargaining, and more recently against race hate" offered the best example of interracial education that would most likely lead to concrete improvement in the lives of Black workers.[127] John A. Davis echoed this view in his examination of interracial education programs in organized labor that stressed "union and worker solidarity" as the most important aspect of any interracial education program.[128]

Finally, Caroline Ware, a history professor and former New Dealer, offered the clearest outline of what an interracial education program that originated from a commitment to economic democracy might look like. Ware argued:

> In particular, students should realize how crucially their position is bound up with general economic conditions, and should recognize a special responsibility to be informed on economic matters, and a special stake in working for measures that involve economic expansion and full employment. Moreover, since the mass labor unions offer the milieu in which the greatest amount of interracial contact and collaboration is taking place, and since Negro and white workers are building common institutions, common experiences, and a common society in meeting their common economic problems, special attention should be given to providing Negro students with an understanding of labor organization.[129]

In addition to the focus on educating Black people on the importance of the economic forces responsible for their subordinate position, Ware also pushed for a corollary program aimed at low-income whites stressing worker solidarity as well as programs aimed at the wealthy informing them of "the extent to which their own lives are dependent upon what happens to others."[130]

Crucially, for Ware, Bond, and Davis, education for racial understanding that stressed the economic foundations of racial oppression could be a useful tool in the broader political struggle. These authors were careful to point out the need for interracial education to focus on the political and economic dimensions behind race prejudice and discrimination, a tendency largely missing from the racial democracy framework. This commitment reflects the difference in the broader political aims of the racial and economic democrats. For the economic democrats, who were committed to the view that prejudice and discrimination were the result of the economic forces of capitalism, it was imperative that any educational program make this link clear. Furthermore, for economic democrats the educational program was secondary to the economic programs like full employment. Economic democrats generally viewed the educational approach as insufficient in the absence of success on these broader fronts.[131] As will become clear, the fundamentally distinct political commitments of economic and racial democrats not only influenced the approach to interracial education but also led different positions on the role that education should play in shaping Black culture and behavior.

Cultural Backwardness and Social Adjustment Through Education

Although interracial education offered a solution to the racial democrats' concern with attitudinal prejudices, it did not represent the full extent of the educational program advocated by racial democrats.[132] While the irrationality of white prejudice was a substantial barrier to be overcome, racial democrats were also deeply concerned with cultural and skill differences between white and Black people that they understood as at least partially responsible for white prejudice.[133] In fact, many racial democrats suggested that the cultural backwardness and poor job skills that characterized the Black population were capable of keeping Black people in an inferior position *even in the absence* of racial prejudice.[134] Like the problem of prejudice, racial democrats looked to the education system to address these potential problems, advancing educational programs that focused on changing the cultural practices and skill level of Black people to help them adjust to the existing institutions and societal expectations.

As the idea of biological race difference became increasingly discredited within the social sciences, inquiries turned to questions of how best to account for the drastically different position of white and Black people in society. One of the points of entry into this question was to examine differences in familial structure and social behavior more broadly. The differences that social scientists appeared to find regarding family structure and behavior was of particular interest to the racial democrats because the political end goal of incorporation left little room for large differences that correlated with race. Furthermore, the majority of studies examining the "Black family" sought to explain why they differed from white people, normalizing the "white family" structure as ideal.[135] This led many to call for the assimilation or acculturation of Black people into the supposed dominant family structures. As Charles Johnson argued, the "manifestations of cultural backwardness, though correctable, are nevertheless strong barriers against acceptability in the common American society."[136] Given the ultimate political aim of equitable incorporation into the existing society, the "cultural backwardness" of Black people represented a problem that needed to be overcome.

The *JNE* reflected this concern with the behavior of the Black family as early as the 1930s. In a 1939 *JNE* article, E. Franklin Frazier outlined the particular deviations that distinguished the Black family, including "loose sexual morals," "widespread illegitimacy," "maternal in organization," ultimately producing children who were illiterate, had problems with impulse control, and were prone to juvenile delinquency. However, critically for Frazier, some Black families, namely, those that had their own land or had "assimilated the culture of whites," had been able to develop a family structure that more closely approximated that of white families.[137] With the end goal of incorporation in mind, Frazier advocated for the elimination of racial barriers to economic success and cultural adjustment of the Black family.[138]

In the same year, anthropologist Allison Davis offered a similar analysis of what he took to be the problematic nature of the Black family.[139] Noting that the "American Negro family, as sociologists have constantly pointed out, is relatively ineffective in training the Negro person to take on the normal sexual and familial behavior of American society," Davis argued this had substantial negative consequences for the "social adjustment" of Black people in the United States.[140] Davis suggested that the main problem of systematic discrimination against Black people was that it confined them disproportionately to the lower class. For Davis, it was not Black culture that was aberrant, it was lower-class culture.[141] Davis, citing Frazier among others, pointed to the "major differences of behavior within the Negro group, according to economic level," as evidence of the class-based nature of the deviant behaviors.[142] Ultimately, the reason that Black families appeared to suffer from so many maladies was due to the fact that the caste system had driven Black people "into lower economic, occupational and educational levels, and thereby fixing upon them the social and educational traits of the lower *class* in America."[143]

The solution, according to Davis, was to raise more Black families into the middle class. Davis suggested that this would involve the gradual elimination of the racial "caste system," but he focused more attention on the "remedial work with individuals, in which we direct them towards new class-goals and show them the techniques for reaching these goals."[144] This was an ideal arena for education, which would be tasked with making lower-class Black students "understand that the social rewards of higher status are satisfying enough to justify hard work and renunciation on their part to change their behavior."[145] Much like Frazier, a major part of Davis's ultimate proscription was changing the behavior of Black people to more closely mirror that of middle-class white people.

The idea that Black people should seek "assimilation" or "acculturation" into the dominant cultural patterns motivated a wide array of educational programs aimed at facilitating this transition. Some of these suggested programs focused on practical skills that were believed to be particular problem areas for Black people. Maudelle Bousfield, the first Black principal of a Chicago public school, pointed to the high rates of morbidity and mortality among Black people and suggested that general health and hygiene should be a central focus of education for Black students. Bousfield pushed for educating about the need for proper "food, sleep, fresh air, personal hygiene; cleanliness of the home and toilets" in school, with the goal that students would "carry-over from the school to the home" these desirable habits.[146] Schools could be an avenue through which Black families began to learn best practices that could help reduce some of the disparities between Black and white people.

Far more common than educational programs focused on changing practical habits were suggestions for educational programs that sought to adjust the psychological outlook and "personality" of Black students. Many educators hoped to make Black students more successful in life through developing certain "personality" traits that were believed to be characteristic of successful white and middle-class students, and necessary for advancing socially and economically. For T. Arnold Hill, this meant education should seek to "develop initiative, aggressiveness, [and] confidence" in order for Black students to eventually match their white counterparts in the workplace.[147] Bousfield stressed that if the Black student was "ever to take his place as a responsible American citizen, he must learn to realize that thrift and frugality must be practiced in all things."[148]

In 1944, Gunnar Myrdal, following in the footsteps of Frazier and Davis, pointed out that the "low standards of efficiency, reliability, ambition, and morals actually displayed by the average Negro" were in part due to the fact that racism and segregation had prevented Black people from adopting white cultural norms.[149] According to Myrdal, this had led Black people in the United States to develop a "distorted" culture characterized by several "forms of social pathology" and "unwholesomeness," including unstable families, underemphasis on education, high crime rates, and "personality difficulties."[150] Myrdal devoted an entire chapter to the personality problems produced by, and characteristic of, Black culture, including a "tendency to be aggressive,"[151] generally likely to be "more indolent, less punctual, less careful, and generally less efficient as a functioning member of society" compared to white people,[152] overly superstitious, a "love of the gaudy, the bizarre, the ostentatious,"[153] "sexual looseness" and "weak family bonds,"[154] more prone to criminal activity,[155] and generally "unfixed moral standards."[156] Like Davis, Myrdal is careful to point out that these characteristics were largely confined to the lower class, arguing that many of the general disparities between white and Black people could be traced to "the fact that the proportion of lower class Negroes is so much greater."[157]

Like Davis and Frazier, Myrdal's suggestion for dealing with the aberrant behavioral differences that caused the myriad "personality difficulties" was to change the culture. Myrdal argued, "*it is to the advantage of American Negroes as individuals and as a group to become assimilated into American culture, to acquire the traits held in esteem by the dominant white Americans.*"[158] For Myrdal, education was the way in which it could be accomplished. His strong advocacy of increasing the general educational level of Black people was based on his belief that "education means an assimilation of white American culture."[159] Ultimately, Myrdal envisioned an education system that would reduce the cultural and personality differences between white and Black people by helping rid Black people of cultural differences that were partially responsible for keeping them politically and economically subordinate. As historian Alice O'Connor notes, this move essentially positioned "Negro" culture as a culture of poverty, only escapable through adopting white cultural norms.[160]

Myrdal's report had a large impact in the pages of the *JNE*, receiving regular mention in a wide variety of articles long after it had been published, and the problems of the "black personality" and cultural difference were a frequent topic of concern. The academic turn to focus on the damaged "Black personality" was driven by many of the same forces that encouraged a focus on white prejudice, namely, the growth in funding and increased prestige of social psychological approaches in the social sciences.[161] Several articles in the *JNE* in the 1950s reflected the increasing concern with the problematic

"Black personality" and attempted to offer specific educational solutions. Walter Daniel, a professor of education at Howard University, argued that "education should develop a personality that can cope with the problems with which it is confronted and can advance social progress." He pushed for schools to develop "frustration-tolerance" in their Black students.[162] Daniel suggested this would encourage "the delaying of gratification" and help build "restraint" and "will power" necessary for the success of Black students.[163] Although Daniel acknowledged that "frustration-tolerance" would be particularly helpful given the barriers that Black students face, it also would address the problem of Black "impulse control" identified by Myrdal, Frazier, and Davis.

Several authors emphasized the importance of building the self-esteem of Black students. After conducting a series of experiments in which they attempted to show a preference for white skin among Black and white children, psychologists Kenneth and Mamie Clark suggested that their results pointed to "the need for a definite mental hygiene and educational program that would relieve children of the tremendous burden of feelings of inadequacy and inferiority which seem to become integrated into the very stricture of personality as it develops."[164] Regina Goff, an education specialist serving the Florida State Department of Education, struck a similar chord as the Clarks, noting that the problems of Black identity made it "apparent that the Negro child needs an enriched program of training which places more emphasis on building of attitudes toward himself, attitudes of worth of self, respect for self, and confidence."[165] Professor Lawrence Nicholson of Stowe Teachers College in St. Louis expressed a similar concern in his article outlining the Urban League's position on the need for the "adjustment of Negro youth" and stressed the importance of an educational program centered on "ministering to the psychological needs of Negro youth for higher levels of aspiration."[166] These suggestions were all driven by the belief that the damaged "Black personality" would limit the ability of Black students to assimilate white cultural norms that were necessary in order to achieve fair incorporation into the existing order. The common solution offered by these *JNE* articles was an educational intervention focused on changing lower-class "Black personality" and culture.

Skills Adjustment

Concern with the skill level that Black workers brought to the workplace garnered the attention of racial democrats from the start of the *JNE*'s existence. The existence of a skill gap between white and Black workers was particularly troubling to this group because it had the potential to relegate Black people to inferior economic positions even in the absence of discrimination on the part of the employer. Therefore, any political project that sought to eliminate racial prejudice would also need to focus on ensuring that Black people were similarly situated when competing with white people. Racial democrats turned to the education system as a means of eliminating important skill gaps between white and Black people.

Several racial democrats pointed to the skills differential as a particularly powerful explanation for the inferior economic and social position of Black people. Some scholars argued that the poor preparation of Black people often meant that employers and professions that were open to hiring Black workers were unable to given the lack of appropriately skilled Black workers.[167] Furthermore, as T. Arnold Hill argued, a rational employer would always select a more skilled employee over a less skilled one, which meant that even in a labor market devoid of racial discrimination, the skill differential between white and Black workers would mean widespread economic advantage for white workers.[168] Some authors, like F. D. Patterson, the director of the philanthropic Phelps-Stokes Fund, defined racial income disparities entirely in terms of skill differential. Patterson argued:

> In 1952 Negroes earned 52 percent as much in salaries and wages as whites. Some 40 percent of all Negro families had incomes of less than $2,000 whereas only 16.5 percent of whites had incomes of less than $2,000; 10 percent of Negro families earned more than $5,000 a year as compared to 35 percent of white families. These discrepancies in earnings reflect the fact that one-half of the Negro male population is unskilled. Only one-sixth of the white population is so classified, yet the white group represents 90 percent of the total population. It is evident, therefore, that the Negro college must continue for a long time to come to hold the door of educational opportunity open to many Negro youth.[169]

This formulation explicitly blamed racial disparity in wages and jobs on the inferior skills that Black workers brought to the marketplace. The solution offered by Patterson and others to these racial disparities was to look to the education system to upgrade the skills of Black workers. This represents a significant difference from the economic democrats' position, which pointed to the structure of the labor market, the lack of government commitment to full employment, and the exploitation of labor as the key explanation for these racial disparities.

It was particularly important for racial democrats, who were committed to the idea of fair incorporation into the existing economic structure, that Black workers bring the same skill level to the labor market in order to ensure fair competition between white and Black workers. Additionally, scholars like Ernest Neal from the Tuskegee Institute suggested that the need for a focus on enhancing the skills of Black workers was reinforced by the shifting demands of a labor market in the midst of a technological transformation. Neal argued "in the future Negroes cannot look for security in agriculture nor the unskilled jobs in industry. Mechanization of agriculture and industry is making cheap unskilled labor unessential in our economy. This means that the traditional function of the Negro is gradually passing out of existence; and if he is to survive, he must survive as a competitor."[170] Racial democrats noted that providing equitable education made economic sense, as the failure to educate capable Black students and workers represented a significant waste of human resources.

The solution proposed by racial democrats to the unfair competition between white and Black workers in the labor market was to use the education system to raise the skill level of Black students so that they might compete with white students to meet the demands of the labor market. Professor of education Leander Boykin argued that "inequality of educational opportunity" was "limiting Negro youth's choice of jobs."[171] For Walter Daniel, another professor of education at Howard University, the clear solution for the skill differential between white and Black workers was "increasing educational opportunities so that they will be equally advisable to all individuals in accordance with their needs, interests and abilities."[172] For the racial democrats, the provision of equal educational opportunity was necessary to the fulfillment of the democratic ideal as it ensured economic reward and differentiation based on one's abilities rather than race.[173]

The importance of a focus on equalizing educational opportunities was magnified by the belief that not only would Black workers be disadvantaged in the marketplace by a skill differential, but this lack of skill would ultimately feed into and justify white prejudice. As several scholars had noted, the lack of income for many Black families, in part driven by skill differences between the races, was associated with deviant family morals and culture that was a critical part of the "vicious circle."[174] Many of the authors concerned about the cultural backwardness of Black people supported skill upgrading as part of a program that would eventually help them assimilate into more appropriate cultural norms. The result of putting Black people on equal footing in competition for jobs would be the fulfillment of democratic ideals, the incorporation of Black people into middle- and upper-class culture, and an economic windfall for the nation. Education could be used to adjust the individual to meet the demands of the existing economic and social structures.

The desire to prepare Black students to compete on equal footing with their white counterparts led several racial democrats to seek to tie the education system closer to the demands of the labor market. For example, Boykin called for the development of a new curriculum and argued that "the new curriculum should be aimed at preparation for life. From this we must conclude that vocational education is implied."[175] Vocational education was seen as a particularly effective way of preparing individuals to enter the labor market. Significantly, racial democrats argued that any vocational education program must take into account the particular problems facing Black people. For Maudelle Bousfield, if "one of the objectives of education is to prepare for efficient service in a chosen vocation, then the education of Negros must be directed towards vocations in which there seems to be reasonable hope of either immediate or remote employment."[176]

While Bousfield stressed the importance that vocational education prepare Black people for the jobs that were actually open to them, Charles Johnson argued that schools needed to prepare students for the changing demands of the labor market given rapid technological change. Johnson argued that these technological changes meant that "on the elementary level it seems essential, along with the simple tools of learning such as are provided in the familiar three 'R's,' that rigid discipline be instilled in the skillful coordination of the mind, hand, and eye."[177] Johnson's desire that Black students learn "highly developed and undifferentiated technical aptitude" was driven by a belief that such skills would be required in the changing marketplace as well as his conviction that the possession of such skill by Black workers would outweigh racial prejudice.[178] Myrdal pressed for a similar approach to educating Black students, arguing, "He needs to be able to read, write, and reckon, and to be lifted so high above illiteracy that he actually participates in modern American society. Before all, he needs not to be specialized, but to be changeable, 'educable.'"[179] These authors pushed a pedagogy that was particularly responsive to the demands of the economy and focused on job preparation, and ultimately was driven by the desire to put Black students in a position to compete fairly with white students in the labor market.

The goal of preparing Black students for the demands of the labor market represented a stance that sought to adjust individuals to the existing economic structure. For racial democrats, this educational focus offered significant promise of individual and group uplift.[180] This position, like those that sought to use education to adjust cultural backwardness or damaged personality, was ultimately concerned with the fair incorporation of Black people into existing social and economic institutions.[181] This was a clear point of difference with the economic democrats, who advocated for a political and educational program focused primarily on challenging these structures, which they identified as inherently problematic. The educational adjustment program of racial democrats was driven by the belief that skill and cultural difference were significantly responsible for the inferior position of Black people in the United States, and that any chance of incorporation for Black people would require adjustment on these fronts.

Standardized Testing and Talent Searches

The commitment to racial incorporation that led racial democrats to advocate for the educational adjustment of Black students to the demands of "white cultural norms" and the labor market also led many to support standardized tests as a pedagogical tool. Tests of intelligence and achievement were embraced by racial democrats as effective means of finding racial leaders and talent, and eventually as a means of evaluating and shaping elementary and secondary school pedagogy. While many progressive educators questioned the pedagogical value of the use of any sort of standardized test, racial democrats seized on racial disparities in standardized test scores as an indication of an unfair and ineffective education system. Given the racial democratic end goal of ensuring white and Black people were fairly able to compete for resources, the ability to reduce racial gaps in test scores became an increasingly important means of evaluating the success of educational programs for racial democrats.

Early discussions of test scores in the *JNE* often centered on the value and interpretation of IQ tests, particularly in regard to their usefulness in sorting out the most intelligent students for special educational attention. Although there was a common endorsement of the view that racial comparisons of IQ tests were problematic given that the differences were merely a reflection of environmental factors or the chosen metrics of comparison, many authors argued that such tests could still be useful in guiding programmatic approaches to Black education. In a 1935 editorial entitled, "Investing in Negro Brains," the *JNE* editorial staff praised the discovery of a girl in Chicago with an IQ of 200 as evidence that high intelligence was distributed across racial categories. While this fact was to be celebrated, the editors lamented the fact that there was not a closer connection between "very superior" intelligence and positions of Black leadership.[182] The editors of the *JNE* were concerned that the failure to identify these "very superior" intellects and train them for positions of racial leadership called into question "whether we are making the best use of our higher educational facilities on the one hand, and whether

we are retarding the progress of the race and nation on the other, by expend-
ing our energy and machinery on raw material of *only* average quality when
'very superior' quality is available."[183] The concern about wasted intelligence
and incompetent Black leadership drove the editors to argue that "there is no
good reason why the graduating class of every high school in the country
could not be canvassed this June, and the 'very superior' students unearthed."[184]
Charles Thompson and the rest of the editorial staff argued that the implementation of such national testing would allow for the discovery and targeting of community and educational resources to those students with "very
superior" intellects.

Daniel P. Clarke, a school psychologist for the New York State Training
School for Boys, echoed this position in a 1941 *JNE* article. Clarke asserted
the need for all schools to employ psychologists and "trained psychome-
trists" in order to discover, through testing, superior children that required
special education. Clarke argued that "modern techniques of education, developed by psychologists, enable estimation (with remarkable accuracy) of
the potentialities for leadership possessed by the child of seven years; we can
even get a fair notion of the pre-school child's abilities and prognose his de-
velopmental limitations."[185] Like Thompson, Clarke positioned the use of
testing to sort out the most intelligent children for special education as necessary for "our salvation as a race,"[186] noting it would be impossible to "attain
racial sufficiency if we fail to exploit fully our reserves of human resources."[187]
For Thompson and Clarke, the tests emerging from the field of psychology
had the potential to be an unbiased means of sorting out the most promising
and deserving candidates for positions of Black leadership. Once these tests
determined which Black students had "very superior" intellect, these authors
suggested that they should receive substantial monetary support from the
Black community in their educational endeavors.[188] The desire to use testing
to single out the "best" Black students for extra resources reflected the belief
that doing so would be beneficial to *all* Black people, even as these scholars
were clearly advocating a tiered or tracked educational system.

While Thompson and Clarke were interested in the ability of a nationally
standardized test to efficiently sort the deserving from the undeserving,
others were more focused on the pedagogical potential of such tools. Kenneth B. M. Crooks, a professor of biology at Hampton University, suggested
in 1939 that while standardized tests could be useful in selecting the most fit,
they also could be essential tools to "*improve our educational processes* in the
grades and secondary schools."[189] Crooks argued that a battery of studies had
shown that certain standardized tests were valid indicators of mental achieve-

ment and consistently revealed "that our schools are now doing poor work in the fundamental tool subjects, reading, writing, and arithmetic."[190] Accepting the standardized tests as a legitimate tool of evaluation, Crooks claimed that standardized college "entrance tests will help the secondary schools by informing them how well their products have made the changes they were trying to bring about. In other words, the curricula of the schools can be guided and the success of schools and teachers can be measured."[191] Crooks argued that test scores could be used for evaluating the performance of educational institutions in addition to sorting individual students. For Crooks, the poor performance of Black students on standardized tests suggested the need for changes to the public elementary and secondary education system.

Crooks articulated a vision of education as a process of perfecting the teaching methods and strategies to bring about desired changes in students, the success of which would be measured by standardized tests.[192] Crooks called for a centralized educational body to agree on the common ends of education and suggested that the rest of the educational process would "be a simple matter to develop means to these ends, and to devise tests to check the prospective pupils' progress in these specific realities."[193] Instead of traditional "subjective" teacher grade evaluations of students, Crooks argued for a "battery of comprehensive, objective tests administered at definite periods by examiners, not influenced by local personalities or prejudices, the pupils and the teachers would have some definite goals at which to aim."[194] The tests would provide students and teachers a clear metric of success or failure and would drive the search for the most effective way of improving student scores on these tests. The educational goal to be aimed for was increasing test scores.

As detailed in the previous chapter, calls for widespread testing existed before World War II; however, the passage of the 1940 Selective Training and Service Act and the nation's first ever peacetime draft brought with it a massive expansion of the use of standardized tests as a sorting mechanism. Although there was no educational or intelligence standard for service in 1940 when the Selective Service first began providing men for the armed forces, technological advances in the "art of war" sparked concerns about the need for "men who had responsibly basic education and intelligence with requisite aptitude and skill."[195] By 1941, driven by a concern about the large number of illiterate service members, the Selective Service established an educational requirement for induction. Beginning on May 15, 1941, selectees were required to "have the capacity of reading and writing the English language as commonly prescribed for fourth grade in grammar school."[196] This new standard was abandoned after a little over a year when it became clear that it was leading to large numbers of rejections and deferrals. More than 143,000 men were rejected on educational grounds in the first four months of the new standard.[197] After a few tweaks, in mid-1943 the Selective Service's standard of "acceptability was changed by both Army and Navy from literacy to intelligence and a new testing procedure based upon intelligence."[198] Despite the fact that the shift to the intelligence test standard was motivated by the belief that many of the men "rejected for military service on literacy grounds ... had sufficient native intelligence to satisfy military needs," rejections for failure to meet the new minimum intelligence standard actually increased.[199] The extent of the problem was captured by the dire warnings of a 1944 Selective Service report that claimed "educational deficiency, or a failure to pass Army intelligence tests primarily because of educational deficiency, has deprived our armed forces of more physically fit men than have the operations of the enemy. Total American war casualties as of the last official announcement were 201,454; total rejected for failure to pass Army intelligence tests primarily because of educational deficiency who have no other disqualifying defect have been about 240,000."[200] The rejection of hundreds of thousands of potential soldiers for failure to pass basic intelligence and aptitude tests called attention to the failures of the education system, and it was clear that the level of educational deficiency exposed by the army's testing regime posed a risk to the nation in times of peace as well as war.[201]

While the exclusion of hundreds of thousands of men on educational grounds was troubling nationally, it was particularly problematic for Black people. Concern about the high level of educational and mental rejections led the American Teachers Association (ATA), a national professional organization of teachers of Black students, to investigate the educational and racial implications of the Selective Service's educational standard for induction.[202] The principal investigators were frequent *JNE* contributors Howard Hale Long and Martin Jenkins and *JNE* editor Charles Thompson.[203] The resulting report, *The Black and White of Rejections for Military Service: A Study of Rejections of Selective Service Registrants, by Race, on Account of Educational and Mental Deficiencies*, found that educational deficiency was by far the single greatest reason for rejection of Black men for military service.[204] Under the fourth-grade literacy standard, the rejection rate for educational deficiency of Black men was almost eleven times that of white men.[205] Although the racial disparity was reduced with the implementation of the intelligence test standard, the differences remained stark, with Black men having an educational deficiency rejection rate six to seven times higher than that of white men and accounting for slightly over half of all such rejections.[206]

The huge disparities in rejections provided a powerful opening for racial democrats to criticize the disparate educational system as a major problem for the nation. The ATA report found that the high and racially disparate rejection rate posed dire problems to the nation, including a smaller and less efficient "reservoir of manpower for the armed forces," an increased draft on well-educated population groups, and "an increased burden being placed on those state and communities which have provided good schools."[207] Through examining educational rejections on a state-by-state basis, the report provided convincing evidence that the disparate rejection rates were due to environmental and institutional factors, as the rejection rates for southern white men was higher than the rejection rate of Black men in several northern states.[208] Furthermore, the authors found a significant relationship between per capita educational expenditures and rejections for low test intelligence, with those states spending less experiencing a much higher rejection rate.[209] The authors suggested that the fact that the per pupil expenditure for Black students was substantially lower than the white per pupil expenditure was a major explanatory factor in the performance on intelligence tests. They ultimately concluded that responsibility for the racially disparate educational deficiency rejection rates could be found "in large measure at least, in the adequacy of the schools."[210]

The broad surveys of intelligence conducted by the Selective Service System gave a portrait of an educational system in disarray and placed hard numbers on the consequences of educational failure.[211] Concern about the problems in the education system extended beyond the immediate wartime crisis, as studies of educational military rejections noted that "good schools do pay; and poor schools are a liability, no less in peace than in war."[212] Indeed, this line of argument about the danger of poor schools was picked up by many Black scholars in the *JNE*, who increasingly relied on disparities in intelligence or achievement test scores as evidence of failing schools.[213] For racial democrats, who viewed equality of educational opportunity as essential for racial incorporation, the testing disparities were particularly problematic. Using the data from the ATA report, George Redd, professor and head of the Education Department at Fisk University, argued that the educational disparities revealed by these tests were distressing because they indicated that the "Negro is placed . . . at a disadvantage in competing with members of the white race for social and economic gains, when these are based on matching certain skills."[214] Increasingly, poor performance on standardized intelligence and achievement tests was used to indict the performance of schools. For racial democrats, the problematic educational system revealed by low and disparate test scores fed racial inequality and represented a threat to the national workforce.

By the 1950s, several groups took concrete steps to encourage the use of standardized tests as a means of identifying potential leaders as well as guiding educational goals and evaluating schools serving Black students.[215] One such effort was the Southern Project of the National Scholarship Service and Fund for Negro Students (NSSFNS). Between 1953 and 1955, the NSSFNS, a nonprofit organization with substantial financial backing from the Ford Foundation and with technical support from the College Entrance Examination Board and the Educational Testing Service, pursued a "South-wide talent search." It sought to "uncover able, college qualified Negro high school seniors and help them find and reach their college objectives."[216] The Southern Project sent workers into forty-five of the largest southern cities, visiting a total of seventy-eight Black high schools in search of talent. After asking the principals and counselors to identify the top 10 percent of students, these students were given scholastic aptitude tests to determine the likelihood of success in college.[217] In total, the Southern Project tested 3,178 high school students, of which 55 percent achieved the minimum score that the NSSFNS believed would indicate likelihood of college success.[218] Those students who met the NSSFNS's threshold received individualized advising on how to apply for colleges and scholarships. The Southern Project pointed to the acceptance of 523 students, and the receipt of more than $215,000 in scholarships (including almost $48,000 from the NSSFNS itself), as evidence of the program's success.[219]

In addition to helping certain Black students enter college, the Southern Project's "collateral objectives were to experiment with the techniques and methods of talent searching."[220] The director of the Southern Project was quick to emphasize the value of the first widespread use of testing among Black students as a means of talent searching. Noting that the Southern Project's use of scholastic aptitude tests as a means of talent searching came at "a most opportune time, when discussions about similar programs on a national scale are under way," the project's final report argued that the "methods and techniques employed in the Project, probably the only one so far of its kind, can be useful in pointing the way for a national talent searching project."[221] The timing was indeed fortuitous, as approximately $40,000,000 in new corporate and foundation scholarships became available to students seeking higher education.[222] In a 1957 report entitled *Blueprint for Talent Searching, America's Hidden Manpower*, Richard Plaut, the director of the Southern Project and the executive vice chairman of the NSSFNS, praised the talent searching function of these new scholarship funds and stressed the need for continued focus on minority students.[223] Arguing that "trained human intelligence is our most valuable resource" and that "we are failing to discover and develop this most valuable resource," Plaut pushed for significant financial and intellectual investment in discovering talent among Black students, which he argued promised the "highest yield for potential ability" given their disparate college attendance.[224] Plaut called for early and extensive use of intelligence and achievement testing in order to identify promising students, who could then be targeted for special attention and scholarships.[225] In an echo of the earlier calls of Thompson and Clarke, Plaut pushed for the widespread adoption of testing as a means of efficiently sorting the manpower resources of the nation.

As the NSSFNS was extolling the virtues of testing as a means of identifying talent, other organizations sought to harness the pedagogical potential of standardized tests. Most notably, the Phelps-Stokes Fund, a philanthropic nonprofit organization with a long-standing commitment to improving education and race relations, in 1955 began a five-year program called the Project of the Improvement of Instruction in Secondary Schools to address what they deemed the most immediate need of Black students. Writing in the *JNE*, project director Aaron Brown noted that justification for the assessment that this was the most pressing need was due to constant reports that Black students consistently scored lower on standardized tests and were entering college unprepared.[226] The primary goal of the project was to "raise the level of academic achievement of students in participating secondary schools to a point more in line with national norms."[227] Evidence of success would come in the form of elimination of racial gaps in standardized test scores.[228]

The testing regime was one of the most prominent features of the Southern Project, with frequent *JNE* contributor Howard Hale Long signing on to design this aspect of the program.[229] The NSSFNS focused on southern states and sought cooperation from state superintendents of education and college presidents. Throughout its five-year history, the Southern Project had a broad reach, with participation from 10,000 high school students, 500 high school teachers, 175 college and university teachers, and 50 administrators.[230] High schools and colleges agreed to a multiyear program of intensive in-service training of teachers by college professors, with particular attention to improving instructional technique and "assisting the schools in developing sound evaluative techniques."[231] Participating high schools were required to administer four standardized exams each year to every entering freshman and graduating student.[232] This evaluation requirement was accompanied by encouraging extensive use of "objective tests" by individual teachers as a means of evaluating pupil achievement and the effectiveness of the teaching method.[233] For many teachers and students, this was their first exposure to standardized tests.[234] In the final report on the Southern Project, director Aaron Brown pointed to "utilization of sound evaluation techniques and reliable instruments" as one of the greatest accomplishments, noting that "this area has been one of the most encouraging outcomes because the growth has been both rapid and substantial."[235]

In evaluating the success of the Southern Project, the final report relied heavily on the effects of its programs on the standardized test scores of Black students. The report touted significantly higher scores by graduating students in 1959 at the end of the project compared to the scores of those that had graduated in 1956, and a reduction in the racial achievement gap.[236] Given that "constant evaluation" was seen as key to improving educational instruction and outcomes, the project widely disseminated these scores, sending each participating school reports of the performance scores of individual students, as well as their comparative ranking among all schools in the project.[237] The final report used test scores to identify underperforming schools and to suggest academic areas in need of improvement.[238]

By the 1950s the appeal of standardized tests to racial democrats was well in place. Racial democrats were firmly committed to fair incorporation into existing economic and social structures, which they believed required equitable educational opportunity. The goal was that merit, rather than race, should ultimately determine one's standing. The overarching concern with establishing equitable outcomes for those of equal merit meant that standardized testing fit quite well with the broader political program of racial democrats. The "objective" metrics of comparison, like standardized intelligence or achievement tests, could help ensure that advancement in education and individual standing resulted from merit. For racial democrats, the gaping racial disparities in test scores provided clear evidence of a lack of equitable educational opportunity.[239] The evidence of disparities contributed to calls for an "educational reconstruction" that was "based on valid evidence successfully translated into practice."[240] Racial democrats argued that standardized tests could be used not only to determine the meritorious but could also point the way toward better educational practice. As the tests became a way to judge the worth of the individual as well as the performance of schools and teachers, Crooks's vision of a system in which "entrance tests . . . become tied up with the aims of education" increasingly represented the racial democratic position.[241] Testing in education became a means by which the goal of fair racial incorporation could be evaluated and eventually realized.

While the use of standardized tests in education was a natural fit with the racial democratic position, they were largely antithetical to the educational program of economic democrats. Economic democrats had long been critics of standardized tests as a tool, arguing that they tended to foster excessive individualism and competitiveness. Calls for talent searching and discovery of "superior intellects" indicated that a significant part of the aim of education for racial democrats involved sorting students on the basis of intellectual capacity and preparation for future leadership. As the final report on the Phelps-Stokes Fund indicated, the tests were designed so that "desirably, the distribution of pupils' achievement test scores should become more variable as pupils progress from grade to grade," and "the function of the school is to develop individual potentialities, rather than group conformity."[242] The role of tests, and by extension the role of the public school, was designed to find variation and reward the high scorers. This vision ran counter to the solidaristic approach envisioned by economic democrats, who tended to advocate for an educational program primarily focused on fostering cooperation and class solidarity.[243] The extent of opposition to standardized tests among economic democrats is evident in a 1938 *JNE* article by Philadelphia AFT vice president Mary Foley Grossman. Grossman argued forcefully against the use of standardized tests for sorting and evaluation, claiming "the use of the I.Q. as an instrument of pressuring children into groups with limited and undesirable curricula is an abuse of their democratic privileges" and noting that such tests tended to dangerously restrict the curriculum, which "suits the purpose of industry to mold belt-line minds in belt-line bodies."[244] The introduction of standardized tests was largely incompatible with the broader educational aims of Grossman and other economic democrats.

THE FUNDAMENTAL CLEAVAGE between economic democrats and racial democrats was over whether improving the situation of Black people in the United States also required substantial changes to the economic landscape. The differences on this central issue drove the development of educational perspectives and programs that were substantially different between the two groups. Economic democrats viewed racial subordination in the United States as fundamentally resulting from exploitative economic arrangements. This group viewed the primary task of education as educating students about these problematic social arrangements and providing tools and strategies, such as worker organization, to address these problems. Importantly, because they viewed the problems facing Black people in the United States as fundamentally economic in nature, the economic democrats placed significantly less faith in the ability of education to address the poor condition of Black citizens. Instead, far more emphasis was placed on the importance of economic policies such as full employment, redistributive foundation, unionization, and democracy in the workplace as the primary means through which the problems facing Black citizens manifested. Given the much more limited faith in the power of education, unsurprisingly, the educational programs of the economic democrats were not nearly as substantial as that of the racial democrats. However, the differences in the educational approaches of the two groups are clear from the strident critiques economic democrats like Oliver Cox levied at the educational politics and ideology of racial democrats.

The ultimate political goal of the racial democrats was fair incorporation into existing social and economic structures, and they viewed the education system as a particularly effective vehicle for achieving this goal. Significantly, racial democrats did not identify economic exploitation or the significant inequalities as the most problematic aspect of the existing economy in the United States. Instead, the racial democrats pointed to the fact that racial categories meant that opportunities for success in the existing economic landscape were distributed unfairly. It was this perspective that caused them to view education as a particularly potent vehicle to effectively ensure that opportunities were based on merit, rather than racial categories. This perspective also suggested a host of educational best practices, including interracial education to combat psychological prejudice, skills education to help Black students effectively compete against white students in the labor market, and racial comparison of standardized test results to evaluate whether true equality of opportunity existed.

Fundamentally, the racial democratic perspective was not critical of significant economic inequality; rather, it was critical of economic inequality that was ineffectively distributed. This was quite close to the ideological perspective of the social efficiency progressives, and, not surprisingly, the educational proposals of the two groups have substantial overlap. Similarly, the critique of the economic order that served as the foundation for the economic democrats placed them in ideological alignment with the social reconstructionist wing of the progressive education movement. Although the educational program of economic democrats was not nearly as extensive as that of the social reconstructionists, both groups advocated for a pedagogy that focused on broad social problems as well as providing students tools to help address these problems.

The economic democracy perspective was in many ways the more popular perspective in the pages of the *JNE* throughout the 1930s and into the early

1940s. By the mid-1940s, this had begun to change, as the racial democracy framework came to increasingly monopolize the discussion of Black politics and education. As the next chapter will show, ensuing political developments would drastically limit the ability of the economic democrats and social reconstructionists to advocate for a politics and educational perspective that centered on a critique of the existing economic order. As these voices were marginalized throughout the 1940s and 1950s, the ideas and policies of the racial democrats and social efficiency progressives increasingly dominated the educational landscape.

CHAPTER THREE

Courts, Communism, and Commercialism

The Rise of the Liberal Incorporationist Coalition

Throughout the 1940s and 1950s individuals and groups on the economic left were ruthlessly cut out of the political mainstream. Although scholars have tended to describe the years between the end of World War II and the 1960s as an "Age of Consensus," historian Thomas Sugrue has argued that it is best understood as "an era of brutality, of attempts to silence dissent."[1] Government loyalty investigations and a resurgent form of business-friendly liberalism curtailed challenges from the left, destroying coalitions and individuals on the way. Simultaneously, the changing international and domestic political context of this era greatly weakened the ability of individuals on the left to effectively advance policies and arguments that were openly critical of existing economic arrangements and made organizing coalitions around such an agenda nearly impossible.

Indeed, the transformation of George Counts—the father of social reconstructionism—was emblematic of these developments. Counts's advocacy that schools and teachers should lead a social transformation quickly made him a target of both the FBI and the infamous House Un-American Activities Committee (HUAC) as Cold War warriors looked for enemies within. Despite becoming an ardent anti-communist who actively purged his former friends from political organizations while openly arguing that communists should not be allowed in the classroom, questions about Counts's loyalty followed him for the rest of his life. By the 1950s, Counts had fully repudiated the social reconstructionist vision. When confronted at a speech in Pittsburgh about his advocacy in *Dare the Schools Build a New Social Order* that teachers ought to lead the nation toward a collectivist social transformation, Counts responded simply with "I once believed that, but I don't anymore."[2] Counts's open rejection of his former views and his participation in the destruction of the careers and reputations of many of his erstwhile allies demonstrates the severity of the attack on the educational left.

The effects of these changes were profound for the educational coalitions described in the previous chapters. There was diminishing space for the ideas of the economic democrats and social reconstructionists as educational visions that called into question the benevolence of capitalism were put on the defensive. As the American left was hobbled, the postwar environment greatly advantaged educational coalitions and ideas that could accommodate the changing political landscape. This new context greatly advantaged racial democrats and scientific efficiency progressives, who were able to articulate a policy agenda for education that was largely divorced from radical critiques of American political and economic structures.

By the end of the 1950s, the liberal incorporationist educational vision provided the dominant understanding of educational methods and purpose. Liberal incorporationism stitched together aspects of racial democracy and scientific efficiency progressivism into an educational ideology that emphasized the role of education in the fair and effective incorporation of individuals into the market economy. The coalition positioned education as a policy area capable of addressing a wide array of social issues including racial prejudice, poverty, and unemployment. The educational methods of liberal incorporationism—often borrowed directly from those of the racial democrats and scientific efficiency progressives—also appealed to emboldened business interests since they did not fundamentally challenge the existing political economy. This vision of educational intervention presented a well-timed alternative to economic intervention.

As this chapter will detail, after the end of World War II cooperation among those on the left began to fracture. With the escalating Cold War and growing Red Scare at home, economic democrats and social reconstructionists—and the coalitions they were a part of—found themselves the subject of brutal suppression in the form of loyalty investigations. Finally, the chapter traces how shifting Supreme Court doctrines helped solidify liberal incorporationism as the dominant educational vision by the end of the 1950s.

International Relations and Shifting Visions of Democracy

The rise of Nazism, the entrance of the United States into World War II, and the onset of the Cold War provided a peculiar mix of opportunity and peril for the individuals and policies of the American left during the 1940s and 1950s. The exigencies of the international situation during this era opened avenues for effective pressure on certain fronts, such as the attainment of civil rights, even as it all but shut the door on radical economic critiques.

Prior to World War II, the ideological center of gravity for left politics was organized around critiques of the exploitative nature of the American economic order. A number of groups and individuals formed a broad coalition of Popular Front organizations that rallied around shared goals of economic justice, unionization and class solidarity, anti-racism, and anti-fascism.[3] Among Black political circles, a group of young Black intellectuals including Ralph Bunche, Abram Harris, Richard Wright, and E. Franklin Frazier advocated for a reorientation of Black political activity along class lines and away from the racialist thinking of the NAACP and NUL. The Second Amenia Conference in 1933 and the 1935 conference on "The Position of the Negro in Our National Economic Crisis" at Howard University that led to the formation of the National Negro Congress (NNC) sought to give organizational strength to a political program focused on uniting Black and white laborers in the hopes of taking on the economic exploitation that flowed from the capitalist economic order. In the late 1930s, the NNC had broad appeal and was frequently at the center of debates and Black political activism.[4] The American Student Union and the League of American Writers were also formed in 1935 and had members from a similarly broad mix of leftist perspectives, including a substantial communist contingent.[5]

With the coming of World War II, international events began to expose cracks in the left Popular Front. Although some Black leftists like Doxey Wilkerson remained committed communists after the signing of the Molotov–Ribbentrop Pact between the Soviet Union and Nazi Germany in 1939, for many others the nonaggression pact was a bridge too far.[6] Ralph Bunche, who had tolerated the significant involvement of communists in the National Negro Congress, was particularly critical. In a 1940 *JNE* article, Bunche criticized the new position of the communists as "sophistry of the cheapest variety" and suggested that this rapid switch was a clear indication of the Communist Party of the United States of America's (CPUSA) true commitments, arguing "the Negro interest for the Communists is tied to uncertain and constantly shifting foreign policy of the Soviet Union."[7] This moment was also pivotal for labor leader and president of the NNC, A. Phillip Randolph, who halted his pragmatic cooperation with the Communist Party after the 1939 pact.[8] The CPUSA lost even more members, including *Native Son* author Richard Wright and his wife, when the party once again embraced anti-fascism after Germany invaded Soviet territory in June 1941.[9] This break between Black leftists and the CPUSA was significant given that the Communist Party had been one of the earliest organizations to support racial equality and was one of its most dedicated proponents.[10]

The Soviet–Nazi pact was not the only international event contributing to a fracturing of the left in the late 1930s. Progressive educators and other prominent intellectuals on the left became increasingly critical of the Soviet Union in the wake of the Great Purge, a widespread program of political repression and elimination of political opposition from 1936 through 1938. Despite earlier work that had largely been sympathetic, *Social Frontier* contributors George Counts, John Dewey, William H. Kilpatrick, and Sidney Hook became openly critical of the Soviet Union after the purges. Dewey and Hooks formed the Committee for Cultural Freedom in 1939, which committed itself to fighting the "totalitarianism" of the Soviet Union in addition to that of Germany and Italy.[11] After hearing about the Soviet–Nazi pact, George Counts, whose relationship with the CPUSA had already soured due to the purges, joined an anti-communist faction of the AFT. With the support of Dewey, Counts was elected president of the AFT in 1939 and steadily limited the influence of communists within the union, including Doxey Wilkerson and Mary Grossman.[12] The renunciation of communism and the effort to sever communists from participation in the Popular Front in the late 1930s represented a significant fracturing of the educational left, and it was largely precipitated by international events.[13]

Although international events strained the Popular Front, many progressive individuals and groups viewed the movement of the United States away from its isolationist stance during 1941 with cautious optimism. This was particularly true for those concerned with improving the condition of Black citizens, as some argued that the United States' entrance into World War II had the potential to be an economic boon for Black workers as the productive demands of war would greatly increase the need for workers.[14] Beyond the possible economic advances, the fact that the United States frequently framed engagement in the war as protecting and advancing the cause of democracy provided a particularly powerful ideological weapon for Black intellectuals and political organizations to criticize the domestic treatment of Black citizens.[15]

As several Black political actors noted, the charges of hypocrisy and inconsistency on the issue of race carried particular significance given the broad geographical scope of World War II. Martin Jenkins pointed out that American "treatment of its darker racial groups is a source of embarrassment to the nation," and that the "counter-propaganda of the Axis nations has not failed to make good use of this weak position of our country to the detriment of our total war effort."[16] The racial practices of the United States also strained relations with allied nations with large or predominantly non-white populations.[17] The hypocrisies represented more than a moral failing on the domestic front: they had the potential to damage the efforts of the United States internationally.

The embrace of racial supremacy by the Nazis also provided an opening to attack racial supremacy ideology and practice in the United States. The Nazi embrace of *Herrenvolk* ideology, which translated as master folk or race, underlined their eugenic policies and also provided justification for excluding non-Aryans from the full benefits of citizenship. This proved an uncomfortable fact in the United States given the early connection between the American eugenics movement and Nazi Germany and the existence of similarly racially restrictive laws in the Jim Crow South.[18] Pointing out similarities between Nazi and American racial ideology, philanthropist Anson Phelps Stokes argued, "we all condemn the *Herrenvolk* idea as both unscientific and unChristian, but in the final analysis the 'white supremacy' doctrine held by large groups of people in the South, and some in the North, is closely akin to it in theory."[19] This fact meant the war provided an opportunity to attack "white supremacy" on the home front. As Stokes argued, "the war, by raising the *Herrenvolk* issue in the case of Germany, has driven home to us in the United States that we are subject to attack on the grounds of inconsistency and insincerity if we ... make any requirements for voting or office-holding that do not treat white men and colored men exactly on the same objective basis."[20] The fact that Anson Phelps Stokes, a former member of the Board of Trustees of the Tuskegee Institute, was openly indicting white supremacy was a clear indication of the shifting political terrain.

Intellectuals recognized the unique political opportunity that these contradictions provided. A variety of Black political organizations such as the Brotherhood of Sleeping Car Porters, the National Association for the Advancement of Colored People, the National Urban League, and the National Negro Congress took advantage of the particular openings provided by the international context. These groups successfully secured long-held policy goals in the early 1940s, including a nondiscriminatory clause in the Selective Service Act, greater opportunities for advancement of Black military officers, greater representation in skilled trades and trade unions, and the creation of the Fair Employment Practices Committee.[21] The international context proved effective helping to advance the domestic agenda of these groups, as they pushed for a "Double Victory" at home and abroad. The success of this strategy led Anson Phelps Stokes to remark, "the progress of the Negro in the United States during the war years has been of epoch-making significance."[22]

Yet even as international events facilitated cooperation between scientific efficiency progressives and racial democrats, they created divisions within social reconstructionist and economic democratic circles. The Nazi embrace of "scientific" racial hierarchy caused many educational progressives to distance themselves from openly embracing similar rhetoric. This was particularly significant for scientific efficiency progressives, who prior to the war had to look to hereditary and genealogy for insights into how to design effective education programs. Although many of the originators of the scientific efficiency progressive position had been committed eugenicists, this position became increasingly untenable during and after World War II. After World War II, scientific efficiency progressives largely abandoned hereditary and eugenic justifications for their educational vision. This ultimately eliminated one of the biggest distinctions between the educational vision of the racial democrats and scientific efficiency progressives. Their educational programs came to look increasingly similar.

The NAACP and Cold War Civil Rights

World War II provided particular openings for advancing priorities of the left and temporarily papered over the divisions that had begun to show between 1939 and 1941. The fact that the Soviet Union and the United States were now allies in the fight against the Axis powers lessened the pressure to purge communists from leftist organizations and reopened a space for limited Popular Front activity. Robert Korstadt and Nelson Lichtenstein have shown how the entrance of the United States into World War II created the space for the communists and their allies in the CIO to make substantial gains in unionization and labor power in unlikely places, with particularly strong gains for Black workers.[23] Michael Kazin captures the unique potential, and temporality, of this opening, noting, "as long as the war continued, a communist could be both a sinner patriot and a follower of Stalin, without tripping over the contradiction."[24] The federal government also sought to incorporate some Black leaders into its international relations apparatus in order to head off charges of racism from the Soviet Union. However, when the war ended in 1945, the opportunities provided by the international context were quickly reconfigured and dramatically changed the prospects of the American left. As anti-communism became a growing part of foreign and domestic policy, mainstream groups like the NAACP shifted their views to align with the new consensus, leaving erstwhile allies on the economic left increasingly marginalized.

The rising conflict with the Soviet Union allowed Black political organizations to continue to make arguments emphasizing that improving the treatment of racial minorities and increasing the protection of civil rights made strategic sense in a globalized conflict involving millions of non-white individuals. However, progress on this front was coupled with a significant limiting of the scope of issues that the left was able to effectively press during this time period. Advancements in civil rights occurred simultaneously with the widespread purges of leftists from left-leaning organizations as the Popular Front collapsed. Individuals on the left were suppressed at all levels of government, leading to the abandonment of anti-imperialism and economic transformation as central tenets of a left politics. The shifting politics of the NAACP provide a good example of the disastrous outcomes for the political—and educational—agenda of the left.

As the United States entered into a new struggle for the hearts and minds of countries that were predominantly not white, the treatment of the non-white citizens within the United States became particularly important to the nation's international agenda.[25] This opening for advancing civil rights protections was quickly seized by many on the left who adapted the arguments they had made during World War II to reflect the new international situation. The NAACP began connecting the fight against communism with the fight against racial subordination almost immediately, with prominent members including Roy Wilkins making this case in *Crisis*.[26] In 1947, the NAACP took the dramatic step of submitting a petition to the recently created United Nations (UN) Commission on Human Rights asking for redress for violations of human rights by the U.S. government. The petition was submitted to the UN by W. E. B. Du Bois, who also authored the petition's introduction.[27] In the petition, Du Bois outlined the instances of violations of human rights and the basic tenets of democracy faced by Black people in the United States. Du Bois continuously pointed to the economic foundation of racial subordination and accused the U.S. federal government of "continuously cast[ing] its influence with imperial aggression," arguing that "it has become through private investment part of the imperialistic bloc which is controlling the colonies of the world."[28] Du Bois continued his radical critique, noting, "It is not Russia that threatens the United States so much as Mississippi; not Stalin and Molotov but Bilbo and Rankin."[29]

The petition was embarrassing to the United States, and to Eleanor Roosevelt in particular, who served as both a delegate to the United Nations and as a board member of the NAACP. Roosevelt and the rest of the U.S. delegation refused to bring up the petition; however, the Soviet Union gladly proposed that the charges be investigated. The petition enjoyed significant domestic support as Du Bois had secured the endorsement of a number of professional organizations and religious groups in addition to leftist support.[30] Despite international support and domestic support within the United States, the UN General Assembly ultimately rejected the proposal to investigate, and no further action was taken on the petition.[31] The submission of this petition was the zenith of the NAACP's radicalism on the international stage, and the last time the organization was formally anti-imperialist.

The NAACP and mainstream Black political leaders adapted Du Bois's radical argument to reflect a closer alignment with the formal international interests of the United States as the contours of the Cold War changed.[32] Several articles in the *JNE* warned that the Soviet Union had effectively weaponized racist practices in the United States, pointing out that the treatment of racial minorities was one of the most encountered questions by Americans traveling abroad, even in allied countries.[33] While most authors maintained that the claims emanating from the Soviet Union were sensationalized and overstated, they did suggest that the United States should combat this international problem through expanding civil rights protections for minorities domestically. Citing recent court decisions and the newfound willingness of federal Justice Department officials to point to international relations in civil rights, several *JNE* authors suggested that the federal judiciary and the civil rights strategy of the NAACP held the most promise for advancing Black interests.[34]

Organization around the opening provided by the international context proved effective in advancing some long-held goals of Black political organizations. In 1948, President Truman pushed for legislation to strengthen civil rights protections including a Civil Rights Division in the Department of Justice, federal protection against lynching, the protection of the right to vote, and prohibition of discrimination in employment and transportation. When Congress failed to act, Truman issued Executive Orders 9980 and 9981, which ordered the desegregation of the federal workforce and the armed services.[35] Truman's actions were just one example of how international context provided substantial impetus for action on civil rights domestically.[36]

Indeed, scholars like Mary Dudziak and Gerald Horne have argued that progress in desegregation throughout the late 1940s and 1950s was to a substantial degree a Cold War imperative.[37]

Nevertheless, though the nascent Cold War provided opportunities to press for certain policy goals of the left, most notably in the protection of civil rights, it quickly proved to be a limiting force for the push for economic changes. The 1948 campaign proved to be a moment where important divisions crystallized. Henry Wallace mounted a challenge to Truman from the left, running as the Progressive Party's candidate. Wallace was the former vice president and secretary of commerce who Truman had fired largely over strong disagreement in the direction of foreign policy regarding the Soviet Union. Wallace's platform coupled domestic policies of "full equality for the Negro people" and strong antidiscrimination legislation, a publicly planned economy, public ownership of critical industries and housing, a strengthening of labor unions, a guaranteed living wage, and full employment with an international agenda committed to disarmament and peaceful relations with the Soviet Union.[38] Even though there was evidence of broad support among Black citizens and NAACP staffers of Wallace's economic progressive campaign,[39] the president of the NAACP, Walter White, was a staunch supporter of Truman. White was of the opinion that the most effective means of advocating for the organization was through lobbying those in the inner circle of power and was concerned with maintaining his relationship and access within the Truman administration.[40]

The effect of the election on Black politics was significant. Truman's campaign was premised on both modest racial reforms and staunch anti-communism internationally and domestically—and a rejection of Wallace's calls for aggressive federal action on egalitarian racial and economic issues. Both during the campaign and after Truman's victory, White moved the NAACP decisively to the right in order to maintain its relationship with the Truman administration. One of the costs of maintaining this access was the repudiation of the organization's earlier anti-imperial stance embodied in its petition to the United Nations. White tied the NAACP tightly to the growing anti-communism of Truman and the Democratic Party—abandoning earlier anti-imperial foreign policy advocacy and severing ties with many on the Black left.[41] Despite the denouncement of the "imperial aggression" of the United States throughout the world in the 1947 petition, by 1948 White had led the NAACP to an open embrace of the United States' efforts to halt the spread of global communism.[42]

The extent to which the NAACP had moved on the issue of foreign policy was evident in 1951 in the organization's response to a petition submitted to the United Nations by the Civil Rights Congress (CRC). The CRC, founded in 1946 as a merger of the NNC and two other Popular Front groups, submitted a petition to the UN General Assembly accusing the United States of the newly defined international crime of genocide. The petition claimed that "the oppressed Negro citizens of the United States . . . suffer from genocide as the result of the consistent, conscious, unified policies of every branch of government."[43] Similar to the NAACP's petition the year before, this new petition argued that the experience of Black people in the United States was at its heart tied to the structure of economic relations in the nation. Claiming that "the object of this genocide . . . is the perpetuation of economic and political power by the few through the destruction of political protest by the many," the petition concluded that "the foundation of the genocide of which we complain is economic."[44] The petition also asserted that the foreign policy of the United States was motivated by the same economic forces, stating "jellied gasoline in Korea and the lyncher's faggot at home are connected. . . . The tie binding both is economic profit and political control."[45] The incendiary charges were roundly condemned by U.S. government officials, who quickly mobilized prominent Black leaders to denounce the petition.

The State Department reached out to Walter White and asked him to publicly repudiate the petition. Although the criticisms of the United States were more extreme than in the NAACP's petition the year before, and the criticism of capitalism much more explicit in the CRC's petition, the two petitions had much in common. A significant amount of the data and specific events that the CRC petition cited had been taken directly from the NAACP's petition.[46] Instead of attacking the data, White released a statement at the behest of the State Department charging that the petition failed to take into account the "phenomenal gains" in civil rights and reducing bigotry that characterized the United States in the most recent decade and accused the CRC of using Black "grievances as a pawn in the world struggle for political domination."[47]

The political context that had facilitated some policy gains and the incorporation of some Black elites and organizations into the United States' international relations apparatus meant that these same groups and individuals were increasingly expected to temper or abandon radical political demands. The increasingly prominent roles occupied by Black individuals such as Edith Sampson as an alternate delegate to the UN assembly, Ralph Bunche as an analyst for the Office of Strategic Services and UN diplomat, and Edward Dudley as the ambassador to Liberia, as well as the more temporary advisory roles given to Charles Johnson and R. P. Weaver, provided the U.S. government with high-profile surrogates to combat criticisms of its racial record.[48] The State Department reached out to Bunche, as well as Phelps-Stokes Fund director Channing Tobias, to help push back against the charges in the petition.[49] Edith Sampson was asked to tour Scandinavian countries to limit any damage from the petition, during which she echoed White's rosy portrayal of the state of race relations in the United States. Sampson claimed that concerns about Jim Crow were overblown, that Black people did not face any barriers to voting, and that the Black people she knew drove Cadillacs and lived in $100,000 houses.[50] The well-organized effort to combat the claims of the CRC petition, many of which were substantially similar to those the NAACP had made just a few years earlier, indicates the extent to which the NAACP and other prominent Black intellectuals had shifted their views to align with Cold War anti-communism in international affairs.

The embrace of anti-communism and an interventionist foreign policy by the NAACP was accompanied by a silencing of those voices of dissent within the organization. Perhaps the most notable instance of this silencing was W. E. B. Du Bois's unceremonious dismissal from the organization in 1948. Du Bois vehemently disagreed with the increasingly close relationship between the NAACP and the Truman administration, and the muting of criticism of Truman's interventionism that this relationship required. This disagreement over the NAACP's position on foreign policy appears to have been decisive in his expulsion from the organization in 1948.[51] The NAACP became increasingly openly critical of other prominent Black leftists, including Paul Robeson and William Patterson, the president of the CRC.[52] The open refusal to associate with Black people on the left was part of a broader effort to separate the NAACP from the Popular Front.[53] At the annual meeting of the NAACP in 1950, members passed a resolution authorizing the national organization to take "necessary steps to eradicate Communist infiltration," including suspension or expulsion of any local branch that came under communist influence.[54] This official stance was organized by Walter White, Roy Wilkins, Thurgood Marshall, and others to combat the influence of communists within the organization and formalized what had been an unofficial policy since 1946.[55]

The distancing of the NAACP and others from those on the left made them particularly vulnerable to the repressive action increasingly employed by the U.S. government. Paul Robeson had his passport revoked due to his criticism of the United States' foreign policy abroad.[56] After submitting the *We Charge Genocide* petition, Patterson was charged with contempt of Congress and had his passport confiscated.[57] In 1951, the eighty-two-year-old Du Bois was charged with being "an agent of foreign principle" for his foreign policy positions and work with the Peace Information Center. Although all charges were eventually dismissed, Manning Marable notes that the NAACP was particularly "conspicuous in its cowardice" in its refusal to offer any legal or public support of the former prominent member.[58] Despite the dismissal of all charges, the indictment did accomplish some of the objectives of the Truman administration, as thousands of libraries removed copies of Du Bois's work and he was increasingly marginalized from organizations that wished to maintain mainstream appeal. Others on the left were not so lucky, and many faced massive material consequences when they were convicted of subversive activities because of their foreign policy views.[59] Although it is certainly true that the NAACP was in part a victim of Cold War anti-communist hysteria, the more conservative politics of those at the top of the organization meant that this hysteria also served as a useful tool to shape the politics of the organization toward the more conservative politics of those at the top.[60]

By severing ties with the left, the NAACP and other mainstream organizations eliminated those members who had been most committed to economic justice through structural transformation. Indeed, this position had become increasingly untenable in organizations strongly committed to anti-communism, as any criticism of the economic organization of the U.S. economy immediately cast suspicion on the loyalty of those making the argument. The strident anti-communism of the United States led to the downfall of the inclusion of strong economic and social equality guarantees as part of the UN's Universal Declaration of Human Rights, largely over concern from the United States that they were a Soviet Trojan horse. The NAACP and other mainstream Black political organizations that prioritized combating Jim Crow largely abandoned these economic commitments in an attempt to maintain legitimacy.[61] By 1948, it was clear that the brief opening provided by World War II to be both a communist and a patriot had closed. The ouster of Du Bois, the purging of communists from the organization, and the abandonment of anti-imperialism and strong demands for economic justice was the price the NAACP willingly paid for the promised support of modest civil rights advancements from Cold War liberals.

As Black political organizations were increasingly channeled into a civil rights framework, commitments to organizing a coalition of interracial working-class people in order to facilitate broad economic structural transformation to achieve economic justice receded into the background. The new imperative of the international context substantially benefited those individuals and organizations who had long been skeptical of the wisdom of closely associating Black political demands with the left. Arguments calling for fair racial incorporation into the existing institutional order were better able to accommodate the changing international context, as their highest priorities could be achieved within the existing institutional and economic landscape. Those pushing for economic reorganization were marginalized, as calls for significant changes to the economic system were increasingly deemed un-American.

The Domestic Constraints of the Second Red Scare

Just as the shifting international context shaped the strategic decisions of organizations and individuals on the left, the brutally repressive domestic suppression of the left facilitated by this shifting context had extensive repercussions for postwar politics. The recovering economy and the strained relationship between the United States and the Soviet Union before, during, and immediately after World War II provided a favorable political environment for conservatives to undermine the influence of the left through challenging their loyalty. As the influence of the rehabilitated business community and congressional conservatives waxed in the postwar era, anti-communism served as a particularly effective tool in attacking political opponents on the left. Stoked by a coalition that found communist witch hunts politically useful, political organizations were increasingly pressured to prove their patriotism through severing all association with anyone deemed too far left or face congressional investigation. During the era of the Second Red Scare, unions and other organizations on the political left paid the price demanded of them in order to maintain access to mainstream politics and purged hundreds of thousands of individuals from membership rolls. Beyond weakening and destroying organizations, the attack on the left during the Second Red Scare had dramatic consequences for the individuals who experienced immense pressure to renounce old positions and abandon social networks and friendships, or else suffer marginalization, substantial fines, or jail time. The anti-communism that shaped much of the domestic politics in the postwar era proved devastating for the organizations, individuals, and ideas of the educational left.

In 1947, President Truman brought the war against communism to the domestic front by signing Executive Order 9835 requiring a loyalty investigation of every individual entering the employment of any department or agency of the executive branch.[62] Five days after this executive order, FBI director J. Edward Hoover testified before the HUAC and proposed a number of tests that would indicate the subversiveness of an organization, including whether an organization criticized American and British foreign policy, whether an organization was endorsed by a communist-controlled labor union, and whether an organization denounced "monopoly-capitalism."[63] Hoover's description of domestic communists as a "fifth column"[64] committed to "the destruction of free enterprise" provided a powerful line that congressional conservatives wielded against individuals and organizations that failed to condemn the party and sympathizers in the most strident terms.[65] A broad range of conservative groups, including the American Legion, the Daughters of the American Revolution (DAR), the National Association of Manufacturers, and the Chamber of Commerce, found red-baiting to be a powerful means of silencing critics and advancing their own political agendas.[66] Calling into question an individual's loyalty became a particularly potent political weapon, and by the early 1950s more than thirty states had their own policies that called for loss of employment for membership in subversive organizations, more than twenty required public servants to sign loyalty oaths, and thirteen had created their own version of HUAC.[67] As the hysteria increased, accusations of disloyalty became a devastatingly effective means of combating individuals, ideas, or policies that might be considered remotely critical of capitalism or American foreign policy.

These loyalty investigations had a significant impact on the direction of postwar education and social policy more broadly, as important individuals were forced to abandon left policies. Policies such as national health insurance, anti-militarism, strong consumer protections, a comprehensive social welfare system, public control of power, and public housing were marginalized as these individuals moved toward the political center and business-friendly positions in an attempt to shore up their anti-subversive credentials.[68] As individuals on the left who had promoted a vision of education grounded in a critique of unfair economic arrangements were targeted by congressional investigations and organizations from across the political spectrum in the 1940s, the space for this alternative vision collapsed. Political suppression destroyed networks and coalitions on the left, eliminated leftist leaders from the political and educational scene, shifted education policy proposals, and resulted in widespread changes to the classroom experience as teachers and books were purged for suspicion of being too far left. The loyalty investigations, and their remarkably effective use by opponents of New Deal–style social and economic programs, contributed significantly to the defeat of more democratic education alternatives and helped forge a postwar consensus that was substantially more conservative. A focus on the experiences of John Dewey, George Counts, Harold Rugg, Mary Foley Grossman, and Doxey Wilkerson illuminates the devastating destructiveness of Red Scare tactics for leftist educators.

John Dewey, the most prominent of the social reconstructionists, presented an inviting target. The FBI had a file on Dewey that dated back to 1930, apparently prompted by Dewey's association with the People's Lobby, a watchdog organization that advocated good government and public disclosure. Despite turning up nothing in their initial search, the FBI kept Dewey's file on hand, and reopened a much more serious investigation in 1943. This time, the investigation was prompted by the FBI office in New York, which noted his membership in twenty-one potentially subversive organizations. The aim of the investigation was to conclude whether Dewey should be officially classified as a "sympathizer," under the Custodial Detention Index, a program used to identify potential subversives that might need to be incarcerated in case of war. Dewey was cleared once again; however, his file remained open and was moved to the "Subversive Control" section of the FBI.[69]

Although never officially charged, Dewey was frequently the subject of attacks by conservative groups. Allen Zoll was perhaps the most infamous of the education red-baiters and the founder of the National Council for American Education (NCAE), whose sole purpose was to root out progressive ideas and educators from the public school system. Zoll took aim at Dewey directly in the late 1940s in one of his more popular pamphlets entitled "Progressive Education Increases Delinquency," which noted that "the purpose of education as conceived by John Dewey, George Counts, and their like" amounted to little more than a denial of "every factor necessary for our survival as a free people." Zoll argued that this vision of education had "robbed growing youth of the ability to think independently," and "blights . . . the moral standards by which alone a people may maintain a secure, free, coherent society."[70] Dewey was also specifically targeted by the American Legion, which published "Your Child Is Their Target" in the *American Legion Magazine*, which accused Dewey and other progressive educators (the article also mentions George Counts, William Kilpatrick, and Harold Rugg) as a group of "pinkos, commies, collectivists, and Marxists" that controlled public schools in the hopes of converting children into communists.[71] Even Dewey's death did not slow the criticisms or the investigations.[72] In 1957, five years after Dewey's death, J. Edgar Hoover, the director of the FBI, requested, "Let me have a summary on John Dewey, the educator who furthered the idea of progressive education."[73] The investigations and accusations of subversive sympathies made Dewey more cautious in his writing and activities;[74] however, the effects of these investigations on Dewey paled in comparison to some of his colleagues.

The attacks on John Dewey and his educational philosophy can be understood as part of a broader campaign by corporate leaders and pro-business groups to attempt "to shape a national consensus that was conducive to unfettered corporate expansion and economic growth."[75] Historian Wendy Wall's work traces the rise of a powerful postwar coalition that frowned on labor militancy and class conflict as un-American, idolized individual liberty and tolerance, and positioned high productivity and mass consumption as central to the preservation of democracy and the economy.[76] Importantly, while this emerging ideology was in part an attempt to head off New Deal–type social welfare programs, the high value it placed on tolerance and consensus did provide an opening for minority groups to seek incorporation into existing structures. In fact, as Wall notes, by the 1950s race and "intergroup relations [had] become a good 'cause' for conservatives to be liberal about. It [was] not basically threatening to their own economic agenda."[77] However, the opening provided was limited, as this ideology could easily be appropriated for purposes like legal and political equality of Black individuals, while forcefully shutting the door on other claims—most importantly, demands for economic equality or economic transformation.[78] These developments were particularly conse-quential for education—as the pro-business coalition provided openings for racial democrats and scientific efficiency progressives, even as it aggressively attacked social reconstructionists and economic democrats.

The Second Red Scare facilitated the rise of this new pro-growth and pro-business political coalition. The loyalty investigations of prominent left-leaning scholars and policy makers in the federal civil service pushed individuals to abandon previous advocacy of expansive government in eco-nomic planning and redistribution. Under the threat of loyalty investigation, important individuals like Leon Keyserling, the head of the Council of Eco-nomic Advisors (CEA) under President Truman, began to advocate for fo-cusing on growth and increasing production rather than redistribution in the early 1950s.[79] As Keyerseling and his wife were investigated, he adopted in-creasingly pro-business rhetoric and policy proposals, at least in part to fend off charges that he was insufficiently loyal.[80] The Keyerselings were certainly not the only individuals who felt this pressure. Historian Landon Storrs has argued that the political right frequently used accusation of disloyalty to "block policy initiatives that impinged on business prerogatives at home and abroad."[81] The growing hysteria and loyalty investigations proved popular tactics in efforts to marginalize certain educational visions and shape policy in a more pro-business direction.

Perhaps the clearest indication of the effects of loyalty investigations and the shifting political context can be seen in the changing views of George Counts. Counts faced questions over his loyalty almost immediately in the wake of the first publication of the *Social Frontier*. The journal dedicated an entire issue to covering the attacks on Counts and other educators from noted newspaper magnate and red-baiter William Hearst.[82] The apparent ini-tial popularity of the social reconstructionist movement prompted heated at-tacks on Counts. For example, a call by the NEA for higher taxation on the wealthy and the proclamation emanating from the 1934 National Convention of School Superintendents that "educational workers of America must band themselves together now in a powerful union to create tens of thousands of citizens groups to study critical economic and social problems" led promi-nent anti–New Deal educator William Wirt to charge Counts with attempt-ing to create an "ultra-radical sentiment among our people, which will force the country over the precipice and into the abyss of Communism."[83] Counts was also subject to continuous attacks from the conservative groups that seemingly specialized in this form of character assassination: the American Legion, the NCAE, the DAR, and the American Council of Churches.[84]

As these accusations put Counts on the defensive, they also drew the attention of the FBI and HUAC. The FBI opened its investigation into Counts
in 1942, largely due to his affiliation with various suspected front organizations.[85] Although the initial investigation found that Counts expressed
"pro-Russian sympathy," it concluded that he was likely not a communist.[86]
Counts continued to face accusations despite his increasingly vocal opposition to the Soviet Union and vigorous efforts to eliminate communist influence from several organizations he was involved with by 1940. Much like
Ralph Bunche (and others), the Molotov–Ribbentrop Pact appears to have
greatly upset Counts and drove him to reconsider his previously sympathetic
view of the Soviet Union. By 1939, Counts had publicly denounced Stalin and
soon turned his attention toward driving communists out of Popular Front
organizations. Perhaps most significantly, he led a coalition in 1940 to challenge the leadership of the national AFT, which he charged with being too
close to the Communist Party.

The leadership Counts sought to oust included Doxey Wilkerson, a professor of education at Howard University, and Mary Foley Grossman, a middle-
school teacher and union leader from Philadelphia. Both Grossman's and
Wilkerson's views on the purpose of education were in line with the social reconstructionist ideals of what Counts had advocated in the early 1930s. Both
had outlined their views in the *JNE*, where Wilkerson also had a recurring
column.[87] Although Wilkerson's and Grossman's educational philosophy was
closely aligned with Counts's, after 1939, Counts was no longer willing to col-
laborate with individuals he considered too close to the Communist Party. He
led a coalition seeking to oust Wilkerson and Grossman, arguing that keeping
the existing leadership in charge would do irreparable harm to the AFT. Counts
and his allies successfully defeated the existing leadership in the 1940 AFT election and Counts took over as president of the organization in 1941.[88]

One year after the election, Counts and the other newly elected officers
moved to revoke the charters of three of the largest and most active local
unions on the grounds that they were dominated by communists. Counts
and the new executive council publicly introduced the charges against Locals
5 and 537 of New York City (one represented elementary and secondary
teachers, the other represented college teachers) as well as Local 192 of Philadelphia in a lengthy and detailed document entitled *The Executive Council's
Proposal to Save the AFT*. Evidence against these locals included the fact that
the union publication had been insufficiently critical of the "Stalin-Hitler
pact" and the fact that they had reported on the activities of pro-communist
organizations such as the National Negro Congress and the American League

for Peace and Democracy. Mary Foley Grossman, who was the president of the Philadelphia local, was one of the few individuals named in the report. She was singled out for particularly harsh treatment in the document because of her continued opposition to the newly elected national officers.[89] This would prove quite damaging for Grossman when she was called before HUAC in the 1950s. The successful effort to revoke the charters of these locals, which by Counts's own admission were some of the most active, is a clear indication that by the early 1940s the changing international context was already creating damaging fissures among left-oriented educators.[90]

In 1944 Counts led a similar effort to rid the American Labor Party (ALP), by then a 400,000-voter-strong organization he had founded a decade earlier, of communist influence. In 1944, Sidney Hillman, the president of the Amalgamated Clothing Workers, challenged Counts for the chairmanship of the ALP. Counts ran a campaign in which he accused Hillman of making common cause with communists. During the campaign, he warned that if he lost, he and his supporters would "not remain in the party and serve as a front for Communists."[91] After Hillman's coalition won an overwhelming victory, Counts and his allies left the party he had founded, vowed to form a splinter group without communists, and declared the "death of the A.L.P."[92] Counts's efforts and public accusations would provide significant fodder for red-baiting members of Congress.

Active participation in anti-communist efforts was not enough to clear Counts's name from suspicion. Counts continued to be a person of interest to congressional committees investigating the influence of subversive individuals in public employment and private organization. Counts's name appeared in a number of reports throughout the 1940s because of his past association with now-suspect organizations including the National Committee for Defense of Political Prisoners, the Union for Democratic Action, the National Committee for Student Congress Against War, the American Student Union, and the Consumers Union.[93] Counts's name and his book *Dare the Schools Build a New Social Order?* were repeatedly invoked in congressional testimony by conservatives as a means of combating federal funding for public education and of smearing political opponents. For example, opponents of the Public School Assistance Act of 1949 pointed to the subversive nature of *Dare the Schools Build a New Social Order?* and Counts's advocacy for greater federal funding of education as a means of attacking increased federal funding and involvement in public elementary and secondary schools.[94]

The situation for Counts became more serious in 1951 when a former European communist claimed Counts was a hidden "member at large" of the

Communist Party.[95] Another investigation was launched as a result of this information and once again investigators concluded that Counts was not a communist. However, this most recent accusation appeared to put Counts on the radar of the HUAC. Although the committee apparently found no new evidence, it still issued nineteen citations against Counts for communist leanings in early 1952.[96] Given that Counts was not employed in the federal government, these citations did not result in loss of employment, but it represented a serious threat to both his reputation and any individual or organizations with which he interacted.

Counts took the latest charges quite seriously as evidenced by his drastic response to the actions of the HUAC. Shortly after the citations were issued, Counts gave speeches in March 1952 at two universities in Pennsylvania where he renounced communism and, more significantly, much of his social reconstructionist positions.[97] In a moment that offered a stark contrast to his earlier writing, Counts excoriated the Soviets for encouraging their populace to pursue "the vision of an ideal society some place just around corner."[98] Counts also used the speeches to outline a new social vision. He claimed that America's best course was to seek "military strength first of all."[99] The role for teachers in Counts's new vision was quite limited, but he did urge educators to teach students about Russia in order to bolster their self-defense against the dangerous Soviet ideology.

Counts's recantation of his earlier views did little to satiate his critics, who still frequently protested his speeches and questioned his political loyalties. Counts continued to move further from his previous positions, eventually claiming in 1954 that "a Communist has no right to teach in the schools of a free society."[100] Although this movement away from social reconstructionism did not quiet his critics, it did strain the relationships he had with former progressive educators. Harold Rugg and Counts had an apparent falling out over Counts's subdued reaction to the dismissal on loyalty grounds of twenty-one teachers from Brooklyn College. According to his widow, Rugg resented Counts for fanning the flames of red-baiting, and their relationship never fully recovered.[101]

This type of damage to personal relationships was a common occurrence during this era, as investigations of individuals resulted in the broader destruction of networks and coalitions on the left.[102] Beyond the hundreds of teachers who lost their positions due to their political beliefs, the suffocating atmosphere of the Second Red Scare greatly limited what could be taught in the classroom. Subjects that were central aspects of a left vision of education such as trade unionism and capitalism became essentially off-limits.[103] The active suppression of the individuals and ideas of the political left dramatically shifted the center of gravity in terms of a national educational vision.

The consequences of red-baiting attacks on Harold Rugg were much more serious than they were for John Dewey and indicate the significant effects of political suppression on the classroom. As educational historian Stephen Foster has noted, "virtually every organization associated with the red scare participated in reflexive assaults on textbooks."[104] Rugg's social studies textbook series was subject to particularly heated criticism, with business groups playing a particularly influential role in the movement to ban them. Perhaps no group was as influential in targeting Rugg's work as the National Association of Manufacturers (NAM). In 1941 the NAM commissioned a comprehensive report of textbooks in an attempt to "determine the attitude or point of view presented by the respective authors with respect to the private enterprise system or the traditional governmental system of the United States."[105] The report evaluated several of Rugg's textbooks and included excerpts that focused on Russia, unemployment, increasing inequality, and economic planning.[106] Although the report remained officially neutral, the quotations were chosen in such a way to give the impression that his books were well outside the mainstream and hostile to free enterprise. The reaction to the report was swift, with immediate calls for the banning of all of Rugg's textbooks.[107] Other business groups soon piled on, with the publisher of *Forbes* magazine stating he would personally "insist that this anti-American educator's text books be cast out," and the American Association of Advertisers joined the effort by asking all of its local affiliates to pressure school boards to no longer buy Rugg's textbooks.[108]

The accusations of subversiveness had an immediate and drastic effect on the use of Rugg's textbooks in public schools across the country. The state of Georgia suspended the use of all of Rugg's textbooks in 1940 after a police officer affiliated with the governor's home defense corps claimed he had found "communistic doctrines" in Rugg's books.[109] In a remarkable case in the central Pennsylvania town of Sunbury, all of Rugg's textbooks mysteriously disappeared from the junior high school after the school board refused demands from the local chapter of the American Legion that they be removed. The books were the only items missing from an apparent break-in over the Christmas break. The case went unsolved, perhaps because the police chief called to investigate the case was also the commander of the local council of the American Legion.[110] In a 1941 editorial, the *Milwaukee Sentinel* approvingly quoted the NAM report, called for a ban, and provided a clear articulation of the reasoning behind much of the attempts to ban Rugg's textbooks. After noting that "public school children are being 'softened' towards Soviet Russia by radical teachers and textbooks," the editorial issued a condemnation of the teaching of any sort of social vision that challenged the status quo, stating "only one doctrine should be taught APPROVINGLY in our schools—that is, AMERICANISM. All other systems but constitutional, free democracy should be condemned unsparingly."[111]

Activity on the local level eventually culminated in attention from HUAC, which held hearings in 1948 to consider a recommendation to officially ban all textbooks written by Rugg and two other progressive educators.[112] Although the committee declined to ban Rugg's books, the accusation of subversiveness was enough to effectively eliminate the textbooks from public schools. As the content of Rugg's work was attacked, circulation of his textbooks declined from 289,000 in 1938 to 21,000 in 1944, to essentially zero by the 1950s. After Rugg's publisher discontinued production of his social studies series under pressure from outside groups, many schools replaced it with a series by Paul Hanna. Hanna had self-consciously crafted his series to avoid serious engagement with the social and political issues of the day and actively attempted to limit the control that social studies teachers had over the parameters of the curricula. The result was a dispassionate series that proved uncontroversial and popular with schools throughout the 1940s and 1950s. The decline of Rugg's textbooks, and the style of those that replaced it, was another damaging blow to the reputation and influence of the social reconstructionists.[113]

The attack on his textbooks were just one of the avenues used to undermine Rugg and his educational positions in this era. Rugg was also investigated as a potential subversive individual by the FBI. Rugg's FBI file did not begin until 1942 and was apparently created in reaction to the accusations of conservative groups that his textbooks contained material designed to indoctrinate students with subversive beliefs. Tellingly, most of the material in the initial file was reprints of articles by conservative critics, including articles from the NAM and a business executive associated with the American Legion. Although no action was taken, Rugg attracted the attention of both the Ohio Un-American Activities Committee and the FBI, which began investigating Rugg under a Security Matter C (Communist) classification.[114] The investigation triggered an immediate outcry from community groups and opposition from the board of trustees, the American Legion, and the governor of Ohio.[115] The 1951 event began a period of sporadic investigation into Rugg's subversiveness that would last until his death in 1960.[116] Despite never having been officially charged, and frequently being found harmless by several investigations, Rugg was deemed a potential risk and faced continuous investigation by the FBI for nearly twenty years.

The investigations proved particularly devastating for the personal and professional careers of many of the educators who had been strong advocates for a pedagogy centered on investigating the inequalities of the capitalist social and economic landscape. In the late 1930s Mary Foley Grossman, the Philadelphia teacher and union leader, was a respected voice in the education and labor community. Grossman had testified before Congress in 1937 as an educational expert, urging Congress to increase federal aid to public education.[117] In 1938, as president of nearly 4,000 organized teachers in Pennsylvania, she led the successful effort to affiliate with the AFT, giving the AFT its first presence in the state.[118] Grossman was a prominent voice warning against the dangers of reducing academic curriculum to "the 3 R's," and encouraging greater education for workers so they could better articulate demands against employers. Grossman was also a strong proponent of teachers unions and greater federal aid to public education.[119]

By 1939 Grossman had already drawn the attention of HUAC, due to both her membership in the American League for Peace and Democracy and for her outspoken opposition to attempts to weaken or overturn the Wagner Act.[120] Grossman's influence was greatly limited in the wake of accusations from Counts's "right-wing" coalition that she held subversive political beliefs. This resulted in her being pushed out of her leadership position in the national AFT and the revocation of the charter of her local union. Although these accusations did not immediately threaten her teaching job, when HUAC turned attention to subversive influences in public education, Grossman was eventually suspended from her teaching position and interrogated by the committee.

Grossman's experience highlights the way in which the Second Red Scare had particularly powerful effects on the membership and programmatic agenda of unions in the postwar era.[121] Passed as the anti-communist hysteria was reaching a fever pitch, the 1947 Taft–Hartley Act greatly undermined the power of the labor movement and contained a provision that required all trade union officials to sign affidavits proclaiming that they were neither members nor supporters of the Communist Party.[122] The passage of the Taft–Hartley Act and the reemergence of HUAC the same year made Popular Front cooperation untenable, and roughly one million members of the CIO were expelled between 1949 and 1950 over their refusal to sign the required anti-communist affidavits.[123] This massive purging of left-oriented unions and members had serious consequences for the political agenda of the labor movement. The Communist Party union workers were often the most

committed and effective organizers when it came to combating racial prejudice and racial exclusion, and their expulsion resulted in a substantial decline
in the priority that the American Federation of Labor–CIO put on fighting
racial segregation.[124] The mass removal of the communist members or sympathizers from the political mainstream significantly limited the influence
and connection the labor movement would have in the dominant left politics
that would emerge in the coming decades.[125]

The elimination of leftists from the labor movement and the increasingly
defensive posture forced by unfriendly legislation and resurgent business influence led to consequential changes in the political demands of unions. The
passage of the Taft–Hartley Act forced labor leaders to shift focus from advocating for expanding New Deal–style welfare programs to a stance that prioritized collective bargaining.[126] The purging of the left flank of the labor
movement was important to this reprioritization, as this was precisely the
part of the labor movement that was most likely to organize around broad
social issues like universal social welfare programs.[127] This fracturing of Popular Front–style cooperation between labor unions and the left resulted in a
labor movement with a narrowed focus, fewer connections with the other left
movements, and a close embrace of the Democratic Party. In a sharp reversal
of the trends of the previous decades, the percent of the workforce belonging
to a union began its lengthy decline in 1953.[128]

In Grossman's 1954 testimony before HUAC, the accusations that Counts's
coalition had used in the 1940 AFT campaign, as well as the suspension of the
Philadelphia local's charter were central to the committee's case against Grossman. Grossman invoked her Fifth Amendment right against self-incrimination
as the committee asked her whether she had ever been a communist or hosted
communist meetings in her home and questioned her about the political loyalties of her fellow union members.[129] The accusations and investigation of Grossman effectively destroyed any influence she may have had over education policy,
and the elimination of her voice from the national scene meant the loss of a
prominent voice advocating for a pedagogy devoted to tackling social injustice.

Doxey Wilkerson, a fellow AFT leader ousted in the 1940 elections, suffered a similar fate. Like Grossman, Wilkerson had been a prominent national
voice on education. After gaining his master's degree from the University of
Kansas, Wilkerson began his career as a professor of education at Virginia
State University, moving to Howard University in 1935. As his prominence
grew with his frequent contributions to the *JNE* throughout the 1930s, in
1937, President Roosevelt's newly appointed Advisory Committee on Education reached out to Wilkerson and hired him as a researcher. Between 1937

and 1939, the committee commissioned Wilkerson for several studies outlining information on federal aid to vocational education, the role of federal, state, and local governments in education, and the particular educational challenges of Black students. In 1939, the Advisory Committee combined Wilkerson's reports into one volume, *Special Problems of Negro Education*, and printed and distributed copies through the Government Printing Office.[130] As a result of his work, Wilkerson was asked to serve on the National Advisory Committee of the Works Progress Administration education program and was eventually hired as an educational specialist for the Office of Price Administration (OPA) in 1942 and 1943.

Wilkerson's national profile as an educational expert was also boosted by his service as a vice president for international affairs of the AFT from 1937–1940, and as a representative of the American Teachers Association, a Black teachers association with more than 4,000 members.[131] By the late 1930s and early 1940s, Wilkerson was one of the most prominent national Black educational figures. Wilkerson publicly advocated for a greater federal role in primary and secondary education, encouraged teachers to expose students to the social injustices of the existing economy, and was firmly committed to the principles of economic democracy.

Wilkerson's actions and writings quickly drew the attention of the FBI, conservative members of Congress, and liberals uncomfortable with his more radical stances. In the late 1930s, as he made multiple appearances as an expert witness on education before the Senate Committee on Labor and Education, Wilkerson's name appeared in a HUAC investigation of "Un-American Propaganda Activities" because of his connection with the International Labor Defense, a suspected communist front group.[132] Wilkerson, along with Mary Foley Grossman, was pushed out of his position at the AFT by George Counts's right-wing coalition. The FBI opened an investigation into Wilkerson following the very public ouster in 1940 of Wilkerson and Grossman from the AFT after George Counts's coalition questioned their loyalties. By 1942, the bureau had concluded that Wilkerson was a communist and issued a report recommending that he no longer be employed by the federal government despite the fact that at the time there was no official prohibition on communists serving as federal employees. Although Wilkerson was not immediately terminated, he ultimately resigned his position a year after the FBI report, at which point he publicly announced his membership in the Communist Party.[133]

Despite no longer being employed by the federal government, Wilkerson continued to draw the attention of congressional investigations. His name showed up frequently in congressional reports of suspected subversive organizations, including the American League for Peace and Democracy, the Washington Committee for Democratic Action, and the Council on African Affairs.[134] Importantly, after Wilkerson announced that he was a communist, his case became a rallying cry for those looking to rid the federal government of communists. In his 1947 testimony before HUAC, J. Edgar Hoover mentioned Doxey Wilkerson's case, and the failure of the OPA to terminate his employment despite an FBI report warning of his communist affiliation, as a cautionary tale.[135] Hoover's testimony resonated with Senator Joseph McCarthy, who began using Wilkerson's case as an example throughout the country of the important work done by the FBI and HUAC.[136]

After 1943, any past association with Wilkerson had the potential to call an individual's political loyalty into question. In his 1950 Senate confirmation hearings to the Third Circuit Court of Appeals, Judge William Henry Hastie was questioned about the years in which he and Wilkerson were both on the faculty of Howard University and were both members of the National Negro Congress.[137] After President Eisenhower nominated former Howard faculty member George Johnson to be a member of the Commission on Civil Rights, Johnson faced similar questions in his Senate confirmation hearing about how well he knew, and how close he worked with, Doxey Wilkerson.[138] Upon being nominated to be a federal circuit court judge in 1962, Thurgood Marshall was questioned over whether he knew or had a relationship with Wilkerson, and if there was any connection between Wilkerson and the NAACP. Despite the fact that Marshall testified that he did not know Wilkerson, the first fifty-four pages of the HUAC file on Wilkerson were read into the records of Marshall's confirmation hearing.[139] Wilkerson also came up when President Johnson requested an FBI background check on Abe Fortas for his potential appointment to the Supreme Court in 1964. Fortas's file included the fact that both he and Wilkerson were members of the Washington Committee for Democratic Action in the early 1940s and a caution that Fortas may have once attended a meeting led by Wilkerson.[140]

In March 1953, Wilkerson was subpoenaed to appear before a Senate committee investigating subversive influence in the educational process. Wilkerson invoked his Fifth Amendment right against self-incrimination as he was asked about his involvement with the Communist Party during his time working for the OPA and Works Progress Administration and as a faculty member at Howard University.[141] However, before invoking his Fifth Amendment privilege, Wilkerson delivered a statement to Senator McCarthy outlining his educational approach and excoriating the committee and its investigation for the damaging effect it had on education in the country. The remarkable statement began:

> I want to make it clear at the outset that I have nothing but contempt for the efforts of this subcommittee to subvert academic freedom in the schools and colleges of our country. I will not cooperate with this subcommittee's aim to reduce the people of our Nation to the intellectual status of robots whose ideas on social and political questions are dictated by certain congressional committees. My whole career as a student and teacher has been one of trying to understand and interpret the history, problems, and development of our society; and I have ever been ready to proclaim what my studies revealed. This I will continue to do. For more than 2 decades I have encouraged thousands of young people in my classes to dig in deeply, to seek answers to the basic questions of our time, and follow with courage the convictions they reach. This, likewise, I will continue to do.[142]

After reaffirming his commitment to a pedagogy centered on investigation of social problems, Wilkerson asked a number of rhetorical questions to highlight what he viewed as the political motivations of the committee. Wilkerson suggested that the subpoena was motivated by his opposition to "the drive to war and fascism which this subcommittee seeks to abet," his history of "investigating and exposing the abominable school conditions to which Negro children are subjected in much of the country," and his public advocacy for "the Socialist reorganization of our society."[143] Finally, Wilkerson hinted that the motivation for his appearance was due to the fact that "this subcommittee believes that, by running me through its inquisitorial mill, it will thereby help intimidate other Negro leaders, other educators, other students into silence."[144]

Wilkerson eventually renounced his membership in the Communist Party in 1957 and was hired as a professor of education at Bishop College, a Black college in Marshall, Texas. After a few quiet years at Bishop, Wilkerson participated in student-led protests and demonstrations against segregation in Marshall in 1960. Before long, Wilkerson's identity and past association were reported by the press and widely publicized by those critical of the demonstrations. Facing intense pressure from the press and donors, the college president requested that Wilkerson resign, and when Wilkerson refused, he was fired. Much like his earlier activities, the events at Marshall were recorded and publicized by a congressional subcommittee investigating subversive individuals.[145] Over a period of twenty years, Wilkerson's political beliefs cost him his semi-regular column in the *JNE*, his leadership position in the AFT, and his ability to work as a public employee. Additionally, Wilkerson became a threat to the personal and professional lives of friends, allies, and organizations with which he had interacted. Wilkerson's former prominence and influence, along with his educational ideas, had been effectively eliminated from the nation's educational scene.

Wilkerson's case was emblematic of the anti-communist fervor that spread to academia, and left-wing professors found their employment on increasingly unstable ground. When congressional investigators turned their attention to communism in higher education in 1953, the Association of American Universities, whose members consisted of the presidents of thirty-seven of the country's most prominent universities, released a statement warning professors that "invocation of the Fifth Amendment places upon a professor a heavy burden of proof of his fitness to hold a teaching position and lays upon his university an obligation to reexamine his qualifications for membership in its society."[146] Charles Johnson, now the president of Fisk University and still a frequent *JNE* contributor, dismissed two faculty members for invoking the Fifth Amendment when called before HUAC, despite widespread support for the two professors on campus.[147] The American Association of University Professors, the main organization committed to defending academic freedom in higher education, largely stayed on the sidelines during the height of the Second Red Scare and did nothing to combat the academic firings that cost hundreds of professors their livelihoods.[148]

The changing domestic political context of the decade and a half after World War II dramatically circumscribed the terrain on which the left could operate in the United States. By the late 1950s, a number of groups advocating for interracial working-class organization and anti-imperialism, including the American Labor Party, the Council on African Affairs, the National Negro Labor Council, and the Civil Rights Congress, had disbanded due in large part to suppression by the federal government.[149] The disappearance of these organizations represented a substantial loss to the ideas and coalitions of the left. Without the intellectual and financial resources, organizing around the political agenda like that advocated by the Popular Front became infinitely more difficult. Furthermore, as historian Ellen Schrecker has argued, "McCarthyism's main impact may well have been in what did not happen rather than in what did—the social reforms that were never adopted, the diplomatic initiatives that were not pursued, the workers who were not organized into unions, the books that were not written, and the movies that were not filmed."[150] There is no way to account for the personal relationships, political allegiances, and new organizations and coalitions that might have emerged in the absence of the widespread suppression of the political left. The repression of the left had an impact not only in the coalitions and policies that disappeared from the political arena but also in the absence of organizational capacity to resist and push back against an increasingly conservative national political agenda.[151]

The loyalty investigation machinery provided a convenient tool for renascent business groups and conservative politicians committed to rolling back many of the New Deal programs and to preventing the passage of similar generous social welfare programs, as they cast individuals on the political left as threats to national security, particularly if they were critical of the economic system. Although this shifting postwar domestic political context was devastating for those on the educational left that centered their politics on a critique of economic inequality and exploitation under the existing economic system, it was substantially more friendly to a politics that could articulate grievances in a manner that did not implicate capitalism. This provided a decisive advantage to those whose educational vision centered on constructing a system that could fairly and effectively incorporate racial minorities into the existing system.

The Changing Court Doctrines

At the moment that the Cold War context was rapidly shrinking the political space for left political organizations and individuals, the courts were providing opportunities for more moderate political approaches to labor and racial equality. Changing federal court doctrines in the 1950s provided an advantage to groups and individuals advancing a political agenda that centered on fair incorporation and equal opportunity. Throughout the 1930s and early 1940s the Supreme Court had appeared open to a conception of civil rights that provided strong protection for the rights of workers and labor, but by the late 1940s this moment had largely passed. Shifting court doctrines had important consequences for the types of legal arguments advanced by groups seeking redress—particularly for those targeting Jim Crow. By the early 1950s, as the Cold War context made cases emphasizing the rights of Black laborers unappealing, the NAACP shifted its focus to attacking the noneconomic consequences of Jim Crow segregation. The increasing openness of the Supreme Court to ruling that segregation violated the Fourteenth Amendment reinforced for many the wisdom of pursuing a political and legal agenda centered on demonstrating the negative psychological effects of segregation and discrimination. Although this approach proved quite successful in eliminating formal barriers to Black participation in existing institutions, it was particularly ill equipped to address the deteriorating economic situation facing Black Americans. The effect of shifting court doctrines filtered down to education coalitions, and by the end of the 1950s, the political context proved much more amenable for educational programs supported by racial democrats and scientific efficiency progressives.

The Supreme Court's shifting stance on labor rights proved significant for the educational visions of social reconstructionists and economic democrats. Since empowered teachers with strong unions were central to both these educational ideologies, the passage of the National Labor Relations Act (NLRA) in 1935 was a welcome development. Passed amid the turmoil of the Great Depression and after a massive wave of strikes and the rise of the CIO, the NLRA promoted collective bargaining, formalized the right of workers to organize, and created the National Labor Relations Board to oversee labor organization and prevent unfair labor practices. The NLRA's author, Senator Robert Wagner (D-NY), asserted the act was essential since "democracy cannot work unless it is honored in the factory as well as the polling booth; men cannot be truly free in body and in spirit unless their freedom extends into the places where they earn their daily bread."[152] This articulation of democracy and its requirements was squarely in line with the educational ideologies articulated by economic democrats and social reconstructionists. The NLRA's promotion of industrial democracy, strong unions, and redistribution of power from corporate leaders to workers had potentially radical implications.[153]

Some initial decisions gave the labor movement hope that the Supreme Court would take an expansive interpretation of protections the NLRA granted to workers, but by the 1940s, the Court was increasingly handing down decisions that "progressively chipped away at labor's rights."[154] The intransigence of the business community, which attempted to undermine the NLRA through refusing to follow the newly established rules and devoting resources to illegal antiunion campaigns, meant that the Court had a decisive role in determining the boundaries of legitimate labor activity.[155] As the Supreme Court limited, or failed to protect, the most effective union tactics, the labor movement was put squarely on the defensive.[156] Shifting court doctrine, much like the purging of labor's left flank, channeled union activity toward bargaining over the wages and conditions of existing members rather than expanding membership and making broad challenges to existing economic structures.[157] The decisions of the Supreme Court had a hand in foreclosing the radical potential of the labor movement as the Court ultimately embraced a

labor doctrine that was "most consistent with the assumptions of liberal capitalism and foreclosed those potential paths of development most threatening
to the established order."[158] The Court's shift away from strong protection of
labor rights became a growing impediment to advocates of social reconstructionism and economic democracy. However, even as the Supreme Court was
unsympathetic to cases that emphasized the material harms of unfair labor
conditions, it proved increasingly open to new arguments emerging from the
NAACP that focused on the harms that stemmed from inequitable treatment
on the basis of race.

The NAACP Legal Strategy at the Supreme Court

Much like the labor rights cases, Supreme Court decisions in the 1940s and
1950s helped shift the political center of gravity for groups seeking legal redress for issues relating to civil rights and racial inequality. This time period
was one in which the legal understanding of civil rights was in flux. Despite
contestation and debate in the early 1940s, a variety of factors, including the
Supreme Court's less sympathetic stance toward labor rights, federal institutions more open to combating racial discrimination, the class commitments
of the NAACP, and the rising Second Red Scare, all contributed to an eventual postwar settlement on a conception of civil rights centered on seeking
redress from the Fourteenth Amendment Equal Protection Clause for the
intangible and psychological harms imposed on Black Americans by Jim
Crow. This settlement, most famously evident in the 1954 *Brown v. Board* decision, greatly strengthened the political hand of racial democrats who
pressed for equal opportunity for success in the existing institutional landscape, and the scientific efficiency progressives who offered a means of evaluating this incorporation.

As Risa Goluboff has shown, this outcome was certainly not inevitable.
Throughout the early 1940s, the Civil Rights Section (CRS) of the Department of Justice pursued a number of cases that focused first and foremost on
the material consequences of exploitation and discrimination for Black laborers. In fact, "the attempts of black workers to build on the labor and economic
rights of the New Deal represented *the most politically promising* civil rights
issues of the 1940s."[159] The CRS successfully pursued a number of cases on
behalf of Black workers, particularly agricultural workers in the southern
sharecropping economy, on the grounds that certain work arrangements had
violated their Thirteenth Amendment right against involuntary servitude and
peonage. Pursuing relief for the economic claims of Black workers allowed the
CRS to navigate the thorny racial politics of the Democratic Party, since these

cases were palatable to Democratic administrations because they did not directly challenge segregation.[160] Furthermore, as Goluboff has argued, relief for the economic consequences of racial discrimination was actually the highest-order grievance for most Black people fighting against racial discrimination.[161] The legal resource and precedents offered by these labor cases suggested a particularly auspicious avenue for pursuing a conception of civil rights that included labor freedom and economic rights in addition to racial equality.[162]

For a brief moment during World War II, the NAACP experimented with a legal strategy that privileged the economic concerns of Black workers, most notably in a number of cases seeking salary equalization for Black teachers teaching in segregated schools.[163] These cases did not attack the segregated nature of workplaces, but rather sought to improve the material conditions of Black workers within segregated workplaces. However, the NAACP had never viewed work-related problems as constituting the primary harm of Jim Crow. The leaders of the organization had always been much more willing to frame the problem of Jim Crow as one in which white people singled out Black people for discriminatory treatment in access to government, hotels, restaurants, theaters, and other social and cultural institutions because this was how *they* were most affected in their personal lives.[164] The view emanating from the elites at the helm of the NAACP was a class-inflected one, as most Black people tended to express more concern about—and were more affected by—the material consequences of Jim Crow.[165] This core commitment by the leaders of the NAACP, coupled with a postwar international and domestic context that was less friendly to both the labor-related cases and the individuals advocating for a focus on the economic consequences of Jim Crow, meant that the NAACP was quick to drop its brief flirtation with a labor-centric notion of civil rights in the 1940s.[166] By 1950, the organization was firmly committed to the goal of overturning *Plessy v. Ferguson* and eliminating segregation as its top priority—regardless of the consequences for Black workers in segregated workplaces.

Significantly, the NAACP's decision to focus on attacking segregation on Fourteenth Amendment grounds was in part due to federal courts increasing receptivity to these arguments. In a 1939 article discussing recent Court cases regarding segregation in education including the 1938 *Missouri ex rel. Gaines v. Canada* decision, which effectively desegregated the University of Missouri School of Law, professor of sociology Henry McGuinn noted that "an indirect effect on the Court's decision was to strengthen the determination of the N.A.A.C.P. to fight segregated educational opportunities."[167] McGuinn argued that the Court's increasing openness to Fourteenth Amendment arguments against segregation "constitutes another reason why those who oppose the inequality and inferiority which Jim Crow schools impose upon Negroes should rally to oppose the spread of separate schools into the North and to wipe them out elsewhere."[168] The strategy used in the *Gaines* case challenging segregation in higher education on Fourteenth Amendment grounds spurred a number of similar challenges in other states.

The increasing success of this legal argument reinforced the belief among many civil rights activists that the Fourteenth Amendment equal protection argument was the best means of challenging racial subordination. In a 1947 *JNE* article, George Johnson, the dean of Howard University School of Law, and law student Jane Lewis argued that the Supreme Court had never decisively settled the question of whether segregation of public education institutions was constitutional under the Fourteenth Amendment. Stating, "in the opinion of the writers of this article, the United States Supreme Court has never squarely held that a state 'separate school' law per se discharges a state's obligation under the Fourteenth Amendment," the authors urged continued pursuit of this line of argument and expressed hope that several cases then working their way through the courts might find segregation unconstitutional on Fourteenth Amendment grounds.[169] In a 1951 *JNE* editorial, Charles Thompson, taking stock of mounting court victories, pointed out that the successful "cases adjudicated thus far have been based upon the 'equal protection clause' of the Fourteenth Amendment."[170] Thompson argued that the result of the NAACP's legal strategy had meant that "the Court has whittled down *Plessy v. Ferguson*," and he urged civil rights organizations to continue to "take full advantage of this opportunity."[171] The growing willingness of the courts to accept these arguments had a feedback effect on the NAACP and others seeking to combat racial subordination. These groups increasingly rallied behind challenging segregation on Fourteenth Amendment grounds and moved away from labor-related cases that had relied primarily on the Thirteenth Amendment.

The class-inflected nature of the NAACP legal strategy was increasingly apparent in the cases and the arguments made by NAACP lawyers. The economic position of individuals influenced the very cases that the NAACP chose to pursue, as the decisions of the organization and the lawyers themselves were constrained by the need to appeal to the wealthy and middle-class Black people and liberal white people that funded their efforts. As NAACP Legal Defense Fund lawyer Leroy Clark noted:

There are two "clients" the civil rights lawyer must satisfy: (1) the immediate litigants (usually black), and (2) those liberals (usually white) who make financial contributions. An apt criticism of the traditional civil rights lawyer is that too often the litigation undertaken was modulated by that which was "salable" to the paying clientele who, in the radical view, had interests threatened by true social change. Attorneys may not make conscious decisions to refuse specific litigation because it is too "controversial" and hard to translate to the public, but no organization dependent on a large number of contributors can ignore the fact that the "appeal" of the program affects fund-raising.[172]

The fact that the organization was run by Black elites and depended on middle-class and wealthy individuals for funding meant that many of the cases pursued by the NAACP were at "the confluence of the personal, professional, class, and racial interests" of well-off Black people.[173] Cases focusing on graduate and professional education, transportation, voting, and the ability to purchase houses were particularly important to Black elites.[174] By the late 1940s, the NAACP and its lawyers in the Legal Defense Fund lined up squarely behind a legal strategy committed to the fair incorporation of Black people into the existing institutional landscape and class structure.

The NAACP's campaign against racially restrictive housing covenants is an excellent example of the class-inflected nature of the organization's legal strategy. Many cities throughout the United States allowed for racially restrictive housing covenants, which were private agreements between white property owners not to sell or lease their property to racial minorities. Ending the practice of these racially restrictive covenants was one of the top priorities of the NAACP legal team in the 1940s, in no small part because it was a practice that was particularly insulting to Black elites who had the desire and resources to move out of racially segregated ghettoes.[175] Thurgood Marshall headed the team of the NAACP lawyers that successfully challenged the state enforcement of racial covenants in the 1948 case *Shelley v. Kraemer*. Marshall and the NAACP had relied heavily on the research of prominent Black social scientists, most notably that of future Secretary of Housing and Urban Development Robert Weaver, sociologists Charles Johnson and E. Franklin Frazier, and psychologist Herman Long. Relying on the work of these social scientists in their petition to the Supreme Court, the NAACP lawyers argued that the segregation of Black people into certain neighborhoods resulted in high-level crime, juvenile delinquency, dependency, psychological and personality damage, mental disorders, and social pathology among Black individuals and families.[176] Furthermore, these social scientists argued that the damages to Black individuals and poor conditions of the neighborhoods and housing to which Black people were relegated ultimately supported the racial preju-dice of white people.[177] As the NAACP embraced these scholars and the ar-guments they put forth about the harm of segregation, the positions of the NAACP and the racial democrats were increasingly difficult to distinguish.

As political scientist Preston Smith has shown, the NAACP's victory in the Court was followed immediately by attempts of Black elites to manage the transition of Black people into new neighborhoods through occupancy standards. These new occupancy standards, supported by the American Council of Race Relations and Robert Weaver, were race-neutral rules and regulations attached to property that limited the ways in which the property could be used and were designed to limit the integration of nicer neighbor-hoods to those that had the economic resources and behavioral habits of the existing neighbors. The turn to occupancy standards was an attempt by Black elites to ensure that only the right class of Black people were allowed into certain neighborhoods and was an effort to find a market-friendly tool to eliminate racial segregation in the housing market while maintaining the stark class segregation of neighborhoods. There was certainly criticism of the NAACP from Black people who realized that the attack on racially re-strictive covenants would mostly benefit the wealthy. The turn to occupancy standards after the victory in the Court was roundly criticized as an attempt to restrict access to housing for poor Black people.[178] Ultimately, the NAACP's legal strategy and victory in the *Kraemer* case disproportionately reflected the class interests of wealthy and middle-class Black people.

The 1948 *Shelley v. Kraemer* case also marked the first time that the federal government intervened as an outside party on behalf of the civil rights groups seeking redress for Fourteenth Amendment violations due to racial discrimi-nation.[179] The increasing willingness of the federal government to intercede on behalf of racial minorities before the Court was in no small part due to negative consequences that continued racial discrimination had on the image of the United States abroad. The amicus brief filed by the Office of the Solici-tor General argued that government enforcement of racially restrictive cove-nants was a "source of serious embarrassment to agencies of the Federal Government" and hindered "the conduct of foreign affairs."[180] The brief in-cluded a statement from the secretary of state warning that instances of racial discrimination were widely publicized internationally and cautioning that "we find it next to impossible to formulate a satisfactory answer to our critics in other countries" and that "the existence of discrimination against minority groups in the United States is a handicap in our relations with other coun-tries."[181] As previously discussed, the international context provided an opening for the pursuit of a civil rights agenda that privileged incorporation of racial minorities into the existing institutional landscape. By the late 1940s, advocates for racial democracy had found powerful institutional support in the NAACP, the federal government, and the Supreme Court.

Perhaps the most important indication of this new settlement in the legal arena was the Supreme Court's 1954 *Brown v. Board* decision. Education provided the NAACP a particularly opportune area to pursue its top priority of overturning the *Plessy v. Ferguson* (1896) precedent. In 1952, Thurgood Marshall outlined the plan of attack at a conference at Howard University hosted by Charles Thompson, editor of the *JNE*. At the conference, which took place as *Brown v. Board* was working its way through the courts, Marshall made it clear that the main thrust of the NAACP's argument would rely on an emerging social science literature that focused on the immaterial consequences of segregation in primary and secondary schools. Instead of focusing on tangible differences between Black and white schools, such as physical facilities, number of teachers, or amount of funding, the NAACP's legal strategy would focus on the evidence that segregation caused "insecurity, self-hate," and "adverse effect[s] on personality development" in Black students.[182] As historian Leah Gordon has shown, the postwar era was a particularly opportune time for this change in legal strategy. Generous federal and foundation funding for studies examining the psychological effects of prejudice and segregation had facilitated a decisive shift in the ideological tenor of the social sciences and led to a proliferation of studies that identified prejudice and attitudes, rather than labor exploitation and class struggle, as the source of racial oppression.[183] It was these studies that would form the heart of the NAACP's argument in *Brown v. Board*.

The focus on the psychological harm of segregation was distinct from the strategy that the NAACP had pursued in previous cases involving higher education and professional schools. The NAACP had experienced some success in cases pursuing integration in institutions of higher education through arguing that the separate opportunities provided to white and Black students were unequal, most notably in the *Sweatt v. Painter* (1950) and *McLaurin v. Oklahoma State Regents* (1950) cases. However, as Marshall pointed out at the conference, it would be much more difficult to win on this argument in primary and secondary education cases, as many states had made an effort (often in response to, or in an attempt to head off, adverse court decisions) to equalize the tangible aspects of Black and white schools.[184] This fact made the turn to the immaterial psychological harm that was the focus of many social scientists particularly attractive to the NAACP lawyers, as it provided them a new avenue of arguing that separate schools did not (and in fact, could not) provide equal educational opportunities.

The decision to focus on the psychological effects of segregation was evident in the oral arguments and briefs submitted by the NAACP in the *Brown* case. The NAACP lawyers submitted an extensive appendix with their briefs, entitled "The Effects of Segregation and the Consequences of Desegregation: A Social Science Statement." This statement, which was represented by the NAACP lawyers as "a consensus of social scientists" and a "summary of the best available scientific evidence relative to the effects of racial segregation" was drafted and signed by a number of prominent social scientists, including psychologists Kenneth and Mamie Clark, anthropologist Allison Davis, and sociologist Ira Reid.[185] The statement emphasized that segregation had the potential to "damage the personality of all children,"[186] which could lead to myriad negative consequences including "anti-social and delinquent behavior," a "defeatist attitude,"[187] and "feelings of inferiority and doubts about personal worth."[188] The focus on the immaterial and psychological harm of segregation featured heavily in Marshall's oral arguments before the Supreme Court as well. Marshall's argument before the justices relied heavily on the claim that segregation in education damaged the personality of children, and thus denied them equal status in schooling. Marshall stated that "Negro children have road blocks put up in their mind as a result of this segregation" and this "stamps [them] with a badge of inferiority."[189] Marshall also drew the justices' attention to the testimony of Kenneth Clark, who had examined Leah Carter and found evidence of psychological injury, and warned of the potential for permanent injury to the mind if students were forced to stay in segregated schools.[190]

The argument that segregation caused psychological damage to students was cited by the justices in their unanimous decision overturning the separate but equal doctrine.[191] Much as Marshall had predicted at the 1952 Howard University conference outlining the NAACP's legal strategy, the justices emphasized that efforts to equalize Black and white schools "with respect to buildings, curricula, qualifications and salaries of teachers, and other 'tangible' factors," meant their decision could not be based "on merely a comparison of these tangible factors."[192] Instead, the decision focused on the immaterial harm of segregation on children, arguing, "to separate them from others of similar age and qualifications solely because of their race generates a feeling of inferiority . . . that may affect their hearts and minds in a way unlikely to ever be undone."[193] In justifying their decision, the justices cited Kenneth Clark, E. Franklin Frazier, and Gunnar Myrdal among others, arguing that new evidence emanating from social scientists had decisively shown that segregation caused psychological damage to children: "Whatever may have been the extent of psychological knowledge at the time of *Plessy v. Ferguson*, this finding is amply supported by modern authority."[194]

The *Brown* decision represented the victory of the NAACP legal vision that focused on the nonmaterial consequences of segregation. The decision also marked a doctrinal shift in the courts that established that government-backed segregation was unconstitutional, even in the absence of material inequality.[195] Law professor Lani Guinier has noted that through the *Brown* decision the Supreme Court converted the problems facing Black people "into a problem of individual psychological dysfunction" and as merely "an aberration in individuals who disregard relevant information, rely on stereotypes and act thoughtlessly."[196] This left little room for legal recourse for the widespread material consequences that Jim Crow had imposed on Black people. Indeed, Oliver Cox had warned about the pitfalls of this approach, arguing that a full-throated pursuit of desegregation ignored possible economic consequences for tens of thousands of Black teachers in segregated schools. Noting that many teachers would be fired if the NAACP was successful on its terms, Cox pointed out that "the right to employment in tax-supported institutions of learning is equally as important as the right to a non-discriminatory form of education."[197] However, this warning went largely unheeded, and the victory in *Brown* helped entrench a significant shift away from earlier conceptions of civil rights that focused on economic and labor rights.[198]

The *Brown* decision galvanized support behind the continued push for a civil rights platform centered on overcoming the specific harms identified by the Court in its decision, the psychological injury imposed by segregation. In a 1955 *JNE* article, Thurgood Marshall and Robert Carter, two of the NAACP lawyers who had argued the *Brown* case before the Supreme Court, urged for the continuation of their program, arguing, "it is important the strongest pressures against the continuation of segregation, North or South, be continually and constantly manifested . . . as much as anything else, this is the key to the elimination of discrimination in the United States."[199] The *Brown* decision, and the many court victories before it, refocused the political agendas of a number of groups and individuals combating racial subordination. The National Council of Negro Women, a council comprised of more than two dozen groups founded by New Dealer and Works Progress Administration administrator Mary McLeod Bethune, announced their new focus, saying that "following the Supreme Court decision of May 17, 1954, the Board of

Directors of the National Council of Negro Women decided that the program emphasis for the organization should embrace a program to further the implementation of the decision."[200] The decision to shift focus was quickly followed by an invitation to Kenneth Clark to give the keynote speech at a national conference and the decision to found a new Interracial Conference to promote interracial understanding.[201]

Part of the broader reorientation of the NAACP around this focus included distancing the organization from association with left-wing groups. Although the NAACP formalized its anti-communist stance in 1950, Marshall had been actively involved in purging suspected communists since the early 1940s. In fact, Marshall developed a close relationship with FBI director J. Edgar Hoover and provided information on subversives within the NAACP in exchange for access to FBI files that helped him push communists out of the organization.

These efforts, although in part driven by the desire to protect the organization from the long arm of the HUAC and the FBI, also reflected the ideological orientation of Marshall and others within the NAACP leadership. As these leaders rejected economic radicalism, the legal victories on terms that sought to facilitate racial incorporation into the existing institutional landscape pushed postwar Black politics toward the racial democratic position.[202]

The court victories of the NAACP lawyers received extensive and overwhelmingly positive coverage in the *JNE* in the late 1940s and 1950s. The articles appearing in the *JNE* increasingly embraced the racial democracy framework and the identification of psychological harm as the paramount harm of racial segregation. This development is particularly significant given the fierce debates between the racial and economic democrats in the 1930s and early 1940s. Indeed, many in the economic democracy camp had made the point that attacking prejudice or segregation without also attacking the exploitative economic system—which they viewed as the source of prejudice—amounted to attacking the symptoms while leaving the cause intact. By the mid-1950s this argument essentially disappeared from the pages of the *JNE*, as the Court decision in *Brown* (and others) reaffirmed the pursuit of desegregation and anti-prejudice as the paramount goal of Black politics. The political agenda shifted accordingly, as programs focused on interracial contact and education to combat prejudice and discrimination and improve race relations began to dominate the political landscape.

The post-*Brown* legal consensus that enshrined psychological damage as the primary consequence of segregation left little room for legal recourse for the material consequences—including poor pay, lack of jobs, and lack of job stability—that were often at the forefront of Black complaints about the harms of Jim Crow.[203] The consolidation of this legal and political consensus came at a particularly perilous economic time for Black workers. The 1930s and early 1940s had been a time of significant improvement in the economic situation of Black workers. There was a fourfold increase in the number of Black people employed by the federal government between 1933 and 1946, and Black union membership exploded from 150,000 in 1935 to 1.25 million by the end of World War II.[204] Although their situation remained decidedly worse than their white counterparts, Black workers continued to make economic gains and considerably reduced the Black–white income gap in the immediate postwar years.[205]

By the early 1950s, the economic prospects of Black workers (and many white workers as well) changed considerably. The fatal blow to the industrial democratic potential of the NLRA dealt by the federal courts and Taft–Hartley legislation greatly weakened the position of workers and the labor movement, leaving them unable to effectively combat the destabilization of millions of jobs as companies turned to automation and moved jobs to open-shop states. As the labor movement was forced into an increasingly defensive position in response to court decisions and hostile legislation, the percentage of the workforce that belonged to unions began to decline by 1953.[206] At roughly the same time, the economic fortunes for Black workers began to shift, and the gap between the wages of Black workers and white workers actually increased from 1952 through the end of the decade.[207] Indeed, although the late 1940s and the 1950s are often regarded as a time of prosperity and affluence, this characterization misses the uneven distribution of the economic gain. By the end of 1950s, more than 22 percent of the population, and 55 percent of the Black population, was living in poverty.[208] As the courts facilitated the disappearance of previous commitments to job guarantees, redistribution of power in the workplace, and strong economic rights from the political and legal landscape, these commitments were replaced by the pursuit of a legal and policy agenda centered on attacking discrimination and prejudice. This new agenda offered considerably fewer avenues for effective redress of immense economic problems facing Black workers.

The Consolidation of the Liberal Incorporationist Order

The Supreme Court's embrace of the NAACP's racial incorporationist arguments occurred at the height of the repression of economic democracy and social reconstructionist visions of education by other arms of the federal government. These developments resulted in a political environment that proved to be particularly amenable to the educational vision and particular pedagogical approaches advocated by racial democrats and scientific efficiency progressives. As the Red Scare eliminated the influence of economic democrats and social reconstructionists and the courts demonstrated increasing responsiveness to arguments relying on the nonmaterial inequities of segregation, the stage was set for the consolidation of a liberal incorporationist educational vision centered on providing equal opportunity for success within the existing economic system. The growth of educational movements advocating for intercultural education, life adjustment education, and greater use of testing in the 1950s was a clear indication that mainstream education ideas had shifted firmly away from the vision of the economic democrats and social reconstructionists.

By the end of the 1950s liberal incorporationsim, an educational vision that stitched together aspects of racial democracy and scientific efficiency, came to dominate liberal understandings of the appropriate methods and purpose of education. This coalition was committed to pursuing equality of educational opportunity as a means of ensuring fair and effective incorporation into the existing market economy. As education was increasingly positioned as social policy that could effectively combat racism, racial inequality, and poverty and effectively prepare individuals for the demands of the workforce, it became increasingly attractive to policy makers looking for a means of addressing these social ills. The stage was set for the consolidation of the liberal incorporationist educational order.

The Court's embrace of social science literature emphasizing the psychological damage of segregation gave substantial support to an intercultural education movement that framed racial subordination as primarily a problem of psychology and attitudes. As detailed in chapter 2, the basis for the intercultural education movement was the belief that racial tensions and prejudice stemmed primarily from fundamental misunderstandings between, and misconceptions about, different races, in part due to the lack of direct interaction of individuals of differing races. These prejudices resulted in the lack of equal opportunities for success for individuals of different races. Advocates of intercultural education had long pushed for integration and greater interaction between students of different races as a means of combating racial prejudice, along with a curricular emphasis on the fundamental similarities of different races, particularly in terms of intellectual ability.[209] The arguments of the NAACP, and much of the basis for the Supreme Court's decision in *Brown*, were fundamentally similar to those of intercultural education advocates, relying heavily on the idea that segregation caused feelings of inferiority in Black students and contributed to the prejudice of white children. Both the intercultural education movement and the *Brown* decision downplayed the idea of an economic dimension to racial prejudice or subordination, instead framing the issue as primarily a nonmaterial, attitudinal one.[210] The ultimate goal was to break down racial misunderstandings to encourage racial harmony, and to ensure that opportunity was not distributed on the basis of an arbitrary category like race, but instead tied closer to a meaningful category such intellectual merit.

The destruction of the personal lives and coalitions on the left also had an effect on education policy. As it became increasingly difficult to openly advocate for a vision of education centered on challenging exploitative economic arrangements and social injustice, the stage was set for the dominance of a vision of education that focused on fairly and effectively adjusting individuals to succeed in the existing institutional landscape. As discussed in chapters 1 and 2, racial democrats and scientific efficiency progressives had long advocated for a form of adjustment education for students that emphasized improving the skills, culture, and behaviors that students brought to the labor market. Racial democrats argued that adjustment education would prepare Black students to compete on equal footing with their white counterparts, ultimately leading to an economic distribution based on merit rather than race. Similarly, adjustment education offered hope to the poor as well, as it could provide the skills needed to earn a living in a changing labor market. Importantly, this educational vision garnered the support of many conservatives who saw the benefit of having the education system carry the burden of workforce training.[211] With their voices marginalized, educators on the left were unable to effectively combat a vision of education that sought to adjust the student to existing structures, rather than challenge them.

The vision of education that stressed fair incorporation of racial groups and gained prominence advocated for only a limited egalitarianism when it came to education. Thurgood Marshall made the limitations clear a year after the *Brown* decision in his arguments before the Court in *Brown II*. Several southern states were seeking to delay implementation of *Brown*, arguing that because the average standardized test scores of Black students were substantially below those of their white counterparts, integration threatened academic standards and should be delayed.[212] Marshall, acknowledging the administrative problems that might arise from disparate educational levels, suggested his own resolution: "So what do we think is the solution? Simple. *Put the dumb colored children in with the dumb white children, and put the smart colored children with the smart white children;* that is no problem."[213] The NAACP's position was that only distinctions based on arbitrary factors like race were problematic; however, there were few qualms about differential educational treatment if it was based on a factor considered nonarbitrary. The differentiation on the basis of intellectual ability and educational merit as nonarbitrary factors that could justify different treatment in education was a cornerstone of the scientific efficiency progressive position, and one that Marshall and other racial democrats increasingly embraced.[214]

The changing political context of the 1940s and 1950s proved to be a boon for advocates of standardized testing in education. The use of intelligence and aptitude tests by the military during World War II convinced many of their potential usefulness for the education system.[215] Scientific efficiency progressives had long pushed for the use of intelligence testing, achievement tests, and student tracking as the best means of developing teaching methods and of aiding in assigning students to jobs that were most appropriate for their skill set. This overlapped with the position of racial democrats, who were proponents of testing as a means of identifying future race leaders and of identifying effective educational methods and teachers. In the aftermath of the *Brown* decision ending segregation in public education, racial democrats were increasingly committed to testing as comparing the educational opportunities between Black and white students through comparing scores on achievement tests.[216] The Nazi embrace of hereditarian racial differences in intelligence made these ideas less popular in the United States and made the merging of the scientific efficiency and racial democracy positions easier.

As the political context facilitated the rise of a liberal incorporationist educational coalition, it pushed alternative visions to the background. The focus on the psychological harms of segregation and the legal push for desegregation pushed other educational consequences to the background. As Oliver Cox feared, the pursuit of desegregation without an attendant push for a right of public employment led to a loss of thousands of educational jobs for Black workers. As newly integrated schools kept white educators while firing Black educators, studies indicated that the percentage of Black teachers throughout the South declined. One study estimated that by the 1972–1973 school year, nearly 40,000 Black teachers and more than 2,200 Black principals had been displaced due to segregation in the South alone.[217] Social reconstructionists and economic democrats were looking to train students to remake existing institutions, not adjust students to them. For these scholars, attacking prejudice was through training students to remake an undemocratic political economy, not adjusting them to the existing landscape. Similarly, the use of standardized testing in education had been vigorously opposed by many on the educational left, who believed that these tests promoted excessive individualism, competitiveness, a narrowing of the curriculum, and routinization that were antithetical to their educational vision.[218] However, by the late 1950s, the political context had become increasingly hostile to individuals and coalitions that pushed for an educational vision centered on the need for changes to the political economy.

The ascendant liberal incorporationist coalition pushed for specific educational policies as *alternatives* to broader structural changes. This ideology helped bind disparate interests together, since these different interests— including those concerned with advancing civil rights and reducing interpersonal racism, those pushing for reducing teacher autonomy and introducing "scientific" methods into the classroom, and business interests looking to the schools to "adjust" students to their needs—could all embrace liberal incorporationism. Fundamentally, this vision positioned education as the key to solving racial disparity, poverty, and unemployment without threatening the capitalist economy. The timing was auspicious for policy makers who would turn to liberal incorporationist ideas as the ideological foundation and justification for a major expansion of the federal education state.

Part II

From Ideology to Institutionalization

The Foundations of the Federal
Education State, 1965–1980

CHAPTER FOUR

The Great Society and the Ideological Origins of the Federal Education State

After his landslide electoral victory in the 1964 election, President Lyndon B. Johnson and an expanded Democratic majority in Congress quickly began pursuing several far-reaching social policy reforms. At the top of the Great Society agenda was education. Just eight days after his State of the Union speech, Johnson submitted his education program to Congress. Johnson positioned education as key to the nation's ongoing war on poverty, low wages, and racial inequality, and he urged Congress to act quickly, noting that "today, lack of formal education is likely to mean low wages, frequent unemployment, and a home in an urban or rural slum. Poverty has many roots, but the taproot is ignorance."[1]

Both the House and Senate eagerly took up his call to action, and congressional committees started hearings by the end of the month. Echoing the president, Secretary of Health, Education, and Welfare Anthony Celebrezze argued federal involvement in education was key to attacking the foundation of the most urgent domestic issues. In his congressional testimony, he pressed lawmakers on the importance of federal funding of education, telling them that "we have come to see the clear link between high educational and high economic attainment—and between poor education and corrosive poverty that affects not only the individual but his city and State and the whole Nation's progress."[2] Remarkably, although federal policy makers had tried and failed to pass federal aid for education since the late 1800s, less than three months after President Johnson submitted his education plan to Congress, the Elementary and Secondary Education Act was signed into law.

The words of President Johnson and Secretary Celebrezze may seem like familiar truisms to the modern ear, but at the time they represented a pivotal transformation of the understanding of the source of social problems and the potential of education to solve them. During the New Deal, the problems of unemployment, inequality, and poverty were largely interpreted as the result of structural failings in the economy, and education policy had been at most tangentially connected to the proposed solutions. As of 1965, a new orthodoxy was ascendant within the Democratic Party, and it pointed to individual characteristics as central to explaining and solving social problems. This new understanding, borrowed largely from social science and the research of large nonprofit foundations, positioned education as a central policy realm for redressing social ills. These new ideas would prove powerful weapons in making the case for the first successful large-scale federal elementary and secondary education legislation.

Uncovering the significance of this moment requires close attention not only to the institutions that Johnson and the Democratic Party built but also to the ideological terms on which they did so. This chapter examines the developments that paved the way for the embrace by the Democratic Party of a liberal incorporationist ideology that positioned education as a key solution to unemployment, poverty, and racial inequality. As these developments provided the ideological basis for federal involvement in elementary and secondary education policy, they also obscured the political economic foundation of social problems.

By the 1960s, the changing political context of the 1940s and 1950s helped cement a liberal incorporationist understanding of the purpose of education firmly in the minds of the education community. The contestation and changes in the dominant understandings of the purpose of education were mirrored by a number of similar developments in other policy areas, most notably broad economic and unemployment policy. Significantly, by the mid-1940s, policy makers within the Democratic Party began to abandon the New Deal commitment to full employment, economic redistribution through progressive taxation, and public job guarantees.

The timing of the ideological victory of the liberal incorporationist educational vision would prove auspicious as policy makers within the Democratic Party increasingly looked for new policy avenues to address the problems of unemployment, poverty, and racial inequality. The liberal incorporationist understanding positioned education policy as an effective means of addressing all three of these pressing social issues without committing the Democratic Party to the massive federal expenditures of a New Deal–type policy agenda. This ideological understanding meant that on the policy front, Democrats eventually embraced approaches that had roots in the earlier visions of racial democrats and scientific efficiency progressives. As the Democratic Party turned its attention to education policy, it relied heavily on liberal incorporationist ideology in crafting the nascent federal education state.

Tracing the story of federal education policy development requires careful attention to the ideological shifts that paved the way for the first major federal law regarding public primary and secondary education policy—the 1965 ESEA. To understand *why* the Great Society coalition embraced education as a solution to a number of social problems requires understanding ideological developments in economic thinking within the Democratic Party in the years preceding the ESEA. As ideologies such as commercial Keynesianism, human capital theory, and culture of poverty theory gained ground within the Democratic Party, policy makers increasingly embraced both the individualized explanations that these ideologies offered for the existence of unemployment, poverty, delinquency, and racial inequality—and the faith that education policy could be a particularly effective tool in addressing these social problems. These new ideological interpretations of social problems helped build a coalition that defeated full employment legislation, pushed Democratic policy makers away from an interventionist economic stance toward more business-friendly economic management practices, and ultimately reframed social problems as the result of individual—rather than structural—deficiencies. These same ideas were also essential constitutive elements in the construction of a coalition that pressed for building the federal education state.[3]

The liberal incorporationist understanding of the purpose of education was able to easily accommodate itself to new ideological explanations of social problems—such as human capital theory and culture of poverty theory—in large part because these new theories also refocused attention and explanations of economic status on the individual rather than the broader economic forces or labor market structures. This ideological context not only helped facilitate the passage of the first major federal education legislation, but also significantly shaped the contours—and expectations—of the educational policies that emerged.

The "educationalization" of the problems of unemployment, poverty, racial inequality, and delinquency took place in a context where Great Society Democratic policy makers increasingly severed these problems from the structure of the economy. This was a distinct contrast with the New Deal coalition, which had focused on the broader structural causes of social problems and had paid little attention to education. This shift in the party—coupled with the consolidation of the liberal incorporationist vision that positioned education as an alternative to broader structural changes that was described in the previous chapter—helps explain why Democrats were so focused on education in the 1960s. Although some have interpreted the passage of the ESEA as a progressive triumph, it is better understood as an indication of a dramatically limited progressive vision.[4] The ESEA was a moment of victory for the liberal incorporationist vision, which individualized the source of social problems, shied away from aggressively redistributive economic policies, and laid the foundation for the punitive accountability policies that dominate federal education policy today. Close attention to the foundations of the federal education state reveals that the origins of current education policies oriented around widespread testing and punitive sanctions can be traced back to the politics and policies of the 1960s.

Reinterpreting Unemployment: Secular Stagnation to Commercial Keynesianism

The events of the Great Depression ushered in a dramatic change in how the Democratic Party understood the relationship between the federal government and the economy. The closing of nearly 40 percent of the nation's banks as well as a 25 percent unemployment rate brought forth a fevered period of legislative activity, including the expansion of social insurance with the Social Security Act and a host of programs aimed at the problem of unemployment.[5] Although President Franklin Roosevelt initially viewed government spending as a means of easing the worst effects of the Depression for the unemployed and vulnerable, the return of economic recession at the end of 1937 ultimately convinced Roosevelt to pursue spending as a tool of stabilization.[6] The 1938 announcement of a plan to expand federal expenditures by $7 billion represented a decisive step toward the use of fiscal policy as a means of economic recovery during the New Deal.[7]

The turn toward this type of economic management found an intellectual basis in John Maynard Keynes's 1936 book, *The General Theory of Employment, Interest and Money*. Keynes provided guidelines for how aggressive fiscal policy could help prevent economic recessions that radically differed from the conventional belief that a general wage reduction was the best means of combating economic depressions.[8] Within Keynes's broad commitment to the maintenance of a market economy, his theory "offered policy formulations which differed significantly in their ideological, political, and economic potentials."[9] These varied policy recommendations, ranging from the maintenance of low interest rates through central control to the more progressive option of active government spending to augment private investment, meant that the Keynesian label was potentially attractive to a broad swath of the ideological spectrum.

The Keynesian policies initially pursued by the federal government in the wake of the recession of 1937 and 1938 stemmed from a group of prominent Keynesians known as "secular stagnationists." According to the stagnationists, the slowing of population growth and technological innovation coupled with the end of territorial expansion meant that the United States had reached a stage of economic maturity in which stagnation was a natural condition of a capitalist economy. The appropriate response to this fundamental disability of the market economy was continued government investment to regenerate growth.[10] On the policy side this meant large programs of social spending and public works funded by highly redistributive taxation that would decrease unemployment and inject money into the economy when required.[11] This was the course advocated by the leading stagnationist, Harvard economist Alvin Hansen, one of many stagnationists who served in an advisory capacity to the Roosevelt administration in the 1940s.[12] Hansen was an advisor on the National Resources Planning Board, a New Deal agency that was a site of institutional strength for the stagnationists. Hansen also helped craft the administration's 1944 endorsement of an economic bill of rights, including the right to work.[13]

The influence of the secular stagnationists and President Roosevelt's focus on addressing the immediate economic problems of the millions of unemployed meant that education policy was largely an afterthought during the New Deal. The economic belief driving New Deal policy was that failures in the market economy were the source of the nation's economic woes, and therefore the federal government should concentrate its efforts on dealing with the inability of the private sphere to provide jobs for those who needed them. The programs pursued by New Dealers—including the Public Works Administration, the Works Progress Administration, the Civilian Conservation Corps, and the National Youth Administration—were created to quickly provide jobs and income to unemployed individuals. Although many of these programs did have educational components, the educational measures were secondary to the primary goal of providing jobs.[14] The Office of Education was largely excluded from any role in the educational measures associated with New Deal programs, and President Roosevelt opposed the direct provision of federal aid to education.[15] As the Depression agencies were shut down by the mid-1940s, what existed of New Deal education policy was shut down as well.[16]

The secular stagnationist interpretation of the source of the Great Depression drove New Dealers to favor direct regulatory intervention to correct market deficiencies. Policies that did not offer the promise of direct intervention—such as education policy—were marginalized when New Dealers were attempting to deal with the crisis. Significantly, much of the ideological framework that would later position education as an ideal policy realm for dealing with social and economic problems during the Great Society had not yet been developed during the 1930s. As Harvey Kantor and Robert Lowe note, "the connection between race and poverty, education, and economic opportunity" was never "a major topic of debate and discussion among policy makers" during the New Deal.[17] Education policy was therefore largely ancillary to the commitment to direct federal intervention in regulating the market economy that dominated the New Deal era.

The introduction of the Full Employment Bill of 1945 by Senator James Murray (D-MT) was the high point of stagnationist influence over economic and employment policy. The Full Employment Bill of 1945 was based on the assumption that private business would be unable to fulfill the required investment to stimulate full employment, thus necessitating federal expenditure to bridge the gap. The bill sought to create a permanent role for the federal government in regulating the economy, committing the government to expenditures necessary to secure the right to work for all Americans seeking employment. Significantly, the bill was based on the belief that unemployment largely represented a fundamental weakness in the market economy rather than in unemployed individuals. The bill explicitly stated that it was the responsibility of the federal government "to assure continuing full employment, that is, the existence at all times of sufficient employment opportunities for all Americans able to work and seeking work."[18] The attempt to build powerful planning agencies capable of injecting large sums into the economy was seen as the most appropriate means of ensuring that Americans were not out of work due to forces beyond their control. This was emblematic of the New Deal coalition's belief that unemployment was generally attributable to problems in the economic system rather than in individual workers.

Despite passing by an overwhelming margin in the Senate, the Full Employment Bill of 1945 was ultimately defeated in Congress by a coalition of business groups, southern Democrats, and Republicans. After passage in the Senate, various business groups led by the Chamber of Commerce mobilized opposition to the bill by charging that it was a form of socialism that threatened free enterprise and "the American way of life."[19] Southern Democrats were also concerned about the potential for the bill to upset existing local economic arrangements. They were particularly concerned about increased federal oversight over local farm labor and wage rates that might ultimately threaten the racial caste system that depended on the economic subordination of Black Americans.[20] The House of Representatives quickly abandoned the 1945 Full Employment Bill, as southern Democrats joined with Republicans to ensure its defeat.

The failure of the Full Employment Bill marked a turning point in the battle over employment policy and over the direction of which style of Keynesian economic management policies would be pursued. Robert Collins argues that as World War II provided "striking evidence of the effectiveness of government expenditure on a huge scale," and Keynesianism gained broad acceptance among economists, many in the business community sought to work within the new consensus to promote more business-friendly Keynesian policies.[21] The defeat of the Full Employment Bill marked a fortuitous moment for this move, as a number of economists began to question the tenets of secular stagnationists in the wake of the strong demand for goods and labor in the postwar years.

Abandoning previous attachments to a strictly balanced budget approach, the business community coalesced around a particular version of Keynesianism that offered a strikingly different interpretation of unemployment and policy prescriptions than the secular stagnationists: commercial Keynesianism. Rejecting the view that unemployment represented a fundamental weakness of the market economy, the advocates of commercial Keynesianism instead argued that "the demand for labor periodically fluctuates, being sometimes excessive and inflationary and at other times deficient."[22] Explaining changes in economic growth and joblessness as the result of economic fluctuations, commercial Keynesians argued that the fiscal role of government should be limited to temporarily moderating these business fluctuations. Commercial Keynesians advocated tax cuts and automatic stabilizers rather than direct spending as the policy mechanisms of choice for dealing with these economic fluctuations. Although nominally committed to pursuing high levels of employment, this goal competed with concerns about inflation and the desire to restrain the growth of the federal budget.[23]

After the defeat of the Full Employment Act of 1945, the rise of commercial Keynesianism facilitated the passage of the alternative Employment Act of 1946. Written by conservative Mississippi Democrat Will Whittington, the new act abandoned the previous act's centralized planning agency committed to federal spending to achieve full employment as well as the idea that the federal government had the responsibility to assure full employment as a right of the American people. In place of the national planning agency the bill established the CEA, which would prove to be an important avenue for the advancement of a more conservative, business-friendly version of Keynesianism in the executive branch. The 1946 Employment Act was endorsed by the Chamber of Commerce and passed by an overwhelming margin in the House and was unanimously approved in the Senate. Alvin Harris, the secular stagnationist author of the 1945 Full Employment Bill, criticized the new act as little more than "window dressing" incapable of addressing the employment problem.[24]

The growing critiques of the stagnationists and the rehabilitated image of business in the postwar years provided an opening for the emergence of a version of Keynesianism that envisioned a drastically limited role for federal government that was much more appealing to the business community. As they abandoned the notion that the market economy was fundamentally flawed, many commercial Keynesians turned toward explanations for unemployment that focused on the individual. Although commercial Keynesians believed that normal business fluctuations would lead to some unemployment, they also believed that it would not affect all workers equally. Commercial Keynesians argued that those affected would largely be the most marginal workers, those with little skill or ability to adapt to the changing demands of the labor market. Throughout the 1940s and 1950s, commercial Keynesian economists and their allies in the Democratic Party increasingly described unemployment not as a function of a flawed economy, but as the result of individual failure to adjust to changing market demands. As the material conditions shifted from dealing with the Great Depression to the post–World War II economic boom, the attractiveness of commercial Keynesianism as an ideology appealed to a growing number of policy makers.

The strength of commercial Keynesianism, and the collapse of the secular stagnationist consensus, was clear by the Kennedy administration. Throughout Kennedy's presidency, the CEA provided a powerful voice for commercial Keynesianism within the executive branch. In a 1964 interview, the members of President Kennedy's CEA—many of whom would go on to serve in the Johnson administration as well—suggested that their influence with Kennedy likely stemmed from the fact that Kennedy felt that "old-style Democratic liberalism in regards to economics and fiscal policy wasn't going to pay off politically," which in turn "influenced the sorts of things and sorts of economists they wanted."[25] One CEA member, James Tobin, noted that Kennedy had deployed him during the 1960 campaign to combat an effort by some to push the Democratic Party to embrace economic policies more reminiscent of the New Deal era. Tobin was effective, and the Democratic Advisory Committee killed the effort to reassert the Democratic Party's commitment to the New Deal economic approach.[26]

Further evidence of the newfound influence of the CEA and commercial Keynesianism was clear in Kennedy's response to fears of an economic recession in 1962. CEA members essentially single-handedly convinced Kennedy of the need to pursue tax cuts to stimulate the economy and help achieve full employment over the objection of members of the cabinet.[27] President

Kennedy, with the backing of the CEA and the business community, responded to the economic downturn of 1962 by proposing a tax cut.[28]

The ability of the CEA and commercial Keynesianism to shape policy was evident by 1964 in President Lyndon B. Johnson's State of the Union address announcing the War on Poverty as well as his Economic Report to Congress. Often overlooked in Johnson's first State of the Union address is that his call for a tax cut takes up nearly half of the speech identified as the launch of the War on Poverty. In his State of the Union address, Johnson argued that "a lack of jobs and money is not the cause of poverty, but the symptom."[29] Johnson claimed that for "far too long, our economy has labored under the handicap of Federal income tax rates born of war and inflation,"[30] and identified the "release of $11 billion of tax reduction into the private spending stream to create new jobs" as the most immediate solution to the problem of unemployment.[31] The CEA praised the Johnson tax bill in its annual report to Congress, echoing the call for "a large reduction in corporate taxes, a cutback of risk-inhibiting top bracket individual tax rates, and a further broadening of the investment credit" as these would "insure the increase in demand necessary to provide markets for our growing productive potential" and "encourage investment."[32]

The adoption of the commercial Keynesian management policy brought education into the spotlight as a crucial piece of the policy solution to the problem of unemployment. In a move that would be repeated by President Johnson and other Great Society liberals, the CEA report coupled the emphasis on tax cuts with policies aimed at easing what it knew would be greater job insecurity for millions of Americans by advocating for an increased focus on vocational education and unemployment insurance. The report also stated: "In our concern with the problems of today's unemployed, it should not be forgotten that a strengthened system of basic education will be the best guarantee against significant problems of displacement and dislocation in tomorrow's full-employment economy."[33] These policies were based on the assumption that jobs were available for all who were qualified, turning the blame for unemployment squarely on the deficiencies of the individual.

This shift was already evident in the 1963 hearings before the Senate Subcommittee on Employment and Manpower, which heard seven days of testimony on the centrality of education policy to the manpower needs of the nation. Francis Keppel, the commissioner of education, described unemployment as in part a problem of "the fit between the educational arrangements in the United States and the nature of the labor market . . . the gears are not joining successfully."[34] He argued that "manpower development is education. Education is manpower development . . . the only way we can develop our manpower resources fully and effectively is to develop our whole educational system."[35] This sentiment was echoed repeatedly throughout the days of testimony, perhaps most forcefully by Dr. Grant Venn, a representative from the American Council on Education. Claiming that an individual's "job is more than ever a function of his education," Venn argued for a renewed focus on the relationship between the labor market and education since "without a job a man is lost and without educational preparation few jobs are available."[36] This testimony helped shape the 1963 Manpower Development and Training Act, which was premised on the belief "that an individual is unemployed because he lacks a marketable skill."[37]

In 1964 attention shifted more directly to education policy and the appropriate role for the federal government. President Johnson promised to focus on education as a first priority and soon followed through by submitting the ESEA to Congress in 1965.[38] In his statement accompanying the bill, Johnson argued:

> The purpose of this legislation is to meet a national problem. This national problem is reflected in draft rejection rates because of basic educational deficiencies. It is evidenced by the employment and manpower retraining problems aggravated by the fact that there are over 8 million adults who have completed less than 5 years of school. It is seen in the 20-percent unemployment rate of our 18- to 24-year-olds. . . . The solution to these problems lies in the ability of our local elementary and secondary school systems to provide full opportunity for a high quality program of instruction in the basic educational skills because of the strong correlation between educational underachievement and poverty.[39]

President Johnson's reasoning reflected that of the CEA, which had argued that "the chief reason for low rates of pay is low productivity, which in turn can reflect lack of education or training, physical and mental disability, or poor motivation."[40] The CEA also suggested the need for a renewed focus on primary and secondary education by noting, "if children of poor families can be given skills and motivation, they will not become poor adults."[41] The increased federal interest in education by Great Society liberals was driven by the reinterpretation of unemployment and underemployment as a problem of individual deficiencies rather than as an indication of a fundamental weakness of the market economy.

Understanding that the interest in federal investment in education was premised on a more limited vision of federal regulation of the economy is critical for comprehending why federal education policies took the form they did. In fact, it is much less likely that the federal government would have been able to establish any authority in this realm had the stagnationist version of Keynesianism been guiding public policy, as evidenced by the marginal role of education policy during the New Deal. By the time that Johnson proposed the ESEA, a new economic understanding had repositioned education as an alternative to more direct government interventions to address unemployment pursued during the New Deal era. Although there was still a significant contingent of executive branch employees calling for public job creation as the solution to unemployment, particularly within the Department of Labor, the turn by Kennedy and Johnson toward tax cuts and human capital investment through education signified that the vision of the commercial Keynesians was the guiding doctrine of the Great Society.[42]

Laborers as Capitalists: Human Capital Theory, Inequality, and Education

The emergence of human capital theory as a dominant economic frame for understanding economic success and failure also significantly contributed to the mid-twentieth-century turn toward the individual as the explanation for unemployment and poverty. Whereas commercial Keynesianism offered a macroeconomic perspective on the issue of unemployment and economic growth, human capital theory sought to offer an explanation as to why particular individuals were economic successes or failures within the existing economic system. Human capital theory posits that resources possessed by the individual such as education, specific skills, or personality traits determine the worth of labor that an individual brings to the marketplace. This view quickly gained acceptance across the political spectrum as an explanation for why individuals were poor or jobless.[43] Human capital theory offered an interpretation of wage earning not as the result of work performed, or as the result of political struggle between labor and management, or of structural conditions imposed by the broader economic system, but rather as a result of the yield on investment in an individual's human capital.[44] Unsurprisingly, as human capital theory gained popularity, education would become a major area of interest to scholars and policy makers alike.

The theory of human capital had been around for centuries, but as political scientist Jennifer Breen notes, it was not understood as resources within the individual worker until the late 1930s, and this view did not gain widespread political popularity until the early 1960s. Although human capital theory quickly gained adherents across the political spectrum, the majority of scholars responsible for crafting and popularizing the theory were conservative academics. Scholars such as Theodore Schultz, Jacob Mincer, Gary Becker, and Milton Friedman were early advocates and were closely aligned with the conservative Chicago school of economics.[45]

In his presidential address to the American Economic Association in 1960 entitled "Investment in Human Capital," Theodore Schultz urged his colleagues to embrace the explanatory power of human capital. Noting that "Laborers have become capitalists . . . from the acquisition of knowledge and skill that have economic value," Schultz argued that human capital theory offered new explanations of, and solutions to, a number of social problems.[46] Schultz suggested that economic growth, unemployment, and wages were all substantially influenced by human capital. Significantly, Schultz also claimed that *racial* patterns of poverty and inequality could largely be traced back to differences in human capital. Schultz argued that "the low earnings of particular people have long been a matter of public concern. Policy all too frequently concentrates only on the effects, ignoring the causes. No small part of the low earnings of many Negroes, Puerto Ricans, Mexican nationals, indigenous migratory farm workers, poor farm people and some of our older workers, reflects the failure to have invested in their health and education."[47] For Schultz, one of the most promising policies to increase human capital was "larger investments in the health and education of disadvantaged Americans."[48] Framing problems such as racial inequality, unemployment, and poverty as the result of failure to invest in human capital implied that policy solutions should focus on how best to increase the human capital of certain individuals rather than the direct provision of jobs or income supplements.

As human capital theory was gaining popularity with economists, large foundations began to provide significant funding and publicity as well. A number of nonprofit organizations promoted human capital theory to a broader audience, and often targeted policy makers directly. The Carnegie Corporation was a significant funder of the National Bureau of Economic Research (NBER), which provided funding and served as a major clearinghouse for the publication of work by prominent human capital theorists. Throughout the 1960s the NBER sought to facilitate the dissemination of research by human capital scholars among other academics as well as policy makers. In December 1961, the Carnegie Corporation hosted a conference funded through the NBER titled "Exploratory Conference on Capital Investment in Human Beings," which included participants from the Ford Foundation and the Brookings Institution. Theodore Schultz chaired the conference and eventually edited a special edition of the *Journal of Political Economy* in 1962 on "Investment in Human Beings" that contained contributions from many of the most influential human capital theorists, including Gary Becker, Jacob Mincer, and George Stigler.[49]

With the support from prominent economists as well as a number of non-profit groups, human capital theory quickly began to influence how Democratic policy makers interpreted the cause of social problems, as well as the most appropriate policy solutions. In a 1963 hearing before the Senate Subcommittee on Education on federal aid to education, Chairman Wayne Morse (D-OR) introduced a summary of recent economic research, noting his desire to provide senators with "the most helpful information in the field of educational legislation."[50] The summary included excerpts of Theodore Schultz's presidential address to the American Economic Association and cited a number of academic articles by Gary Becker.[51] The report before the Senate Subcommittee on Education concluded by arguing, "The evidence is compelling that lack of schooling and poor schooling are associated with such social problems as low earning capacity, unemployment, rejection from military service, and dependence upon public relief in its various forms."[52] As Democratic policy makers increasingly interpreted unemployment, poverty, and racial inequality as a function of individual shortcomings rather than structural failures of the economy, they embraced alternatives to the interventionist economic policies that characterized the approach of the New Deal coalition.

By the 1960s, education quickly became one of the preferred policy arenas in which Democrats sought to address social problems. In congressional hearings on federal aid to elementary and secondary education, members of Congress drew directly from human capital theory to justify the need for federal involvement in primary and secondary education. In February 1965, as Democrats were considering early versions of what would become the ESEA, both the House and Senate Subcommittees on Education heard testimony from economist Tom Lantos, who served as an economic consultant for the National Education Association.[53] In his prepared statement, Lantos told both the House and Senate committees that "it is generally recognized that economic growth is in large measure attributable to investments in human capital," and that "the time has come to recognize that when we devote resources to education we are in fact investing in human capital."[54] In reference to congressional plans to increase federal educational funding, Lantos proclaimed that "the bill before you does not deal with the symptoms of the ailments of our society, but strikes at the root cause."[55] According to Lantos, investing in human capital through increasing federal support for education would help lower unemployment and increase economic growth, and represented one of the most effective ways of dealing with social problems.

Congressional Democrats were quick to embrace the human capital framing of Lantos's testimony. Congressman John Brademas (D-IN), a coauthor of the ESEA, remarked after Lantos's statement, "I am especially pleased at the fact that you have called attention to the concept of investment in human capital which this legislation represents. I know Professor Shultz of the University of Chicago did some pioneering work in this."[56] Congressman William Ford (D-MI) praised Lantos for his portrayal of the cause of unemployment, noting, "I have come to the conclusion myself. I am happy to have people like you tell us, those of us who believe this way, that the answer to the employment future and the possibility of the people in a district . . . depending on a mass production industry, lies in the field of education, and at a level we have not heretofore attacked from a Federal vantage point, the elementary and secondary school."[57] Congressman James Scheuer (D-NY) made clear Lantos's statement also reflected the thinking of a number of congressmen regarding the connection between education and poverty, proclaiming, "I think those of us from the big cities have felt clearly the economic impact of poverty-stricken population groups from the point of view of education. There has been an increasingly clear consciousness of the pure economic impact of impoverished education. But I have rarely heard a statement as classical, beautifully distilled, and clearly thought out, as yours. My great problem is that I have no question marks. I have only exclamation marks."[58] The language from Democratic congressmen clearly indicates the extent to which human capital theory helped guide the thinking of policy makers in terms of both how they understood the root causes of social problems and the particular promise of education in addressing these problems.

Human capital theory, much like commercial Keynesianism, ultimately individualized the cause of unemployment and inequality. Human capital theorists offered an explanation of unemployment, poverty, and racial inequality as primarily the result of individuals failing to adjust to new market demands, rather than as evidence of inherent failures of the broader economic structure. This ideological shift suggested that previous approaches to dealing with these social problems that were more directly redistributive in nature would be ineffective, since the problem was not with the inability of the economy to provide jobs and decent wages, but rather with a workforce that was ill equipped to meet the demands of the labor market.[59] As policy makers increasingly embraced this understanding, many looked to the education system as the most effective way of addressing unemployment and inequality through boosting individual human capital.

Cultural Understandings of Poverty:
Race, Poverty, and Education

As commercial Keynesians and human capital theorists were pushing the Democratic coalition to rethink the sources of—and solutions to—unemployment and inequality, the early 1960s also brought the emergence of poverty as a central area of policy focus. As the popular press began to cover poverty as a pressing issue, the Kennedy administration quickly turned its attention to the issue. President Kennedy asked Walter Heller, the chairman of the CEA, to investigate what could be done about the problem of poverty, in part due to a concern about having a policy program for those who would not benefit directly from the proposed tax cuts.[60] The programmatic approach to poverty that developed was driven by social science theories that asserted that poverty was largely a cultural phenomenon. These cultural theories of poverty suggested that deviant cultures among particular groups resulted in warped values and family structures, which in turn ultimately led to widespread poverty and other social problems within these groups. This understanding—which reinforced the notion from human capital theory that the proper focus of policy attention was addressing deficiencies within the individual—was particularly powerful in an era where policy makers were increasingly concerned about high levels of Black poverty and unemployment. The interpretation of poverty as primarily attributable to an individual's culture would lead the Kennedy and Johnson administrations to attempt to solve poverty through policies that could correct cultural deficiencies. It is in this context that Democrats in the early 1960s turned to education as a particularly promising poverty policy.

Cultural understandings of poverty held particular sway with those seeking explanations for racial inequality. Although the postwar period did coincide with an expansion of the middle class, the growth was uneven. Whereas the percentage of unemployment among white and Black people was relatively comparable in 1940, by the 1960s, the unemployment rate for Black people was more than twice that of white people, and Black people represented more than one-third of the total long-term unemployed.[61] As genetic explanations for racial inequality became increasingly unfashionable, many social scientists turned toward culture to explain divergent racial outcomes.[62] During the

1930s and 1940s, these cultural accounts competed with alternative social science accounts that situated racial inequality more squarely as a result of political economic arrangements. However, by the 1950s federal and foundation aid and a shifting political context helped give rise to the dominance of explanations of racial inequality that identified individual culture, prejudice, and attitudes, rather than labor exploitation and class struggle, as the source of racial oppression.[63]

Much like human capital theory, policy makers adopted cultural theories of poverty from academia. In the post–World War II era, nonprofit organizations began heavily investing in the social sciences largely based on the belief that the study of individual behavior offered the key to solving pressing social problems. For example, the Ford Foundation announced the establishment of a new behavioral sciences program based on the idea "that all problems—'from war to individual adjustment'—could be traced to individual behavior and human relationships."[64] The Ford Foundation poured $24 million into funding behavioral science research between 1951 and 1957, and it was hardly alone as other foundations including the Carnegie Corporation, the Brookings Institution, the Rockefeller Foundation, and the Russell Sage Foundation all followed suit.[65] Historian Alice O'Connor points out that these new funding streams helped shape the "political economy of knowledge" in the mid-twentieth century, and the resulting social science research put forth theories that tended to "individual[ize] poverty as a social problem, locating its origins in individual behavior rather than in economic and social arrangements, and tracing 'pathology' to individual personality."[66] As with human capital theory, policy makers eagerly embraced cultural theories of poverty emerging from the social sciences, and the individualized understanding of social problems they provided. This framing would ultimately prove significant for the development of federal education policy.

One of the clearest conduits for introducing federal policy makers to the cultural understandings of poverty came through the President's Commission on Juvenile Delinquency (PCJD). Created by executive order in 1961, the PCJD was a cabinet-level body chaired by Attorney General Robert Kennedy, and the secretaries of labor and health, education, and welfare both served on the commission. The PCJD was charged with investigating and tackling the problem of juvenile delinquency, and the commission quickly reached out to academics for guidance on what kind of programs might best address the issue. Chicago sociologist Lloyd Ohlin was a major influence on the PCJD's interpretation of juvenile delinquency and the programs it proposed. Ohlin joined the PCJD as the chief research consultant and also began personally advising the attorney general.[67] Ohlin and fellow sociologist Richard Cloward had published their influential book, *Delinquency and Opportunity: A Theory of Delinquent Gangs,* just a year before the formation of the PCJD. Ohlin and Cloward argued that delinquency was primarily the result of a deviant subculture that arose among a lower class frustrated over their inability to realize their aspirations because of blocked opportunities.[68] This "opportunity theory" was fundamentally a cultural explanation of delinquency, and as Lloyd Ohlin directly advised many of the most powerful policy makers in Washington, D.C., this idea gained widespread traction as the explanation for delinquent behavior by the early 1960s.[69]

Although Cloward and Ohlin's book did not offer specific policy suggestions, the clear implication was that expansion of opportunities for youth would "close the gap between aspiration and achievement" and thus attack the aberrant culture at its source.[70] The authors also singled out access to education as an important source of, and solution to, the origins of delinquent cultures. According to Cloward and Ohlin, lower-class individuals valued education less because they had fewer educational opportunities than their better-off peers.[71] This fact was damaging, as "the lower-class boy who fails to secure an education is likely to discover that he has little chance of improving his circumstances," at which point "discontent may be generated, leading in turn to aberrant behavior."[72] The clear implication was that a concerted focus on increasing the educational opportunities of the lower class could attack the problem of deviant subcultures at the source. The close association of Ohlin with the PCJD, the strong support of this type of social science from the nonprofit world, and the active movement of members of the PCJD into other executive departments meant that cultural understandings of poverty— and the important position they ascribed to education—guided the policy approach of the broader War on Poverty.[73]

Cloward and Ohlin's theory meshed well with other cultural explanations of poverty that tended to take the focus off of the broader economic structures and concentrate on the individual. The 1965 report by Assistant Secretary of Labor Daniel Patrick Moynihan entitled *The Negro Family: The Case for National Action* represented another version of a cultural theory of poverty that influenced policy makers. *The Negro Family,* published in the midst of congressional hearings on the ESEA, attributed significant responsibility for racial inequality to defective cultural adaptations and warped family structures within the Black population. According to Moynihan's report, children raised in these deviant households were mostly doomed to perpetuate the failings of their parents, resulting in the passage of a culture of poverty from one generation to the next. Moynihan argued that the source of poverty among Black people was a vicious cycle in which "low education levels in turn produce low income levels, which deprive children of many opportunities, and so the cycle repeats itself."[74] According to Moynihan, addressing poverty meant breaking this cycle, and like most other culture of poverty theorists, he believed that education was a critical component of breaking the cycle.

Moynihan's analysis in *The Negro Family* was largely drawn from the liberal social science consensus in the early 1960s, and indicative of the degree to which theorizing about poverty had become synonymous with theorizing about Black Americans.[75] In search of arguments to justify race-conscious compensatory programs, liberal social scientists embraced the notion that the history of slavery and Jim Crow had created a damaged Black psyche and culture.[76] Through his role within the executive branch, Moynihan was able to influence President Johnson's thinking around the issue of race and poverty, perhaps most apparently in Johnson's commencement address at Howard University in 1965. In an indication of Moynihan's intellectual sway, Johnson argued that Black poverty was distinct from white poverty because of "a cultural tradition which had been twisted and battered by endless years of hatred and hopelessness" and the "breakdown of the Negro family structure" that this history of oppression had caused.[77] Johnson ended his speech by announcing a White House conference—called "To Fulfill These Rights"—of scholars and experts to produce policy recommendations to address racial inequality.

Moynihan and Johnson approached these race-conscious solutions with the goal of perfecting the market economy rather than fundamentally challenging it. As historian Daryl Scott notes, "Moynihan had a conception of race-conscious policies that avoided using the state to intervene in hiring to ensure equality of results," instead favoring the use of "the state to create conditions that would allow the black community to pursue equality of results."[78] For Moynihan, federal involvement in education was desirable as a means of putting Black Americans in a position to compete on equal terms with their white counterparts, which in turn would help break the culture of poverty.

The promotion of cultural theories of poverty was not limited to white academics and policy makers, as Black social scientists and leaders also embraced some central tenets of culture of poverty arguments in order to justify federal attention and support.[79] Kenneth Clark, a prominent psychologist perhaps most well known for his psychological research cited in the Supreme Court's *Brown v. Board* decision, was a prominent example. In his writing about the origin of racial inequality, cultural distinctiveness, and poverty, Clark directly implicated the schools and the education system in the perpetuation of the problems of the Black poor. Clark's arguments and thinking are particularly relevant, as he had direct contact with several members of the Johnson administration and was chosen by the White House to lead the educational group of the conference announced by Johnson in his Howard University commencement address.[80]

Although some have interpreted Clark as rejecting the notion of cultural distinctiveness and pathology that were central features of cultural theories of poverty, a close reading of his writing reveals something different. Clark was wary of any notion of the "culturally deprived child" that might be interpreted as requiring a distinct form of education. According to Clark, poor Black children were just as capable of learning as their wealthier peers, and teachers in urban schools had relied on the notion of cultural deprivation as an alibi for their own failures to adequately teach these children.[81] Clark's theoretical approach is therefore best understood as an attempt to center educational institutions as key sites in the production of the distinctive behavior of the poor.

For Clark, the term *cultural deprivation* was limited in that it "masks the significant aspects of the process, masks the fact that these are human beings who are not in just some God-given state, but are deliberately and chronically victimized by the larger society in general, and by educational institutions, specifically."[82] Clark largely agreed with other cultural theories of poverty in his identification of the consequences of educational failure and suggested it was at the heart of the "cycle of socio-economic pathology—poor education, menial jobs, unemployment, family instability, group and personal powerlessness."[83] According to Clark, poor educational performance did not flow from cultural distinctiveness but rather reflected the failure of the educational institutions. The inadequate performance of teachers and educational institutions serving the poor ultimately were the foundation of the social pathology of the poor.

Given this understanding, Clark was especially biting in his assessment of the public education system. Clark argued that elementary and secondary schools serving poor children were "very effective instruments in widening socioeconomic and racial cleavages in our society."[84] For Clark, the role that educational institutions played in the origin of racial inequality and social pathology pointed to the need to "reorganize public education as a whole to obtain maximum educational efficiency for all children."[85] Failure to reform educational institutions risked leaving individuals poorly prepared for the "increasing industrialization and automation of our economy" and also risked increasing "crime, delinquency, and urban decay."[86] Successful educational reform would therefore need not only more federal funding but would also require efforts to ensure that educational institutions and teachers were not failing their poor students and serving as the source of social pathology.

Clark, like other cultural theorists of poverty, received substantial federal support for his studies of urban youth. Much of Clark's thinking about the issues of the urban youth and the role of educational institutions came from his time as chairman of the board of directors at Harlem Youth Opportunity Unlimited (Haryou), an organization that received substantial funding from the PCJD.[87] Clark also was viewed as an educational expert within the Johnson White House.[88] Through his prominence as an academic and his direct advising of the executive branch, Clark served as a powerful voice calling for greater federal attention to education as central to the fight against poverty and racial inequality.

The cultural understanding of poverty, much like human capital theory, directly linked education to the economic success of the individual. Indeed, human capital theory was frequently formulated as "the belief that a good education would lead to individual financial success, higher personal status, and the benefits of a flourishing economy."[89] With human capital theory and cultural theories of poverty both pushing similar interpretations of poverty and inequality, policy makers naturally turned policy focus toward "youth, who human capital theorists argued were in the best position to reap the rewards of greater investment in themselves . . . in the hopes that doing so would break the 'cycle of poverty.'"[90] These ideologies ultimately shaped not only how policy makers interpreted the source of unemployment, poverty, and racial inequality but also shaped the preferred policy solutions.

President Johnson clearly drew on tenets from both human capital and cultural theories of poverty in justifying the need for a federal role in education. In his message accompanying the delivery of the ESEA to Congress, Johnson proclaimed that, "with education, instead of being condemned to poverty and idleness, young Americans can learn the skills to find a job and provide for a family."[91] Johnson also warned of the "cost in other terms" of failing to invest in education, noting "we spend $1,800 a year to keep a delinquent youth in a detention home—$2,500 for a family on relief—$3,500 a year for a criminal in a State prison."[92] In congressional hearings on the bill, Robert Kennedy, now a Democratic senator from New York, agreed on the need for an early educational focus in breaking the cycle of poverty, noting, "by the time you start to focus the attention on them at the age of 12, they are already lost to society."[93] The particular understanding of the potential for education to address social problems led the Johnson administration to advocate for a federal educational policy approach focused on the disadvantaged.

The CEA also proved to be an important source of support for pushing education as a poverty program. By the 1960s, the CEA was firmly dominated by commercial Keynesians and actively pushed both the Kennedy and Johnson administrations to pursue tax cuts as a means of stimulating the economy and reducing unemployment and poverty.[94] Given this commitment, the CEA was attracted to education as poverty policy in part because it aligned with their ideological understanding of the cause of social problems. Additionally, because it was a substantially cheaper approach to dealing with unemployment, poverty, and racial inequality than direct redistributionary policies, it was also compatible with the CEA's proposed tax cuts.[95] In a particularly revealing statement of the degree to which education policy could be positioned as an alternative to direct aid programs for the poor, the 1964 CEA-authored *Economic Report of the President to Congress* asserted that "tax reduction is the first requisite in 1964 of a concerted attack on poverty" and praised the focus on education as an attack on the root cause of poverty:

> Conquest of poverty is well within our power. About $11 billion a year would bring poor families up to the $3,000 income level we have taken to be the minimum for a decent life. The majority of the Nation could simply tax themselves enough to provide the necessary income supplements to their less fortunate citizens. The burden . . . would certainly not be intolerable. But this "solution" would leave untouched most of the roots of poverty. Americans want to *earn* the American standard of living by their own efforts and contributions. . . . We can surely afford greater generosity in relief of distress. But the major thrust of our campaign must be against causes rather than symptoms.[96]

Significantly, the $11 billion a year estimate that the CEA suggested could raise all families in the country to an acceptable standard of living was the precise amount of the tax cuts that the CEA successfully persuaded the Johnson administration to pursue.[97] Thus, the appeal to the cultural understanding of poverty served as a powerful weapon for the CEA to argue against directly redistributive programs. This understanding positioned the individual as the proper policy focus, and further allowed the CEA to claim that policies of direct redistribution and job creation would not only degrade recipients but would likely only perpetuate the poverty problem. In its place, the CEA advocated attacking the "roots" of the problem through educational investment aimed at breaking the intergenerational cycle poverty.

By the 1960s, Democratic policy makers were increasingly citing education as a key policy in the fight against unemployment, poverty, and racial inequality.

In the same report that made the case for tax cuts as a poverty and unemployment policy, the CEA also pressed for greater federal involvement in education. In order to fight poverty, the CEA suggested that "most vitally, and with Federal support, we must upgrade the education of the children of the poor, so that they need not follow their parents into poverty."[98] According to the CEA, an educational focus also offered a particularly promising approach to addressing racial inequality, arguing that "to reduce the abnormally high and stubborn unemployment rate for Negroes requires a major improvement in their education and training and an attack on racial discrimination."[99]

The belief that education could address these problems began to increasingly drive action within the executive branch by the mid-1960s. President Kennedy and his administration, worried that high rates of unemployment and impoverishment in Black communities represented potential "social dynamite," called for a "massive upgrading" of public schools and efforts to combat juvenile delinquency.[100] Similar concerns drove President Johnson to announce his support for the first major federal expansion in primary and secondary education policy early in his administration. In his first public policy paper after winning election, Johnson proclaimed "I pledge now to put education at the head of our work agenda."[101] Johnson wrote that "we must concentrate our teaching resources in the urban slums and the poor rural areas" because the "war on poverty can be won only if those who are poverty's prisoners can break the chains of ignorance."[102] By the start of the Johnson administration, education had become the preferred policy choice to fight back against the cultural foundation of poverty, racial inequality, and unemployment.

Ultimately, much like commercial Keynesianism and human capital theory, cultural understandings of poverty refocused blame for the existence of social problems onto individuals. Both the Kennedy and Johnson administrations launched national interventions aimed at poverty and unemployment that framed these issues as attributable to cultural deficiencies and pathology, which reinforced the notion that these were essentially problems of individual behavior.[103] The new focus on education was indicative of this turn, as Great Society liberals sought to eliminate the damaging impact of racism and cultural deficiencies on individuals through changes to the educational system rather than pursuing more robust and directly redistributive political economic reforms.

The Intellectual Foundations of Federal Education Policy

The broad acceptance of commercial Keynesianism, human capital theory, and cultural theories of poverty among Democratic policy makers by the

1960s reflected a significant ideological realignment. Commercial Keynesianism shifted the Democratic coalition away from the New Deal approach of addressing unemployment through regulatory interventions and toward a strategy of stimulating aggregate demand through tax cuts and an educational agenda that was driven by the demands of the labor market. Human capital theory helped reinterpret difference in wages as simply the result of market forces rewarding individual skills and suggested the way to increase wages and reduce inequality was to provide better and more equitable education. Cultural theories of poverty posited that aberrant behavior—particularly among the Black poor—largely explained entrenched poverty and pointed to the potential of education to help individuals escape the cycle of poverty. These ideological visions represented fundamental shifts from the height of the New Deal era, where Democrats largely ignored education at the federal level and were much more likely to attribute unemployment and poverty to failures of the market economy. The turn away from directly interventionist economic policies was supported by a powerful coalition of business groups, wealthy nonprofit foundations, and social scientists that pushed the Democratic Party to focus on adjusting individuals to the existing economy.

Although Great Society Democratic politicians still sought to expand the capacity of the federal government to mitigate the worst effects of the existing economic arrangements, as Kantor notes, "the expansion of state activity was undertaken within limits that precluded attempts to reorganize and modify the market itself."[104] In this context, education proved to be a particularly attractive policy realm that offered the potential for addressing social problems without fundamentally altering existing economic arrangements. The "educationalizing" of social problems like unemployment, poverty, and racial inequality minimized and obscured the role of broader political economic forces in the creation of the problems and created a powerful argument for federal involvement in K–12 education policy.

The passage of ESEA represented a significant achievement for the Johnson administration and the broader Democratic Party. By positioning education as a particularly effective policy vehicle for addressing some of society's most pressing problems, the Johnson administration was able to overcome years of failed attempts to pass general aid legislation. In an indication of the significance of this institutional development, the ESEA continues to provide the basis for federal education policy to this day. However, understanding the full significance of the ESEA requires grappling with the ideological legacy that serves as the foundation of the federal education state. The ESEA represents a dramatic shift in ideology within the Democratic Party about the source of, and potential solutions to, the problems of unemployment, poverty, and racial inequality. The passage of the ESEA therefore also serves as an indication of the diminished willingness of Great Society Democrats to address social problems through direct intervention to reorganize the market economy. Investment in education was in no small part an alternative to a more direct federal response to the shortcomings of the market economy.

As this coalition succeeded in its goal of institutionalizing a federal role in education, the ideological shifts that paved the way for this achievement would significantly shape contours of the specific federal education policies that emerged. Whereas the federal educational programs of the New Deal were largely incidental by-products of direct employment programs, the nascent belief that education policy could potentially solve unemployment, poverty, and racial inequality meant that by the 1960s federal policy makers were much more willing to provide substantial monetary support to educational programs. As lawmakers looked to craft policy, they embraced the liberal incorporationist vision and pushed for education policies that were centered on fairly and effectively incorporating individuals into the existing system. However, as chapter 5 will show, even as the faith in education brought greater federal resources, the ideological basis for funding meant that federal policy makers would begin to demand evidence of effectiveness and quickly embraced increasingly punitive consequences for failure.

CHAPTER FIVE

From Belief to Blame

Federal Funding and the Punitive Policy Shift

The passage of the ESEA was a landmark event that poured billions of badly needed dollars into the nation's underfunded schools. Although the liberal incoporationist ideology proved remarkably efficient at constructing a coalition that supported building the federal education state, this development did not come without peril for the public school system. The ideological foundation and programmatic structure of the federal education state that emerged with the passage of the ESEA was one that incorporated an understanding of public education's purpose as correcting individual deficiencies in order to improve economic outcomes and reduce racial disparities. The faith that schools *could* solve social problems not only helped justify increased funding but also led to the expectation that increased school funding *should* solve these problems. This chapter traces how these new expectations placed on the public school system also quickly led to blaming the public school system for the continued existence of these problems. By the late 1960s, the liberal incorporationist foundation of the ESEA and the resilient faith that education could solve poverty and racial inequality meant that the nascent federal education state began to support punitive accountability policies.

Efforts to provide federal funding for public schools were accompanied by suspicion that schools were partially responsible for the existence of myriad social problems in the first place. This tension was evident even prior to the passage of the ESEA. In a 1965 hearing on the bill, Senator Robert Kennedy boldly stated, "Most of us, 95 percent of us, are doing well, but there are 5, 8, or 10 percent of our young people who, through no fault of their own, are never going to be able to live decent lives. I just do not believe that we can meet our responsibilities here as Members of Congress or others, or as American citizens, and let that kind of situation exist. I think it is the fault of the school system that has been permitted to exist as long as it has."[1] As early evaluations of the ESEA raised a number of questions about the effectiveness of federal funding, rather than reexamine their faith in education, liberal incorporationists blamed teachers and schools themselves. The result was a number of early amendments to the ESEA that demanded more accountability, expanded and enshrined the use of standardized tests as *the* preferred means of evaluating educational success, and introduced sanctions for states that spent funds in ineffective ways.

Federally funded experiments in punitive accountability education policy soon followed. Frustration over what some perceived to be the failure of the ESEA to effectively push schools to address racial inequality and prepare students for the demands of the labor market led a number of prominent academics and activists to challenge the public education system itself. In his testimony before the National Commission on Tests in Washington, D.C., just two short years after the passage of the ESEA, Kenneth Clark issued a call to action to address continued educational inequality, arguing:

> If I were doing any studies now . . . concerned with getting the American people to understand the enormity of the injustice inherent in differential educational quality of our biracial school systems, I would search for the most rigorous, objective, standardized test that was relevant to the question of educational achievement, and I would administer it to all of the children in public schools. [Then] I would present . . . the stark differential results and say to the American people: "This is what you are doing by way of damming up human potential and human resources. . . . You can either continue this and know . . . that you are spawning hundreds of thousands of human casualties, or you can make the necessary changes in the educational system to narrow this gap, and hopefully obviate it."[2]

Eventually, Kenneth Clark and other prominent Black leaders began to openly point to the public school system as a central source of racial inequality and pushed for reforms, including more testing, tying teacher pay to student achievement scores, and alternatives to public schools. Many liberal social scientists and policy makers embraced the argument that there was a need for experiments that would challenge the public school monopoly, including performance contracting and vouchers. At the behest of liberals, federal education dollars were funneled into a number of state and local pilot programs that funded efforts to introduce market incentives into the nation's education system.

This chapter's account of the connection between ideas, coalitions, and institutions seeks to shed light on why the liberal incorporationist vision—which positions schools as sites of potential promise but also the embodiments of failure—has remained so firmly affixed. The liberal incorporationist coalition, which blended ideas and pedagogical methods from both social efficiency progressives and racial democrats, was a broad and durable coalition that was ascendant as policy makers built the federal education state. This coalition of policy makers, Black political activists, social scientists, and large foundations that helped build the federal education state also began to push it in a punitive direction. The result was a new array of punitive policy prescriptions that aimed to hold schools accountable for failing to solve the broad array of social problems that liberal incorporationists believed they could. Ultimately, liberal incorporationists continued to push more direct efforts to address racial inequality, poverty, and unemployment to the background and instead demanded more punitive accountability for schools and teachers. The same basic institutional and ideological structure that first helped justify federal intervention in public K–12 education continues to guide federal education policy today.

From Ideas to Institutions: Educational Accountability in the Great Society

The consensus that education was the most effective means of addressing the issue of unemployment, poverty, and racial inequality created a powerful coalition in Congress to push for compensatory education. In an important shift, and as a consequence of ideological developments described in the previous chapter, the bill put forth by the Johnson administration in 1964 focused specifically on the disadvantaged rather than general aid bills that had been proposed and defeated since the late 1800s. In his 1964 Economic Report to Congress, President Johnson outlined education as his first priority in the War on Poverty. Arguing that education was key to earning power through the acquisition of marketable skills, he implored Congress to "upgrade the education of the children of the poor, so that they need not follow their parents in poverty."[3] The interpretation of poverty and unemployment as largely attributable to individual deficiencies in skill or culture drove the compensatory approach of ESEA, in which funds were targeted toward the disadvantaged poor.

The centerpiece of the compensatory strategy was Title I, which accounted for between 75 and 85 percent of total ESEA funding.[4] Title I was a categorical grant that provided schools funding based on the concentration of low-income families, defined as families earning less than $2,000 annually. This design ensured that although Title I funds would be targeted toward the poor, funding would also be widely distributed with more than 94 percent of school districts ultimately receiving Title I money.[5] The funding mechanism enabled substantial discretion for local educational agencies to pursue a variety of approaches aimed at increasing the educational opportunity of the disadvantaged. The goal was that schools, with the help of federal funding, would help to ensure that no individual was arbitrarily relegated to economic squalor due to discrimination, cultural deprivation, or technological displacement.

In addition to inspiring support for greater education funding, ideological developments that pointed to education as the central mechanism for overcoming poverty and unemployment also drove many Great Society liberals to criticize schools and teachers as responsible for these problems in the first place and demand accountability for any federal funds distributed by the ESEA. No member of Congress represented this tendency more than New York senator Robert Kennedy. Reflecting the concerns of many of his constituents, particularly his constituents of color,[6] Senator Kennedy repeatedly expressed his belief that the schools and teachers themselves bore a substantial portion of the blame for the state of education for the poor.[7] In questioning Commissioner of Education Francis Keppel, Senator Kennedy charged, "would you agree . . . that from your experience of studying the school systems around the United States, that the school system itself has created an educationally deprived system?"[8] After Commissioner Keppel agreed, Kennedy questioned the wisdom of giving these schools more money, saying, "if you are placing or putting money into a school system which itself creates this problem or helps to create it . . . are we not just in fact wasting the money of the Federal Government and of the taxpayer?"[9] Kennedy's concern was not that education was incapable of helping the disadvantaged, but rather that absent a mechanism of accountability, schools would continue to contribute to the "economic educational deprivation of the child," a concern shared by Commissioner Keppel.[10]

Senator Kennedy argued that funds distributed by Title I of ESEA should be accompanied by "some standardized test that could be given in these areas where the money has been invested to determine whether, in fact, the child is making the kind of progress that we hope."[11] Kennedy made clear to Commissioner Keppel and Wilbur Cohen, the assistant secretary of the Department of Health, Education, and Welfare (DHEW), that his support for ESEA was dependent on modifications to the bill that would "hold educators responsive to their constituencies and to make educational achievement the touchstone of success in judging ESEA."[12] In a private meeting, Kennedy told Keppel, "Look, I want to change this bill because it doesn't have any way of measuring those damned educators like you, Frank."[13] Kennedy's refusal to support the bill absent an evaluation amendment came close to derailing the legislation. Keppel agreed with Kennedy on the need for some sort of evaluation provision. He helped draft an amendment that required any local educational authority wishing to receive a federal grant to prove "that effective procedures, including provision for appropriate objective measurements of educational achievement, will be adopted for evaluating at least annually the effectiveness of the programs in meeting the special educational needs of educationally deprived children," as well as make these results public.[14]

Realizing that this type of evaluation provision would likely provoke a strong backlash from conservatives and professional education organizations such as the American Federation of Teachers, Commissioner Keppel asked Samuel Halperin, the director of the Office of Legislation of the U.S. Office of Education (USOE), to quietly insert the new provision into the bill. Professional education groups were broadly against evaluations of the type mentioned in the Kennedy amendment. Organizations such as the National Education Association argued that such requirements would undermine the professionalism of teachers by reducing teacher autonomy, lead to destructive comparisons among teachers, schools, and school districts, and narrow the focus of education to only tested subjects. These concerns meant that "educators were in almost complete agreement that standardized tests were insensitive and inappropriate measures of the effectiveness of a Title I program."[15] Republicans, some southern Democrats, and religious organizations were also suspicious of the type of evaluation proposed by Kennedy, as the use of such standardized measures could eventually lead to national standards and curriculums, ultimately threatening local autonomy. Furthermore, the educational research community was largely in agreement that changes in education strategies had little effect on academic achievement, prompting some members of the American Educational Research Association to ask that the association officially go on record as opposed to the Kennedy evaluation requirement of Title I at their 1966 annual meeting. Had the evaluation requirement received open debate when it was included in the ESEA, it is perhaps probable that these groups would have prevented its inclusion in the final bill.[16]

In the Senate hearing, Senator Kennedy made sure to emphasize to Commissioner Keppel that he expected the USOE to follow through on holding schools accountable.[17] The commissioner assured Kennedy that the evaluation amendment, and the requirement that the results be shared and disseminated, would mean that "we can really depend on the competitive instinct, the competition of American school systems" to assure accountability for raising educational achievement. If this did not work, Keppel argued, "I think we have some instruments here frankly to needle a lot of the schools."[18] Secretary Anthony Celebrezze of the DHEW told Kennedy that local educational agencies would have to submit plans that complied with the evaluation provisions, "or they get no funds."[19]

In congressional hearings on appropriations for the DHEW in February 1965, the Office of Education made clear to lawmakers that they were serious about developing standardized tests that would allow for comparison of education success nationally. Keppel lamented to members of Congress, "we don't have a reporting method on how well kids have learned subjects, that cuts across State lines," which left him in the position of being unable to report whether particular educational efforts were successful.[20] Keppel noted that the Office of Education had been working with the Carnegie Corporation, which had actually introduced the idea of a broad test of student achievement to the Office of Education, on this front.[21] Indeed, the Carnegie Corporation had already been involved in "discussions with school officials and agencies to determine interests in testing procedures to assess student achievement."[22] The Office of Education requested $100,000 to help support Carnegie's effort in developing an assessment test of educational achievement.[23]

Foundations such as the Carnegie Corporation and Ford Foundation were significant advocates of expanding testing in schools as a means of measuring and improving educational outcomes. Commissioner of Education Francis Keppel was a former Ford Foundation associate, and his replacement Harold Howe had been a Ford Foundation vice president. Similarly, prior to becoming Johnson's secretary of health, education, and welfare, John W. Gardner was president of the Carnegie Corporation at the time it was pushing for the Office of Education to develop standardized assessment.[24] Beyond their influence through grants, think tanks, and policy studies, the fact that so many top federal policy makers came directly from foundations meant that these organizations' desire for more testing and their close cooperation with powerful lawmakers was particularly significant during the early days of the nascent federal education state.

Although Kennedy was primarily responsible for the inclusion of the evaluation provision and the raised achievement test score standard of success in the ESEA, his view was shared by several of his fellow liberal senators and several important members of the executive branch who would be responsible for implementing the bill. Senator Wayne Morse (D-OR), the chairman of the Subcommittee on Education, repeatedly endorsed Kennedy's line of questioning.[25] During Keppel's testimony outlining the need for an assessment test, Congressman Robert Duncan (D-OR) noted that "I think I am almost to the point where I am prepared to say that certain minimum standards at least would be highly desirable."[26] Both Secretary Celebrezze and his assistant Wilbur Cohen supported the strong evaluation requirements, as did Celebrezze's replacement, John Gardner. Secretary Gardner also created the position of assistant secretary of program evaluation filled by William Gorham, who became a powerful advocate for evaluation based on achievement scores within the DHEW.[27]

The business community was also a voice of support for more testing. A report by the Chamber of Commerce entitled *The Disadvantaged Poor: Education and Employment* reflected the liberal incorporationist vision and declared the importance of education for the efficient incorporation of poor and minority students into the nation's economy. The report stated that "education is necessary to prepare the minority poor to take advantage of the opportunities a fair and efficient free economy presents."[28] The same report lamented that "American education has been subject to few tests of its efficiency. . . . there is little information to measure the quality of the public school 'output'—the student."[29] The chamber encouraged greater federal investment for the development of "tests that measure a graduate's employability" and "pupil preparedness for entry into employment."[30] From the business perspective, testing could not only be used to evaluate equal opportunity but also as a means of pushing schools to prepare and sort the future workforce.

There was also pressure for greater accountability from groups outside of government that were critical of schools and teachers, most notably prominent social psychologist Kenneth Clark. Clark, who had served as a member of the Chamber of Commerce task force that produced *The Disadvantaged Poor* report, argued that any reform needed to address the fact that the low expectation of schools and teachers for "culturally deprived" students contributed to their poor performance.[31] Clark called for "rigorous, objective, standardized tests" to be administered to all public schoolchildren as an important tool of demonstrating, and rooting out, racial inequality.[32]

Clark's call for increased testing and measurement of educational effectiveness was echoed by Democrats at the federal level who were anxious for evidence that increased federal expenditure was improving educational outcomes. Voices such as Clark's combined with those of Senator Kennedy, large nonprofit organizations, and business groups to form a powerful coalition in favor of greater testing. This coalition was confident that schools could help address the problem of joblessness, poverty, and inequality, but only if schools were held accountable for the achievement scores of their students. In a reflection of the importance of the legacy of racial democracy and social efficiency progressivism to the liberal incorporationist order, this coalition positioned standardized tests as the ideal pedagogical tool to ensure more effective teaching, closer alignment between schools and the labor market, and more racially equitable outcomes. The result of the active maneuvering of this like-minded group was the establishment of evaluation and reporting requirements that were unprecedented for a piece of social legislation.

The required evaluations of compensatory education programs quickly began to shift the focus of the ESEA toward the goal of increasing achievement scores of disadvantaged students on standardized tests. The 1966 Equality of Educational Opportunity Survey (EEOS), popularly known as the Coleman Report after its lead author James Coleman, cast doubt on whether compensatory funding could raise the achievement of poor and minority students. Commissioned as part of the 1964 Civil Rights Act, the EEOS reported "it appears that differences between schools account for only a small fraction of the differences in pupil achievement."[33] The conclusion that inequalities in school resources, variations in curriculums, and teacher experience had little effect on student achievement scores measured by standardized tests sent shock waves through the educational community. The report's finding that 80 percent of variation in student achievement occurred within schools rather than between them appeared to directly rebut the intellectual foundation of compensatory funding: the belief that greater funding would result in greater achievement.[34]

The findings of the Coleman Report were soon confirmed by a study commissioned by the DHEW and conducted by E. J. Mosbaek of the General Electric Company. Known as the G.E. TEMPO report, it had been authorized and funded by the "Kennedy amendments" to the ESEA[35] and drew its data from the achievement test evaluations mandated by the same amendments. The G.E. TEMPO report looked at the effect on standardized test scores of Title I funds on five school districts, finding that scores increased in one district, remained the same in three districts, and decreased in the final district despite the increased funding.[36] The high-profile reports shocked congressional liberals and quickly put them on the defensive.

These findings should not have been surprising. Prior to the passage of the ESEA, the social science evidence indicated that when it came to achievement scores, factors outside of school mattered significantly more than what happened within the classroom.[37] The existing evidence at the time of the ESEA's passage did suggest that the social class composition of students could affect achievement scores, but the compensatory strategy of the ESEA did nothing to alter existing classroom composition.[38] However, the faith that education was the key to solving important social problems and the belief that greater funding was central to raising educational achievement meant that much of this earlier evidence was ignored. Congressional Democrats and others interpreted this new evidence of the failure of compensatory education programs to raise achievement as an indication of failing institutions, rather than the result of a flawed educational (and broader social welfare) strategy. For example, Alice Rivlin, an assistant secretary of planning and evaluation under President Johnson, argued that the poor results indicated the need for larger data sets and "a longitudinal data system for keeping track of individual students as they move through school."[39] The negative reports that followed the passage of ESEA therefore had the effect of enshrining the raising of standardized test scores and the closing of achievement gaps as the primary purpose of the ESEA, and the standard by which it would be judged.

This development was not a forgone conclusion, as Title I had never specified that improvement on standardized tests of achievement was the legislation's objective. Indeed, this topic had been intentionally avoided because of the likely backlash such an objective would have provoked. Furthermore, as Milbrey McLaughlin notes, there were many other metrics by which Title I could have been judged. Researchers easily "could have looked at the efficiency of the delivery of Title I services or examined the effects of Title I on the redistribution of educational services between socioeconomic groups," and in fact "such study designs [were] more typical of evaluations conducted in other areas of DHEW."[40] Congressional liberals did not raise any of these issues. Instead, after the Coleman and G.E. TEMPO reports, many adopted the view that improvement in achievement test scores and the narrowing achievement gaps should be the standard of success for Title I and the ESEA.

As several reports focused on the limited effect of compensatory education on achievement scores, others focused on where the ESEA funds were actually being spent. A particularly influential report sponsored by the NAACP's Legal Defense and Educational Fund and the Washington Research Project questioned whether Title I funds were being used for their intended purposes. The 1969 report, entitled *Title I of ESEA: Is It Helping Poor Children?*, argued that although "the central purpose of Title I is to raise academic achievement . . . Title I in some school systems is not being used at all, or only in a limited way, for academic programs for the special educational needs of children from poor and minority communities."[41] The report noted several instances in which Title I funds were being used for programs that had existed before ESEA, not targeted specifically at the disadvantaged, or diverted into programs that were not specifically education related. Claiming that many states were treating Title I funds as if it were general aid rather than compensatory, the authors urged Congress, the Department of Justice, and the USOE to crack down on school systems that had misused funds. They suggested "immediate action" in demanding "restitution of misused funds" against local education authorities that were not in compliance.[42] To aid in restitution, the report also suggested a congressional oversight hearing, additional staff members within the USOE devoted to enforcing state and local compliance, and additional audits and evaluation of Title I programs.[43] The report positively cited action taken by the USOE to sanction the state of Mississippi for ineffective use of Title I funds.

The cumulative effect of these reports was significant. Although earlier debates on federal support of education had tended to focus on funding equalization as the purpose of compensatory education efforts, the decision by Coleman and others to focus on the effect of funding on test scores redefined the measure of ESEA's success. The new metric of effectiveness of educational programs was whether they could demonstrate improvement in test scores and eliminate differences for students from different racial and economic backgrounds.[44] Policy makers were quick to adopt this new standard.[45] In addition to demanding repayments for misspent funds, Congress also began to stress the need for more evaluations, and funding for educational evaluation ballooned from a few hundred thousand dollars prior to ESEA to more than $5 million per year by 1970.[46] John F. Jennings, a long-time Democratic staffer on the House Subcommittee on Education, noted that by the 1970s, "success came to be measured by achievement. Democrats who in 1964–65 had looked to Title I as a poverty program had to try to find achievement data with which to defend it. We were forced into wanting data."[47] Throughout the 1970s, federal Democrats supported a number of amendments to the ESEA that increased the state reporting requirements and sanctioning power of federal education officials. The continued liberal incorporationist faith in education to solve social problems helps explain why a broad coalition demanded increased evaluation and sanctions for noncompliance despite serious evidence that the educational approach of the ESEA could not lead to the educational outcomes they desired.

As the immediate reports examining the ESEA strengthened the standardized test as the preferred measure of educational success, they also gave rise to demands that Congress devise new means to hold states accountable for ineffective use of federal education funding. The state of Mississippi was an early example. In response to several complaints, the USOE conducted a review in the summer of 1969 of the state's administration of Title I funds and found that it had violated several federal policies. Commissioner of Education James Allen subsequently ordered that no Title I projects be approved in Mississippi for

1970 until remedial action had been taken and froze Title I expenditures for several broad areas such as construction, supplies and equipment, and custodial services.[48] The report endorsed a more muscular federal enforcement of ESEA provisions, and sanctions for those who violated them, as the best means of "fulfilling a long-needed promise to our Nation's poor children."[49]

Mounting evidence of compensatory funding's limited effects on achievement and misspent funds resulted in quick congressional action. Through the 1969 amendments to the ESEA, Congress increased the focus on standardized tests and sought to strengthen and encourage the USOE to sanction states and localities that did not comply with Title I provisions. This approach reflected the growing understanding that standardized achievement tests were the best means of evaluating effective use of compensatory education spending. Despite testimony by some academics and policy specialists expressing concern over the extent to which the ESEA had come to be judged by standardized tests,[50] Congress passed amendments that provided funding for states and the USOE to help localities develop and implement these tests,[51] and required local educational agencies to set objectives and report annually on their progress.[52] Additionally, Congress also extended the "objective measurement of education achievement" requirements to sections of the legislation targeting handicapped children[53] and districts receiving additional funds for having the highest concentration of disadvantaged students.[54] By 1974, Congress moved decisively to orient the ESEA around improving academic performance, requiring DHEW to "develop and publish standards for evaluation of program effectiveness," including "goals and specific objectives in qualitative and quantitative terms," and required annual reports on the "effectiveness" of compensatory programs.[55]

Along with increasing the focus on purportedly objective educational achievement measures, the 1969 ESEA amendments also encouraged more aggressive oversight, including sanctions on noncompliant states, by the USOE. Citing the NAACP Legal Defense and Educational Fund report, the Senate Committee on Labor and Public Welfare expressed its "deep concern about the necessity for stronger enforcement of Title I requirements by both Federal and State agencies in monitoring the legitimate and effective use of Title I funds by local educational agencies."[56] Praising the action the USOE had taken in the case of Mississippi, the committee pushed for "vigorous action" and increased prioritization and staff devoted to compliance, and a greater focus on auditing and state program reviews within the USOE.[57] The USOE appeared to get the message from Congress, and the following year the commissioner of education sent out letters to states outlining violations from the previous three years, and expected to request a total repayment as high as $30 million from the nearly thirty states that were not in compliance.[58] By 1977, the total amount of repayment of Title I funds sought by the USOE had reached $240 million.[59] Although much of the compliance action had been geared toward misspent funds, the 1974 ESEA extension required that the USOE report on plans for "implementing corrective action" for those programs that had not met their specific qualitative or quantitative effectiveness objectives.[60] As Samuel Halperin, the former director of the Office of Legislation of the USOE who helped pass the Kennedy amendments in the original ESEA, pointed out, this clearly oriented the federal education state around "ensur[ing] that public funds result in gains in learning, particularly in reading and mathematics."[61] Given that policy makers had embraced the "objective measure" standard of evidence, schools were increasingly expected to demonstrate gains in standardized tests as evidence of effective use of federal funds.

The quick alignment of the ESEA around the goal of increasing achievement as measured by standardized test scores, and the emerging strategy of sanctions as a means of insuring progress toward this goal, was the result of understanding education as an unemployment and poverty program. The reason that Senator Kennedy, Commissioner Keppel, and other liberals supported the extensive evaluation requirements and standardized tests as the ideal metric was due to a belief that education could eliminate these problems if educational opportunity was equalized. Moreover, as this belief triggered widespread liberal support for investment in education, it also triggered suspicions of the role the existing educational structures had played in perpetuating disadvantage and heightened demands for accountability.[62] The disappointing results of the initial reports on the effectiveness of ESEA programs at raising the test scores of low-income children did not result in a questioning of the appropriateness of test scores as a measure of success or a reexamination of the ability of compensatory education to raise achievement scores. Instead, the early results strengthened the use of standardized tests as a yardstick, increased the evaluation of ESEA programs, and led to calls to enforce strict sanctions on states who failed to deliver.

The Punitive Turn: The Federal Government Funds Experiments

Frustration and disappointment over the findings on the effectiveness of compensatory education began to fracture the unified support for education funding with little oversight. The dispiriting reports did not shake the faith in education that was central to the liberal incorporationist vision. Rather, policy makers interpreted these results as largely the result of lax oversight and an intransigent public school system. Therefore, instead of questioning the ability of education to help solve poverty, unemployment, delinquency, and racial inequality, lawmakers began to turn toward punitive accountability policies designed to force schools to do better. By the late 1960s, the liberal incorporationist faith in education that proved central to the establishment of the federal education state was increasingly used as a justification for shifting federal education policies in a more punitive direction. In fact, early versions of education policies that are hallmarks of the twenty-first-century education landscape first began appearing as federal pilot programs in the late 1960s and early 1970s, including high-stakes testing, merit pay for teachers, vouchers, and early efforts at privatization. The strongest proponents for these policies were frequently the same liberals who had advocated for the ESEA.

The remainder of this chapter traces the federal origin of a number of punitive education policies. The 1960s and early 1970s saw growing Black support for alternatives to public schools, merit-based teacher pay, performance contracting, and vouchers. Even though some Black activist voices rejected incorporationism and disciplinary educational policies, within the context of a system completely in the grip of liberal incorporationism, these dissents fed into broader critiques of the public schooling system and contributed to demands for punitive reforms. A careful examination of these events reveals that the increased federal funding for education quickly gave rise to attacks on the system of public education itself.

The publication of several reports calling into question the effectiveness of compensatory education caused a reevaluation among many Black political leaders and social scientists. Frustration with the slow pace of desegregation, a curriculum largely devoid of Black history and people, a desire for greater control over local institutions, and new evidence of continued group differences on standardized achievement tests all contributed to a growing dissatisfaction with the state of education among Black leaders. Growing evidence of lackluster results on achievement tests and limited integration provided fodder for some Black political leaders to attack public schools directly.

As the economic democracy view within Black political thought was increasingly marginalized throughout the 1960s and 1970s, voices from within the Black political circles called for increasingly dramatic education reforms. Many activists and scholars rejected the findings from reports that seemed to indicate the limited effectiveness of schools in raising standardized test scores, pointing out that this line of argument essentially excused the schools from any responsibility for inferior outcomes.[63] In the late 1960s, Black educators and school administrators were key founders of the Effective Schools Movement. The Effective Schools Movement was a response to a "discontent with schools and their product, the perception of a lack of professionalism and accountability on the part of teachers and administrators, a feeling of general distrust, and the failure of schools to provide appropriately trained laborers for the workforce through providing dysfunctional schools for poor urban children."[64] Black school administrators and scholars like Ronald Edmonds argued that all students could succeed if schools were properly organized around a set of best principles, regardless of the socioeconomic situation outside the schoolhouse walls.[65] In a move that clearly echoed the approach of scientific efficiency progressives of the early twentieth century, the movement drew directly from organizational theories and principles emanating from the business world as inspiration for developing new "best practices" for education. The movement advocated for strong central leadership, high expectations of staff and students, an orderly climate, and careful and continuous evaluation of progress in order to ensure the best educational product.[66] Although the motivation of early advocates of the Effective Schools Movement was to improve the education of Black students, as Elizabeth Todd-Breland notes, they pressed for "solutions that required relatively little additional funding, and were generally confined within the walls of the schools themselves, rather than linking school issues to larger-scale calls for economic redistribution."[67] The emphasis on treating schools and students as akin to shop floors and products meant that the Effective Schools Movement eventually found powerful allies in the business community, while the emphasis on constant evaluation helped spur calls for more frequent testing as the movement gained popularity in the later decades of the twentieth century.[68]

While some called for more effective and efficient school organization, other voices from within the Black political circles became fierce critics of the public school system. The growing strength of Black power and Black nationalist voices ironically found some of their greatest support from liberal social scientists and large foundations. United by faith that education was the key to Black advancement, this group coalesced around a critique of public schools as a sclerotic bureaucracy that represented one of the most significant barriers to Black progress. The continued faith of both Black power advocates and racial democrats that school was key to Black advancement (a shared belief, even if the end goals were different) quickly led to calls for dramatic changes to the public school system. Black leaders and social scientists—and their liberal counterparts—began to advocate for early versions of today's punitive education policies—including privatization, merit pay for teachers, and the expansion of standardized testing—as necessary for racial justice. By the late 1960s, a growing chorus of Black power advocates, mainstream civil rights groups, and liberal philanthropic groups began to attack public schools more directly as obstacles to racial justice.

Perhaps most prominent among those critiquing the public school system were members of the new Black power movement. Reflecting a broader frustration with the pace and demands of liberal integration as a political strategy, Stokely Carmichael—by then a supporter of Black separatism—was elected as the new head of the Student Nonviolent Coordinating Committee (SNCC) in 1966.[69] Carmichael was clear that the Black power agenda required a dramatic shift in the approach to public schools that centered on taking control of institutions that were not acting in the interests of Black children. In a 1968 speech, Carmichael blamed schools for failing to prepare Black youth for success and proclaimed, "We have to understand that unless we control the education system, where it begins to teach us how to change our community where we live like human beings, no need to send anybody to school—that's just a natural fact."[70]

Charles Hamilton, who coauthored *Black Power: The Politics of Liberation* with Carmichael in 1967, expanded the critique of schools in a 1968 article entitled "Race and Education: A Search for Legitimacy" in the *Harvard Education Review*. Hamilton argued that in the wake of the Coleman Report and others with similar findings, "There comes a point when it is no longer possible to recognize institutional failure and then merely propose more stepped-up measures to overcome those failures."[71] While some social scientists and policy makers were looking for ways to improve the compensatory approach, Hamilton argued that "black people are questioning, evaluating the *legitimacy* of existing educational institutions, not simply searching for ways to make those institutions more *effective*."[72] Hamilton called for an end to compulsory busing for integration and a new educational agenda that emphasized community control of schools led by Black parents, teachers, and principals with a curriculum that centered the Black experience. As Hamilton himself had noted, the concept of community schools had its most recent proponents among white opponents to integration. However, this concept found increasing support within some Black circles, particularly with the ascendance of Black power ideology.[73]

The critique of public education was not limited to a call for community schools. In a 1967 *New York Times* editorial, the national director of the Congress of Racial Equality (CORE), Floyd McKissick, suggested that the education system itself was foundational to racial inequality.[74] According to McKissick, schools should no longer be allowed to displace blame for the failure of Black students, noting that the current system had been "disastrous for the black population, who can least afford to be without the skills and knowledge needed to eke out a living in this vicious, competitive society." McKissick argued that because "public education is a monopoly . . . Black people have no alternative to public education," which meant that they were trapped in a failing system.[75] McKissick expressed particular frustration with the "lack of accountability of teachers and administrators" who he argued were quick to blame broader societal forces for learning inequities rather than examining their own deficiencies. According to McKissick, new structures needed to be put in place to ensure that teachers were "directly accountable to the black community in which they serve, not to the union or the Board of Education." For McKissick—much like Stokely Carmichael—changing the education system was key to Black advancement. According to McKissick, the focus on the education system made sense because "when that system is set aright we can begin to rid our other institutions of racism."[76]

An array of Black nationalist scholars and activists built off the critiques of McKissick, Hamilton, and Carmichael and sought to build independent Black educational institutions in the late 1960s and early 1970s. The very real frustration over an existing school system that delivered inferior services to Black students led to the establishment of a number of pan-African nationalist schools in cities with large Black populations. The educational philosophy on which these schools were based rejected the idea of integration and incorporation on its face, and instead viewed Black control of educational institutions as key to building the intellectual and cultural autonomy required for Black independent sovereignty and liberation.[77]

Although in their early instantiations many pan-African independent schools were driven by commitments to anti-imperialism and anti-capitalism, Russell Rickford notes that these institutions struggled to offer robust models of political change in the face of intense external pressure.[78] These schools tended to accept the *Brown* decision's framing of psychological stigma as a significant educational barrier and adopted a pedagogy that focused on cultural and psychological uplift. Divorced from earlier radical tendencies, by the 1970s an "entrepreneurial ethos" increasingly prevailed and these independent Black educational institutions sought to "prepare minority youth for the technologically sophisticated, capital intensive economy of the future."[79] As Rickford notes, by the mid-1970s, "no viable critique of political economy remained" in the Afrocentric pedagogy as many of these schools "sought no basic transformation of social and economic relations" and leaned into the objective of "psychological fortification, not mass mobilization or resistance."[80] These independent educational institutions were inspired in part by a rejection of liberal incorporationism; but by the 1970s, many in practice had come to be advocates of a remarkably similar educational agenda.[81]

More broadly, as scholars Dean Robinson and Touré Reed have argued, advocates of Black nationalism during this era produced a political program that largely replicated existing liberal policies. These groups, with some notable exceptions, did not focus on radically altering existing institutions, but sought Black control of anti-poverty and other government programs.[82] And as Cedric Johnson notes, even though they disagreed strongly about the value of integrated schools, both Black power advocates and liberals like Kenneth Clark and Daniel Patrick Moynihan tended to share a common understanding of the cultural roots of Black poverty.[83] Additionally, Karen Ferguson notes that while "black activists may have initiated the notion of community control," the Ford Foundation quickly expressed an interest in the idea and through massive funding "indelibly shaped its execution according to its assimilationist aims."[84] The Ford Foundation funded the Kenneth Clark–led Metropolitan Applied Research Center (MARC), through which it also funded a fellowship for Floyd McKissick.[85] Although the critiques of McKissick, Carmichael, and Hamilton appeared to be dramatic at first blush, their calls for community control, greater accountability, and alternatives to public schools largely replicated—or unintentionally fed into—the education agenda of liberal incorporationism while emphasizing the need for Black leadership.

By the end of the 1960s, a broad coalition of Black organizations—the NAACP, CORE, SNCC, and the Urban League—all supported an education agenda that emphasized community control.[86] This support for alternative forms of schooling was not entirely new for Black parents or the left more generally.[87] However, the support for community school was in large part motivated by a frustration over the perceived failure of the federal government's compensatory education strategy and desegregation efforts. The conviction that traditional public schools were failing Black students led directly to attacks on the public school system and the teachers who worked within it. This understanding of a public school system in crisis positioned the introduction of greater teacher accountability, greater community control, and the end of the public school monopoly as critical steps toward racial equality. The community schools movement ultimately had significant overlap with a growing movement from both the left and right that began calling for rethinking public schools altogether via the introduction of "free market incentives."

In a demonstration of the shifting center of gravity, by the late 1960s, Kenneth Clark—whose research had been cited by the Supreme Court in *Brown*—began to articulate a critique of public schools that echoed those of the Ford Foundation and Black power activists. In a series of articles and op-eds, Clark excoriated the "criminally inferior education of the ghetto schools."[88] He argued that public schools were producing "thousands of functional illiterates each year," and a generation of Black youth that were "so damaged, so scared, so inadequately prepared that they cannot hope to compete with other races for either higher education or better paying jobs."[89] According to Clark, public schools had become such significant barriers to economic mobility for Black youth that "it is now no longer necessary for even the most prejudiced personnel director to exercise directly his personal prejudices in order to exclude the majority of Negro youth from white collar jobs or from any job which requires adequate education; it's no longer necessary for the decision-maker in the actual business or industry to have his own personal prejudice be the basis for the exclusion of Negro youth from skilled jobs or jobs which require education, because the public schools do a most effective job of racial discrimination at the very source."[90] For Clark, the education system—and the clear inequities of Black schools—was now at the heart of racial inequality. Although he had long been critical of schools, Clark argued that emerging social science evidence suggested that the "relationship between long-standing urban problems of poverty, crime and delinquency, broken homes—the total cycle of pathology, powerlessness, and personal and social destructiveness which haunts our urban ghettos—and the breakdown in the efficiency of our public schools is now unavoidably clear."[91]

Clark's belief that the ESEA's compensatory education program had failed led him to call for dramatic changes to the existing school system. Teachers in urban schools in particular drew Clark's ire. In a 1970 op-ed for the *New York Times* entitled "Answer for 'Disadvantaged' is Effective Teaching," Clark proclaimed that the results from compensatory experiments had demonstrated that "the answer to the question of the best way to teach 'the disadvantaged' is embarrassingly simple—namely, to teach them with the same expectations, the same acceptance of their humanity and their educability and, therefore, with the same effectiveness as one would teach the more privileged child."[92] Clark argued that one of the central drivers of inequity was teachers failing to hold Black students to the same standards as their white counterparts, either due to racist belief in their inferiority or well-intentioned efforts to not hold back their advancement through school.[93] In order to overcome the failing of teachers, Clark advocated for "the development of more rigorous procedures of supervision, reward of superior performance, and the institution of a realistic and tough system of accountability."[94] For Clark, this system of accountability would require stronger educational standards and a new form of merit pay where teachers' compensation and advancement were closely tied to student achievement.[95]

Clark also expressed frustration that public schools had become essentially "protected public monopolies with only minimal competition from private and parochial schools," and therefore had little incentive to change.[96] Clark argued that competition was necessary in order to spur change in the bureaucracy of public schools. It was time for policy makers to make this case directly to business leaders, and he called for enlisting their help in introducing competition to spur greater efficiency within the public school system. According to Clark, business should welcome this change as the current education system offered them "shoddy products" in the form of unprepared workers, and represented a form of double taxation since the poor educational outcomes of the current system meant businesses had to spend additional money to prepare workers for their own needs.[97] Clark called specifically for "strong, efficient, and demonstrably excellent parallel systems of public schools, organized and operated on a quasi-private level, and with quality control and professional accountability maintained and determined by Federal and State educational standards and supervision."[98] For Clark, the failure of existing educational policy required these radical steps, particularly since he believed that educational disadvantage helped perpetuate all other forms of social disadvantage.[99]

Clark and the D.C. Schools Experiment

Beyond his stature as one the most prominent mid-twentieth-century Black social scientists, Clark's thinking on the issue of public education is significant because in 1970, the Washington, D.C., public school system attempted to implement his vision. Testifying before Congress in 1970, president of the Board of Education Anita Allen indicated that a concern about the lack of achievement of Washington, D.C., children had led the board to seek out Kenneth Clark. The board asked Clark to help develop a plan for improvement that centered on building a system of accountability within the city's schools.[100] Clark, in his role as head of MARC and with financial support from the Ford Foundation, Carnegie Foundation, and a number of other nonprofit foundations, developed a plan called "A Possible Reality: A Design for the Attainment of High Academic Achievement for the Students of the Public Elementary and Junior High Schools of Washington, D.C." The Board of Education accepted this plan in 1970 and retained both Kenneth Clark and MARC to help implement the plan in the 1970–1971 school year.

The plan, informally referred to as the "Clark Plan," was adopted by the Board of Education and had many of the hallmarks of Clark's critique of the existing school system. The Clark Plan proclaimed that urban public school systems produced a group of individuals incapable of competing with more educationally privileged peers, and that "neglected and inefficient public schools have become the principal, the most specific, and the most direct agent for the perpetuation of the cycle of social, racial, and economic injustices, of community pathology, and of urban instability."[101] The Clark Plan explicitly rejected the argument that environmental and broader economic factors could explain disparities in achievement, arguing that effective educational policy could overcome these structural barriers.[102]

The Clark Plan called for a number of specific policies designed to increase accountability and introduce competition as a spur to efficiency and effectiveness. The overall goal of the plan was "observable and measurable improvements in student achievement," which required "clear, specific, and high standards" for schoolchildren.[103] At the heart of the Clark Plan was frequent testing of students, and it stated that standardized tests in math and reading "should be administered at least three times a year" in grades 1 through 9.[104] It also suggested that the "competitiveness of these children be tapped as a source of motivation for high academic achievement," by connecting "academic success to *concrete rewards* such as certificates, medals, plaques, and books."[105] Standardized testing would also be integral in changing teacher behavior and motivation as well. The Clark Plan argued that frequent testing would allow for continuous evaluation of teacher performance and should be the basis for rewarding teachers. The Clark Plan called for a shift from the existing system of teacher pay that was based on experience and credentials to a merit-based system of pay and advancement based on the "demonstration of the teacher's ability to raise academic achievement of his pupils."[106]

Although the Clark Plan had strong support from the Board of Education, it faced immediate resistance from Washington, D.C., teachers. William Simons, the president of the Washington Teachers' Union (WTU), led the opposition.[107] Simons, an educator who had taught for eighteen years at one of the city's all-Black junior high schools, had a radically different perspective to Clark on the problems in D.C. schools. Contrary to Clark, who believed that teachers alone could overcome structural impediments if properly incentivized, Simons argued that "if there is to be a major change in education, there must also be a major change in the overall society."[108] The WTU, which had been calling for the increased funding to address teacher shortages, increased class sizes, and a lack of basic classic supplies, expressed strong opposition to the Clark Plan's proposal to focus on increasing standardized testing and tying teacher pay to the results.[109] After the board ignored teacher opposition, one-third of district teachers refused to give their students the standardized test on the first day of testing.

The immediate crisis passed when the board and the WTU reached an agreement that the standardized tests would not be used to rank teachers. However, the Clark Plan quickly faced another hurdle when Superintendent Hugh Scott began to express sympathy with the teachers' criticism of the belief that changing teacher behavior alone could reduce racial inequality within schools. Kenneth Clark began to openly denounce the superintendent, at one point saying, "I used to think that a man could only talk that way because he is not black. These are the same things I've heard from white segregationists and white liberals and condescending whites."[110] Clark resigned from his position as paid consultant to the Board of Education but published a follow-up memo through MARC that criticized Superintendent Scott for ignoring the recommendations of the reform plan.[111] By the end of the 1971–1972 school year, the Clark Plan was essentially dead in the D.C. school district.

Although the plan failed, Clark remained steadfast in his belief that changing the incentives and behavior of teachers remained key for racial equality within schools and society more broadly. In a 1973 interview with the *New York Times*, Clark argued that the reason for the failure of the Clark Plan was not due to its policy proposals, but rather because it was "effectively sabotaged."[112] Clark pointedly noted that the "teachers' union in Washington is predominantly black, headed by a black person," and was perhaps the central culprit in the plan's defeat. Throughout the interview, Clark lamented that the continued lack of competition and accountability for teachers was among the most pressing issues for racial equality in the United States.

Clark's advocacy for an expanded federal presence in public education policy in the mid-1960s and his fierce criticism of existing public schools and teachers by the 1970s were both driven by his adherence to a liberal incorporationist view of education. Clark believed that schools were *the* key institution that could advance racial equality and upward mobility. Clark also argued that schools were capable of reducing inequality even in the absence of broader structural change. Indeed, it was this belief that led Clark to his sharp criticism of public schoolteachers. Clark argued, "I'm saying that teachers probably have the most important role and responsibility in our society, and it's not being fulfilled for these children because of a whole lot of alibis."[113] If education was at the heart of racial inequality, then continued inequality was evidence of the failure of the educational system. Clark's faith that education could effectively address social and racial disadvantage led him to propose increasingly punitive policies directed at public schools and teachers.

As indicated by the opposition of the predominantly Black WTU, the educational agenda of Clark and Black power advocates was not universally embraced, particularly among Black teachers. Bayard Rustin, who continued to advocate for economic democracy, was particularly critical of these new educational proposals.[114] In a 1967 speech that focused on Black activists, Rustin identified the limitations of attempting to address economic problems through the schools:

> Every year there has been a new gimmick. First it was buses; the next year it was the Allen Plan. Now these are forgotten. The following year it was talk about education parks. Last year it was the More Effective Schools program. This year it's decentralization. Next year it will be still another gimmick. The fundamental reasons educators have become involved in this gimmickry is that they do not seem to understand that unless there is a *master plan* to cover housing, jobs, and health, every plan for the schools will fall on its face. No piecemeal strategy can work.[115]

For Rustin, the decision of Black activists to attack teachers was an indication of political weakness; although schools might be susceptible to pressure tactics, they were incapable of addressing problems that were fundamentally economic in nature.[116] In a 1968 speech to the United Federation of Teachers, Rustin pushed activists to recognize the significance of "the teaching process as an integral part of the effort to bring about social change and social justice in our society" and argued that teachers could be particularly effective coalition partners.[117] Rustin urged activists to reconsider the approach of the ESEA more generally, arguing that "compensatory education, isolated from adequate housing, decent living conditions, and good neighborhoods, is useless."[118]

Even as Rustin continued to advocate for a broader program, the center of gravity in Black educational thinking was clearly on the side of Clark and other educational reformers. Although Clark's Washington, D.C., experiment largely failed, it was an indication of how easily the faith in education as a panacea could be turned in a punitive direction when schools failed to live up to expectations. Additionally, the calls from Black power advocates and liberals for drastic changes to the education system offered early evidence of how concerns about racial inequality could quickly slip into punitive and market-driven responses to public education. The Black critiques of schools in the wake of a number of early evaluations of the ESEA were in part driven by the fear that if policy makers accepted the notion that schools were incapable of equalizing opportunity, a natural response would be to abandon attempts to make schools more fair.[119] This was a legitimate concern given how hard-fought the gains in education funding had been and the unresponsiveness of many of these institutions to Black parents and students; but this dynamic did have the effect of doubling down on the expectations of schools and generating more calls for dramatic changes to the existing system. The convergence of Clark, Carmichael, Hamilton, and McKissick—with the generous support of the Ford and Carnegie Foundations—around demands for greater accountability for teachers and alternatives to public school is indicative of the prominence of liberal incorporationist approaches among Black educational reformers. As Elizabeth Todd-Breland notes, the radical demands for self-determination and independent institutions eventually "collided with, and contributed to, neoliberal models of school choice, competition, and privatization."[120] As the next section shows, the federal policy makers embraced a similar understanding and began to fund a number of experiments to challenge the public school "monopoly."

Performance Contracts

By the late 1960s, frustration with the disappointing results of evaluations of compensatory education programs led to calls for new approaches in federal education programs. In 1970, Leon Lessinger, the associate commissioner for elementary and secondary education in the U.S. Office of Education, argued that the "increased and accelerating costs, poor academic performance of minority children, and inconclusive results of federal compensatory education projects" created a "growing demand to link dollars spent for education to results achieved from students."[121] As improved achievement scores became the metric by which ESEA programs were judged, federal policy makers increasingly attempted to tie federal funding of education programs to the demonstration of student progress on objective measures and were increasingly willing to consider "penalties and rewards" since "accountability without redress or incentive is mere rhetoric."[122] The continued faith that properly designed education programs could solve social problems led federal policy makers to take a more combative stance with schools that had failed to deliver. According to Lessinger, "Accountability is the coming sine qua non for education in the 1970s."[123]

One way that federal policy makers sought to increase accountability of public schools was through the private sector in the form of performance contracts. Originating in the Department of Defense, the performance contract was embraced by a number of officials in the Office of Education in the late 1960s and early 1970s.[124] The basic design of a performance contract was a private contractor signing an agreement to improve student achievement test scores by set amounts, with payment to the contractor dependent on the success in improving test scores. The contractors were given broad latitude in instruction method, classroom materials, and class size with the idea that this would encourage educational innovation.[125]

The performance contract model was embraced by the business community, who believed that they could educate disadvantaged students at a reduced cost and make a substantial profit in this new market.[126] Federal officials in the Office of Economic Opportunity (OEO) and the Office of Education were enthusiastic about the potential of introducing this type of private sector accountability. In a 1969 coauthored essay, Lessinger proclaimed that "contracts for federal funds, wherever possible, should be performance contracts."[127] Both federal officials and for-profit firms believed that the failure of previous federal efforts to help educate disadvantaged student was due in part to inefficiencies and ineffective teachers in traditional public schools. The potential for for-profit involvement extended well beyond instruction within the classroom, as federal policy makers called for ESEA funds to be used by school districts to contract with private firms to perform a host of other duties, including managing the application process for contract bidders, the evaluation process, and the payment process.[128] Federal policy makers paved the way for private companies to enter the public school market, and in the late 1960s school districts began to use federal money to pay for-profit companies to increase the test scores of disadvantaged students.

The first federal performance contract in education took place in Texarkana, Texas. The Texarkana school district used a grant from the ESEA to hire Dorsett Educational Systems, a small audiovisual equipment firm, to educate a number of students that were two grade levels behind their peers. The contract stipulated that the for-profit firm would be paid a base payment for raising student performance by one grade level after eighty hours of instruction, with the possibility for additional money if students gained more than one grade level.[129] Dorsett pulled the selected students out of traditional classrooms for two hours at a time and trained them only in English and math—which were the only two subjects in which Dorsett was contractually obligated to show improvement.[130] At the end of the year, federal policy makers were unable to evaluate the success of the program as it became clear that before the final test, students had been allowed to see in advance the very questions that served as the basis for judging improvement as well as Dorsett's success.[131] Although the school board attempted to withhold payment from Dorsett, a federal court ultimately required the school board to pay the company even though it found that tests had indeed been compromised.[132]

Despite a lack of evidence for the efficacy of performance contracting, the federal government continued the practice in Texarkana and began to expand it nationally.[133] The number of performance contracts grew from two in the 1969–1970 school year to sixty in the 1970–1971 school year, to more than 150 in the 1971–1972 school year.[134] In the 1970–1971 school year, the OEO spent nearly $6 million on eighteen different performance contracts that covered roughly 27,000 students in an effort to determine whether for-profit firms could educate disadvantaged children more cheaply and effectively than public schools.[135] Performance contracts were targeted specifically at the same group of students covered by the ESEA, and the first qualification for school district eligibility for the OEO experiment was that it qualified for Title I assistance under the ESEA.[136] The OEO relied on Education Turnkey Systems, the same management support firm it had contracted with in Texarkana, to run the nationwide performance contract experiment.[137]

As the OEO was funding performance contracts nationwide, other school districts used Title I funding from the ESEA to implement their own performance contracts. In 1970, the school district in Gary, Indiana, entered into a four-year contract with Behavioral Research Laboratories (BRL) to take over an entire Title I school within the district. The school, Banneker, had a majority Black student body and majority Black faculty.[138] BRL had been founded with a Carnegie Corporation grant and was a for-profit educational business that already had performance contracts in other school districts. Given broad control of personnel and curriculum, BRL put a former systems analyst from Lockheed Martin with no formal degree in education in charge of the project.[139] The president of the local school board argued that the performance contract and takeover was necessary because the schools had hit "rock bottom,"[140] and BRL pitched itself as willing to work with "students that nobody else wants."[141]

Despite high hopes, evaluations of the Banneker project were mixed at best. Early evaluations showed students in second through sixth grade showed improvement on math scores but fell further behind their peers in reading scores.[142] However, the consequence of the BRL model became even more concerning when looking beyond the standardized test scores. Independent evaluations of the Banneker experiment found that BRL appeared to only be teaching students reading and math, the two subjects on which BRL would be evaluated.[143] Another analysis found that teachers at Banneker tended to ignore students at the high and low extremes of achievement and focused most attention on the mid-level students. This phenomenon—which scholars would subsequently refer to as focusing on "bubble students"—was driven by the belief that the midrange students were the ones most likely to meet the required testing minimums—as the more advanced students could achieve the necessary scores on their own and the worst students would likely never achieve the required test score.[144]

One of the first moves the company made was to replace thirteen certified teachers with uncertified aides, and pay them substantially less money.[145] One evaluation estimated that although BRL reduced costs by roughly $77,000 annually through employing noncertified teachers, large payments to other private entities—including $25,000 annually for consultants and $20,000 for an evaluation of effectiveness—meant it was likely that the company ended up spending more per student than traditional public schools.[146] The exact amount that BRL spent per pupil is unknown because the company claimed that its expenditures and costs were proprietary and refused to release this information.[147] Underlining the lack of transparency and perverse incentives introduced by for-profit companies in the public education sector, BRL went bankrupt in 1978 after a scandal involving accusations of bribes to public officials in order to secure contracts for reading materials.[148]

The experience at Banneker was emblematic of the problems of other performance contracts throughout the nation. Multiple reports examining performance contracts found that they were broadly ineffective in raising test scores. A 1972 OEO study found "the results of the experiment clearly indicate that the firms operating under performance contracts did not perform significantly better than the more traditional school systems."[149] A 1972 RAND report found that nearly all of the contracting firms had "follow on contracts" to continue into the next year despite little evidence of effectiveness.[150] These conclusions of ineffectiveness were largely backed up by reports released by the General Accounting Office (GAO) and the RAND Corporation in 1974.[151] The Brookings Institution put forth its own report on performance contracting in 1975 and bluntly stated that all of "the objective evidence, whether from achievement test gains in reading or mathematics, gains in other subjects, or daily attendance records indicates little ground for enthusiasm about the contractors' performance."[152] There was no evidence that any firm had been able to produce their initial goals of consistently outperforming traditional public schools, and in fact, many performed worse than their public counterparts.

Beyond lack of effectiveness in raising scores, there was also reason to be concerned on the fiscal front. There was evidence that many of the firms that signed performance contracts kept federal money despite failing to meet their contractual obligations. The GAO report found that payments to the performance contracting firms "bore little, if any, relationship to the achievement of students they instructed although this was to be the crux of the performance contracting concept."[153] Since firms were advanced up to 80 percent of the value of their contracts, the OEO was put in a position of seeking repayment from a number of firms that had failed to meet the terms of contract.[154] In 1975, three years after the end of the OEO experiment, half of the performance contracting firms had still not returned to the federal government what they were contractually obligated to repay.[155] Finally, despite promising a way to effectively educate for less money, one program evaluation of the OEO experiment found that the performance contracts cost at least twice as much per pupil as traditional instruction.[156]

Although the OEO had been at the heart of the performance contract push, the ideological belief that drove the turn toward performance contracts had spread to several states and local education authorities. Congress invited Charles Blaschke, of Education Turnkey Systems (the management support firm the OEO had contracted with to run both the Texarkana and nationwide performance contract experiments) to testify as it was considering amendments to the ESEA in 1973. Blaschke argued that the ESEA could be made to work if policy makers included "incentive structures" and "accountability techniques" that would push "those responsible to increase student performance."[157]

Several state and local authorities had in fact begun to use ESEA funds to implement accountability programs in the early 1970s. In 1971, Michigan passed an "accountability-compensatory" education program that complemented Title I of the ESEA.[158] According to the state superintendent of public instruction, John Porter, the plan required that the "compensatory education program . . . demonstrate measurable growth based upon either standardized norm referenced or criterion-referenced tests."[159] If schools failed to meet the standards set by the state, then they would have their funding reduced. Porter justified reducing compensatory funds by noting "our emphasis is on student output rather than school inputs."[160] Some schools in Florida adopted a similar strategy to increase "accountability," with teachers being given bonuses if students met certain benchmarks in reading and math, but "teachers risk having to repay all or part of this money if students achieve less than 50% above expected gains."[161] Congressman William Lehman (D-FL), who had been integral in helping to implement the Florida plan, told his colleagues, "I think that we are going to have to accept some form of accountability, some form of incentives, some form of high-type performance in the public sector in the Federal funding of education in order to continue public support."[162] Even as the evidence was mounting that performance contracts were at best ineffective in improving student performance, several local authorities sought to introduce market-based accountability policies in public education.[163]

Vouchers

The same dynamics of blaming schools for poor results that resulted in liberal support for performance contracting led a number of liberals to embrace a new educational reform that had originated from free market conservatives: school vouchers. These liberals led the charge in pushing the federal government to implement the first widespread studies and demonstration project of school vouchers in the early 1970s. Although the initial efforts around school vouchers were largely considered failures, they helped introduce and popularize the ideas of parental choice and free market competition as spurs to greater educational outcomes that would later become hallmarks of the school choice movement.

The idea of school vouchers was first popularized by Milton Friedman in the 1950s. Under a voucher plan, public money for education would be given to parents of schoolchildren in the form of a voucher that would be redeemable for a specific amount of money for educational services. Parents, using the voucher, would then be able to choose which school their children attended. According to Friedman, this system would allow for the introduction of private enterprise and nonprofit competitors to the existing public schools. Friedman, an ardent free market conservative, argued that this competition in education would lead to greater efficiency, a reduction in government activities, and greater choice for parents.[164] Early support for educational vouchers was limited largely to those who saw them as a way to prevent integration and those in favor of channeling public dollars toward parochial schools.[165]

Despite muted initial support, the growing dissatisfaction of liberals with the perceived failure of compensatory education programs brought a powerful new group into the school voucher fold. By the mid-1960s, Friedman was welcoming a number of liberals to the realm of those advocating for school vouchers.[166] Christopher Jencks, a social scientist associated with the progressive Institute for Policy Studies, lent a prominent liberal voice to the call for school vouchers and the introduction of private market competition as a means of addressing the problems of education for the disadvantaged. In a 1966 article entitled "Is the Public School Obsolete?" Jencks argued that "so far as the slum child is concerned, the present system of 'socialized education' has failed, and that some kind of new departure, either 'capitalist' or 'syndicalist,' is needed."[167] According to Jencks, the public control of schools in big cities had resulted in a public school "monopoly," "organizational sclerosis," and schools that were "less educational than penal institutions," with devastating results for poor children.[168] As a solution, Jencks pushed for "tuition grants to children who opted out of the public-controlled schools, equal to what would be spent on them if they stayed in" as a way of introducing increased parental choice and private sector educational options.[169] According to Jencks, if "the public schools could not survive in open competition with private ones, then perhaps they *should* not survive."[170]

Jencks's call for school vouchers was soon joined by other high-profile liberal social scientists. James Coleman, in an article written just one year after the publication of his bombshell Equality of Educational Opportunity Survey, advocated for "open schools" as a way to improve education for poor children. Echoing the criticism of Jencks and Kenneth Clark, Coleman suggested that the public school monopoly and its organizational weight were barriers to educational innovations that would help lower-class children. Coleman argued for opening up the teaching of reading and arithmetic to "entrepreneurs outside the school . . . paid on the basis of increased performance by the child on standardized tests."[171] Parents would have the choice to keep their children in the existing public school, or to send them to a number of private programs outside the school, meaning "the parent could, for the first time in education, have the full privileges of consumer choice."[172] Coleman, like Jencks, suggested that this competition would mean "some schools might lose most of their teaching functions—if they did not deserve to keep them."[173]

Thomas Sizer, the liberal dean of the Harvard Graduate School of Education, made a similar case in his 1969 article, "The Case for a Free Market," that appeared in a special *Saturday Review* issue on "Education in the Ghetto." Sizer also pointed to the value of introducing vouchers as a way of combating the pitfalls of the "public education monopoly." Sizer pushed for a voucher scheme that "discriminate[s] in favor of poor children" by ensuring that the value of the voucher for poor children was worth more than the vouchers of children who were not disadvantaged.[174] According to Sizer, this would allow for poor parents to enjoy "the real freedom of choice enjoyed by the middle class" and give them greater leverage over their school.[175] The voucher plan would also require a massive expansion in standardized testing so that the performance of schools was not "left wholly to gossip and unsupported assumption."[176] Sizer recognized that his proposals were dramatic departures from existing educational practice, but nonetheless argued they might be necessary as "school systems are, particularly in many large cities, close to collapse."[177]

The liberal turn toward vouchers not only was driven by disappointment over the perceived failure of compensatory education but was also a reaction to the educational critiques articulated by Black nationalists and Black parents frustrated with poor schools. Sizer argued that although vouchers and the introduction of competition into public education might have some shortcomings, "the political claims of the black community have become more persuasive than these educational draw-backs."[178] In 1968, Jencks expressed a similar sentiment in a *New York Times Magazine* article entitled "An Alternative to Endless School Crisis: Private Schools for Black Children," in which he acknowledged that liberals' increasing willingness to attack the public school bureaucracy was "in large part a response to black nationalism."[179] Jencks suggested that a voucher-like system could help address the concerns of Black nationalists, arguing the best option would be to "allow nationalists to create their own private schools, outside the regular public system and to encourage this by making such schools eligible for substantial tax support."[180] The frustration with the slow pace of desegregation, and the growing number of Black activists who questioned the desirability of desegregation as an end goal, pushed liberals to consider these drastic educational reforms.

The appeal of vouchers was not limited to liberal academics, but increasingly found a foothold with federal policy makers. A 1970 Congressional Research Service report noted that "criticism of our schools has become increasingly vehement and widespread," but, despite this, "public schools in many areas have been slow to reform, because they have little incentive to change."[181] Congressional policy makers also held hearings on the needs of education for the 1970s, and much of the testimony was critical of public education and several witnesses advocated for greater parental choice and financial support for alternatives to public schools, including some who specifically pushed for school vouchers. A notable exception to this trend came from teachers' unions. Both the American Federation of Teachers and the National

Education Association steadfastly opposed the voucher proposals, which they viewed as likely to destroy public education.[182]

The critiques articulated by liberal academics were also echoed by President Nixon. In a special address to Congress on education reform in 1970, Nixon argued that "the most glaring shortcoming in American education today continues to be the lag in essential learning skills in large numbers of poor families," and, citing the Coleman Report, proclaimed that "the best available evidence indicates that most of the compensatory education programs have not measurably helped poor children catch up."[183] Nixon asked Congress to establish the National Institute of Education to serve as a hub for educational research and experimentation, with a particular focus on measuring and reducing inequities in education for poor students and racial minorities. In the same speech, Nixon indicated the importance of "non-public schools" in preventing an educational monopoly and lauded the value of these schools, including giving the "spur of competition to the public schools."[184] Nixon claimed these schools provided "parents the opportunity to send their children to a school of their own choice" and offered "a wider range of possibilities for education experimentation and special opportunities for minorities, especially Spanish-speaking Americans and black Americans."[185] Later that year, a Congressional Research Service report indicated that the "idea of a Federally-funded educational voucher plan seems to be receiving serious consideration by the Executive branch."[186]

By 1970, liberal academics, Black activists, Democratic congressional policy makers, and the executive branch all expressed increasing openness to the idea that introducing competition to break up the public school monopoly represented a particularly promising way of reducing education inequalities and improving educational outcomes. Given the growing support, the Office of Economic Opportunity made a grant to the Center for the Study of Public Policy (CSPP) for a detailed study of education vouchers in December 1969. Christopher Jencks was the president of the CSPP and one of the principal authors of the study and Kenneth Clark, James Coleman, and Theodore Sizer all served on the study's advisory committee that offered direct feedback on the proposal and final report.[187] The final CSPP report, *Education Vouchers: A Report on Financing Elementary Education Grants*, was issued in 1970 and articulated a familiar set of critiques.[188] The report criticized the monopolistic control that the public schools had over the current system, pointed to the lack of choice available to poor parents as a significant problem, and lauded the potential of vouchers to "substantially improve the education of elementary school children, especially the disadvantaged."[189]

The report advocated for the OEO to fund a number of voucher experiments in local school districts throughout the country. Specifically, the CSPP report recommended building off the ESEA's framework with what it referred to as a "regulated compensatory model." Under this model, vouchers for disadvantaged children would be worth more than vouchers for non-disadvantaged students. The report argued that this voucher proposal had a number of potential advantages, including the likelihood of closing the achievement gap,[190] giving poor parents more choice and control,[191] and ultimately making poor children more attractive to new schools and "entrepreneurs who think they can teach children better and cheaper than the public school."[192] The report concluded that OEO should fund a demonstration project of the regulated compensatory voucher model, and provided extensive instructions on how to set up a selection lottery, evaluations, and the administrative structure.[193] Before the end of 1970, the OEO had sent out letters to the superintendents of large school districts throughout the country soliciting applications for grants to investigate the feasibility of setting up a voucher demonstration in their district.[194]

Between 1970 and 1972, the OEO awarded six grants to school districts to study the feasibility of implementing vouchers. Intense opposition from local parent groups and teachers' unions meant that only one of the six districts, the Alum Rock School District in San Jose, California, opted to move forward with implementation after the feasibility studies.[195] The Alum Rock School District was a majority non-white district and was one of the poorest districts in the entire state of California, with more than half of its students meeting the threshold for free and reduced lunch.[196] The federally funded voucher experiment began in the 1972–1973 school year and largely followed the "regulated compensatory voucher" design outlined in the CSPP report. When the demonstration started, California had not passed the necessary legislation to allow nonpublic schools to receive public education funding, and there were no existing private schools in Alum Rock, so the Office of Economic Opportunity attempted to build alternative education options within the existing public school system. Schools participating in the voucher experiment were required to develop at least two distinct educational programs, called "mini-schools," that would operate relatively autonomously with regard to budget, curriculum, pedagogy, and staff. Parents could then choose to enroll their children in any "mini-school" within the district and these "mini-schools" would receive funding based on the student vouchers.[197] The vouchers had a compensatory component, with students who met the Title I threshold given a higher value voucher.[198] By May 1972, the district had twenty-two different "mini-schools" ready to accept students for the upcoming school year.[199]

Just three years after it began, the voucher demonstration project in Alum Rock was largely viewed as a failure. One of the biggest obstacles was the general lack of parental interest in vouchers. Parents in Alum Rock were generally satisfied with their existing public schools, and the third year of the experiment saw a substantial drop-off in the number of parents that registered for voucher programs.[200] In the second year of the demonstration, after California passed enabling legislation, the district approved a plan to admit a private school into the experiment but too few parents signed up, and the school never opened its doors.[201] A RAND evaluation of the voucher experiment after three years concluded that "the underlying assumption of a voucher system that parents would actually use their choice, causing schools to compete with each other, did not hold up over time in Alum Rock."[202]

In addition to a lack of participation, there was little evidence that the introduction of vouchers had improved educational performance. As part of the demonstration project, all voucher students and some non-voucher students in the district were given standardized tests in reading and math.[203] The RAND Corporation, which had been contracted to evaluate the test scores, found conflicting results. Voucher students scored better on some tests and worse on others when compared with non-voucher students. A reevaluation of test score data a few years later found slight negative effects for all vouchers, with more substantial negative effects on the reading test scores of students who attended the voucher "mini-schools" that most deviated from the curricular and instructional patterns of traditional public schools.[204] Although scholars cautioned about drawing conclusions from the data, Daniel Wieler, the head of the RAND study evaluating test scores, stated, "I am making the personal political prediction that vouchers are not in the cards."[205] Despite $7 million in federal funding spent over the first three years on demonstration projects, a 1975 *New York Times* story on Alum Rock reflected a growing sentiment when it reported that "many persons familiar with the voucher situation are not overly optimistic about the future."[206] The Alum Rock voucher demonstration project was ultimately disbanded with little fanfare after five years.

The California Enabling Legislation— Ronald Reagan and School Vouchers

Although the Alum Rock experiment itself failed, the nation's first federally funded school voucher project did have a significant long-term impact by introducing the idea to a much broader audience of policy makers. As mentioned previously, one of the obstacles to the voucher demonstration project was that in most states it was not legal to channel public funds to private elementary and secondary education institutions. This limited the ability to test the expansive voucher program proposed by the CSPP study—which included private alternatives to the existing school system. To overcome this issue, the OEO encouraged states to pass "enabling legislation" that would allow for public education funds to go to private educational institutions, and the final CSPP report provided "model legislation" for states to implement. This issue became particularly important in California after the Alum Rock School District became the only district in the country to decide to participate in the OEO voucher experiment.

In 1969, the California Assembly considered its first version of a voucher project introduced by Assemblyman Leon D. Ralph of South Los Angeles. In addition to Assemblyman Ralph, several of the other sponsors were Black, including Yvonne Brathwaite (the first Black woman elected to the California Assembly), John J. Miller (former president of the Berkeley Board of Education), and future San Francisco mayor Willie Brown Jr.[207] Framed as a way to increase both accountability and local control over primary and secondary education, the Self-Determination in Education Act would have applied only to "economically disadvantaged areas" and would have given parents tuition vouchers when their local public schools fell below performance standards in reading and math scores. If a school fell below the performance standards, parents would be able to use their vouchers to send their children to any approved educational provider, including private schools and private contractors. Although the bill never advanced past the education committee, it did indicate that a potential constituency did exist for school vouchers, particularly among the Black assembly members.[208]

Although this initial bill had little traction, the following year Dennis Doyle, a consultant to one of the legislative joint committees on education, became interested in the CSPP study and its voucher proposal. In 1970, inspired by the CSPP report, Doyle drafted an enabling bill for the California Assembly that provided for demonstration voucher school districts and waived state requirements on curriculum, teacher salary schedules, class size, minimum length of the school day, and certification requirements for voucher schools.[209] Assembly Bill 2471, which opened by claiming that the current system "severely limits the range of educational opportunity available to the vast majority of students and discriminates against economically disadvantaged children," also required reports on the progress of students determined by standardized tests.[210] Although the bill failed to pass in 1970, it had substantially more support than the bill from the previous year, and a more restrictive version did eventually pass in the fall of 1973.[211] In 1972, the year after writing California's enabling legislation, Dennis Doyle was appointed as the assistant director of the OEO, and then the assistant director of National Institute of Education after the OEO was disbanded. In his capacity as assistant director of the NIE, he oversaw the Alum Rock demonstration project and continued to be an advocate for greater "choice" in primary and secondary education.[212]

Perhaps most significantly, the federally funded CSPP report and Alum Rock demonstration project helped introduce then-governor of California Ronald Reagan to the notion of school vouchers. Just a few months after the CSPP submitted its preliminary report on school vouchers, Reagan ordered a state-level study of vouchers, noting the potential of vouchers to spur innovation and allow parents the "freedom of choice in selecting between competing schools."[213] After winning reelection, Reagan announced that education would be one of his top priorities in his 1971 State of the State address. Reagan argued that educational reforms were needed to ensure "schools are held accountable for quality and results," and pushed for replacing tenure for school-teachers with merit pay and called on state lawmakers to pass legislation allowing for a pilot voucher program.[214] After the legislature failed to pass a bill in 1971, Reagan claimed in his 1972 State of the State address that the "most urgent unfinished tasks before us involve our educational system" and once again called for the passage of a voucher demonstration legislation.[215]

Despite the fact that the voucher demonstration at Alum Rock was largely considered a setback for voucher advocates, it helped lay the groundwork for later advocates of school choice and privatization. The call for vouchers originated from both a liberal incorporationist faith that education could solve broad social problems as well as a growing tendency to blame schools and teachers for failing to address these issues as compensatory education approaches did not close testing gaps. It was therefore liberals in the late 1960s and early 1970s who were the most vocal advocates of school vouchers, arguing that this means of introducing competition into the public school monopoly coupled with rigorous testing held the key to holding schools accountable and improving educational outcomes for poor and Black students. The willingness to increasingly point to the "public" aspect of public schools as problematic meant that the education reforms pushed by some liberal academics during this time period resonated with many conservatives who had long been critical of the "monopoly" of public schools and teachers' unions. As the popularity of vouchers and school choice grew in conservative circles, it would eventually become one of the major components of Republican efforts to win minority votes for privatization of the public education system.[216] Ironically, Ronald Reagan, who would go on to be one of the most prominent advocates for school vouchers, adopted many of his arguments and advocacy language from a federally funded education experiment designed by liberals.

The Punitive Liberal Incorporationist Education State

The persistent liberal incorporationist faith in education as a key to racial and social equality and the frustration over the continued existence of widespread inequality increasingly drove liberal academics and policy makers to look to dramatic educational reforms. By the 1970s, the federal push for punitive accountability education policies had become thoroughly bipartisan and had begun to influence education policy at the state level as well. Republican governor Ronald Reagan and Black Democratic assembly members pushed for voucher legislation in California. Similarly, Scott Baker notes that a whole generation of New South politicians, including governors Jimmy Carter (D-GA), Reuben Askew (D-FL), Linwood Holton (R-VA), Lamar Alexander (R-TN), and James Hunt (D-NC), "turned to accountability as a politically expedient alternative to the task of confronting the structural sources of racial inequality."[217] With the support of Black legislators and civil rights groups several of these governors pushed for expanded testing and punitive policies, such as diploma denial for poor standardized test scores, in an effort to increase accountability in education.[218] Excoriating public schools and calling for more testing and free market incentives proved a particularly effective message in building a broad coalition of business leaders, Black politicians, and large foundations across the country.

The efforts of Reagan and his southern counterparts built on both the ideological, pedagogical, and institutional capacity provided by the federal education state. The ESEA enshrined the liberal incorporationist understanding that the purpose of education lay in building human capital in order to secure individual economic security and altering individual behavioral deficiencies in order to reduce inequality, poverty, and racial disparity. Liberal incorporationists quickly turned their attention to the creation of institutions focused on measuring how well education accomplished these goals, and an increasingly harsh variety of alternatives when schools and teachers failed to meet expectations.

Despite having been only recently created, the federal role was crucial. For example, southern governors relied directly on federal grants provided by an

ESEA reauthorization in order to establish high-stakes exit exams for high school students,[219] and Reagan's initial embrace of vouchers was prompted by a federal pilot program. As some of these state-level politicians moved into federally elected positions, they pushed for greater federal support of punitive accountability policies. As president, Jimmy Carter sought to establish a mandatory national achievement test and signed the 1978 ESEA reauthorization that provided federal grants to expand testing and the capacity of state testing agencies.[220] Ronald Reagan successfully won election to the presidency on a Republican platform that called for federal support of a voucher-like program and channeled Christopher Jencks, James Coleman, and other liberal incorporationists by noting that this was "a matter of fairness, especially for low-income families, most of whom would be free for the first time to choose" a school for their children.[221]

The policy experiments of the late 1960s and 1970s foreshadowed the future of education reform in the United States. The redefinition of racial inequality, poverty, and unemployment into educational issues ultimately created a perilous environment for public education. As the federal role was justified in new ideological terms, public funding of education did in fact increase, but it simultaneously pushed more direct means of addressing inequality into the background and raised expectations for schools. Failure to meet these new expectations resulted in attacks on teachers and public education and calls for new measures designed to ensure accountability. Black educators and activists, frustrated by a system that frequently offered an inferior education to Black students, pushed for measures and alternatives that intentionally and unintentionally fed into broader attacks on the public school system. As policy makers grew frustrated with what they perceived to be languishing test scores and lingering racial achievement gaps, they ratcheted up demands for more testing, test score–based teacher pay, and market-based alternatives to public schools. This feedback loop, undergirded by the misplaced faith that education is the most appropriate place to intervene on what are fundamentally political economic issues, is the hallmark of the liberal incorporationist education order.

The Enduring Legacy of the Liberal Incorporationist Education State

Persistence and Possibility in the Current Era

Less than a year after his landslide victory, President Obama was welcomed with chants of "¡Sí se puede!" as he strode up to the lectern to address the annual legislative meeting of the U.S. Hispanic Chamber of Commerce. With the country's focus still squarely on the devastating consequences of the Great Recession, President Obama was quick to tie the economic crisis to the nation's education crisis. After telling the crowd that "we know that economic progress and educational achievement have always gone hand in hand in America," the president denounced the educational status quo. President Obama noted that "despite resources that are unmatched anywhere in the world, we've let our grades slip, our schools crumble, our teacher quality fall short, and other nations outpace us." Acknowledging the chosen audience for the speech, the president was careful to point out that the situation was particularly dire for students of color, as "year after year, a stubborn gap persists between how well white students are doing compared to their African American and Latino classmates." Now was the time to "stop making excuses" for bad teachers and "demand results" from the beleaguered education system, because, as the president exclaimed, "education is no longer just a pathway to opportunity and success, it is a prerequisite for success."[1]

Seven years after this speech, the man who was in many ways President Obama's political antipode and eventual successor voiced a remarkably similar critique. As he spoke to small crowd in the cafeteria of a charter school in Cleveland in May 2016, then-candidate Donald Trump promised to turn the page on "a failed education policy" and "a failed economic policy." He lamented that despite spending "more per student than almost any major country in the world," student performance in the United States lagged behind that of other countries. Having chosen a charter school that served an almost all-Black student body, candidate Trump pointedly asserted that poor performance of Black students on standardized tests was evidence of an education system in crisis. After noting that "nearly 40% of African-American children live in poverty," he placed the blame squarely on schools, arguing that "failing schools then contribute to failing economies." Claiming that "our public schools are failing to put young Americans on a path to success," Donald Trump called for merit-based pay to replace the tenure system and promised to "provide school choice to every disadvantaged student in America."[2]

The words of these recent presidents reflect the curious reality that in an age often derided as one of unparalleled polarization, both major American political parties have notably similar understandings of the problems and potential of the education system. There is a bipartisan consensus on the foundational importance of education for individual and national economic success, and for addressing social problems such as racial inequality. Both political parties couple this belief in the power of education with criticism of the education system for contributing to existing social ills. Public K–12 schools are frequently positioned as facing a crisis of poor achievement, low standards, and bad teachers, and therefore requiring new policies to hold various actors accountable. The calls for accountability have been decidedly punitive, with politicians from across the aisle threatening loss of funding, loss of teaching jobs, or school closure for failure to live up to expectations. This bipartisan consensus is beyond rhetorical, as major federal education legislation pairing greater funding with harsh accountability policies has consistently received overwhelming bipartisan support.[3]

This book has contended that liberal federal policy makers built an education order in which faith in education as a solution to poverty, unemployment, and racial disparities helped pave the way for the development of a powerful federal education state characterized by punitive accountability policies. In a departure from existing accounts that focus on the 1980s and the political right, this book traces the origins of the current educational order to debates among progressive educators in the 1930s through 1950s, and the first major federal intervention in K–12 education during the height of the Great Society.[4] What appears superficially to be a progressive triumph of mid-twentieth-century state building in fact represents the triumph of an educational consensus with a distinctly limited social vision. Examining the fierce ideological debates between different coalitions over the purpose of education in the mid-twentieth century reveals that the construction of the federal education state marked a distinct turn away from more radical possibilities, and eventually resulted in an embrace of punitive education policies.

The dominance of liberal incorporationist ideology among policy makers and intellectuals during the construction of the federal education state can be traced to the settlement of fierce ideological battles in the decades preceding the passage of the ESEA. Throughout the 1930s and 1940s, the progressive education movement was divided by a debate over whether schools and teachers should lead the effort to fundamentally change an unfair social and economic order, or whether the education system should attempt to fit students into the existing social order. As the social efficiency progressive vision proved better able to accommodate the changing political context of the 1940s, its vision of the purpose of education came to dominate the progressive education reform landscape. This vision articulated an incorporationist function for education and promoted a particular set of policies, including extensive use of testing, educational tracking, and routinization of teaching methods.

A similar divide characterized Black political organizations and thought throughout the same era, as one coalition argued that advancing the concerns of Black Americans required fundamental changes to the economic order, and another argued that justice could be achieved through fair racial incorporation into the existing economic and social structures. The educational vision of the racial democrats was much more amenable to the international and domestic developments of the 1940s and 1950s. The Cold War, shifting Supreme Court doctrines, and brutal political repression of the economic democrats during the Second Red Scare all helped position the racial democratic vision as the most influential articulation of Black political interests by the 1960s. Much like the social efficiency progressive vision, the racial democratic educational vision was centered primarily on the incorporation of students into the existing economic and social order, with the central difference being that racial democrats demanded that this incorporation not be unfairly structured on the basis of race. The ideological concerns of the racial democrats also drove their preferred educational policies, including equal educational opportunities for Black and white students, intercultural education to combat racial prejudice, and strong accountability policies to ensure equal opportunity across racial lines.

The two perspectives that proved best suited for the changing political context had substantial ideological similarities. Both the racial democrats and the social efficiency progressives viewed the function of schools as preparing students for successful integration into the labor market. The two ideological perspectives placed great faith in the ability of efficient and fair educational organization to significantly improve human welfare and social goods. Both also warned of the long-term consequences and significant human suffering that could result from a poorly organized educational system. These commonalities in broader education vision meant that there was also significant overlap in the programmatic approach of the two groups. Both supported the implementation of standardized testing, curriculum tied to the skills demanded by the labor market, and increased accountability for schools and teachers.

Importantly, racial democrats had few qualms with the differentiation sought by social efficiency progressives, as long as the differentiation was not based on race. Many racial democrats openly embraced differentiation on the basis of factors such as intelligence or merit as both wise and, more importantly, fair. By the end of World War II, the broader acceptance of the fundamental similarity of the distribution of intelligence levels between Black and white people meant that the differentiation of educational opportunities on the basis of intelligence or merit did not necessarily imply the creation of racial disparity. Both the racial democrats and the social efficiency progressives embraced the usefulness of markers such as merit, talent, and intelligence in distributing opportunity and power. Shorn of racial overtones, psychologist Henry Goddard's ideal of "Aristocracy *in* Democracy"[5] is fundamentally similar to Phelps-Stokes Fund director F. D. Patterson's call to transform college admissions to ensure that "the aristocracy of such institutions must be an aristocracy . . . of talent."[6] As these two perspectives increasingly dominated the educational landscape, both positioned merit, talent, and intelligence as legitimate means of differentiation in the education system, and in social destiny more broadly.

Perhaps most significantly, neither of these groups pressed for substantial changes to the existing economic order. While the transformation of the fundamentally unfair and undemocratic economic order was central to the vision of economic democrats and social reconstructionists, the social efficiency progressives and racial democrats sought relatively minor adjustments. The social efficiency progressives wanted schools to prepare students for success in the existing institutional landscape. Racial democrats also wanted schools to prepare students for success within the existing social order but wanted to make sure that this preparation was the same across racial lines. The compatibility of both positions with the capitalist organization of the economy proved greatly advantageous as the radicalism of the New Deal years gave way to the more conservative post–World War II era and provided the foundation for the emergent liberal incorporationist consensus.

The changing political context of the 1940s and 1950s also led the Democratic Party to look to different economic management techniques than the ones relied on by the New Deal coalition. By the mid-1940s, the consensus within the Democratic coalition around high levels of taxation, centralized economic planning, and extensive public job creation had begun to crack. Persistent economic problems such as poverty and unemployment were increasingly explained by pointing to deficiencies within individuals that prevented their success in the existing labor market. The turn to the individualized explanation for economic inequality and disparities also positioned education as a particularly effective and relatively inexpensive means of addressing these concerns. As the Democratic Party turned away from the most expansive and redistributive policies of the New Deal, it increasingly positioned education as a means of addressing myriad social problems such as poverty, unemployment, and racial disparity.

By the end of the 1960s, a powerful coalition backed the liberal incorporationist education order. Faith in the ability of education to meaningfully address the persistent issues of poverty, unemployment, and racial disparity had united a coalition of policy makers to pass the first major federal intervention in primary and secondary education policy. The programmatic approach chosen by federal policy makers was *liberal* in its attempt to ensure that all students, regardless of race or economic status, were given equal opportunity to reach their potential. The approach was also explicitly *incorporationist* in that justification for targeting aid to poor students was done in the attempt to give all students an equal chance for success within the existing economic order. Within the Democratic Party, positioning education as one of the most effective solutions to poverty, unemployment, and racial disparities largely replaced more directly redistributive policies—such as public job guarantees and a progressive taxation system.

AS THE FEDERAL GOVERNMENT was pushing for its most substantial involvement in education, the public education system was positioned as a root cause of poor economic outcomes and as the foundation of racial inequality. This faith in education not only fueled the growth of the federal education state but also led to policies focused on punishing teachers, students, and schools for failing to live up to expectations. These lofty expectations meant that funding was attached to increasingly harsh measures to ensure accountability. A litany of punitive measures in the education system stem from this dynamic, including high-stakes testing, tying teacher pay to test performance, and privatization or closure for schools that fail to achieve benchmarks. Many of these policies looked remarkably similar to those that had first been advocated by social efficiency progressives and racial democrats decades earlier. The educational commitments that were institutionalized during the Great Society have driven the rise in increasingly punitive education policies supported by both political parties.

Although many accounts of neoliberalism point to the 1970s as the critical moment for its emergence in policy, careful attention to the origins of the federal education state shows that developments in the 1940s and 1950s did much to set the ideological stage for the later neoliberal turn in American politics.[7] A resurgent form of business-friendly liberalism moved to curtail challenges from the left, destroying coalitions, individuals, and certain policy courses on the way. The turn toward education policy helped Great Society liberals square concerns about the continued existence of inequality with their newfound hesitancy to engage in interventionist economic policies. As a result, the underlying logic of the nascent federal education state and its attendant policy prescriptions contained early versions of what scholars have subsequently identified as mechanisms of neoliberal governance—including broad testing requirements, sanctions for failing to demonstrate measurable achievement, and calls for alternatives to public schools.[8] Tracing mid-twentieth-century ideological debates between education scholars, Black political thinkers, and liberal policy makers provides new insight into the development of the disciplinary apparatus and punitive governmentality of the social welfare state in the United States.

The liberal incorporationist educational ideology positioned education as a particularly effective social policy arena for addressing problems within the existing economic order, demanded accountability when educational institutions "failed" to address these problems, and pushed alternative educational and political economic approaches to the background. Understanding this history is critical for comprehending that continued attempts to solve social problems through the education system cannot succeed, but the continued faith that reorganizing the education system can reorganize society is likely to fuel increasingly punitive education polices. Despite this reality, the liberal incorporationist ideology continues to shape education policy with increasingly negative consequences.

The Punitive Educational Landscape: 2000 through 2020

The modern education policy landscape and its surrounding rhetoric reflects the consequences of the incorporationists' vision. The NCLB Act passed under President George W. Bush, and the RTT initiative and Every Student Succeeds Act (ESSA) passed under President Obama have solidified the liberal incorporationist ideology that has driven federal education policy since the passage of the ESEA. These post-2000 federal education policies have made the receipt of federal funds contingent on the implementation of statewide standards, frequent student evaluations, and harsh turnaround methods for schools failing to meet standards. The NCLB Act, RTT, and ESSA have all positioned standardized achievement tests scores as the method of choice for evaluating the success of students, teachers, and schools. A brief examination of the structure and policies of recent federal reform efforts reveals the ideological continuity of the liberal incorporationist vision that provided the foundation for the 1965 ESEA.

Passed with widespread bipartisan support in 2001 as a reauthorization of the ESEA, the NCLB Act represented a dramatic expansion of federal influence in education policy. The act required states to develop subject area standards to determine what students should learn throughout their elementary and secondary school years, with the goal that every student would reach a minimum level of proficiency as determined by these new standards. In order to hold schools accountable, the new law also required that states test every student in grades 3 through 8, and once more in high school to ensure that every student reached the standards set by the state. The law also required that schools keep track of the scores of "subgroup" populations, most notably racial minorities, in order to ensure the elimination of test score achievement gaps. Critically, the new federal law required states to intervene in schools whose students failed to meet proficiency standards (determined by standardized test scores) and implement "turnaround" strategies. These turnaround strategies included many punitive measures, including forcing schools to pay for private tutors for students out of already strained budgets, mass firing of teachers, or closing the school completely. The ultimate goal that the NCLB set for states was that 100 percent of students would meet proficiency levels by 2014.[9]

Although the NCLB Act faced widespread criticism after implementation, the measure that replaced it—the 2015 ESSA—maintains much of the NCLB Act's programmatic structure and clearly shares the same ideological understanding of the purpose of education and the perceived shortcomings of public schools. Like the NCLB, the ESSA requires states to test all children in grades 3 through 8 and once in high school and continues the practice of requiring separate subgroup testing records. Unlike the NCLB, the ESSA allows states to determine their own accountability goals (doing away with the 100 percent proficiency goal). However, it does require that states submit their accountability plans to the Department of Education for approval and also requires that test scores be given greater weight than more subjective measures. The law also requires that states implement turnaround strategies for any schools with persistent disparities in subgroup test scores, a graduation rate lower than 67 percent, or if they fell in the bottom 5 percent of state assessment scores.[10]

In a review of the first approved state accountability plans, one report found that although some states cut back on the harshest accountability policies, most states continued to rely heavily on test scores and planned to "impose penalties, some potentially severe, on schools that do not test at least 95% of their students."[11] Several years after passage, states continued to reward and punish schools on the basis of test scores, and educators were still concerned about curricular narrowing, teaching to the test, and the tremendous pressure to raise test scores above all else. After pointing out that the ESSA had done little to change the practical reality or the way policy makers and the public view educational success, one group of scholars noted, "The new boss is the same as the old boss, just with a different name."[12]

Although the RTT initiative differs from NCLB and ESSA in structure and origin, there are many similarities in the policies and overall vision of reform it promotes. At the request of the Obama administration, the 2009 American Recovery and Reinvestment Act set aside $4.35 billion for the creation of the RTT fund. The Obama administration committed to use these funds to provide grants to motivate states to create "the conditions for education innovation and reform . . . including making substantial gains in student achievement, closing achievement gaps, improving high school graduation rates, and ensuring student preparation for success in college and careers."[13] Grant winners were determined on the basis of a points system, with states getting points for adopting rigorous standards, eliminating barriers to the expansion of charter schools, implementing extensive new teacher evaluation plans, turnaround plans for poor-performing schools, promotion of and emphasis on STEM (science, technology, engineering, and math) education, and expanding the use of data systems. Facing dire financial straits in the wake of the 2008 recession, many states enthusiastically passed reforms in an attempt to be competitive for RTT funds.[14] Ultimately, RTT proved to be a dramatically effective means of inducing states to enact substantial changes in education policy, regardless of whether these states ultimately received RTT funds.[15]

These latest federal efforts reflect the liberal incorporationist faith and understanding of the purpose of education. Expansive and punitive reforms are pursued based on the belief that public schools are failing children and are the root cause of a number of social ills such as unemployment and racial disparities. These federal policies are responsible for the development of a number of policy reforms at the local level with particularly pernicious consequences for teachers, students, and communities.

The reliance on standardized test scores as a metric of evaluation has provided a reliable line of attack on public school teachers. Nearly a century after

John Franklin Bobbitt praised the usefulness of standards and frequent testing in the identification of good and bad teachers (and suggested tying
teacher pay, promotion, and retention to the test scores of their pupils), policy makers have again turned to tying teacher evaluation to student test
scores. A coalition of large-city school superintendents, including Michelle
Rhee in Washington, D.C., and Joel Klein in New York City, and national nonprofit organizations, such as the Gates Foundation, argued that persistent low
student test scores were a reflection of poor teaching.[16] Arguing that teachers
needed to be held accountable and could no longer be allowed to rely on
the poverty of students as an excuse for poor performance, this coalition
pressed for greater teacher evaluation on the basis of standardized test
scores and greater administrative freedom to fire teachers whose students
scored poorly.[17] This demand for greater administrative authority to fire teachers with low performance scores is often framed as a necessary reform to ensure quality education in schools serving high numbers of poor students and
students of color.[18]

The Obama administration was responsive to these arguments and made
the receipt of RTT funds and NCLB waivers contingent on the implementation of teacher evaluation systems that included evaluation on the basis of
improvement in student standardized test scores.[19] This organized support
has led to the rapid expansion of this type of teacher evaluation, with the
number of states requiring that student standardized test scores be a part of
teacher evaluation growing from fifteen in 2009 to forty-three by 2015.[20] With
active support of large philanthropic foundations, such as the Gates Foundation's "Measures of Effective Teaching Project," forty-nine states and the District of Columbia have made significant changes to their teacher evaluation
methods since 2009.[21] Indeed, advocates like the Gates and Broad Foundations saw widespread and standardized teacher evaluation as a necessary first
step in advancing other goals, such as tying teacher pay to performance.[22]
Long after their initial promotion by the likes of John Bobbitt and Kenneth
Clark, policies encouraging the direct connection between teacher performance and pay and promotion is the reality in many classrooms throughout
the country.

Although educational tracking of the type envisioned by the social efficiency progressives, where students would be grouped by ability and placed
in entirely separate educational tracks aimed at preparing them for their
future professions, is not a major aspect of the educational landscape today,
elementary and secondary schools *do* still use forms of tracking.[23] Placing
students in different classes on the basis of ability or prior performance con-

tinues to be a widespread practice. At the elementary level, although students of differing ability are housed in the same classroom, they are frequently grouped with children of similar ability (known as ability grouping), with each group receiving instruction based on the group's perceived ability. Tracking today is predominantly used in high school and is determined on a subject-by-subject basis, with students assigned to different classrooms based on past performance.[24] Although getting a firm grasp of the extent of tracking in schools is difficult, recent comprehensive surveys of teachers indicates that between 70 and 90 percent of elementary classrooms use ability grouping, and 65–85 percent of high school students experience tracked classrooms.[25]

Recent federal reforms have also ushered in a decisive shift in the definition of educational research and what types of research schools and educators are allowed to rely on in guiding pedagogy. NCLB included provisions that made receipt of federal funds for turnaround schools contingent on schools and districts using these funds to develop educational programs based on the best available evidence of effectiveness, or "scientifically based research."[26] Much like the social efficiency progressives' importation of the scientific methods of industrial organization to the schools, the term *scientifically based research* originates in the medical field and is seen as a way of rationalizing and improving a disorganized education system. The importance of this requirement is reflected by the fact that the term *scientifically based research* appears more than one hundred times in the NCLB Act.[27] The act also outlined what constituted "scientifically based research," ultimately settling on an extremely narrow definition that limits research to "testing hypotheses and using experimental and quasi-experimental designs only, and preferring random assignment."[28] This narrow definition of what counts as research is particularly consequential as it provides support for educational research that frames success in education as determined by whether educational methods have effects that can be detected through easily quantifiable and replicable observations. This approach to education research is a legacy of the victory of early social efficiency progressives such as Edward Thorndike.[29]

Standardized test scores provide ideal observations, and the desire for the "certainty" of scientifically based research reinforces the proliferation of testing in education. Furthermore, as education professor Suzanne Franco has pointed out, the definition adopted by the NCLB inevitably "leads one to the conclusion that forms of research that do not conform to SBR [scientifically based research] are invalid."[30] The 2015 ESSA similarly emphasizes the value of scientifically based research and continues to point to experimental studies as the gold standard in education research.[31] Defining the boundaries of education research in terms that support limited conceptions of educational success bolsters the liberal incorporationist order by reinforcing narrow individualist approaches to education, increasing demands for quantification, delegitimizing research that might challenge its ideological foundations, and preventing schools from implementing an alternative policy approach.

Aspects of social efficiency ideology are also present in the justifications used for the push to implement the so-called Common Core State Standards nationwide. The original standards were first developed in 2009, with considerable support from the testing industry, which dominated the working groups that wrote the standards, and the Gates Foundation, which spent millions of dollars on efforts to get states to adopt the standards.[32] The Obama administration also got on board, requiring states competing for the $4 billion in RTT funds to adopt rigorous "standards that build toward college and career readiness" and that were "supported by evidence."[33] The Common Core website describes the standards as "research and evidenced based," "aligned with college and career expectations," and designed to prepare all students for "success in college, career, and life in our global economy and society."[34] The website notes that the standards would impact teachers by providing them "with consistent goals and benchmarks to ensure students are progressing on a path towards success in college, career, and life."[35] Remarkably, by 2011, forty-five states and the District of Columbia had adopted the Common Core State Standards.[36] In an echo of the scientific progressives of the past, major promoters like Bill Gates portray themselves as little more than technocrats looking to implement the latest data-proven techniques. Gates dismissed criticism of the standards, saying, "these are not political things," but rather simply attempts to "apply expertise to say, 'Is this a way of making education better?'"[37]

The development and implementation of these standards followed a top-down approach with little initial input from the public or teachers. These new "evidenced-based" standards, the evaluation of teachers on the basis of student test scores aligned with these standards, and the design of standards that reflect the needs of the labor market or "global economy" were pushed heavily by large foundations. Foundations supporting these reforms included the Gates Foundation, the Broad Foundation, and the foundation intimately involved in pushing the federal government to fund the first nationwide standardized test in the 1960s—the Carnegie Corporation.[38] The Gates Foundation alone poured $200 million into building support for Common Core across the political spectrum, and the standards were instituted in many states without a single vote by an elected lawmaker.[39]

The Common Core standards movement also has echoes of racial democracy ideology, as advocates have framed it as a way to ensure racial equity.[40] Reform advocates like Bill Gates have argued that ensuring that all schools were holding students to the same high standards and punishing those schools and teachers that failed to improve student scores would not only improve education but would help combat poverty and racial disparity. As Gates remarked in a speech before the National Urban League, "let's end the myth that we have to solve poverty before we improve education. I say it's more the other way around: Improving education is the best way to solve poverty."[41] And as with the reforms in the 1970s, these new efforts promise new opportunity for private profit through educational reform.[42]

Recent federal education policy efforts have also been at the forefront of the twin developments of rapid expansion of charter schools and the closings of traditional public schools. The NCLB specifically named transfer to charter school as one of the school choice options that must be given to children in low-performing schools. The promotion of charter schools as a turnaround strategy continued under RTT, which made elimination of state barriers to charter school expansion a significant factor in determining which states won grants.[43] Much like the OEO's encouragement of states to change their laws to allow public education funds to flow to private providers in the 1970s, the federal government again pushed states to change laws to expand "choice" in education. Since the start of RTT, fifteen states have lifted caps on charter school growth and one state enacted its first charter law.[44]

The rapid growth of charter schools shows little sign of slowing down. In September 2015, the U.S. Department of Education announced that it would give $157 million to expand charter schools nationally, and the passage of the ESSA in 2015 channeled even more federal funds to charter expansion.[45] The massive federal subsidies of charter schools continued unabated during the Trump administration, with two of the nation's largest charter networks—KIPP and IDEA—getting federal expansion grants totaling more than $200 million in 2019 alone.[46] Since 1995, the federal government has given charter schools nearly $4 billion for opening and operating expenses, and these charter schools serve disproportionately poor and non-white students.[47] Much like the proponents of alternatives to public schools in the 1960s and 1970s before them, charter advocates today position themselves as taking on an unresponsive public school monopoly in order to improve education for disadvantaged students.[48]

As charter schools expand, the requirements that states intervene in poor-performing schools has pushed a number of states and local school districts to pursue a strategy of mass school closure. Spurred by these federal requirements, cities such as Chicago, Philadelphia, Detroit, and Columbus have aggressively closed low-performing schools as a central aspect of their reform agendas. The closure of traditional public schools often goes hand in hand with the expansion of charter schools. In a recent twelve-city study, the Pew Charitable Trust found that more than 40 percent of closed school buildings were ultimately reopened as charter schools.[49] The shift toward charters is also evident in enrollment numbers. In Chicago, between 2005 and 2013 enrollment in traditional public schools fell by 14 percent while charter school enrollment grew by 219 percent over the same period.[50]

The move toward widespread school closure and rapid expansion of charter schools is particularly concerning given growing evidence of the pernicious effects of these reform strategies. Studies have consistently shown that expansion of charter schools comes with a significant risk of increasing segregation by race, ethnicity, and income. The expansion of charter schools is also associated with increased segregation for special education and language minority students.[51] The reform strategy of school closure and charter expansion has also been tied to diminished teacher effectiveness and working conditions, increased student conflict, and a weakening of community connection to local schools.[52] There is little evidence that charter schools offer better student outcomes, even on the standardized testing metrics preferred by reform advocates.[53] And similar to the push for performance contracting in the 1970s, federal funding of charter schools has been a ripe target for fraud, with one study estimating that roughly $1.17 billion federal dollars went to charter schools that either never opened, or closed within a few years of opening.[54] The expansion of charter schools has provided the opportunity for the private sector to reap massive profits even as hundreds of traditional schools are closed down in part due to lack of funds.

Despite growing evidence of the negative consequences, the bipartisan punitive education reform agenda has proceeded full speed ahead at the federal level. The continued popularity of these reforms among federal policy makers can be explained by the dominance of the liberal incorporationist ideology. Both parties continue to articulate an educational vision that couples calls for equal educational opportunity for all with an understanding that the central purpose of education is providing individuals with the skills needed to successfully compete in the existing labor market. Republicans and Democrats continue to agree that primary and secondary education is key to solving the persistent problems of poverty, unemployment, and racial disparity—and there is substantial overlap in educational policy agendas of both parties. As with earlier eras, the faith in education helps funnel funds to this policy area and pushes more direct efforts to address political economic problems into the background. In a particularly egregious recent example, the director of the Ohio Department of Job and Family Services justified reallocating $500 million in federal money intended for direct relief for the poor into early education programs by arguing, "directing federal anti-poverty funds toward systemic issues, primarily education, is a better use of the money because poorer families will be more prosperous in the long term if children are better educated."[55] Beyond obscuring the political economic foundations of social problems, the liberal incorporationist order justifies the punitive reforms targeted at public schools when these problems persist.

The expansion of high-stakes testing, destabilization of the teaching force, and increasing privatization and charterization of public schools represent the latest destructive extension of the institutional and ideological commitments of the liberal incorporationist order in education. The federal government continues to rely on essentially the same institutional mechanism to induce change as it has since the 1960s, the threat of withholding compensatory funds from states failing to demonstrate objective gains in student achievement and the promotion of alternatives to public schools. The common ideological foundations explain why so many of the reforms of the current era look similar—in some cases nearly identical—to those proposed more than fifty years ago. The continued support of this reform agenda despite mounting evidence of negative consequences for vulnerable populations demonstrates the thoroughly entrenched nature of the liberal incorporationist order.

Moving Forward

Despite the dominance of the liberal incorporationist educational vision and the punitive reforms it justifies, there is growing evidence of organized efforts to push back against the education policies that have flourished under this hegemonic educational ideology. Although the ideas of the social reconstructionists and economic democrats were marginalized by the 1960s, the vision put forth by these coalitions never completely disappeared from the national discussion. Coalitions pushing against the liberal incorporationist education order and the policies it has supported have shown signs of growing mobilization in the past decade. The most prominent organized opposition to the bipartisan liberal incorporationist order has come from a number of progressive teachers' unions situated in large cities that have borne the brunt of the negative consequences of punitive education policies. Frustrated with the traditional approach of supporting the Democratic Party as the "lesser of two evils" only to see enthusiastic Democratic support for punitive reforms, progressive groups such as the Caucus of Rank and File Educators in Chicago, the Progressive Educators for Action Caucus (PEAC) in Los Angeles, and Educators for a Democratic Union (EDU) in San Francisco have successfully pushed their unions toward a more combative approach to the liberal incorporationist order.[56]

Karen Lewis, a member of the Caucus of Rank and File Educators who was elected president of the Chicago Teachers Union (CTU) in 2010, was one of the most visible national leaders of teacher-led efforts to combat the bipartisan punitive reform consensus. In her 2010 election victory speech, Lewis announced, "Today marks the beginning of the end of scapegoating educators for all the social ills that our children, families and schools struggle against every day."[57] Lewis outlined an educational vision that placed the CTU in clear opposition to the liberal incorporationist ideology and harkened back to the ideas of the economic democrats and social reconstructionists. Lewis called for greater teacher autonomy,[58] substantial reduction in the use of testing,[59] and renewed teacher activism outside the classroom.[60] In a reflection of the new activist stance, Lewis led the CTU on a strike in 2012 and won substantial concessions from Mayor Rahm Emanuel. Notably, the CTU halted the implementation of merit pay, limited the use of student standardized test scores in teacher evaluations, stopped the city's plan to increase class sizes, and won a pay raise.[61]

In language sounding distinctly similar to the social reconstructionists of the 1930s, Lewis and the CTU have expanded their political agenda and suggested a role for teachers as agents of political change. In 2015, Lewis gave a speech drawing attention to the limited and politically problematic nature of the liberal incorporationist educational vision, arguing that "they want 'Stepford Teachers' and 'Children of the Corn'—kids who are compliant and will not challenge authority or the system on eradicating inequality, poverty, and injustice."[62] In the same speech, Lewis announced her endorsement of a number of progressive challengers to Democratic City Council members, including a number of teachers from the ranks of the CTU. The CTU emphasized its commitment to expand the involvement of teachers in bringing about social change through the 2015 release of *A Just Chicago: Fighting for the City Our Students Deserve*, a report detailing an expansive political agenda. In addition to calling for greater and more equitable funding of schools, the CTU pointed to the need to take on broader economic issues and called for expansive reforms including "increas[ing] the numbers of affordable and homeless housing units built across the city"[63] and "guarantee[d] jobs that pay a living wage and provide health insurance for families of Chicago's students."[64] The report channels the analytical outlook of both the economic democrats and social reconstructionists by framing the existing economic and social order as fundamentally unfair and positioning teachers as powerful agents in the fight for a just future.[65]

The CTU strike was followed several years later by remarkable displays of teacher power in surprising places. In a show of exceptional political solidarity in 2018, teachers in West Virginia, Oklahoma, and Arizona coordinated statewide multiday work stoppages that won significant concessions from oppositional state lawmakers. In addition to winning hundreds of millions of dollars of new school funding, these teachers won expansive victories for working people more broadly. In West Virginia, the striking teachers won a 5 percent pay raise for *all* public employees in the state.[66] In Oklahoma, teachers won the first tax increase in the state in twenty-eight years, with millions of dollars in support for crumbling school infrastructure and support staff.[67] In Arizona, teachers stopped cuts to Medicaid and a proposed tax cut.[68] Across these states, fights that originated in demands for greater funding of education raised more radical questions about the distribution of wealth and power in this country.[69] The thousands of workers that led these fights embodied the notion central to earlier education radicals that teachers could be the central component of broad social transformation.

Within the past few years, the efforts of activist teachers' unions to combat punitive education reform has been accompanied by a number of community groups that have become increasingly critical of the liberal incorporationist education order. Groups such as Parents United for Public Education in Philadelphia have organized to push back against the privatization, rapid charterization, and widespread school closings that have served as the backbone of the school reform efforts in Philadelphia for the last fifteen years. Helen Gym, a cofounder of Parents United for Public Education who had criticized the reform approach as a "brand of disaster capitalism," won a seat on the Philadelphia City Council in 2015, largely on a platform of halting punitive education reforms.[70] Additionally, in a remarkable turn, the NAACP came out forcefully against the public funding of private charter schools in 2014 and two years later called for a complete moratorium on charter school expansion.[71]

In an effort to resist punitive reform policies, Journey for Justice (J4J), an alliance of thirty-six community-based organizations from twenty-one different cities, released a report entitled *Death By a Thousand Cuts: Racism, School*

Closures, and Public School Sabotage. This report explicitly criticized President Obama, Secretary Duncan, Bill Gates, Michelle Rhee, and others of promoting educational reforms that attempted to "driv[e] a wedge between low-income communities of color and the teachers that serve their schools," reducing schools to "fungible businesses,"[72] and ultimately perpetuating a social order in which "wealth, ideology, and political opportunism have been allowed to triumph over the interests and well-being of our communities."[73] This coalescing of groups and unions from cities throughout the country not only underscores the degree to which the dominance of the liberal incorporationist ideology at the federal level has produced problems for schools across the nation but has also generated pushback.

Teachers have also been central to fighting against the most punitive aspects of reform in Washington, D.C.—outlined at the beginning of this book. The mayor of Washington, D.C., Adrian Fenty, had to face voters in 2010 after he and his chosen education chancellor Michelle Rhee oversaw the firings of more than 1,000 teachers, the closure of twenty-seven schools, and a radical restructuring of D.C. schools. Fenty ultimately lost his reelection bid in an election that was largely a referendum on Rhee's education reform agenda.[74] The Washington Teachers' Union, the same union that ultimately defeated Kenneth Clark's push for frequent standardized testing and tying teacher pay to student test score, endorsed Fenty's opponent and was central to his defeat.[75] Rhee resigned shortly after Fenty's ouster, a substantial victory for opponents of punitive education reform. However, in an indication of how difficult the liberal incorporationist education order will be to dislodge, Michelle Rhee did not disappear from the education scene. With the help of millions of dollars from the Broad and Walton Foundations and other billionaire funders, Rhee started StudentsFirst, an organization dedicated to school vouchers and the elimination of teacher tenure through pouring money into local state house and school board races.[76]

Teacher and community resistance to the liberal incorporationist understanding of education and the policies it produces is a promising development. However, these developments have yet to meaningfully shift federal education policy from the liberal incorporationist ideology that motivated the first significant federal intervention in primary and secondary education policy back in 1965. At the national level, both political parties continue to broadly articulate a liberal incorporationist understanding of the function of public education, as evidenced by overwhelmingly bipartisan support of the ESSA in 2015.[77] In his remarks at the bill signing, President Obama noted the fundamental ideological continuity of the new bill with earlier federal efforts, stating, "The goals of No Child Left Behind, the predecessor of this law, were the right one: High Standards. Accountability. Closing the achievement gap."[78] Invoking the spirit of President Johnson, Obama proclaimed, "With this bill, we reaffirm that fundamental American ideal that every child, regardless of race, income, background, the zip code where they live, *deserves the chance to make out of their lives what they will.*"[79] Obama's remarks indicate the continued popularity of the belief that the purpose of education is limited to providing students with the tools to compete equally in the labor market.

President Obama's successor did little to indicate a fundamental break with the liberal incorporationist order. President Trump justified pouring millions of dollars into alternatives to public schools by arguing that "for decades, countless children have been trapped in failing government schools," and that "now is the is the time to fight for the forgotten child."[80] There is some hope that President Biden will push back against the excessive punitiveness of the most recent era; however, in the past he voted for NCLB, suggested an openness to performance-based pay,[81] and has claimed that education was a central to addressing racial inequality.[82] When Biden argued on the 2020 campaign trail that "the public school system in this country is in trouble. . . . The idea you can make it in the middle class and sustain yourself there with just 12 years of education is not accurate,"[83] and that more federal education spending was "one of the single best instruments and investments that we can make to address systemic inequality,"[84] the reverberations of the 1960s were clear. Although pledges to increase teacher pay, stop funding for-profit charter schools, and end high-stakes testing are welcome developments, the grandiose expectations for education remain—always threatening a punitive turn when schools don't measure up.

Moving forward, a more just education system requires a fundamental reconceptualization of the purpose of education, and of the role of the federal government. Education must be understood as something valuable beyond its ability to provide marketable skills for students. Societal ills that are fundamentally problems of political economy must no longer be laid at the doorstep of education. Efforts to address the problems that have been blamed on education require expansive federal efforts to shift profoundly unfair economic arrangements that are the real causes of unemployment, poverty, and racial disparity. Absent these fundamental shifts in ideology and political commitment, the cycle of blaming schools leading to ever more punitive reform measures is likely to continue to dominate the education landscape in the United States.

Notes

Introduction

1. Lewin, "School Chancellor Fires 241 Teachers."
2. Turque, "Foundations Reserve the Right"; Hopkinson, "Why Michelle Rhee's."
3. Osbourne, "A Tale of Two Systems."
4. Chu, "Obama and McCain Fight Over a Woman"; "How to Fix America's Schools."
5. Hopkinson, "Why Michelle Rhee's."
6. Stamm, "23 Philly Schools Slated to Close"; DiSanto, "17K Students Will Be Moved."
7. McGill, "Jindal Signs Education Reforms." Jindal was seeking to build on the extensive educational reforms that had already occurred in New Orleans. In the wake of Hurricane Katrina, the school district of New Orleans fired more than 4,300 teachers, shut down all of its traditional public schools, and transitioned to an all-charter school district. Dreilinger, "Most Katrina Laid-off Teachers." Praising these reform efforts, President Obama's secretary of education Arne Duncan proclaimed that Hurricane Katrina was "the best thing that happened to the education system of New Orleans." Anderson, "Education Secretary Duncan Calls Hurricane Katrina Good."
8. Todd-Breland, *A Political Education*, 221.
9. For example, in New Orleans, the percent of Black teachers in the district was 71 percent prior to Hurricane Katrina, but dropped to 49 percent after the implementation of education reform efforts. Barrett and Harris, "Significant Changes"; see also Todd-Breland, *A Political Education*, 225. As several examples from Washington, D.C., indicate, these mass terminations of teachers often end up firing teachers erroneously deemed poor performers. Stein, "'I've Been a Hostage for Nine Years.'"
10. Stein, "'It's Absolutely Terrible.'"
11. Burris and Bryant, "Asleep at the Wheel"; Long, "Hidden Crisis."
12. Jamison, "A Short Guide."
13. Cockerham, "We Knew Michelle Rhee."
14. Strauss, "What Michelle Rhee Has Been Up To."
15. Kalb, "St. Hope Taps Michelle Rhee." In a sign that Rhee's approach may not have changed much from her days as chancellor of Washington, D.C., schools, in 2018 students at one of the charter schools walked out in protest of dismissal of teachers, school dress codes, and other arbitrary rules. Johnson, "Sacramento High Students Hold Walk-Out." The principal of the school resigned a few days later, stating that "upper leadership does not appreciate education as a collaborative enterprise," and a "sustained history of neglect from above." Smith, Amezcua, and McGough, "Sac High Boss Resigns."
16. I use *order* here in the same sense as Karen Orren and Stephen Skowronek, meaning, "the constellation of rules, institutions, practices, and ideas that hang together over time." Orren and Skowronek, *The Search for American Political Development*, 14.

17. The centerpiece of the compensatory strategy was Title I, which accounted for more than 80 percent of total ESEA funding. Title I was a categorical grant that provided schools funding based on the concentration of low-income families. This design ensured that although Title I funds would be targeted toward the poor, funding would also be widely distributed, with more than 94 percent of school districts ultimately receiving Title I money. Superfine, *Equality in Educational Law and Policy*, 51.

18. My conceptualization of punitive governmentality is similar to that of Soss, Fording, and Schram in their book tracing the development of what they understand as the disciplinary regime of neoliberal paternalism. They argue that in the realm of "poverty governance," policy makers have embraced and redirected social programs for the poor "around a disciplinary agenda that emphasizes self-mastery, wage work, and uses of state authority to cultivate market relations." Soss, Fording, and Schram, *Disciplining the Poor*, 6. See also Wacquant, *Punishing the Poor*; Katz, *The Undeserving Poor*; and Piven and Cloward, *Regulating the Poor*.

19. Berliner, "Rational Responses to High Stakes Testing"; Crocco and Costigan, "The Narrowing of Curriculum"; Amrein and Berliner, "An Analysis of Some Unintended and Negative Consequences"; Madaus and Russell, "Paradoxes of High-Stakes Testing"; Smith, Miller-Kahn, Heinecke, and Jarvis, *Political Spectacle*; Darling-Hammond, "Race, Inequality and Educational Accountability."

20. Booher-Jennings, "Below the Bubble"; McNeil, *Contradictions of School Reform*; Madaus, *The Influence of Testing*; Amrein and Berliner, "An Analysis of Some Unintended and Negative Consequences."

21. Heilig and Darling-Hammond, "Accountability Texas-Style"; Amrein and Berliner, "An Analysis of Some Unintended and Negative Consequences"; Booher-Jennings, "Below the Bubble."

22. Mehrens, "Consequences of Assessment"; Sheldon and Biddle, "Standards, Accountability, and School Reform"; Goldstein, *The Teacher Wars*; Crocco and Costigan, "The Narrowing of Curriculum and Pedagogy"; Gerson, "The Neoliberal Agenda."

23. Orfield and Wald, "Testing, Testing"; McNeil, "Faking Equity"; Madaus and Russell, "Paradoxes of High-Stakes Testing"; Heilig and Darling-Hammond, "Accountability Texas-Style"; Darling-Hammond, "Race, Inequality and Educational Accountability"; Smith, Miller-Kahn, Heinecke, and Jarvis, *Political Spectacle*.

24. Au, *Unequal by Design*; Darling-Hammond, "Race, Inequality and Educational Accountability"; Smith, Miller-Kahn, Heinecke, and Jarvis, *Political Spectacle*; McNeil, *Contradictions of School Reform*.

25. Ben-Porath, "Deferring Virtue"; Molnar, *School Commercialism*; Fabricant and Fine, *Charter Schools and the Corporate Makeover*.

26. See Cuban, *The Blackboard and the Bottom Line*; Lipman, *The New Political Economy of Urban Education*; Weiner, *The Future of Our Schools*.

27. Winfield, "Resuscitating Bad Science," 154. For a similar periodization, see Watkins, "The New Social Order"; Berliner and Biddle, *The Manufactured Crisis*; Smith, Miller-Kahn, Heinecke, and Jarvis, *Political Spectacle*; Robinson and Lugg, "The Role of the Religious Right"; Cohen and Moffitt, *The Ordeal of Equality*.

28. See Robinson and Lugg, "The Role of the Religious Right"; Cuban, *The Blackboard and Bottom Line*; and Apple, *Educating the "Right" Way*.

29. See Kristen L. Buras, *Rightist Multiculturalism*; Apple, *Educating the "Right" Way*; and Berliner and Biddle, *The Manufactured Crisis*.

30. Saltman, *Capitalizing on Disaster*; Saltman, *The Failure of Corporate School Reform*; Smith, Miller-Kahn, Heinecke, and Jarvis, *Political Spectacle*; Lipman, *The New Political Economy*; Watkins, "The New Social Order"; Gerson, "The Neoliberal Agenda"; Ravitch, *Reign of Error*; Henig, "Education Policy from 1980 to the Present; Molnar, *School Commercialism*; Boyles, *American Education and Corporations*.

31. Debray, *Politics, Ideology, and Education*; Ravitch, *Reign of Error*; Fabricant and Fine, *Charter Schools and the Corporate Makeover*.

32. Rhodes, *An Education in Politics*; Pedroni, *Market Movements*; Apple and Pedroni, "Conservative Alliance Building"; Henig, "Education Policy from 1980 to the Present."

33. Watkins, "The New Social Order," 10. See also Hess and McGuinn, "Seeking the Mantle of Opportunity"; and Debray, *Politics, Ideology, and Education*, 150.

34. For example, political scientists Patrick McGuinn, Paul Manna, and Jesse Rhodes characterize the early federal education state established in the 1960s as an equity regime focused on targeting funds to disadvantaged students. These accounts map a distinct shift in the 1980s from a progressive focus on educational equality to policies promoting excellence through standards and accountability. See Manna, *School's In*; McGuinn, *No Child Left Behind*; Rhodes, *An Education in Politics*; and Petrovich and Wells, *Bringing Equity Back*, 3.

35. This is not to say that there is no difference between the 1960s and 1980s: there are important institutional and coalitional differences. However, the ideological understanding of the purpose of education as the cure to economic hardship remained largely consistent throughout the time period.

36. Katznelson, "Was the Great Society a Lost Opportunity?" See also Chen, *The Fifth Freedom*.

37. Marie Gottschalk demonstrates how the political context and strategic decisions in the 1940s and 1950s tied the U.S. labor movement to support of job-based health benefits and the private welfare state model, a political settlement that proved to be a substantial barrier to the development of universal insurance over the long run. Gottschalk, *The Shadow Welfare State*. Southern Democrats and conservative Republicans turned to a "delegated welfare state" model of private, state, and local operation as a means of state-building in the post–World War II context that was no longer supportive of a broad expansion of the federal welfare state. Although this was politically expedient in the 1960s, this institutional structure hampered effectiveness and exposed the program to political attacks and market-based reforms as the political environment shifted. Morgan and Campbell, *The Delegated Welfare State*. Detailing the transition from welfare to workfare, Eva Bertram demonstrates that the foundations of the punitive workfare state were laid in the 1960s by powerful Southern Democrats in Congress. Bertram, *The Workfare State*. Margaret Weir argues that the possibility for robust public employment programs was undercut by the War on Poverty, which constructed policies based on an understanding that attributed poverty to individual attributes rather than larger structural forces. Weir, *Politics and Jobs*.

38. In his examination of New Deal social welfare policy, Robert Lieberman argues that "race inhibited the development of a strong, unitary, centralized welfare state in the United States," as the desire to maintain racial hierarchies that drove policy makers to develop decentralized, non-contributory social welfare programs designed to push Black people to the margins of the

welfare state. Lieberman, *Shifting the Color Line*, 6. Similarly, Judith Russell argues "institutional racism" shifted the approach of the War on Poverty to a service delivery model of largely ineffectual programs, despite the overwhelming preference of Black leaders that the federal government focus on jobs and employment issues. Russell suggests the refusal of federal officials to acknowledge the demands of the Black community limited the programs that emerged from the Great Society. Russell, *Economics, Bureaucracy, and Race*. In her study of the federal penal state, Naomi Murakawa demonstrates how the state-building activities of racial liberals in the 1940s through 1960s combined with conservative hard-liners to build a "fairer" penal system, but one that was capable of locking up significantly more citizens, especially poorer non-white citizens. Murakawa, *The First Civil Right*. Finally, Lani Guinier has noted that the legal strategy of the racial liberals pursuing desegregation through the courts in the 1950s limited the direction of subsequent social policy by reframing the structural origins of racism as a problem of individual psychology. Guinier, "From Racial Liberalism to Racial Literacy," 61.

39. Several scholars have demonstrated how the embrace of particular racial ideologies had important consequences for the political demands of Black Americans. In his study tracing the marginalization of class-based accounts of racial oppression among prominent Black intellectuals in the 1920s through the 1940s, historian Jonathan Holloway demonstrates the way in which "people have used 'race' to constrain the possibilities of radical politics and social science thinking." Holloway, *Confronting the Veil*, 17. Touré Reed demonstrates how the Urban League's embrace of assimilationist theories emerging from the social sciences led to a racial uplift agenda that focused on changing individual behavior rather than structural transformation as the best means of addressing racial and economic inequality. Reed, *Not Alms but Opportunity*. Similarly, historian Leah Gordon demonstrates how the post–World War II retreat from New Deal economic liberalism and the rise in antidiscrimination and anti-prejudice policies were facilitated by federal and foundation support of social science research that identified prejudice and attitudes, rather than labor exploitation and class struggle, as the source of racial oppression. Gordon, *From Power to Prejudice*. Adolph Reed, Robert Korstad, Nelson Lichtenstein, and Risa Goluboff have shown how these developments in the understanding of race facilitated a shift in Black political demands from a focus on union organizing and redistributive economic demands in the 1930s and 1940s to a politics centered on legal administrative demands for equal inclusion into existing social structures by the 1960s. Reed, *Stirrings in the Jug*; Korstad and Lichtenstein, "Opportunities Found and Lost"; and Goluboff, *The Lost Promise of Civil Rights*. In his examination of housing policy in Chicago, Preston Smith demonstrates how the post–World War II adoption of "racial liberalism" by Black elites legitimized their claim to leadership and helped consolidate a liberal politics that limited political demands to "equal treatment in the marketplace." Smith, *Racial Democracy and the Black Metropolis*, 5. Smith traces the class-inflected nature of this politics, showing how Black elites targeted racial segregation reform while accepting the class-segmented housing arrangements promoted by progrowth white business and political elites. Tracking the consequences of these settlements for the current political landscape, Lester Spence examines the neoliberal turn in Black politics over the past few decades. Spence argues that the "neoliberalization of black politics" replaced political organization and mobilization with a politics "in which racial inequality is managed through black elite-promoted techniques designed to get black people to act according to market principles." Spence, "The Neoliberal Turn in Black Politics," 146.

40. Several scholars have noted the importance of analytical approaches that include both ideas and institutions in explanations of political change. Rogers Smith argues that ideas are crucial "constitutive elements" of political order, but that accounts of political development must also include the institutional focus as "ideas can produce political change only when particular, identifiable political institutions, groups, and actors advance them." Smith, "Which Comes First," 109. For scholars that take a similar view of the need to focus on both ideas and institutions, see Lieberman, "Ideas, Institutions, and Political Order"; Schmidt, "Taking Ideas and Discourse Seriously"; Weaver, *Blazing the Neoliberal Trail*; and Smith, *Political Peoplehood*, 30.

41. Counts, *Dare the Schools.*

42. Although I use slightly different terminology, my concentration on the ideological debates within Black political thought during this era largely follows the divisions identified by Preston Smith. See Smith, *Racial Democracy and the Black Metropolis.*

43. Reddick, "What Should the American Negro Reasonably Expect," 569.

44. Indeed, many of these authors openly embraced a capitalist economy as essential to protecting individual freedom.

45. See Dudziak, *Cold War Civil Rights*; and Klinkner and Smith, *The Unsteady March.*

46. See Goluboff, *The Lost Promise of Civil Rights*; Gordon, *From Power to Prejudice*; and Guinier, "From Racial Liberalism to Racial Literacy."

47. See Storrs, *The Second Red Scare*; Schrecker, *Many Are the Crimes*; and Hartman, *Education and the Cold War.*

48. See Collins, *The Business Response*; Katz, *The Undeserving Poor*; Mucciaroni, *The Political Failure*; and Weir, *Politics and Jobs.*

49. Not everyone abandoned the economic democracy position. Several authors and public servants continued to maintain this position well into the 1960s. For example, Willard Wirtz, President Lyndon Johnson's secretary of labor; Leon Keyserling, former head of the Council of Economic Advisors under President Harry Truman; and Bayard Rustin, a lead organizer of the 1963 March on Washington for Jobs and Freedom, offered spirited but unsuccessful advocacy of full employment and aggressive public job creation as the most effective poverty program during Johnson's administration. The shifting political context and shifting positions of many previous supporters meant that these holdouts were increasingly marginalized and their effect on federal education policy was minimal. As labor historian Judith Stein argues more generally, the economic crises of the 1970s saw the last gasps of those advocating for broad structural reform, as the federal government turned to supply-side solutions instead. See Stein, *Pivotal Decade*; Russell, *Economics, Bureaucracy, and Race*; Keyserling, "Economic Progress and the Great Society"; and Rustin, "From Protest to Politics."

50. U.S. Senate Committee on Labor and Public Welfare, *Report on Elementary and Secondary Education Act of 1965*, 3.

51. See Clark, *Dark Ghetto*; Harlem Youth Opportunities Unlimited, *Youth in the Ghetto*; and Halperin, "ESEA Ten Years Later."

52. Blanc, *Red State Revolt.*

Chapter One

1. Puzzanghera, "A Decade After."
2. Obama, "Remarks by the President on Education Reform."

3. Obama, "Remarks by the President on Education Reform."

4. Obama, "Remarks by the President on Education Reform."

5. The conservative Heritage Foundation issued a report on education reform that argued that the nation's ability to meet "challenges will depend on our economic strength, our ability to innovate, and our ability to produce highly skilled workers. And all of these will depend, in turn, on how well we educate our children." Lips, Marshall, and Burke, "A Parent's Guide to Education Reform," 11. One of the most recent Republican Party platforms claimed that education was the surest means of "maintaining America's preeminence" in the global economy. Republican National Convention, "Platform of the Republican Party, 2012."

6. For example, the 2011 annual report from the National Association for the Advancement of Colored People (NAACP) claimed, "education is the great leveler; it allows the recipient to overcome any circumstances of birth." NAACP, "Affirming America's Promise," 16. The 2012 Democratic Party platform argues that education is "the surest path to the middle class" for individuals, and the NEA recently promised to help "fulfill the purpose" of education by "prepar[ing] all students to thrive in college, careers, and life." Democratic National Convention, "Platform of the Democratic Party, 2012"; National Education Association, "ESEA Reauthorization."

7. Indeed, unequal rewards based on educational merit is a central aspect of the existing system.

8. Several scholars have noted a similar general division within the progressive education movement, but disagree about the terms used to describe the different coalitions. Stephen Tomlinson refers to the division of conservative and liberal visions, which is similar to the liberal progressive and conservative progressive terminology used by Robert L. Church and Michael W. Sedlak. Both David Tyack and David Labaree use the terms *administrative* and *pedagogical progressives* to draw a similar distinction. My use of social efficiency and social reconstructionist labels is closest to Herbert Kliebard's, who actually distinguishes three groups, social reconstructionists, social efficiency, and child-centered progressives. For the time period this chapter examines, the terms *social reconstructionist* and *social efficiency* most clearly capture the most significant division of interest. Church and Sedlak, *Education in the United States*; Kliebard, *The Struggle for the American Curriculum*; Labaree, "The Ed School's Romance," 92–100; Tomlinson, "Edward Lee Thorndike and John Dewey"; and Tyack, *The One Best System*. See also Lagemann, "The Plural Worlds of Educational Research."

9. Social reconstructionism traces many of its roots to romanticism and the child-centered pedagogy of John Dewey's early writings that appeared well before the Great Depression. However, social reconstructionism, and its theorized relationship between education, existing institutions, and political change was a distinctly post-1929 phenomena. This examination of these coalitions builds off earlier scholarship that has traced how broader political visions shape educational values, and, in turn, educational policy. The revisionist turn in the history of education scholarship positioned schools largely as agents of social control that help secure economic and political stability over a culturally heterogenous and large working-class population. See Bowles and Gintis, *Schooling in Capitalist America*; Katz, *The Irony of Early School Reform*; Spring, *The Sorting Machine*; Nasaw, *Schooled to Order*; Karier, Violas, and Spring, *Roots of Crisis*; and Kozol, *Savage Inequalities*. More recently, scholars employing critical race theory have made similar arguments surrounding

the connection between schools and the criminal justice system, arguing that schools are intentionally designed to funnel some students into prisons. See Stovall, "Schools Suck, But They're Supposed To"; Allen and White-Smith, "Just as Bad as Prisons"; Heitzeg, "Education or Incarceration"; Dancy, (Un)doing Hegemony in Education"; and Fasching-Varner, Mitchell, Martin, and Bennett-Haron, "Beyond School-to-Prison Pipeline." Contrarily, Ravitch pushed back against the notion from the revisionist schools and suggested that federal reforms after World War II meant that disorder in schools was a more significant problem than too much order. See Diane Ravitch, *The Revisionists Revised*; and Diane Ravitch, *The Troubled Crusade*. Alternatively, others have positioned schools—if properly ordered—as the site of the great hope of economic advancement. See Goldin and Katz, *The Race Between Education and Technology*; Klein, *Lessons of Hope*; Rhee, *Radical: Fighting to Put Students First*; Becker and Chiswick, "Education and the Distribution of Earnings"; U.S. National Commission on Excellence in Education, *A Nation at Risk*; Kristof, "Democrats and Schools"; Betts and Loveless, *Getting Choice Right*. As chapter 2 examines in more depth, others have pointed to education as the site of potential racial uplift and liberation. See Herbert, "Education, Education, Education." Hochschild and Scovronick synthesize these traditions and argue that education reform is spurred by an unresolvable tension between desire for an equitable starting point for all children and desire to pass advantage on to one's own children, which is the fundamental paradox of schooling in America. Hochschild and Scovronick, *The American Dream and the Public Schools*. As Katzenelson and Weir have convincingly argued that the tendency for schools to be sites of control or of liberation is historically contingent—with the dominance of one tendency or the other dependent on the particular economic and political forces of a given point in time. Katznelson and Weir, *Schooling for All*. These perspectives point to the value of examining educational visions and policies in their particular historical and material moments.

10. Significantly, these discussions and debates about education have the potential to shape, shift, or stunt the developments in other social and economic policy arenas. In her masterful account of the development of the education state in the early twentieth century, Tracy Steffes shows how public schooling became the policy area of choice at the state and local level to address the consequences of industrialization and the tensions that arose between democracy and capitalism. As European countries sought to address these conflicts through redistributive welfare states, Americans turned to schools, and in doing so saddled them with unrealistic expectations and stunted other areas of the American welfare state. Steffes, *School, Society, and State*. See also Cohen, "Reconsidering Schools and the American Welfare State"; Katz, *Reconstructing American Education*; and Cremin, *The Transformation of the School*. Nancy Beadie similarly focuses on this relationship in an earlier historical period, examining the role of schools in the political and economic integration of the liberal state during the market revolution and capitalist transition of the early American republic. Beadie, *Education and the Creation of Capital*. See also Kaestle, *Pillars of the Republic*. As this historical scholarship makes clear, understanding the ideological debates about education and the political economy can offer significant insights into education policy—but also the broader structure of the welfare state itself. Debates within education circles inevitably reflected—and influenced—the broader debates about the structure of the welfare state, the requirements of democracy, and notions of equality. The perspective advanced here is most similar to a body of scholarship that has focused on the notion that the faith in

schools as solvers of social ills is misplaced and has harmful consequences. As Tyack and Cuban have noted, the American faith in schools quickly made teachers into nearly universal scapegoats. Tyack and Cuban, *Tinkering Toward Utopia*. Several scholars have since followed up on the consequences of "educationalizing" social problems, for both the public education system and its employees, and social policy more broadly. See Labaree, "The Winning Ways of a Losing Strategy"; Kantor and Lowe, "From New Deal to No Deal"; Kantor and Brenzel, "Urban Education and the Truly Disadvantaged"; Grubb and Lazerson, *The Education Gospel*; Kantor and Lowe, "The Price of Human Capital,"; Labaree, *Someone Has to Fail*; and Marsh, *Class Dismissed*. For additional scholarship that analyzes education as part of the broader welfare state, see Kantor and Lowe, "Educationalizing the Welfare State"; Katz, "Public Education as Welfare"; Garfinkle, Rainwater, and Smeeding, *Wealth and Welfare States*; and Ansell, *From the Ballot to the Blackboard*.

11. Smith, "Ideas and the Spiral of Politics."

12. Laats, *The Other School Reformers*, 13–23.

13. Mirel, "Old Educational Ideas, New American Schools." See also Fallace, *Race and the Origins of Progressive Education*, 3.

14. Labaree, "The Ed School's Romance," 93.

15. Taylor, *The Principles of Scientific Management*.

16. Ohles, *Biographical Dictionary of American Educators*, 143–44.

17. Bobbitt, "The Supervision of City Schools," 12.

18. Bobbitt, 50.

19. Bobbitt, 14, 43.

20. Thorndike and Courtis, "The Nature, Purposes, and General Methods," 16.

21. Bobbitt, "The Supervision of City Schools," 34.

22. Bobbitt, 36.

23. Bobbitt, 26.

24. Bobbitt, 26.

25. Bobbitt also believed that the measurement of students and the differentiation of standards was an important aspect of holding teachers and principals accountable, particularly for schools serving disadvantaged areas. Bobbitt argued that once differentiated standards were developed and students assigned to their appropriate tracks, teachers and principals could no longer "hide behind the plea that he has an inferior social class in his school, and therefore, high performance should not be expected of him or his teachers." Bobbitt, "The Supervision of City Schools," 29.

26. Thorndike, "The Distribution of Education," 343, 345.

27. Bobbitt, "The Supervision of City Schools," 23.

28. Bobbitt, 52.

29. Bobbitt, 89, emphasis added.

30. Tomlinson, "Edward Lee Thorndike and John Dewey," 367.

31. Bobbitt, "The Supervision of City Schools," 46, 73.

32. Bobbitt, 28. This was a clear reference to, and argument against, teacher tenure, which Bobbitt viewed as inefficient and inappropriate for a well-managed educational system.

33. Bobbitt, "The Supervision of City Schools," 45–47.

34. Labaree, "The Ed School's Romance," 95; Karier, "Testing for Order and Control," 158–61; Callahan, *Education and the Cult of Efficiency*.

35. Cubberley, *Public School Administration*, 338.

36. Carson, "Army Alpha, Army Brass." See also Yoakum and Yerkes, *Army Mental Tests*; and Goddard, *Human Efficiency*.

37. Goddard, *Human Efficiency*, 28. Another reason that social efficiency progressives and other testing advocates dominated the World War I landscape was due to the widespread repression and elimination of the influence of radical populists and socialists during the First Red Scare. The general demoralized state of the American left meant that it provided little pushback to the efforts of the social efficiency progressives during and immediately after the war effort. See Karier, "Testing for Order," 158; Cremin, "John Dewey and the Progressive-Education Movement," 164.

38. Yoakum and Yerkes, *Army Mental Tests*, 191.

39. Yerkes, "News Items and Communications," 321.

40. Thorndike, "Scales and Tests," 395, emphasis added.

41. Goddard, *Human Efficiency*, 116.

42. Goddard, 48.

43. See Goddard, "The Bearing of Heredity"; Goddard, "A Scientific Program"; Yoakum and Yerkes, *Army Mental Tests*, 191–93; and Thorndike, "The Distribution of Education."

44. Thorndike, "Intelligence and Its Uses," 234.

45. Thorndike, "Scales and Tests," 396.

46. Goddard, "The Bearing of Heredity," 492.

47. Thorndike, "The Goal of the Social Effort," 166.

48. Thorndike, "Racial Inequalities," 134.

49. Thorndike, 133.

50. Thorndike, "Intelligence and Its Uses," 233. According to the hereditarians, the reverse was also true. Goddard argued that the actions of criminals, misdemeanants, delinquents, and other antisocial groups could be attributed to low levels of intelligence. Goddard, *Human Efficiency*, 72.

51. Thorndike, "Intelligence and Its Uses," 232; see also Goddard, "A Scientific Program," 264.

52. Yoakum and Yerkes, *Army Mental Tests*; Goddard, *Human Efficiency*; Goddard, "A Scientific Program"; Snedden, "Seeking Realistic Objectives," 455–59.

53. Goddard, "A Scientific Program," 264.

54. Thorndike, "Racial Inequalities," 134.

55. Thorndike, 137.

56. Goddard, "A Scientific Program," 257, 259. Goddard also praised the benefits of eugenics, a common position among hereditarians and many social efficiency progressives. In addition to strong advocacy of sterilization, Goddard claimed that those with lower-grade intelligence were social liabilities, and that the most rational and efficient approach would be to "put out of existence" those individuals with low grade intelligence. Goddard, "A Scientific Program," 259; see also Goddard, *Human Efficiency*.

57. See Thorndike, "The Distribution of Education"; Goddard, *Human Efficiency*; Goddard, "A Scientific Program"; and Snedden, "Seeking Realistic Objectives."

58. Goddard, *Human Efficiency*, 96. According to Goddard, the tendency of those with low levels of intelligence to seek and follow the advice of those with high levels of intelligence was a law of human nature. Goddard, *Human Efficiency*, 97. And, of course, Goddard did

not believe that democracy required the participation of all citizens. He advocated for intelligence-based restrictions to the rights of citizenship, arguing "while we all believe in democracy, we may nevertheless admit that we have been too free with the franchise and it would seem a self-evident fact that the feeble-minded should not be allowed to take part in civic affairs; should not be allowed to vote." Goddard, *Human Efficiency*, 99.

59. Goddard, *Human Efficiency*, 99.

60. Goddard, 126–27.

61. Thorndike, "Intelligence and Its Uses," 235.

62. Thorndike, 235.

63. Thorndike, 235.

64. Indeed, Thorndike pointed to the superior intelligences of the European monarchical families as an explanation for how they had gained and maintained power.

65. Goddard, *Human Efficiency*, 101. After criticizing the arguments of those advocating for better housing, Goddard dismissed economic redistribution, stating, "As for the equal distribution of the wealth of the world that is equally absurd."

66. Goddard, "Anniversary Address," 59. Goddard was not alone in blaming those suffering the worst effects of the Depression for their own situations. In a remarkable 1934 essay in *Scientific American*, Secretary of Agriculture Henry Wallace criticized the laissez-faire political orientation of scientists that had resulted in the tendency to turn "loose upon the world new productive power without regard to the social implications." Wallace argued that the scientific efficiency reforms and new productive technologies not only had contributed to increased production but also substantial unemployment, which was a particularly pressing concern in the Depression. Wallace, "The Scientist in an Unscientific Society," 287. Two months after the Wallace article was published, biologist Charles Davenport, who worked closely with Yerkes, Thorndike, and Goddard at the Eugenics Records Office, responded to Wallace. Davenport blamed the economic hardships that many were facing on the fact that many individuals had grown too soft during prosperous times and were now unwilling to work in positions that did not pay as well. Appearing to completely miss the implications of the collapse of the labor market, Davenport's main suggestion for the improvement of economic conditions was to note that "it would be better if every person with normal mentality had two or more occupations" and also to cut down on "extravagance in governance" by reducing taxes. Davenport, "Science Replies to Secretary Wallace," 77–78.

67. Thorndike, "The Goal of the Social Effort," 165–66. Thorndike echoed this sentiment two years later in an article about the consequences of economic disparity in city life, claiming "parity for parity's sake is a false god. There may conceivably be a magic potency in economic equality which would show itself in certain sorts of civilization and in our cities if life were fundamentally different from what it is. It does not show itself in the facts for our cities." Thorndike, "The Influence of Disparity," 35.

68. Thorndike, "The Goal of the Social Effort," 166. Thorndike reiterated this claim a few pages later, warning that "lacking omniscience, we should experiment very carefully with the redistribution of wealth, concerning ourselves chiefly with increasing it." Thorndike, "The Goal of the Social Effort," 168. Thorndike's argument that the central focus should be put on growing the broader economy rather than redistribution as a response to the terrible conditions facing the working class is substantively similar to the argument of growth liberalism.

69. Thorndike, "The Goal of the Social Effort," 168.

70. Bowers, *The Progressive Educator and the Depression*, 15.

71. Counts, *Dare the Schools*, 33.

72. Counts, 34–35.

73. Counts, 26–27.

74. Counts, 47.

75. Counts, 46.

76. Counts, 54.

77. Counts, 28.

78. Counts, 24.

79. Counts, 37.

80. Counts, 6.

81. Counts, 54.

82. Counts, 15.

83. Counts, 28.

84. Counts, 19.

85. Lagemann, *An Elusive Science*, 110–11. Kilpatrick's article "The Project Method" was turned into a pamphlet which sold more than 60,000 copies. Also, in his long tenure as a professor of education at Teachers College, Kilpatrick lectured to more than 35,000 students, a major source for the dissemination of his ideas about education.

86. Lagemann, *An Elusive Science*, 127.

87. Rugg, "Social Reconstruction Through Education," 11.

88. Rugg, 13.

89. Rugg, 13–15.

90. As quoted in Bowers, *The Progressive Educator*, 23.

91. Moore, "Applying Ethics to Economics," 158–59.

92. Moore, 158–59.

93. Donovan, "Teacher Training for the New Age," 96.

94. Donovan, 100.

95. Kilpatrick, "Speech Before Annual Meeting," 58.

96. American Historical Association, *Conclusions and Recommendations*, 1

97. American Historical Association, 16.

98. American Historical Association, 30, emphasis added.

99. American Historical Association, 35.

100. American Historical Association, 46.

101. This is not to say that the NEA explicitly endorsed the social reconstructionist position; it did not. In fact, the annual conventions also often had speeches from representatives of the American Legion and Daughters of the American Revolution, two groups who would grow to be some of the most virulent critics of leftist influence in education. The point, rather, is that there was time in which the social reconstructionist vision of the purpose of education was viewed as a serious and viable alternative path of reform.

102. Bowers, *The Progressive Educator*, 38–39.

103. Bowers, 44, 96.

104. Kilpatrick, "Launching *The Social Frontier*," 2.

105. The cover of the first journal carried a quote from the previously cited AHA report on social studies about the transition to the age of collectivism.

106. Editorial Board, "Orientation," 4.

107. John Dewey had a standing column in every issue for many years.

108. "The assumption is—or was—that we are living in a free economic society in which every individual has an equal chance to exercise his initiative and his other abilities, and that the legal and political order is designed and calculated to further this equal liberty on the part of all individuals. No grosser myth ever received general currency." Dewey, "Can Education Share in Social Reconstruction?" 11.

109. "The plea that teachers must passively accommodate themselves to existing social conditions is but one way—and a cowardly way—of making a choice in favor of the old and the chaotic." Dewey, "Can Education Share in Social Reconstruction?" 12.

110. Dewey, "Can Education Share in Social Reconstruction?" 12.

111. For just a few examples, see Dewey, "The Teacher and His World," 7; Dewey, "The Meaning of Liberalism," 74–75; Dewey, "The Social Significance," 165–66; and Dewey, "Education and Social Change," 235–38.

112. "Editorial Comments on *The Social Frontier*," 22. Although not all of the editorial reaction to the first edition was positive, the *Social Frontier* did receive encouragement from several prominent newspapers, including the *New York World-Telegram*, which noted, "the contents of the first number are indeed gratifying," the *Portland Oregonian*, which proclaimed that if the contents of "the first issue are a fair indication of what is to come, at least the new collectivism is to have a brilliant and clear advocacy." "Editorial Comments on the Social Frontier," 22.

113. For example, the commissioner of education for Puerto Rico noted the need for reform and expressed confidence that, "*The Social Frontier* should contribute the sort of sympathetic leverage needed." Padden, "Correspondence: Prodding the Educational Worm," 34. Positive reviews also streamed in from other progressive organizations like the *Consumer Research Bulletin*, whose editor exclaimed, "I think your journal has by far the best combination of intelligence and social drive . . . in what it is talking about, of any periodical published today." Schlink, "Correspondence, 28.

114. Editorial Board, "'Class' and Social Purpose," 134–35.

115. An entire volume of the *Social Frontier* (volume 2, number 6) was dedicated to examining and advocating for the academic freedom of teachers, and a more limited role for administrators.

116. Editorial Board, "The Social Order Desired by Society," 133–34.

117. Editorial Board, 133–34.

118. Judd, "Is Contact with Logically Organized," 657. Elsewhere, Judd referred to this group as a "small cult." Judd, "The Training of Teachers," 577.

119. Judd, "New Standards for Secondary Schools," 15.

120. Judd, "Programs of Social Studies," 22.

121. Judd, "Is Contact with Logically Organized," 659.

122. Judd, "This Era of Uncertainty in Education," 357, emphasis added.

123. According to Judd and his coauthor Howard Bell, "the curriculum of these schools has not been changed to keep up with changes in the population and in vocational opportunities; it is still largely organized to prepare students for the professions." Bell and Judd, "Occupational Adjustments of Young Adults," 526. This formulation was substantially similar to that of Goddard, Thorndike, and Snedden. See also National Conference on Life Adjustment Education, *Life Adjustment Education for Every Youth*.

124. Unlike many of the social efficiency progressives, Judd did support some of the political and economic reforms of the New Deal. However, his overall educational perspective and reform proposals placed him squarely in the social efficiency camp.

125. Carr testified that "there is always going to be this ambition to rise, but I would like to point out that this so-called ambition to rise in the professions is due partly to the halo of prestige which attaches to professions and partly to the fact that the professions are, on the whole, very much better off economically." U.S. Senate Temporary National Economic Committee, *Investigation of Concentration of Economic Power*, 17181.

126. U.S. Senate Temporary National Economic Committee, Investigation of Concentration of Economic Power, 171–81.

127. Laski, "A New Education Needs a New World."

128. U.S. Senate Temporary National Economic Committee, Investigation of Concentration of Economic Power, 171–72.

129. Goddard, "The Gifted Child."

130. The most notable challenge to the ideological commitments of the social efficiency progressives in the post–World War II context was their hereditarianism. The Nazi ideology and extermination efforts had made this position politically unpalatable for much of the country. Although many social efficiency progressives dropped the strict hereditarianism of Thorndike and Goddard, the educational policies they advocated remained fundamentally similar, with more nebulous definitions of intelligence or merit replacing the earlier fixed and hereditarian definitions.

131. Lagemann, "The Plural Worlds of Educational Research," 185. Lagemann is not the only one who has noted the apparent victory of the social efficiency progressives. Although David Labaree notes that the social reconstructionist vision lingers in the way that many people talk about education, particularly those who teach in education schools, at the level of school practice the social efficiency progressive vision remains dominant. Labaree, "The Ed School's Romance."

Chapter Two

1. Bunche, "Education in Black and White," 355.

2. Bunche, 352.

3. Bunche, 358.

4. Long wrote "It is our thesis here, which will not be fully defended, that education provides eugenic selection in mental ability and the selection is more effective in a disadvantaged group like the Negro than it is in the dominant group." Long suggested that as educational opportunity expanded, it could help distinguish the most intelligent students, who would then be more likely to marry among themselves. Therefore, according to Long, "on a whole eugenic improvement follows as a result of democratic education." Long, "The Position of the Negro," 610.

5. Long, "The Position of the Negro," 609.

6. Long, 615.

7. In another indication of difference in their broader political disagreement, Long was critical of the effects of the New Deal's relief efforts on the Black population, noting "His morale has been undermined to an uncomfortable degree by relief and the dole." Long, "The Position of the Negro," 606.

228 Notes to Chapter Two

8. Woodson, *The Education of the Negro*; Horton and Horton, *In Hope of Liberty*; Hughes, *Refusing Ignorance*.

9. Williams, *Self-Taught*; Moss, *Schooling Citizens*; Jones, *Soldiers of Light and Love*; Morris, *Reading, 'Riting, and Reconstruction*; Butchart, *Northern Schools, Southern Blacks, and Reconstruction*; Gutman, "Schools for Freedom."

10. Bond, *The Education of the Negro*; Bond, *Negro Education in Alabama*.

11. Anderson, *The Education of Blacks*; Todd-Breland, *A Political Education*; Walker, *The Lost Education of Horace Tate*; Anderson and Kharem, *Education as Freedom*.

12. Goluboff, "'Let Economic Equality Take Care of Itself.'"

13. Although I use the term *economic democracy* rather than *social democracy*, the distinction between these groups follows the broad division identified by Preston H. Smith II. I use the term *economic democracy* because some education scholars used this term in the *Journal of Negro Education*. See Smith, *Racial Democracy and the Black Metropolis*.

14. Following Preston H. Smith, I use the term *racial democracy* to describe this ideological outlook. Racial democracy is distinct from accommodationism and assimilationism. Accommodationism is an ideological outlook that suggests Black people should accept the reality of current racial domination and adapt to this system in the hopes of achieving the full rights of citizenship in the future. The author most associated with accommodationism, Booker T. Washington, argued that the condition of being enslaved had hindered racial development and led to racial inferiority and backwardness. Indeed, Washington urged Black people to abandon the political arena to focus on racial development. See Washington, "Atlanta Exposition Address"; Washington, "My View of Segregation Laws"; and Washington, "The Rights and Duties of the Negro." The focus of assimilationism is cultural, with proponents suggesting the need to adopt majority culture in order to advance racial interests. Critics of assimilationism suggest that the concept requires abandoning Black cultural forms. Alternatively, racial democracy is an outlook that directly challenged existing racial discrimination and inequality, never accepted racial inferiority, and argued for immediate fair racial incorporation into the existing institutional and political landscape. Although some racial democrats stressed the need for abandoning perceived backward cultural practices, these actors did not perceive the cultural practices to be abandoned as distinctly Black cultural forms (if anything, they were perceived as the cultural practices of the poor). Additionally, in their active challenge of Jim Crow and racial exclusion, racial democrats were not arguing for assimilation into the dominant culture and institutions, but for a change to the culture and institutions that actively excluded Black people.

15. Du Bois, "Does the Negro."

16. Du Bois was probably the most visible supporter of the position, arguing that segregated institutes offered certain advantages. Du Bois noted that "when our schools are separate, the control of the teaching force, the expenditure of money, the choice of textbooks, the discipline and other administrative matters of this sort ought, also, to come into our hands." Du Bois also argued that Black students might require and benefit from a different type of education than their white counterparts, suggesting, "Negroes must know the history of the Negro race in America, and this they will seldom get in white institutions." Du Bois, "Does the Negro," 333, 335.

17. Bunche, "A Critical Analysis." Of course, the proposed solutions of these two groups differed radically. The Garveyites and other "racial separatists" advocated physical and

political separation in an autonomous nation. Bunche notes that the "economic separatists" were often Black business owners who in part depended on Black business and racial loyalty to survive, and the political program of this group was limited to advocacy to create mirror images of white institutions in the Black community.

18. Gallagher, "Reorganize the College."

19. Du Bois, "Does the Negro," 335. Again, this was clearly a strategic choice to embrace what he saw as a situation that was unlikely to change. He knew that some would take his article as a positive endorsement of segregated schools, to which he responded, "It is not. It is simply calling a spade a spade. It is saying in plain English: that a separate Negro school, where children are treated like human beings, trained by teachers of their own race, who know what it means to be black in the year of salvation 1935, is infinitely better than making our boys and girls doormats to be spit and trampled upon and lied to by ignorant social climbers, whose sole claim to superiority is the ability to kick 'niggers' when they are down." Du Bois, "Does the Negro," 335.

20. This journal was the official organ of the National Urban League, an organization that operated on the conservative wing of the broader civil rights movement.

21. Rudwick, "Du Bois' Last Year."

22. National Negro Committee, "Platform." Both Du Bois and John Dewey were members of the National Negro Committee, the committee responsible for planning the permanent advocacy organization that eventually became the NAACP. See also the National Association for the Advancement of Colored People, "A Letter to President Woodrow Wilson."

23. This appears to be due in no small part to the more confrontational approach adopted by T. Arnold Hill who headed the Urban League from 1933 to 1936. Hill was eventually pushed out of the leadership of the Urban League due to rising tensions with the organization's leader, Eugene Kinckle Jones. Jones and prominent white allies of the Urban League were increasingly dissatisfied with the direction that Hill had set for the Urban League, particularly his willingness to push the organization toward a closer association with labor and a more politically confrontational engagement. Jones "slammed on the brakes" when he returned to reassume the leadership position of the organization. Armfield, *Eugene Kinckle Jones*, 74.

24. Ford, "The Communist's Way Out"; Thomas, "The Socialist's Way Out"; McKinney, "The Workers Party's Way Out."

25. Smith, *Racial Democracy and the Black Metropolis*, 5. I have chosen the term *economic democracy*, but substantively it is similar to the terms *industrial democracy* and *social democracy* that other authors have chosen to employ.

26. Smith, *Racial Democracy and the Black Metropolis*, 10.

27. Note here that it was assumed that the commitment to equality of outcomes at schools would take care of the disparities that currently existed in the labor market.

28. Reed, *Toward Freedom*, 15–47.

29. Davis, "A Survey of the Problems," 11.

30. Lewis, "The Economic Position of the American Negro," 446.

31. Bunche, "A Critical Analysis," 308.

32. Unsurprisingly, many of the most vocal advocates of industrial democracy were well positioned in the labor movement.

33. Bunche, "The Programs of Organizations," 549.

34. Bunche, 549.

35. Weaver, "The Role of Organized Labor," 420.

36. Townsend, "Full Employment and the Negro Worker," 6.

37. Weaver, "The Role of Organized Labor," 414–15.

38. As Professor Lloyd Bailer articulated, the focus on full employment was thus driven by the belief that "the most important single issue facing the non-white population is the attainment of economic equality and that in so doing numerous other disadvantages presently suffered will be eliminated automatically." Bailer, "The Negro in the Labor Force," 298; see also Bunche, "The Programs of Organizations"; Hartley, "Psychological Investigations"; Townsend, "Full Employment"; Weaver, "The Role of Organized Labor"; and Cox, "An American Dilemma."

39. Randolph, "The Trade Union Movement," 58.

40. Grossman, "Redefining the Relationship," 450.

41. Mason, "The CIO and the Negro," 561.

42. Cox, "Modern Democracy," 156.

43. Cox, 162.

44. Cox, "The New Crisis," 463.

45. Cox, "An American Dilemma," 145.

46. Lewis, "The Economic Position," 446.

47. Cox, "An American Dilemma, 147.

48. Dorsey, "The Negro and Social Planning," 107; McKinney, "The Workers Party's Way"; Randolph, "The Trade Union Movement"; Bunche, "The Programs of Organizations"; Cox, "An American Dilemma"; Cox, "The New Crisis"; Neal, "Two Negro Problems."

49. Bunche, "The Programs of Organizations," 546.

50. Neal, "Two Negro Problems."

51. Dorsey, "The Negro and Social Planning," 107; see also Cox, "The New Crisis."

52. McKinney, "The Workers Party's Way," 98.

53. Randolph, "The Trade Union Movement," 58.

54. See Cox, "The New Crisis," for more on this distinction.

55. Reddick, "What Should the American Negro Reasonably Expect," 569. As the next chapter will demonstrate, not every individual who adopted either the economic or racial democracy position in the 1930s and 1940s continued to hold those same positions as the political and economic circumstances shifted. For a careful account of the later development of Reddick's political philosophy, see Varel, *The Scholar and the Struggle*.

56. Thompson, "Editorial Comment: FEPC Hearings Reduce Race Problem," 588, emphasis in original.

57. Beittel, "Some Effects of the 'Separate but Equal' Doctrine," 146.

58. Deutsch, "Equality in Life," 500, emphasis added.

59. Patterson, "Colleges for Negro Youth," 114. See also, Myrdal *An American Dilemma*, 672–74.

60. Long, "Some Psychogenic Hazards," 350.

61. See Long, "Some Psychogenic Hazards," 350; Horowitz, "Racial Aspects of Self-Identification"; Clark and Clark, "The Development of Consciousness"; Clark and Clark, "Segregation as a Factor"; Clark and Clark, "Emotional Factors in Racial Identification."

62. Goodman, "The Education of Children," 404. See also Goff, "Problems and Emotional Difficulties"; and Daniel, "The Responsibility of Education."

63. For example, see Johnson, "The Next Decade"; and Goodman, "The Education of Children," 407.

64. Cox, "An American Dilemma," 143.

65. Brown, "Race Prejudice as a Factor," 358.

66. Townsend, "Full Employment," 9.

67. Cox, "An American Dilemma," 143. And indeed, racial democrats like Mary Foley Goodman did argue that one of the virtues of an intercultural education program was that it "supports the constructive and problem-solving rather than the combat orientation toward society." Goodman, "The Education of Children," 407.

68. Frazier, "Problems and Needs of Negro Children," 269.

69. Frazier, 276. Frazier's colleague in education, Marion T. Wright, echoed his focus on the family, noting that the family was an important site in the development of the "stigma of inferiority" from segregation and discrimination, as adults transmitted destructive attitudes and disorganization to their children, which ultimately "further handicapped . . . personality development." Wright, "Some Educational and Cultural Problems," 320–21.

70. The types of education and programs varied widely, including encouraging better mental and physical hygiene (see Bousfield, "Redirection of the Education of Negroes"; Clark and Clark "Emotional Factors"; Banks, "Changing Attitudes Towards the Negro"), education on the need for strong father figures given the large number of single mothers (see Frazier, "Problems and Needs of Negro Children"; and Long, "The Relative Learning Capacities"), improving parenting skills (Blalock, "Educational Achievement"), raising self-esteem of young Black people (Goff, "Problems and Emotional Difficulties"), and teaching better habits regarding money management (Canady, "The Social Psychology of Youth").

71. Blalock, "Educational Achievement," 546.

72. See Canady, "The Social Psychology of Youth"; Blalock, "Educational Achievement"; and Clark, "Color, Class, Personality and Juvenile Delinquency." The class-inflected nature of these programs was sometimes quite explicit. For example, Herman G. Canady, the chair of the Psychology Department at West Virginia Collegiate Institute, argued that "when low-status people become more like middle- and upper-class people, they can compete on more nearly equal terms for the good things America has to offer." Canady, "The Social Psychology of Youth," 123.

73. Canady, "The Social Psychology of Youth," 122.

74. Cox, "An American Dilemma," 143.

75. Hill, "Educating and Guiding Negro Youth," 25, emphasis added. Columbia professor Robert Smuts offered a similar analysis, noting, "Those who have been actively engaged in attempting to break down employment discrimination in the North know that it is often harder to find a Negro who is fully qualified for a job requiring skill and training than it is to find employers who are willing to employ qualified Negroes." Smuts, "The Negro Community," 458. Charles Johnson had also suggested improving Black skills could lead to Black advancement in the 1930s, arguing, "Negro youth should assure themselves of that superior competence which in many cases outweighs purely racial advantage." Johnson, "On the Need of Realism," 382, emphasis added.

76. Charles Johnson stressed the potential opportunity and dangers offered by the changing economy, noting, "A problem facing this race today is one of mastering the techniques imposed by technological changes. It is in this world that the Negro must live by competition with others who are geared to the tempo of the new age." Johnson, "On the Need of Realism," 377. See also Boykin, "The Vocational Education"; Neal, "Two Negro Problems"; and Johnson, "Some Significant Social and Educational Implications."

77. Johnson, "The Negro and the Present Crisis." See also Banks, "Changing Attitudes"; Beittel, "Some Effects"; Deutsch, "Equality in Life"; Hughes, "What About Human Equality?"; Patterson, "Colleges for Negro Youth"; Reddick, "What Should the American Negro"; and Thompson, "Editorial Comment," 1943.

78. Hughes, "What About Human Equality?" 60.

79. The framing of segregation and discrimination as leading to unfair competition was not unique to the pages of the *JNE*. In his influential 1944 book, *An American Dilemma*, Gunnar Myrdal argued that democracy in America required, "*free competition*, which in this sphere of social stratification represents the combination of the two basic norms: 'equality' and 'liberty.' And it is prepared to accept the outcome of competition—if it is really free—though there be some inequality." Myrdal, *An American Dilemma*, 672. Additionally, Myrdal quoted Donald Young, the future president of the American Sociological Association, who argued, "Democracy is an empty word unless it means the free recognition of ability, native and acquired, whether it be found in rich or poor, alien or native, black man or white." As quoted in Myrdal, *An American Dilemma*, 672.

80. Johnson, "The Negro and the Present Crisis," 585.

81. For example, Monroe Deutsch warned the newly minted NAACP chapter of the University of California, Berkeley, "I am sure that you all know that wherever Communism has become master, freedom (yes, all the freedoms) have vanished." Deustch, "Equality in Life," 501. Additionally, in justifying the specific programs central to racial democracy ideology, many authors stressed that they were alternatives to communism. Mary Goodman noted that "perhaps nothing could be more constructive in a democracy hard-pressed by communism" than a carefully tailored intercultural education program. Goodman, "The Education of Children," 405.

82. Long, "The Position of the Negro," 616.

83. At times, scholars and educators used both *interracial education* and *intercultural education*. Although there are differences between the terms, I use the term *interracial education*. Whereas intercultural education referred to education aimed at improving relationships between religious, cultural, ethnic, and racial groups, interracial education referred more specifically to education focused on improving racial understanding. Importantly, the pedagogical and ideological forces behind both programs were nearly identical.

84. Zeligs, "Children Explain Their Intergroup Attitudes," 534; Hartley, "Psychological Investigations"; Clark and Clark, "Emotional Factors"; Zeligs, "Growth in Intergroup Attitudes"; Amerman, "Perspective for Evaluating Intergroup Relations."

85. Founded in 1934, the New York City–based bureau was formed to provide teachers with intercultural education resources. Lal, "1930s Multiculturalism."

86. Among the prominent supporters of this version of interracial education was Gunnar Myrdal. Myrdal openly endorsed this educational strategy in his highly influential 1944 report, *An American Dilemma*.

87. See Vickery and Cole, *Intercultural Education.*

88. "Second National Conference on Intergroup Relations," 188.

89. "Second National Conference on Intergroup Relations," 188.

90. See Goodman, "The Education of Children"; Goff "Problems and Emotional Difficulties"; and Daniel, "The Responsibility of Education."

91. Jenkins, "Editorial Comment: Education for Racial Understanding," 265–66.

92. Jenkins, 267.

93. Jenkins, 267, emphasis added.

94. McCulloch, "Educational Programs for the Improvement of Race Relations: Seven Religious Agencies."

95. Clement, "Educational Programs for the Improvement of Race Relations: Interracial Committees."

96. Wright, "Educational Programs for the Improvement of Race Relations: Negro Advancement Organizations."

97. Brownlee, "Educational Programs for the Improvement of Race Relations: Philanthropic Foundations."

98. Davis, "Educational Programs for the Improvement of Race Relations: Organized Labor and Industrial Organizations."

99. Reddick, "Educational Programs for the Improvement of Race Relations: Motion Pictures Radio, the Press, and Libraries."

100. Smith, "Educational Programs for the Improvement of Race Relations: Government Agencies."

101. As Alaine Locke noted, "It is not too utopian, however, to assume that as we correct the deficiencies of the social education aspect of formal education there will remain much less to be done (and undone) by informal adult educative efforts." Locke, "Whither Race Relations?" 398.

102. Powdermaker, "The Anthropological Approach," 301.

103. See Brown, *Problems of Race and Culture*, 14–15.

104. Wilkins argued that "the textbook treatment of the Negro cries aloud for revision, and we will make little progress in education for racial understanding until the average boy and girl stops absorbing this poison from the first grade through high school." Wilkins, "Next Steps in Education," 437. Wilkins was particularly adamant in pointing to the responsibility of inadequate education for the circumstances of Black people in the United States, arguing, "In so complex a problem as the adjustment of a pigmented minority with a slave background to American life, it is, of course difficult to place a finger on the chief cause of misunderstanding and continued proscription; but certainly the 'education' which generations of white Americans have received on the Negroes in their schools and colleges must rank high on the list." Wilkins, "Next Steps in Education," 435.

105. Wilkins, "Next Steps in Education," 438.

106. For example, interracial education advocate Regina Goff concluded after one such study, "It is apparent that the Negro child needs an enriched program of training which places more emphasis on building of attitudes toward himself, attitudes of worth of self, respect for self, and confidence." Goff, "Problems and Emotional Difficulties," 158. See also Bousfield, "Redirection of the Education"; Clark and Clark, "Emotional Factors in Racial Identification"; and Johnson, "On the Need of Realism." The calls for changed textbooks or

special attention to the contributions and achievements of minorities were also present in the manuals produced by the Intercultural Bureau for Intercultural Education.

107. For example, arguing that a "psychological emphasis would aim that education should teach that the best hope for complete integration lies in the advancement of human understanding," Jeanne Noble advocated for an education that "seeks primarily to release the inner potentialities of the Negro." Noble, "Future Educational Emphasis," 407, 409. For Noble, the material consequences like "better jobs, better homes" would proceed from the emphasis on the Black inner self, and so should be secondary to an education program. Noble, "Future Educational Emphasis," 409.

108. Powdermaker and Storen, *Probing Our Prejudices*, 68.

109. Powdermaker, "The Anthropological Approach"; see also Goodman, "The Education of Children."

110. Vickery and Cole, *Intercultural Education*, 81. Powdermaker made essentially this same point as Vickery and Cole a year later in her *JNE* yearbook piece.

111. Vickery and Cole, *Intercultural Education*; Powdermaker and Storen, *Probing Our Prejudices*; Wilkins, "Next Steps in Education"; and Powdermaker, "The Anthropological Approach."

112. Vickery and Cole, *Intercultural Education*, 82.

113. Gordon, *From Power to Prejudice*, 132–60.

114. Vickery and Cole, *Intercultural Education*, 140. See also Powdermaker and Storen, *Probing Our Prejudices*.

115. Powdermaker, "The Anthropological Approach," 67.

116. Vickery and Cole, *Intercultural Education*, 139–47.

117. See Myrdal, *An American Dilemma*; Powdermaker, "The Anthropological Approach"; Vickery and Cole, *Intercultural Education*.

118. Powdermaker, "The Anthropological Approach," 301.

119. Powdermaker, 301. See also Powdermaker and Storen, *Probing Our Prejudices*, 70.

120. Vickery and Cole, *Intercultural Education*, 99.

121. Vickery and Cole, 103.

122. Brown, *Problems of Race and Culture*, 163.

123. Vickery and Cole, *Intercultural Education*, 87.

124. Powdermaker and Storen, *Probing Our Prejudices*, 12.

125. Bond, "Educational Programs."

126. Bond, 392. In fact, Bond derisively defined this brand of "Americanism" as "that paradoxical social patter which includes at the same time, the Constitution and The Bill of Rights of the disfranchisement of the Negro, economic exploitation, and the consignment of lesser peoples to a place of degradation and shame."

127. Bond, "Educational Programs," 395.

128. Davis, "Educational Programs," 342.

129. Ware, "The Role of the Schools," 427.

130. Ware, 427–28.

131. For example, Caroline Ware was careful to frame her discussion of interracial education with the caveat, "In considering the direct contributions of education to race relations, one should never lose sight of the fact that unemployment and economic frustration can tear down everything that has been built up." Ware, "The Role of the Schools," 421.

132. Although the term *adjustment* was not widely used, it does reflect the common focus on the need to change or adjust something about Black students in order to facilitate their equitable incorporation into existing social and economic structures. It also reflects the emerging field of "life adjustment education" that began to take off in the late 1940s (after the more radical social reconstructionist arguments had largely disappeared from the progressive education movement) that focused primarily on adjusting students to the world they would find upon exiting school (rather than prepare students to change the institutional structures, life adjustment sought to adjust the students to the institutional structure).

133. As Alice O'Connor has argued, much of the writing in the racial democracy camp over the problems facing Black people focused on two causes, white prejudice and Black disorganization. O'Connor notes that these two explanations existed in some degree of contradiction throughout much of the 1930s. Myrdal's notion of the "vicious circle" and "dual causation" essentially allowed both explanations to fit comfortably alongside one another. Rather than *either* white racism or Black disorganization as causes of Black poverty, *both* caused poverty while also causing each other. O'Connor, *Poverty Knowledge*, 96.

134. See Johnson, "The Present Status"; and Myrdal, *An American Dilemma*.

135. Some authors (Myrdal in particular) acknowledge this and denied any connotation of superiority of one form over the other and explained the move as simply recognizing the strategic value of getting Black families to mirror the dominant social structures—although the highly moralistic tones in which these authors tended to discuss the differences of Black families should give one pause before accepting the claim.

136. Johnson, "The Next Decade," 444. Johnson's concern here reflected his class position, as he noted the particularly problematic position this posed for upper-class Black people, arguing, "no one is more intimately involved in the results than the culturally advanced Negroes who are all too readily classed with their backward brothers in the American race system." Johnson, "The Next Decade," 444.

137. Frazier, "The Present Status," 378, 380.

138. Frazier was quite explicit on this point, arguing that "in the competitive life of America, the success of the Negro in achieving a new and more intelligent adaptation to American civilization will depend upon his incorporation into the economic organization at large, upon his own cultural resources, and finally upon the extent to which he is able to incorporate in his own family traditions and heritage the patterns of behavior requisite for survival." Frazier, "The Present Status," 382.

139. See chapter 3 of O'Connor, *Poverty Knowledge*, for a more in-depth discussion of the differences between the academic commitments of Davis and Frazier.

140. Davis "The Socialization of the American Negro," 264–65. Davis identified many of the same disparities between Black and white families as Frazier, noting Black families were more likely to "have illegitimate children," "desert their mates," be characterized by parental abuse, eventually producing children that easily gave into impulse, were aggressive, truant, delinquent, and "retarded in school achievement." Davis "The Socialization of the American Negro," 265.

141. For example, Davis argued that "the importance of the Negro-white positional system is great. . . . It operates so as to fix upon the overwhelming majority of Negro families the social and economic traits and goals of *lower-class* people in America. When the details of this process, and its effect upon the habit structures of the Negroes subjected to it are understood,

the origin of the atypical behavior of relatively large numbers of Negro as compared to white adolescents becomes clear." Davis, "The Socialization of the American Negro," 268.

142. Davis "The Socialization of the American Negro," 267. Davis also used the difference of behavior by income level to attack the idea that the observed behavioral differences could be ascribed to racial biology.

143. Davis, "The Socialization of the American Negro," 271.

144. Davis, 274. Alice O'Connor notes that the American Council of Education commissioned a series of studies seeking to uncover the effect of racial caste on personality development in the 1930s, which ended up with similar conclusions and a similar suggestion of "rehabilitative social engineering, aimed at changing lower-class child rearing patterns." O'Connor, *Poverty Knowledge*, 87.

145. Davis, "The Socialization of the American Negro," 274.

146. Bousfield, "Redirection of the Education," 414. For additional articles focusing on the deficient hygiene habits of Black families, see Frazier, "Problems and Needs"; and Banks, "Changing Attitudes."

147. Hill, "Educating and Guiding," 30.

148. Bousfield, "Redirection of the Education," 415. See also Canady, "The Social Psychology of Youth."

149. Myrdal, *An American Dilemma*, 208. Myrdal's work was heavily influenced by the work of Frazier, Johnson, Davis, and others whose work had been prominently featured in the *JNE*, and he cites them liberally.

150. Myrdal, *An American Dilemma*, 928–29.

151. Myrdal, 957.

152. Myrdal, 959.

153. Myrdal, 962.

154. Myrdal, 976.

155. Myrdal, 978.

156. Myrdal, 978.

157. Myrdal, 979. Myrdal was careful to note that "upper and middle class Negroes make a special effort to be law-abiding just as they try to avoid most of the typical and stereotyped patterns of behavior associated with the Negro lower classes."

158. Myrdal, *An American Dilemma*, 929, emphasis in original.

159. Myrdal, 879.

160. O'Connor, *Poverty Knowledge*, 96.

161. Gordon, "The Question of Prejudice," 278.

162. Daniel, "The Responsibility of Education," 391.

163. Daniel, 391.

164. Clark and Clark, "Emotional Factors," 350.

165. Goff, "Problems and Emotional Difficulties," 158.

166. Nicholson, "The Urban League," 450, 455. Another part of the Urban League's broader educational strategy was to build support for the incorporation of Black people into the workforce "on the basis of individual merit." Nicholson, "The Urban League," 455.

167. Boykin, "The Vocational Education"; Smuts, "The Negro Community."

168. Hill, "Educating and Guiding." See also Johnson, "On the Need of Realism"; and Daniel, "The Responsibility of Education."

169. Patterson, "Colleges for Negro Youth," 110.

170. Neal, "Two Negro Problems," 219. Gunnar Myrdal made a similar point in *An American Dilemma*, arguing, "if the American economy and economic policy are not going to stagnate, Negroes are going to work in new occupations within the next generation. *What is needed is an education which makes the Negro child adaptable to and movable in the American culture at large.*" Myrdal, *An American Dilemma*, 906, emphasis in original. See also Bousfield, "Redirection of the Education"; and Johnson, "On the Need of Realism."

171. Boykin, "The Vocational Education," 42.

172. Daniel, "The Responsibility of Education," 397.

173. See Johnson, "The Negro and the Present Crisis"; and Hughes, "What About Human Equality?" As Myrdal wrote in *An American Dilemma*, "The American nation will not have peace with its conscience until inequality is stamped out, and the principle of education is realized universally." Myrdal, *An American Dilemma*, 907.

174. See Myrdal, *An American Dilemma*; Davis "The Socialization of the American Negro"; Daniel, "The Responsibility of Education"; and Nicholson, "The Urban League."

175. Boykin, "The Vocational Education," 46.

176. Bousfield, "Redirection of the Education," 417.

177. Johnson, "On the Need of Realism," 379.

178. Johnson, 378.

179. Myrdal, *An American Dilemma*, 906; see also Neal, "Two Negro Problems," on the need for schools to teach minimal tools of survival in a changing economy.

180. See Daniel, "The Responsibility of Education"; and Nicholson, "The Urban League."

181. The similarity of these positions is underlined by the fact that many of the authors who argued for addressing skill differential through education also argued for an educational focus on Black cultural backwardness.

182. "Editorial Comment: Investing in Negro Brains," 153–55. The editors suggested that this situation represented a serious problem for Black people, arguing, "Whatever else may be at the root of the Negro's troubles in this country, it is fairly obvious that one of his difficulties is in the fact that he has more than his *necessary* share of mental incompetence in high places." "Editorial Comment: Investing in Negro Brains," 154.

183. "Editorial Comment: Investing in Negro Brains," 154. The editors argued that because intelligence was roughly equally distributed across racial categories, that Black people had roughly an equal percentage of "very superior" individuals as whites—a figure they put at roughly 3 percent of the population. The editors calculated there were approximately 50,000–75,000 "very superior" Black school children whose gift could be identified and "developed for the benefit of the race and nation." "Editorial Comment: Investing in Negro Brains," 154.

184. "Editorial Comment: Investing in Negro Brains," 155.

185. Clarke, "The Role of Psychology," 51.

186. Clarke, 51. For Clarke, a trained psychologist, this belief suggested that "the school psychologist is as important to racial existence as are the school doctor and the school itself." Clarke, "The Role of Psychology," 53.

187. Clarke, "The Role of Psychology," 52. Clarke was concerned that rather than focusing on the highly intelligent students, in most schools "the dull child seems to be getting the lion's share of attention." Clarke, "The Role of Psychology," 52.

188. This line of argument was not unique to Black educators. During the same era, James Bryant Conant, president of Harvard, argued that as much as 50 percent of college students were unqualified and argued forcefully for the use of the SAT scores to help place "others of more talent in their place." As quoted in Lemann, *The Big Test*, 43. Journalism professor Nicholas Lemann points out that Conant's main goal (and the impetus behind his support for standardized entrance exams) was his desire to replace the hereditary elite with an elite determined by academic merit. Lemann, *The Big Test*, 42–52.

189. Crooks, "Is Negro Education Failing?" 20.

190. Crooks, 23. Crooks noted that there was wide agreement that the public schools were not doing their job when it came to Black students. Crooks wrote that "most colleges for Negroes acknowledge that something is wrong with our primary and secondary schools," and there was a common understanding that the achievement of "educational objectives and ideals . . . in the education of Negroes is seriously to be doubted." Crooks, "Is Negro Education Failing?" 20.

191. Crooks, "Is Negro Education Failing?" 22–23.

192. This vision is essentially that expressed by the scientific efficiency progressives. Crooks's article has a lengthy citation from Edward Thorndike, one of the founding academics who advocated for a scientific efficiency approach to education. Crooks's faith in the ability to measure intelligence was so great, he claimed, "We ought then to be able to measure our pupils' mindpower as accurately as engineers measure machines in terms of horsepower." Crooks, "Is Negro Education Failing?" 24.

193. Crooks, "Is Negro Education Failing?" 22.

194. Crooks, 21. It was clear that part of Crooks's desire for implementing these tests was due to his dissatisfaction with the performance of teachers. Crooks noted teacher responsibility for poor student outcomes, claiming, "There is no doubt that teachers are doing their level best, but until teaching can be made more attractive by state or federal or philanthropic funds, there will be poor teachers for poor, low-salaried jobs, and poor pupils will result." Crooks, "Is Negro Education Failing?" 25.

195. Selective Service System, *Special Monograph No. 10*, 143.

196. Selective Service System, 145.

197. Selective Service System, 145.

198. Selective Service System, 147. This was the first time the armed forces had used an intelligence test as a means of screening who would be accepted for service. The Army General Classification Test and its progenitors had been administered after an individual had been inducted and was used largely to assign recruits to particular military jobs.

199. Selective Service System, *Special Monograph No. 10*, 151. See also, Jenkins, *The Black and White of Rejections*, 4.

200. As quoted in Selective Service System, *Special Monograph No. 10*, 167. This appears to be a conservative estimate, as a report by the American Teachers Association concluded that roughly 341,200 registrants had been excluded because of educational deficiency by September 1943. Jenkins, *The Black and White of Rejections*, 5.

201. Selective Service System, *Special Monograph No. 10*, 166. The report noted that "in peacetime, it [educational deficiency] prevents the effective participation of large numbers of citizens at a productive level." Selective Service System, *Special Monograph No. 10*, 166.

202. The mission of the ATA was "the achievement of the American goal of EQUALITY OF EDUCATIONAL OPPORTUNITY for all children without respect to Economic Circumstance, Place of Residence, Sex, or RACE." Jenkins, *The Black and White of Rejections*, iv.

203. The other two principal investigators were high school principal Francis Gregory and Jane E. McCallister, a professor of education at Miner Teacher College. The influence of the ATA report can clearly be seen in the Selective Service monograph on special groups, which cites the report extensively and relies on much of its data.

204. Jenkins, *The Black and White of Rejections*, 5. Under the intelligence test standard, the ATA report calculated that educational deficiency rejections accounted for 34.5 percent of all rejections of Black selectees (almost three times as much as the second highest reason, mental disease).

205. Jenkins, *The Black and White of Rejections*, 2. In the first four months of the fourth grade literacy requirement, Black people accounted for 58 percent of the total rejections for educational deficiency (83,480 of the 143,493 rejected for this reason). Selective Service System, *Special Monograph No. 10*, 145.

206. Jenkins, *The Black and White of Rejections*, 5–7. This was a calculation based on total rejections as of September 1, 1943. See also U.S. Senate Committee on Military Affairs, *Lowering the Draft Age to 18 Years*, 31–32.

207. Jenkins, *The Black and White of Rejections*, 10. The argument that high educational deficiency rejection rates of Black people was unfair for white people was a common refrain. The Selective Service monograph on special groups pointed out that part of the justification for racial inclusion in the draft was "that if a Negro was not selected, accepted or inducted because of his race and a white registrant had to take his place, the discrimination was in relation to both men. In such instance, the white registrant was required to serve ahead of the proper sequence for his liability." Selective Service System, *Special Monograph No. 10*, 4. This sentiment created strange bedfellows, as civil rights groups were joined by southern segregationists in calling for greater Black participation in the draft. In a 1942 Senate hearing, Mississippi senator Theodore Bilbo urged the deputy chief of staff of U.S. Army General J. T. McNarney to lower the educational standard, arguing, "In my state, with a population of one-half Negro and one-half whites . . . the system that you are using now has resulted in taking all the whites to meet the quota and leaving the great majority of Negroes at home, or they are sent back, because there is the literacy test. . . . That is the result of the present system, and that was the reason I was anxious that you develop the reservoir of illiterate class." U.S. Senate Committee on Military Affairs, *Lowering the Draft Age to 18 Years*, 31–32. The fact that progress in racial incorporation did not always proceed on noble grounds is further highlighted by the fact that several white draftees sued the federal government alleging discrimination when "the disproportionately small number of Negroes appearing in the early calls issued throughout the System on requisitions from the War Department resulted in advancing white men so that they were inducted into the armed forces before their order numbers would ordinarily have been reached." Selective Service System, *Special Monograph No. 10*, 53.

208. One example highlighted in the report was the fact that educational rejection rates in Alabama for white people was nearly four times that of the rejection rate of Black people in Illinois (8.5 percent for white people in Alabama and 2.5 percent for Black people in Illinois). Jenkins, *The Black and White of Rejections*, 5.

209. Jenkins, *The Black and White of Rejections*, 32.

210. Jenkins, 33. The authors also looked at school attendance and school persistence in reaching this conclusion. The Selective Service System Report reached a very similar conclusion regarding racial disparities in rejection, arguing, "substandard schools, equally poor physical facilities, teachers with inadequate preparation and a lower per capita expenditure of school funds . . . were foremost among the factors creating this condition." Selective Service System, *Special Monograph No. 10*, 189.

211. Herbert Aptheker referred the situation as a "the dream experiment" for educational and social psychologists. Aptheker, "Literacy, the Negro and World War II," 595.

212. Jenkins, *The Black and White of Rejections*, 46. See also page 10 where the ATA investigators concluded that the most important implication of the high and disparate educational rejection rate was its long-term indication of a "reduced social efficiency of large elements in the population and consequently of the Nation. . . . people who are not sufficiently competent to participate in the war effort, are likewise unable to make their best contribution to a peacetime economy."

213. See Davenport, "Implications of Military Selection"; Boykin, "The Vocational Education"; Redd, "The Educational and Cultural"; and Miller, "The Price of Educational Inequality."

214. Redd, "The Educational and Cultural," 252.

215. It was clear that the widespread use of standardized aptitude and intelligence tests during World War II convinced many of their usefulness for peacetime education. The report of President Truman's Commission on Higher Education provides a useful example. The report advocated for moving beyond traditional criterion for college entrance (like a high-school diploma) and toward a reliance on "general tests of intelligence and aptitude" that "can take adequate account of the wide disparities in high-school education even within individual States" in order to lead to a "wiser selection of students by the institutions." President's Commission on Higher Education, *Higher Education for American Democracy*, 41. For evidence of the desirability and feasibility of such a move, the report noted that "the program for accrediting the educational experience of men in the armed forces has abundantly demonstrated that objective tests of mastery of knowledge and skill are adequate measures of potential success in college." President's Commission on Higher Education, *Higher Education for American Democracy*, 42.

216. Plaut, *Southern Project Report*, 1.

217. The College Entrance Examination Board provided the NSSFNS with copies of the SAT at printing cost.

218. Plaut, *Southern Project Report*, 4.

219. Plaut, 4.

220. Plaut, 1.

221. Plaut, 1–2. The report also emphasized that it was the "first use of a scholastic aptitude test as a screening device for a large, culturally and economically deprived group." Plaut, *Southern Project Report*, 2.

222. Plaut, *Blueprint for Talent Searching*, 3. Much of this new money was reserved for those who demonstrated scholastic ability, which often meant performance on some sort of standardized test. The largest scholarship organization to emerge from this time period is the National Merit Scholarship, which was founded in 1955, two years *after* the Southern

Project. Like the Southern Project, the National Merit Scholarship relied primarily on standardized test scores to identify potential scholarship recipients.

223. This report, like the Southern Project, was funded by the Ford Foundation's Fund for the Advancement of Education. Kenneth Clark was also a member of the board of directors of the National Scholarship Service and Fund for Negro Students.

224. Plaut, *Blueprint for Talent Searching*, 6.

225. Although Plaut noted that the lower scores of disadvantaged students were not particularly useful in predicting college success, he still advocated for such tests as the best means of identifying talent, arguing, "We do know that tests of verbal and quantitative aptitude and school achievement are among the best predictors of scholastic attainment in high school and college. For these reasons such tests are suggested for use in identifying talented pupils." Plaut, *Blueprint for Talent Searching*, 34.

226. Brown, "The Phelps-Stokes Fund." The article cites an unnamed college professor who claimed, "At our university a group of tests is given to the high school students and on practically any standard test 80% of the students is below the national norm." Brown, "The Phelps-Stokes Fund," 456. The article also cites the NSSFNS report on their Southern Project in which 50–60 percent of top Black students were able to achieve minimum qualifying scores (for a prognosis of college success) on aptitude tests. Brown, "The Phelps-Stokes Fund," 457.

227. Brown, "The Phelps-Stokes Fund," 457.

228. In justifying the project, Brown also pointed specifically to the racial gap on median achievement test scores in elementary and secondary school students. Of particular concern was the widening of the gap in the years after the fourth grade. Brown, "The Phelps-Stokes Fund," 456.

229. See Brown, "The Phelps-Stokes Fund"; and Brown, *Ladders to Improvement*. Long died shortly after, with much of the duties being taken over by Frank A. DeCosta, the director of student teaching at Morgan State College, another contributor to the *JNE*.

230. Brown, "Ladders to Improvement," A-iii. This represented sixteen public high schools and sixteen private and public colleges as well as three resource universities.

231. Brown, "The Phelps-Stokes Fund," 459.

232. Brown, "Ladders to Improvement." These four tests were portions of the Iowa Tests of Educational Development that focused on reading, social studies, natural science, and quantitative reasoning. DeCosta, "The Use and Results of Standardized Tests."

233. DeCosta, "The Use and Results of Standardized Tests," C-16. These included, but were not limited to, ability tests, aptitude tests, achievement tests, comprehensive tests, diagnostic tests, and intelligence tests. Brown, "Ladders to Improvement," A-iii.

234. Brown, "Ladders to Improvement," A-32, B-6.

235. Brown, A-41.

236. DeCosta, "The Use and Results of Standardized Tests," C-11.

237. Brown, "Ladders to Improvement," A-iii.

238. DeCosta, "The Use and Results of Standardized Tests," C-8.

239. This conclusion was reached because of an understanding that Black and white people possessed more or less equal intellectual capacity. The implication was that in an ideal world, there should be no racial difference in distribution of test scores. The fact that disparity did exist therefore constituted evidence of inequitable opportunity. There were

several racial conservatives who interpreted the disparities as evidence of biological inferiority.

240. Good, "The Social Crisis," 271.

241. Crooks, "Is Negro Education Failing?" 20.

242. DeCosta, "The Use and Results of Standardized Tests," C-8.

243. Davis, "Educational Programs"; Thomas, "The Socialist's Way"; Wesley, "Education for Citizenship"; Wilkerson, "The Vocational Education," 1938; Wilkerson, "The Vocational Education, Guidance and Placement," 1939; Wilkerson, "The Vocational Education," 1942; Wilkerson, "The Vocational Education and Guidance of Negros" 1938; and Wilkerson, "Russia's Proposed New World Order."

244. Grossman, "Redefining the Relationship," 450–51. Grossman was concerned that the "reduction of academic content in the curricula" and "the increased emphasis on vocational training . . . are all pieces of one pattern—'Strip public education to the 3 R's.'" Grossman, "The Education of Children," 451. Ultimately, Grossman argued that this would threaten worker solidarity by making it less likely that poorly educated workers would join unions or express opinions contrary to employers.

Chapter Three

1. Sugrue, "Reassessing the History," 505. The common interpretation of these years as an "Age of Consensus" flows from the fact that one side—a resurgent business community that joined with anti-communist liberals from both political parties—was the overwhelming victor in the conflict between visions.

2. As quoted in, Wright, "Once Pro-Russian."

3. Lieberman and Lang, "Introduction," 5; Rossinow, *Visions of Progress*, 143–44, 166; Kazin, *American Dreamers*, 170; Reed, *Toward Freedom*, 15–47.

4. Holloway, *Confronting the Veil*; Rossinow, *Visions of Progress*, 153–57; Miller, *Born along the Color Line*.

5. Kazin, *American Dreamers*, 172–74.

6. The Molotov–Ribbentrop Pact put the Communist Party USA in the position of shifting stances from one of cooperation with a broad coalition in resisting the spread of fascism to advocating for isolation almost overnight. Doxey Wilkerson, a member of the Communist Party and a frequent contributor to the *Journal of Negro Education* (*JNE*), was emblematic of this switch. In a 1941 article, Wilkerson urged against involvement in a conflict of "rival imperialisms" and argued that "the government of this newer America has placed our nation 'beside' Britain, again to prosecute an imperialist war under the guise of a great 'moral' crusade." Wilkerson, "Russia's Proposed New World," 396–97.

7. Bunche, "The Role of the University," 577.

8. Both Bunche and Randolph ceased their relationship with the NNC in 1940 after it followed the communist line and switched from strong support of Roosevelt and antifascism to noninterventionism. Arnesen, "No 'Graver Danger.'"

9. Significantly, despite the fact that Richard Wright renounced his membership in the party, he continued to maintain that he still agreed with the communist position ideologically on the economic front. Wright, *The God That Failed*, 148; Arnesen, "No 'Graver Danger'"; Lang, "Freedom Train Derailed," 166. Doxey Wilkerson remained committed to the

CPUSA line throughout this time. In a 1942 article appearing in *JNE* just months after he had strenuously objected to joining what he called an imperialist war, Wilkerson urged full cooperation in the war effort, citing the necessity to "crush the fascist aggressors with their state-sponsored ideologies of race hate and persecution." Wilkerson, "The Vocational Education and Guidance of Negroes," 230.

10. Marable, *Race, Reform, and Rebellion*, 19–20; Kazin, *American Dreamers*, 192; Rossinow, *Visions of Progress*, 153.

11. Counts and Kilpatrick also signed the committee's manifesto, as did Abram Harris and Norman Thomas among others. Foundational to the committee was the denouncement of the actions of the Soviet Union. In fact, it appears to have been formed in part as an alternative organization to the Committee for Democracy and Intellectual Freedom, led by Franz Boas, Secretary of Agriculture Henry Wallace, and Secretary of the Interior Harold Ickes, that had been critical only of Germany and Italy. See "New Group Fights Any Freedom Curb"; Adler and Paterson, "Red Fascism," 1048; Anderson and Herr, *Encyclopedia of Activism*, 399–400.

12. In fact, after his election, Counts and the AFT executive council pressed for the revocation of the charters of certain local organizations because they were dominated by communists, including the New York branch and Philadelphia local, which was headed by Mary Grossman. Both these locals had their charters revoked in 1941. Taylor, *Reds at the Blackboard*, 61–74; Hartman, *Education and the Cold War*, 37–40.

13. The AFT was not alone in seeking to counteract the influence of communists in the wake of the 1939 pact. A number of liberal groups and other unions passed so-called Communazi resolutions aimed at excluding supporters of "totalitarianism," either from the right or the left, from membership. The fact that communists were the dominant organized group in the Popular Front meant that this backlash left it weakened, and several groups, including the American Student Union and League of American Writers, disbanded in the early 1940s. Kazin, *American Dreamers*, 174; Rossinow, *Visions of Progress*, 144.

14. Johnson, "The Impact of War Upon the Negro," 596, 610–11.

15. In a 1942 commencement address, Charles Thompson, the editor of *JNE*, drove this point home, noting that the "paradoxical situation of our country at war to save the world for democracy, denying a substantial part of its population at home a full share of democracy for which it was fighting abroad." Thompson, "The Basis of Negro," 454. See also McMillan, "Light Which Two World Wars," 437; Bunche, "The Negro in the Political Life"; Embree, "The Status of Minorities"; McCulloch, "What Should the American Negro"; Jenkins, "Editorial Comment: Education for Racial Understanding"; Wilkins, "Next Steps."

16. Jenkins, "Editorial Comment: Education for Racial Understanding," 266. See also Borstelmann, *The Cold War and the Color Line*, 36–41; Thompson, "The Basis of Negro Morale," 459; Daniel and Wright, "The Role of Educational Agencies"; and Chaffee, "William E. B. Dubois' Concept."

17. Freyre, "Brazil and the International Crisis"; and Johnson, "The Negro and the Present Crisis," 594.

18. In fact, there is some evidence that the Nazi lawmakers may have drawn directly from Jim Crow statutes when constructing the racial laws of the Third Reich. Ezzell, "Laws of Racial Identification"; Kuhl, *The Nazi Connection*, 36; Rossinow, *Visions of Progress*, 168.

19. Stokes, "American Race Relations," 537.

20. Stokes, 538. Martin Jenkins, a professor of education at Howard University, also noted the significance of race in the war, writing, "the present war, based as it is in part at least, on differing racial ideologies, has made *race* a paramount issue throughout the world." Jenkins, "Education for Racial Understanding," 265. See also Borstelmann, *The Cold War and the Color Line*, 27–29.

21. Roberts, "The Negro in Government War Agencies"; Lewis, "The Role of Pressure Groups," 468; McCulloch, "What Should the American Negro," 563; and Chen, *The Fifth Freedom*, 33–38.

22. Stokes, "American Race Relations," 540.

23. Korstad and Lichtenstein, "Opportunities Found and Lost."

24. Kazin, *American Dreamers*, 176.

25. This new reality was quickly grasped by Secretary of State Dean Acheson, who in a 1946 letter to the Fair Employment Practices Committee (FEPC) wrote, "the existence of discrimination against minority groups in this country has an adverse effect upon our relations with other countries. We are reminded over and over by some foreign newspapers and spokesmen, that our treatment of various minorities leaves much to be desired.... We will have better international relations when these reasons for suspicion and resentment have been removed." As quoted in the U.S. President's Committee on Civil Rights, "To Secure These Rights," 146. This international reality was part of the impetus for President Truman's decision to establish the President's Committee on Civil Rights (PCCR) in 1946 to investigate the status of civil rights. The PCCR's 1947 report, *To Secure These Rights: The Report of the President's Committee on Civil Rights*, pointed repeatedly to the international rationale for taking action to improve the protection of civil rights for racial minorities. The PCCR argued that "our civil rights record has growing international implications," and that "throughout the Pacific, Latin America, Africa, the Near, Middle, and Far East, the treatment which our Negroes receive is taken as a reflection of our attitudes toward all dark-skinned peoples." U.S. President's Committee on Civil Rights, "To Secure These Rights," 133, 147.

26. Dudziak, *Cold War Civil Rights*, 29.

27. The petition, entitled *An Appeal to the World: A Statement on the Denial of Human Rights to Minorities in the Case of Citizens of Negro Descent in the United States of America and an Appeal to the United Nations for Redress*, was largely Du Bois's idea. Du Bois had been inspired by a similar, although much less in-depth, submission the year before by the NNC, a petition which had been essentially ignored. Dudziak, *Cold War Civil Rights*, 43–44.

28. Du Bois, *An Appeal to the World*, 11.

29. Du Bois, 12.

30. Horne, *Black and Red*, 76.

31. Dudziak, *Cold War Civil Rights*, 44–45.

32. This was particularly true as China transitioned to communism in 1949 and the subsequent Korean War shifted the focus of the Cold War to Asia in the early 1950s. In a 1951 *JNE* article sociologist St. Clair Drake noted that in Asia, the "Communist movement attempts to define the situation as one in which '*white* imperialist powers' are decimating '*oppressed Colored* peoples.'" St. Clair Drake argued that the communists pursued a strategy of "publicizing its own repudiation of racism and all theories of biological determinism," while it simultaneously "exposes, attacks, and ridicules any evidences of racism among

the 'free nations.'" St. Clair Drake, "The International Implications," 263–64. Psychologist Howard Hale Long echoed this point, noting that the treatment of Black people meant that the "USSR has several advantages over the West in its approach to the Asians," most notably the fact that "she had decisively abolished race prejudice and ostensibly at least accepted the Asians on equality." Long pointed out that it was not only the domestic treatment of Black people that was harming the United States' international interests, but also the fact that the United States continued to treat non-white allies as inferior creating the impression that Soviet propaganda was true. Long, "Cultural and Racial Tension," 14.

33. Snowden, "The Italian Press Views"; Eells, "The Higher Education of Negroes"; Dudziak, *Cold War Civil Rights*, 30–43.

34. Drake, "The International Implications"; Long, "Cultural and Racial Tension."

35. Truman, Executive Order 9980; Truman, Executive Order 9981, 4313.

36. Truman ended his 1948 appeal for congressional action by noting, "If we wish to inspire the peoples of the world whose freedom is in jeopardy, if we wish to restore hope to those who have already lost their civil liberties, if we wish to fulfill the promise that is ours, we must correct the remaining imperfections in our practice of democracy." President Truman also acknowledged the report of the President's Committee on Civil Rights in justifying his proposed new legislative protections. Truman, "Special Message to the Congress on Civil Rights," 2.

37. Dudziak, "Desegregation as a Cold War Imperative"; Horne, "Race from Power."

38. Associated Press, "Text of the Platform," 29.

39. Marable, *Race, Reform, and Rebellion*, 21. Du Bois and Robeson were also Wallace supporters. A 1947 poll of the NAACP national office found that roughly 70 percent of NAACP staffers intended to support Wallace over Truman in the 1948 election.

40. Janken, "From Colonial Liberation," 1075.

41. Truman ultimately garnered two-thirds of the Black vote, which in the close election provided him his margin of victory in several states. Marable, *Race, Reform, and Rebellion*, 23.

42. Du Bois. *An Appeal to the World*, 11; Janken, "From Colonial Liberation," 1086–87.

43. Patterson, *We Charge Genocide*, xi.

44. Patterson, 5, 23.

45. Patterson, 7.

46. This proved to be an uncomfortable reality when Walter White attempted to initially discredit the CRC's petition through challenging the facts it presented, a position he backed off only after Roy Wilkins pointed out that "many of the citations in that book are from the records and other publications of the NAACP. How can we 'blast' a book that uses our records as source material?" Wilkins, "Memorandum to Mr. White."

47. White, "Statement by Walter White," 1, 5. White recognized the value of his statement to the State Department, given that the "experience and prestige" of the NAACP meant that his statement regarding the treatment of Black people in the United States would be "accepted as truth by the non-communist people of the world." White, "Memorandum from Mr. White to Mr. Wilkins." White followed his official statement with a column for the *Saturday Review of Literature* entitled "Time for a Progress Report," in which he pointed to fifteen specific areas that constituted a "solid body of achievement" in bettering the lives of racial minorities throughout the 1940s. White, "Time for a Progress Report," 41.

48. Drake, "The International Implications," 261; White, "Time for a Progress Report."

49. Significantly, Ralph Bunche's strident critiques of the foreign policy of the United States and the NAACP subsided around the same time he was hired by the Office of Strategic Services. The State Department also reached out to Professor Rayford Logan who was representing the NAACP at the Paris UN session, but Logan refused to denounce the petition. Janken, "From Colonial Liberation," 1087.

50. Anderson, "Bleached Souls and Red Negroes," 103–4.

51. Janken, "From Colonial Liberation," 1083.

52. Du Bois, Robeson, and Patterson had all been critical of the NAACP's embrace of Truman in the 1948 election, and all three were signatories to the *We Charge Genocide* petition. Janken, "From Colonial Liberation," 1086; Patterson, *We Charge Genocide*.

53. Despite disagreements, there was some attempt by Patterson to cooperate on common political goals with the NAACP. Patterson had reached out to White in 1949 in an attempt to work together on the UN petition, but White refused and criticized the communist nature of the CRC. Jonas, *Freedom's Sword*, 144; Anderson, "Bleached Souls and Red Negroes," 93.

54. Jonas, *Freedom's Sword*, 148.

55. Jonas, 145. In addition to aligning ideologically with the leaders of the NAACP, the strident anti-communism of the organization's leaders was likely given a boost by Arthur Schlesinger's public accusation that the Communist Party was "sinking its tentacles" into the NAACP. Rossinow, *Visions of Progress*, 214.

56. Redding, *Turncoats, Traitors, and Fellow Travelers*, 65.

57. Anderson, "Bleached Souls and Red Negroes," 103–6.

58. Marable, *Race, Reform, Rebellion*, 27.

59. Marable, 26–28. See also Borstelmann, *The Cold War and the Color Line*, 67.

60. Lang, "Freedom Train Derailed," 164. By the mid-1950s, several top NAACP officials, including Thurgood Marshall, had become informants to the FBI. Jonas, *Freedom's Sword*, 149.

61. Anderson, "Bleached Souls and Red Negroes," 107.

62. The order outlined disqualifying offenses for which employees could be fired, including "membership in, affiliation with or sympathetic association with" any organization "designated by the Attorney General as totalitarian, fascist, communist, or subversive." Truman, Executive Order 9835.

63. U.S. House of Representatives Committee on Un-American Activities, *Investigation of Un-American Propaganda*, 42. Hoover's testimony focused almost exclusively on domestic communism as one of the most serious threats facing the nation, warning the committee that "literally hundreds of groups and organizations have either been infiltrated or organized primarily to accomplish the purposes of promoting the interests of the Soviet Union."

64. U.S. House of Representatives Committee on Un-American Activities, *Investigation of Un-American Propaganda*, 43.

65. Congressman Richard Nixon (R-CA) was present at the HUAC hearing and expressed particular concern about communist infiltration and reiterated the pressing need "to expose them, to drive them out of labor unions, out of other institutions." During Hoover's testimony, Republican congressman Karl Mundt of South Dakota, who would become one of Senator Joseph McCarthy's (R-WI) staunchest allies, argued that it was "liberal and progressive" forces that had the responsibility to be the most vigilant and out-

spoken, noting that "it is necessary for them to take vigorous and active steps to expose and defeat the activities of communists, and not simply to damn communism with faint praise, as some have done in the past." U.S. House of Representatives Committee on Un-American Activities, *Investigation of Un-American Propaganda*, 44–47.

66. Wall, *Inventing the "American Way"*; Storrs, *The Second Red Scare*; Foster, *Red Alert!*; Hartman, *Education and the Cold War*; Korstad and Lichtenstein, "Opportunities Found and Lost," 800.

67. Storrs, *The Second Red Scare*, 288; Schrecker, *The Age of McCarthyism*, 71.

68. Storrs, *The Second Red Scare*, 205–58.

69. Nelson and Singleton, *Governmental Surveillance*, 9.

70. As cited in Foster, *Red Alert!*, 64.

71. As cited in Foster, 76–77.

72. Dewey died at age ninety-two on June 1, 1952, the same month of the publication of "Your Child Is Their Target."

73. Nelson and Singleton, *Governmental Surveillance*, 10.

74. For example, see Zimring, Dunham, and Dewey, "Notes and Documents."

75. Wall, *Inventing the "American Way,"* 190–91.

76. Wall, 9, 192.

77. Wall, 283.

78. Wall, 235, 279–85.

79. This new "guns and butter" strategy positioned economic growth, in large part through increased military spending to combat communism, rather than redistribution of wealth as the top economic priority of Cold War liberals. Storrs, *The Second Red Scare*, 164–72.

80. Storrs, *The Second Red Scare*, 164–72.

81. Storrs, 206.

82. *Social Frontier*, volume 1, number 5.

83. Holles, "Wirt's Warning."

84. For example, see "Anti-Red Speaker Hit as Pro-Red."

85. In an illustration of how wide this label was, the list of suspected front groups that led to Counts being targeted included the American Civil Liberties Union, the NAACP Legal Defense and Educational Fund, and, tellingly, the People's Committee Against Hearst. Nelson and Singleton, *Governmental Surveillance*, 18–22.

86. Nelson and Singleton, *Governmental Surveillance*, 18.

87. See Grossman, "Redefining the Relationship"; Wilkerson, "The Vocational Education and Guidance of Negroes"; and Wilkerson, "The Vocational Education and Guidance of Negroes."

88. U.S. Senate Committee on Education and Labor, *Federal Aid for Education Hearings*, 782–84.

89. U.S. Senate Subcommittee to Investigate the Administration of the Internal Security Act and other Internal Security Law, 82nd Cong., *Subversive Influence in the Educational Process Hearings*, 305–22.

90. U.S. House of Representatives Committee on Un-American Activities, *Investigation of Communist Activities in Philadelphia Area*, 3994–97.

91. "Rightists Bolt N.Y. Labor Party." See also "Hillman Elected Party Chairman."

92. "Rightists Bolt N.Y. Labor Party."

93. U.S. House of Representatives, *Special Report on Subversive Activities*, 1–22; U.S. House of Representatives Special Committee on Un-American Activities, *Investigation of Un-American Propaganda Activities*, 3179; U.S. House of Representatives Committee to Investigate Campaign Expenditures, *Hearings on Campaign Expenditures*, 148–64.

94. U.S. House of Representatives Special Subcommittee of the Committee on Education and Labor, *Hearings on the Public School Assistance Act of 1949*, 575. See also U.S. House of Representatives Special Subcommittee of the Committee on Education and Labor, *Hearings on the Public School Assistance Act of 1949*, 834, 894.

95. As quoted in Nelson and Singleton, *Governmental Surveillance*, 20. Importantly, Storrs notes that the informants used by the FBI and HUAC at this time were notoriously unreliable, a fact of which both these organizations were well aware.

96. Nelson and Singleton, *Governmental Surveillance*, 20.

97. The anti-communist nature of his public speaking is evident by the title of one of his speeches, "The Soviet System of Thought Control." See "Accused Educator Blasts Reds"; "Anti-Red Speaker Hit as Pro-Red"; "Squabble over Accused Red's Appearance."

98. As quoted in Wright, "Once Pro-Russian But Not Now."

99. As quoted in Wright, "Once Pro-Russian But Not Now."

100. As quoted in "Claim Reds Make Poor Instructors." See also Cahill, "No Room for Commie Teacher." Counts joined his fellow *Social Frontier* contributor Sidney Hook in taking the position that communists should not be allowed to be employed as teachers.

101. Nelson and Singleton, *Governmental Surveillance*, 19.

102. Storrs, *The Second Red Scare*, 181.

103. Holloway, "Ralph Bunche," 132.

104. Foster, *Red Alert!*, 92.

105. As quoted in Rippa, "The Textbook Controversy," 52.

106. Robey, *Abstracts of Social Science Textbooks*, 420–30.

107. For example, see "An Exhibit," 12.

108. As cited in Lagemann, *An Elusive Science*, 127. The involvement of the American Association of Advertisers appears to have been prompted by their dissatisfaction of a section of Rugg's textbook that noted that expenditure on advertising tended to mean higher prices for the consumer.

109. "Intellectual 'Hot Potato' Stirs Row." In the charged atmosphere, even coming to Rugg's defense represented a danger, as a professor at Georgia Tech found out when an angry crowd erupted into calls for the faculty member to be "thrown out" before a meeting of the Georgia State Board of Education. See "Georgia School Board Meeting Has 'Red Row.'"

110. United Press, "Books Criticized By Legionnaires Reported Stolen."

111. "An Exhibit," 12.

112. Foster, *Red Alert!*, 91. In a telling example of how little it took to cause suspicion, the primary objection to one of the social studies textbooks being consider by the committee was the fact that it carried a picture of Joseph Stalin.

113. Lagemann, *An Elusive Science*, 127–29.

114. Nelson and Singleton, *Governmental Surveillance*, 14.

115. Schoedel, "OSU Speaker Controversy." The 1951 investigation again found little basis for these attacks and there was apparently no mention or objection to the contents of his 1951

speech at Ohio State University; however, the file was filled with attacks on Rugg's writings from the 1930s and 1940s. These were largely local editorials and pamphlets from conservative groups, including some from the DAR and the American Legion. A good demonstration of just how little it took to be subject to charges of subversiveness is the fact that one of the charges that apparently justified Rugg's investigation is that he had once written "our land is not an opportunity for all." Nelson and Singleton, *Governmental Surveillance*, 15.

116. Nelson and Singleton, *Governmental Surveilance*, 14–17. Of particular concern to the FBI during this period was his vocal criticism of the loyalty investigations in education, and his defense of fired teachers, a practice that Rugg had engaged in since his affiliation with the *Social Frontier*.

117. U.S. House of Representatives Committee on Education, *Hearings on Federal Aid to the States for the Support of Public Schools*, 295–97.

118. "Teacher's Union Holds Convention"; "Charter Presented to Teachers' Unit."

119. Grossman, "Redefining the Relationship," 450–53.

120. U.S. House of Representatives Special Committee on Un-American Activities, *Investigation of Un-American Propaganda Activities in U.S.* Volume 10, 6278; U.S. House of Representatives Special Subcommittee on Appropriations, *Hearings on the Fitness for Continuance in Federal Employment*, 204, 220; U.S. House of Representatives Special Committee on Un-American Activities, *Investigation of Un-American Propaganda Activities*, 400, 651–53.

121. U.S. House of Representatives Special Committee on Un-American Activities, *Investigation of Un-American Propaganda Activities*, 40, 47.

122. The legislation contained several provisions that made it much more difficult for labor unions to maintain and expand membership. The limitation on the right to strike, limitations on the use of the boycott, and a provision allowing states to ban "closed shops" all substantially weakened the political position of labor in the postwar era. Lichtenstein, "Taft-Hartley," 788; Gottschalk, *The Shadow Welfare State*, 43–44.

123. The industrial unions of the CIO were by far the largest organizations that had continued to maintain the rough outlines of Popular Front–style cooperation with communists. In 1948, the president of the United Electrical, Radio and Machine Workers (UE) was arrested after he refused to cooperate with HUAC in an investigation of another Popular Front organization. The UE and ten other union affiliates were expelled over refusal to cooperate in the purges. The CIO Resolution on Expulsion of the UE stated emphatically "there is no place in the CIO for any organization whose leaders . . . would betray the American workers into totalitarian bondage." See Schrecker, "Resolution on Expulsion," 197; Rossinow, *Visions of Progress*, 197–98; Marable, *Race, Reform, Rebellion*, 18.

124. Marable, *Race, Reform, Rebellion*, 19–28.

125. As labor historian Nelson Lichtenstein has noted, prior to their exclusion, communist union members had often provided the "organic leadership" for many left-oriented movements, including opposition to the Cold War, defense of civil liberties, and early feminism. Lichtenstein, "Taft-Hartley," 782. Additionally, the Second Red Scare and the broad purges foreclosed the possibility of a clear independence from the Democratic Party and ultimately served to bind the leadership of the labor movement tightly to the Democratic Party leadership. Rossinow, *Visions of Progress*, 144.

126. Marie Gottschalk shows that this was largely a reaction to an unfavorable political climate in which union leaders made the strategic decision to prioritize the maintenance of

member loyalty and the protection of existing unions rather than active expansion and organization of new members. The passage of the Taft–Hartley Act and the political context of the postwar era created an alliance of labor and employers around job-based health and pension benefits that limited labor's active advocacy for universal benefit programs. Gottschalk, *The Shadow Welfare State*, 42–44. See also Forbath, "Civil Rights and Economic Citizenship," 707–8.

127. Korstad and Lichtenstein, "Opportunities Found and Lost," 792–800; Lieberman and Lang, *Anticommunism and the African American*, 8.

128. Sugrue, "Reassessing the History," 497.

129. U.S. House of Representatives Committee on Un-American Activities, *Investigation of Communist Activities in Philadelphia Area*, 3994–97. Incidentally, the house where Mary Foley Grossman was accused of hosting communist meetings, 2302 Delancey Street, was roughly two blocks from the author's residence during graduate school.

130. Wilkerson, *Special Problems of Negro Education*.

131. U.S. Senate Subcommittee to Investigate the Administration of the Internal Security Act and other Internal Security Law, *Subversive Influence in the Educational Process*, 83rd Cong., 637–43.

132. U.S. House of Representatives Special Committee on Un-American Activities, *Investigation of Un-American Propaganda Activities*, 76th Cong., 5981–6001; U.S. House of Representatives Committee on Education, *Hearings on Federal Aid to the States for the Support of Public Schools*, 297–305; U.S. Senate Subcommittee of the Committee on Education and Labor, *Hearing on American Youth Act*, 65–67; U.S. Senate Subcommittee of the Committee on Education and Labor, *Hearing on Federal Aid to Education Act of 1939*, 204–9.

133. U.S. House of Representatives Committee on Un-American Activities, *Investigation of Un-American Propaganda*, 41.

134. U.S. House of Representatives Special Committee on Un-American Activities, *Investigation of Un-American Propaganda Activities*, 671, 772–74, 839, 1676, 1695, 1697, 1700, 1713.

135. U.S. House of Representatives Special Committee on Un-American Activities, *Investigation of Un-American Propaganda Activities*, 41.

136. U.S. Senate Permanent Subcommittee on Investigations, *Hearings on Communist Infiltration Among Army Civilian Workers*, 23–40.

137. U.S. Senate Committee on the Judiciary, *Hearing on the Confirmation of the Nomination of Honorable William Henry Hastie*, 192–204.

138. U.S. Senate Committee on the Judiciary, *Hearing on the Nomination of George M. Johnson*, 15–17.

139. U.S. Senate Subcommittee of the Committee on the Judiciary, *Hearing on the Nomination of Thurgood Marshall*, 124–63.

140. U.S. Department of Justice, "Abe Fortas, Special Inquiry," 6.

141. U.S. Senate Subcommittee to Investigate the Administration of the Internal Security Act and other Internal Security Law, *Subversive Influence in the Educational Process*, 83rd Cong., 637–43.

142. U.S. Senate Subcommittee to Investigate the Administration of the Internal Security Act and Other Internal Security Law, *Subversive Influence in the Educational Process*, 83rd Cong., 638.

143. U.S. Senate Subcommittee to Investigate the Administration of the Internal Security Act and Other Internal Security Law, *Subversive Influence in the Educational Process*, 83rd Cong., 638.

144. U.S. Senate Subcommittee to Investigate the Administration of the Internal Security Act and Other Internal Security Law, *Subversive Influence in the Educational Process Hearings*, 83rd Cong., 638. Despite the fact that the committee learned little from Wilkerson's March testimony, he was called before a different Senate subcommittee investigating communist infiltration of army civilian workers six months later, where he again invoked his Fifth Amendment rights. U.S. Senate Permanent Subcommittee on Investigations, *Hearings on Communist Infiltration Among Army Civilian Workers*, 23–40.

145. *Nomination of Thurgood Marshall*, 127–63.

146. As quoted in Schrecker, *The Lost Soul of Higher Education*, 51–52.

147. Marable, *Race, Reform, and Rebellion*, 27–28.

148. Schrecker, *The Age of McCarthyism*, 90.

149. Additionally, groups such as the Emergency Civil Liberties Committee, which had been formed by civil rights activists unhappy with the unwillingness of the American Civil Liberties Union (ACLU) to defend accused communists, and the National Lawyers Guild who actively opposed anti-communist repression, were actively targeted and marginalized for combating McCarthyism. The National Lawyers Guild lost roughly four-fifths of its members after HUAC issued a report calling it "the Legal Bulwark of the Communist Party," and the Eisenhower administration's unsuccessful attempt to list it as a subversive organization. Schrecker, *The Age of McCarthyism*, 90–91. In addition to infiltration, surveillance, and harassment, many left-leaning groups (including all those listed above) were added to the attorney general's list of subversive organizations by 1953. The act of adding an organization to this list was essentially a death blow, as individuals seeking employment with the federal government were required to sign a statement certifying that they had no past or present connection with any of the listed organizations. Lieberman and Lang, *Anticommunism and the African American*, 9; Lang, "Freedom Train Derailed," 172. The pressures leading to the destruction and disbandment of these groups after World War II was similar to those that had forced similar disbandment of left groups in the early 1940s, such as the National Negro Congress, the American Student Union, and the League of American Writers. Kazin, *American Dreamers*.

150. Schrecker, *The Age of McCarthyism*, 92–93.

151. Indeed, the focus of many groups turned inward. Many groups that had tolerated or welcomed the participation of Communist Party members in the early 1940s began targeting and purging these individuals by the end of the decade. The ACLU ousted communists and sympathizers and actively supported federal suppression efforts. Jonas, *Freedom's Sword*, 147. The American Bar Association (ABA) passed resolutions against permitting communists to practice law and actively cooperated with federal officials to investigate members and begin disbarment proceedings against those deemed subversive. Schrecker, *The Age of McCarthyism*, 85–86.

152. U.S. House of Representatives Committee on Labor, *Proposed Amendments to the National Labor Relations Act*, 277.

153. Klare, "Judicial Deradicalization," 284–85. Klare notes that it easily could be read as overtly anti-capitalist.

154. In the late 1930s and early 1940s, the Court handed down several decisions favorable to labor, including the protection of the right of unionists to speak in public, protection for union advertisements, and protection of the right of unions to picket. However, these early victories were interspersed among other Court decisions that narrowed the rights of unions and workers, including decisions that allowed employers to hire permanent replacement workers, outlawed sit-down strikes, and required employees suing for wrongful termination to mitigate damages while waiting for a ruling. Pope, "Labor and the Constitution," 1090; Kimeldorf and Stepan-Norris, "Historical Studies of Labor Movements," 500; and Klare, "Judicial Deradicalization," 319.

155. Klare, "Judicial Deradicalization," 285–89. Klare notes that illegal tactics included company unionism, espionage, surveillance, and lockouts, as well as violence and terrorism.

156. Pope, "Labor and the Constitution," 1071–72, 1078–82.

157. Pope, 1072; Klare, "Judicial Deradicalization," 320–21; and Gottschalk, *The Shadow Welfare State*, 42–44.

158. Klare, "Judicial Deradicalization," 292.

159. Goluboff, *The Lost Promise of Civil Rights*, 9, emphasis added.

160. Goluboff, 111–40.

161. Goluboff, 85, 105–7.

162. Goluboff, 172, 206.

163. Goluboff, "'Let Economic Equality," 1431.

164. Bunche, "A Critical Analysis," 316; and Goluboff, *The Lost Promise of Civil Rights*, 176, 180.

165. Goluboff, *The Lost Promise of Civil Rights*, 85, 105–7.

166. Goluboff, 219. In fact, pursuing cases that focused on improving the economic conditions of Black workers within segregated workplaces became impossible once the organization prioritized eliminating segregation.

167. McGuinn, "Equal Protection of the Law," 158.

168. McGuinn, 158–59.

169. Johnson and Lucas, "The Present Legal Status," 280.

170. Thompson, "Editorial Comment: How Imminent," 495.

171. Thompson, 498.

172. Clark, "The Lawyer in the Civil Rights Movement," 469. See also Bell, "Serving Two Masters," 470–516; and Bunche, "A Critical Analysis."

173. Smith, *Racial Democracy*, 191.

174. Neal, "Two Negro Problems"; see also Goluboff, *The Lost Promise of Civil Rights*, 198, 237.

175. Smith, "The Quest for Racial Democracy."

176. "Brief for the United States as Amicus Curiae," 61–70. The lawyers appear to accept that these were accurate descriptors of Black families and individuals in racially segregated communities.

177. "Brief for the United States as Amicus Curiae," 67; Smith, *Racial Democracy*, 191–206.

178. Smith, *Racial Democracy*, 202, 211.

179. Dudziak, *Cold War Civil Rights*, 91.

180. "Brief for the United States as Amicus Curiae," 4–5.

181. "Brief for the United States as Amicus Curiae," 20.

182. Marshall, "An Evaluation of Recent Efforts," 322.

183. Gordon, *From Power to Prejudice*.

184. Marshall, "An Evaluation of Recent Efforts," 321–22.

185. Carter, "The Effects of Segregation," 68. The statement also cited a number of other prominent social scientists, including Gunnar Myrdal and E. Franklin Frazier, and was reprinted in full in *JNE* in 1953.

186. Clark, Chein, and Cook, "The Effects of Segregation," 495.

187. Clark, Chein, and Cook, 496.

188. Clark, Chein, and Cook, 497. The statement noted that in a recent questionnaire, the view that racial segregation damaged the segregated population was supported by roughly 90 percent of social scientists that had responded. Clark, Chein, and Cook, "The Effects of Segregation," 497.

189. Marshall, "Opening Argument," 310.

190. Marshall, 312, 315. Marshall's cocounsel Robert Carter sounded similar themes, arguing that segregation slowed the "emotional and mental development" of children and that the "emotional impacts of segregation . . . does impair the ability to learn." Carter, "Opening Argument," 284–85.

191. Although Warren would later claim that the case did not hinge on the social science evidence, Daryl Michael Scott notes that it is difficult to comprehend "what the case hinged on if not the damage imagery generated by social science." Scott, *Contempt and Pity*, 135. Significantly for the NAACP, Thurgood Marshall believed that the social science evidence was critical for many of their victories. See Marshall, "Marshall to George Beaver, Jr.," 236.

192. *Brown v. Board of Education of Topeka*, 347 U.S. 483, 492 (1954).

193. *Brown v. Board of Education of Topeka*, 347 U.S. 483, 494 (1954).

194. *Brown v. Board of Education of Topeka*, 347 U.S. 483, 494 (1954).

195. Goluboff, *The Lost Promise of Civil Rights*, 240.

196. Guinier, "From Racial Liberalism," 116.

197. Cox, "Vested Interests," 113.

198. Daryl Michael Scott argues that the "emphasis on black egos marked a shift . . . away from the interwar racial liberals' economic approach to securing the civil rights of black folk." Scott, *Contempt and Pity*, 97.

199. Carter and Marshall, "The Meaning and Significance," 404.

200. Williams, "The Interracial Conference," 204.

201. Williams, 204.

202. Moak, "Thurgood Marshall," 397–401.

203. Goluboff, *The Lost Promise of Civil Rights*, 244.

204. Marable, *Race, Reform, and Rebellion*, 13–14.

205. Marable, 51–52.

206. Sugrue, "Reassessing the History," 497.

207. Marable, *Race, Reform, and Rebellion*, 51–52.

208. Sugrue, "Reassessing the History," 497.

209. Powdermaker and Storen, *Probing Our Prejudices*.

210. See Noble, "Future Educational Emphasis"; Hartley, "Psychological Investigations"; Lane, "Report of the Committee"; and "Second National Conference on Intergroup Relations."

211. See United States Office of Education, *Life Adjustment Education for Every Youth.*

212. See "Brief of Harry McMullan," 1015–17; "Amicus Curiae Brief of the Attorney General of Florida," 883; and Almond, "Argument on Behalf of the Attorney General of Virginia," 119.

213. Marshall, "Argument of Thurgood Marshall, Esq., on Behalf of Harry Briggs," 1154, emphasis added.

214. See Moak, "Thurgood Marshall," 405–7.

215. U.S. President's Commission on Higher Education, *Higher Education for Democracy,* 41–42.

216. Clarke, "The Role of Psychology"; and Thompson, "Evaluation as a Factor." Somewhat ironically, the *Brown* decision also increased support for the use of standardized tests in evaluating teachers in the South, as southern educational officials turned to tests like the National Teacher's Examination as a race-neutral way of firing thousands of Black teachers as schools consolidated in the wake of the Court rulings. Baker, "Testing Equality."

217. Ethridge, "Impact of the 1954 *Brown vs. Board.*" It is important to again note that this is not a full reflection of the extent of displacement. Not only do these numbers not capture demotion and salary reductions, but they also only reflect displacement in the southern states. Ethridge noted the most flagrant perpetrators of displacement were the school systems of Boston and New York City, numbers that are not fully reflected in the statistics above. For the 1970–1971 school year, Ethridge estimated that displacement of Black educators represented a loss of more than $240 million in salary. By the mid-1960s the prescience of Cox's earlier warning was clear, and Herman Long lamented that "the great advance in school desegregation under the impetus of Federal sanctions may well result in what we feared when desegregation began; namely, the use of the Negro teacher as a pawn, as the dispensable element with which gains in desegregation can be bought." Long, "On the Emergence," 13. For more on the consequences of desegregation for Black educators, see Haney, "The Effects of the *Brown* Decision"; National Education Association, *School Desegregation*; National Education Association of the United States and National Commission on Professional Rights and Responsibilities, *Report of Task Force*; Baker, "Testing Equality"; Fultz, "The Displacement of Black Educators"; Hooker, "Displacement of Black Teachers."

218. Grossman, "Redefining the Relationship," 450–53.

Chapter Four

1. U.S. Congress House of Representatives Committee on Education and Labor, *Message from the President of the United States Transmitting Educational Program.*

2. U.S. Senate Subcommittee on Education, *Hearings on a Bill to Strengthen and Improve Educational Quality,* 78.

3. Uncovering the continuity between the federal education landscape of the 1960s and the current moment requires paying close attention to the ideas about the purpose of education that drove the development of the federal education state in the mid-twentieth century. As scholars of American political development have shown, ideas are constitutive

elements in stitching together coalitions that shape the way that the public and policy makers interpret the world. Ideas are thus critical for understanding political development, as the success of an idea in shaping the interpretation of social problems and their potential solutions can drive institutional change. On the importance of ideas in political development, see Smith, "Which Comes First," 109; Lieberman, "Ideas, Institutions, and Political Order"; Schmidt, "Taking Ideas and Discourse Seriously"; Smith, "Ideas and the Spiral of Politics"; and Weaver, *Blazing the Neoliberal Trail.*

4. In keeping with the efforts of other scholars of American political development to broadly reconsider the mid-twentieth century, this chapter challenges the notion that the ESEA represented a progressive victory that was only subsequently pushed in a punitive direction by conservatives. Several scholarly accounts point to the ESEA as a pinnacle of the Great Society's attempt to attack inequality and poverty, with initial success rolled back by a later conservative mobilization around the school choice and standards movement, and a renewed focus on "excellence" rather than "equity" in education. See Apple, *Educating the "Right" Way*; Debray, *Politics, Ideology and Education*; Fabricant and Fine, *Charter Schools and the Corporate Makeover of Public Education*; Henig, "Education Policy from 1980 to the Present"; Manna, *School's In*; McGuinn, "Education Policy from the Great Society to 1980"; Rhodes, *An Education in Politics*; Saltman, "The Rise of Venture Philanthropy"; Saltman, *The Failure of Corporate School Reform*; and McGuinn, *No Child Left Behind*. Similarly, recent scholarship from the field of education has interrogated the consequences of "educationalizing" social problems, noting that the belief that education is the key to social transformation downplays or completely ignores the role of political economy in the creation and maintenance of these problems. See Labaree, "The Winning Ways of a Losing Strategy." See also Grubb and Lazerson, *The Education Gospel*; Kantor and Lowe, "The Price of Human Capital"; Kantor and Lowe, "Educationalizing the Welfare State"; and Imbroscio, "Urban Policy as Meritocracy." This broader reevaluation of the foundation of the federal education state joins the efforts from a number of other scholars of American political development to examine the role of the mid-twentieth century in constraining future progressive developments and setting the stage for punitive developments. See Gottschalk, *The Shadow Welfare State*; Katznelson, "Was the Great Society a Lost Opportunity?"; Chen, *The Fifth Freedom*; Morgan and Campbell, *The Delegated Welfare State*; Bertram, *The Workfare State*; Murakawa, *The First Civil Right*; Hinton, *From the War on Poverty to the War on Crime*; and O'Connor, *Poverty Knowledge.*

5. These programs included the Public Works Administration, the Federal Emergency Relief Act, the Farm Security Administration, the Civilian Conservation Corps, the Civil Works Administration, the Works Progress Administration, and the National Youth Administration.

6. Mucciaroni, *The Political Failure*, 21. Mucciaroni notes that in the early part of his second term, with decreasing unemployment rates, President Roosevelt immediately took steps aimed at balancing the budget. See also Collins, *The Business Response*, 5.

7. Mucciaroni, *The Political Failure*, 22.

8. Collins, *The Business Response*, 6–7.

9. Collins, 10.

10. Mucciaroni, *The Political Failure*, 22–26.

11. Weir, *Politics and Jobs*, 40–41. Robert Collins notes that Alvin Hansen and other stagnationists appeared to envision a "state dedicated to continuously high spending for education,

social welfare, public works, regional development, public health, and urban renewal." Collins, *The Business Response*, 97.

12. Weir notes that by 1940, many of Hansen's students served in important positions in the executive branch, a result of the active recruitment by those in the administration who favored increased spending as well as the specific orientation toward policy represented by Hansen and his students. Weir, *Politics and Jobs*, 41.

13. Mucciaroni, *The Political Failure*, 23.

14. Fass, "Without Design," 43. For example, throughout the New Deal, the federal government spent millions in school construction and school repair, largely as a means of providing work relief.

15. Fass, "Without Design," 51.

16. According to Paula Fass, the New Deal "left no immediate instrumental legacy" in terms of education. Fass, "Without Design," 61.

17. Kantor and Lowe, "Class, Race, and the Emergence of Federal Education Policy," 6.

18. Full Employment Act of 1945, section 2, c.

19. Mucciaroni, *The Political Failure*, 24. Business opposition was also grounded in a broader strategy to curb organized labor's political power. Weir, *Politics and Jobs*, 50.

20. Weir, *Politics and Jobs*, 48–49.

21. Weir, 12.

22. Mucciaroni, *The Political Failure*, 26.

23. Mucciaroni, 26. Robert Collins, Gary Mucciaroni, and Margaret Weir all point to the importance of the Committee for Economic Development in crafting the central tenets of commercial Keynesianism and creating support for this economic vision within the larger business community.

24. Collins, *The Business Response*, 108.

25. Council of Economic Advisers, *Oral History Interview*, 49.

26. Council of Economic Advisers, 33.

27. Council of Economic Advisers, 424–54.

28. Weir, *Politics and Jobs*, 59–60. Congressional concern about the effect of tax cuts on the budget deficit delayed passage until President Johnson's administration.

29. Johnson, "Annual Message to the Congress."

30. *Economic Report of the President*, 7.

31. Johnson, "Annual Message."

32. *Economic Report of the President*, 104.

33. *Economic Report of the President*, 111.

34. U.S. Senate Subcommittee on Employment and Manpower, *Hearing Relating to the Training and Utilization of the Manpower*, 1871.

35. U.S. Senate Subcommittee on Employment and Manpower, *Hearing Relating to the Training and Utilization of the Manpower*, 1865.

36. U.S. Senate Subcommittee on Employment and Manpower, *Hearing Relating to the Training and Utilization of the Manpower*, 1938.

37. U.S. Senate Subcommittee on Employment and Manpower, *Hearing Relating to the Training and Utilization of the Manpower*, 1968.

38. Johnson, "Presidential Policy Paper No. 1: Education."

39. U.S. Senate Committee on Labor and Public Welfare, *Report on Elementary and Secondary Education Act of 1965*, 4.

40. *Economic Report of the President*, 66.

41. *Economic Report of the President*, 75.

42. See Katz, *The Undeserving Poor*; see also Weir, *Politics and Jobs*; and Muciarroni, *The Political Failure*.

43. Breen, "Capitalizing Labor."

44. Breen, 92.

45. Breen, 92.

46. Schultz, "Investment in Human Capital," 14.

47. Schultz, 14.

48. Schultz, 14.

49. *Journal of Political Economy*, volume 70, number 5.

50. U.S. Senate Subcommittee on Education, *Hearings on Bills to Improve Education Quality and Opportunity*, 4023.

51. The summary had been put together by Agnes Meyer, the chair of the recently formed National Committee for Support of Public Schools. Meyer's ability to influence the educational thinking of policy makers extended beyond Congress as indicated by President Lyndon Johnson's memoir, in which he noted, "My determined efforts on behalf of education bills were stimulated and inspired by Mrs. Agnes E. Meyer, an old friend who, I believe, did more to influence me on federal education measures than any other person." Agnes E. Meyer was well known to policy makers in Washington, D.C. She had served on the 1946 Zook Commission on Higher Education, and her husband was Eugene Meyer, a former chairman of the Federal Reserve, the first president of the World Bank, and part owner of the *Washington Post*. Johnson, *The Vantage Point*, 219.

52. U.S. Senate Subcommittee on Education, *Hearings on Bills to Improve Education Quality and Opportunity*, 4034.

53. Lantos would later go on to serve for twenty-seven years as a Democratic member of the House of Representatives from California.

54. U.S. Senate Subcommittee on Education, *Hearings on a Bill to Strengthen and Improve Educational Quality and Educational Opportunities*, 1738. Lantos also argued that "our public school system is by far the most effective instrument of securing an adequate rate of economic growth for our future." U.S. Senate Subcommittee on Education, *Hearings on a Bill to Strengthen and Improve Educational Quality and Educational Opportunities*, 1738.

55. U.S. Senate Subcommittee on Education, *Hearings on a Bill to Strengthen and Improve Educational Quality and Educational Opportunities*, 1742.

56. U.S. House of Representatives Subcommittee on Education, *Hearings on Bills to Strengthen and Improve Educational Quality and Educational Opportunities*, 1347. Brademas also applauded Lantos for connecting the issue of unemployment directly to education, noting, "I am especially glad you talked about the relationship between education and the problem of unemployment. I think it has only been since the passage of the Manpower Development and Training Act that we have started to give adequate attention to these two problems." U.S. House of Representatives Subcommittee on Education, *Hearings on Bills to Strengthen and Improve Educational Quality and Educational Opportunities*, 1347.

57. U.S. House of Representatives Subcommittee on Education, *Hearings on Bills to Strengthen and Improve Educational Quality and Educational Opportunities*, 1348.

58. U.S. House of Representatives Subcommittee on Education, *Hearings on Bills to Strengthen and Improve Educational Quality and Educational Opportunities*, 1349.

59. In his Senate testimony advocating federal support for primary and secondary education, Tom Lantos made this point to Senator Robert Kennedy, noting, "I think what we are discovering is that, we have a new kind of poor in American society, or perhaps I should put it this way—the relationship between the poor and society today is different than what, it had been historically. Historically this economy was eager to absorb large numbers of unskilled, unschooled, uneducated people because there were millions of jobs available for these people. What we are discovering now, and I agree with you we are discovering it too late, that the new poor are going to be permanently alienated from the mainstream of American society because in an increasingly automated society, there will never be room for them." U.S. Senate Subcommittee on Education, *Hearings on a Bill to Strengthen and Improve Educational Quality and Educational Opportunities*, 1745–46.

60. Weir, *Politics and Jobs*, 68; Muciarroni, *The Political Failure*, 53.

61. Hinton, *From the War on Poverty to the War on Crime*, 28.

62. For more on the history of the relocation of assumed Black deviancy from genetics to culture, see Muhammad, *The Condemnation of Blackness*.

63. See Gordon, *From Power to Prejudice*. Significantly, these developments also facilitated a shift in how Black political organizations and social scientists articulated their political positions as well. Several scholars have shown a shift from a focus on union organizing and redistributive economic demands in the 1930s and 1940s to a politics centered on legal administrative demands for equal inclusion into existing social structures by the 1960s. See Korstad and Lichtenstein, "Opportunities Found and Lost"; Smith, *Racial Democracy and the Black Metropolis*; and Goluboff, *The Lost Promise of Civil Rights*.

64. O'Connor, *Poverty Knowledge*, 103.

65. Hauptmann, "The Ford Foundation," 156. One of the earliest examples of this type of foundation funding social scientific investigations into social problems was the Carnegie Corporation's funding of Gunnar Myrdal's *An American Dilemma: The Negro Problem and Modern Democracy*. Significantly, Myrdal's analysis contained early versions of cultural explanations of racial inequality. Myrdal was also an early advocate of the power of education to address cultural pathologies responsible for racial inequality.

66. O'Connor, *Poverty Knowledge*, 104.

67. See Schmitt, *President of the Other America*, 69–72; O'Connor, *Poverty Knowledge*, 128.

68. Cloward and Ohlin, *Delinquency and Opportunity*.

69. O'Connor, *Poverty Knowledge*, 128.

70. Katz, *The Undeserving Poor*, 121.

71. Cloward and Ohlin, *Delinquency and Opportunity*, 103.

72. Cloward and Ohlin, 98.

73. Community action programs of the 1964 Economic Opportunity Act were modeled programs that the PCJD had developed to address delinquency. See Katz, *The Undeserving Poor*; and Weir, *Politics and Jobs* for accounts of the importance of the PCJD and "opportunity theory" to the policies of the War on Poverty.

74. Moynihan, *The Negro Family*.

75. Scott, *Contempt and Pity*, 144.

76. Scott, 137–59.

77. Johnson, "Commencement Address at Howard University."

78. Scott, *Contempt and Pity*, 152.

79. Scott, 148.

80. Clark, "American Education Today," 51.

81. Clark, "Clash of Cultures in the Classroom," 13–14.

82. Clark, 13–14.

83. Clark, "American Education Today," 52. Indeed, at times, Clark's discussion about pathology of the ghetto appeared indistinguishable from his fellow social scientists that centered cultural difference more directly. For example, in *Dark Ghetto: Dilemmas of Social Power*, Clark wrote, "The dark ghetto is institutionalized pathology; it is chronic, self-perpetuating pathology. . . . Not only is the pathology of the ghetto self-perpetuating, but one kind of pathology breeds another. The child born in the ghetto is more likely to come into a world of broken homes and illegitimacy; and this family and social instability is conducive to delinquency, drug addiction, and criminal violence." Clark, *Dark Ghetto*, 81.

84. Clark, "Clash of Cultures in the Classroom," 10.

85. Clark, "American Education Today," 53.

86. Clark, 52.

87. Clark, *Dark Ghetto*, xxvii.

88. Johnson, "Commencement Address at Howard University"; Clark, "American Education Today," 51.

89. Cuban, *The Blackboard and the Bottom Line*, 10.

90. Breen, "Capitalizing Labor," 107.

91. U.S. Senate Committee on Labor and Public Welfare, *Report on Elementary and Secondary Education*, 3.

92. U.S. Senate Committee on Labor and Public Welfare, *Report on Elementary and Secondary Education*, 3–4.

93. U.S. Senate Subcommittee on Education, *Hearings on a Bill to Strengthen and Improve Educational Quality and Educational Opportunities*, 901.

94. Council of Economic Advisers, "Oral History Interview," 424–54.

95. Muciarroni, *The Political Failure*, 55.

96. *Economic Report of the President*, 77–78.

97. Council of Economic Advisers, "Oral History Interview," 292.

98. *Economic Report of the President*, 16.

99. *Economic Report of the President*, 111.

100. Hinton, *From the War on Poverty*, 28–30. In describing the behavior of urban youth, Kenneth Clark also picked up on the language of "social dynamite," but suggested the schools were more directly responsible. Clark argued in discussion of social dynamite that it was important to note that it was "dynamite that is planted by educators themselves and by a society that seems incapable of understanding its problems of justice; that the dignity and integrity of the human being can not be flagrantly violated in an institution which is called educational." Clark, "Clash of Cultures," 11.

101. Johnson, "Presidential Policy Paper No. 1: Education."

102. Johnson, "Presidential Policy Paper No. 1: Education."

103. Hinton, *From the War on Poverty*, 31.

104. Kantor, "Education, Social Reform, and the State."

Chapter Five

1. U.S. Senate Subcommittee on Education of the Committee on Labor and Public Welfare, *Hearings on a Bill to Strengthen and Improve Educational Quality and Educational Opportunities*, 3014.

2. As quoted in Manning, "The Measurement of Intellectual Capacity," 261.

3. Johnson, *Economic Report of the President*, 15–16.

4. Urban and Wagoner, *American Education: A History*, 373.

5. McGuinn, *No Child Left Behind*, 31.

6. For example, see *Youth in the Ghetto*.

7. Indeed, Kennedy argued, "If you are going to judge [the school system] on whether the children are keeping up with their reading, reading ability, whether they are dropouts, whether they are involved in juvenile delinquency, all of these matters in these various communities at the present time, including my own city of New York, you would have to say that the school system is flunking." U.S. Senate Subcommittee on Education of the Committee on Labor and Public Welfare, *Hearings on a Bill to Strengthen and Improve Educational Quality and Educational Opportunities*, 2729–30.

8. U.S. Senate Subcommittee on Education of the Committee on Labor and Public Welfare, *Hearings on a Bill to Strengthen and Improve Educational Quality and Educational Opportunities*, 511.

9. U.S. Senate Subcommittee on Education of the Committee on Labor and Public Welfare, *Hearings on a Bill to Strengthen and Improve Educational Quality and Educational Opportunities*, 511. Kennedy publicly voiced similar concerns during Tom Lantos's congressional testimony. Kennedy remarked to Lantos, "I do not think money in and of itself is necessarily the answer. I have seen enough school districts where there has been lack of imagination, lack of initiative, and lack of interest in the problems of some of the deprived children which causes me concern. My feeling is that even if we put money into those school districts, then it will be wasted."

10. U.S. Senate Subcommittee on Education of the Committee on Labor and Public Welfare, *Hearings on a Bill to Strengthen and Improve Educational Quality and Educational Opportunities*, 511. Later on in the hearings, noting poor reading ability test scores, dropout numbers, and juvenile delinquency, Kennedy argued, "the school system must have something to do with it, and if the program they have had in effect over the period of the last decade has produced such poor results and *destroyed the lives of these children, then I think that whoever is responsible for that should be held responsible.*" U.S. Senate Subcommittee on Education of the Committee on Labor and Public Welfare, *Hearings on a Bill to Strengthen and Improve Educational Quality and Educational Opportunities*, 3086, emphasis added.

11. U.S. Senate Subcommittee on Education of the Committee on Labor and Public Welfare, *Hearings on a Bill to Strengthen and Improve Educational Quality and Educational Opportunities*, 512. See also U.S. Senate Subcommittee on Education of the Committee on Labor and Public Welfare, *Hearings on S. 370, 1298, 2663, 2727, 2875, and 3085*.

12. Halperin, "ESEA: Five Years Later."

13. Graham, *The Uncertain Triumph*, 78–79. See also McLaughlin, *Evaluation and Reform*, 3.

14. Senate Committee on Labor and Public Welfare, *Report on Elementary and Secondary Education*, 40. See also Halperin, "ESEA Ten Years Later," 8; and McLaughlin, *Evaluation and Reform*.

15. McLaughlin, *Evaluation and Reform*, 10.

16. McLaughlin, 8–11.

17. U.S. Senate Subcommittee on Education of the Committee on Labor and Public Welfare, *Hearings on a Bill to Strengthen and Improve Educational Quality and Educational Opportunities*, 511.

18. U.S. Senate Subcommittee on Education of the Committee on Labor and Public Welfare, *Hearings on a Bill to Strengthen and Improve Educational Quality and Educational Opportunities*, 901.

19. U.S. Senate Subcommittee on Education of the Committee on Labor and Public Welfare, *Hearings on a Bill to Strengthen and Improve Educational Quality and Educational Opportunities*, 515.

20. U.S. House of Representatives, *Departments of Labor, and Health*, 333.

21. John Hughes, the executive officer of the Office of Education, made clear to members of Congress that the idea of the assessment test came directly from the Carnegie Corporation, noting, "As a matter of fact, we do not wish to claim credit for it, because the Carnegie Corp. had this idea before we came along. But we were able to encourage their participation in this field." U.S. House of Representatives, *Departments of Labor, and Health*, 622.

22. U.S. House of Representatives, *Departments of Labor, and Health*, 333.

23. U.S. House of Representatives, *Departments of Labor, and Health*, 659.

24. Roelofs, *Foundations and Public Policy*, 70–71.

25. For example, see U.S. Senate Subcommittee on Education of the Committee on Labor and Public Welfare, *Hearings on a Bill to Strengthen and Improve Educational Quality and Educational Opportunities*, 528.

26. U.S. House of Representatives, *Departments of Labor, and Health*, 334.

27. McLaughlin, *Evaluation and Reform*, 5–6.

28. Task Force on Economic Growth and Opportunity, *The Disadvantaged Poor*, 26. This report also demonstrated how business could employ liberal incorporationist rhetoric to square calls for racial advancement with capitalism. The report argued "systemic exclusion of any ethnic group from full participation is not only morally and politically wrong, but economically wasteful as well." Task Force on Economic Growth and Opportunity, *The Disadvantaged Poor*, 12.

29. Task Force on Economic Growth and Opportunity, *The Disadvantaged Poor*, 60.

30. Task Force on Economic Growth and Opportunity, 61.

31. See Clark, *Dark Ghetto*. See also Cohen and Moffitt, *The Ordeal of Equality*, 71; and Kantor, "Education, Social Reform, and the State," 66. For another example of a voice outside of government that agreed with Kennedy's analysis, see the testimony of Lindley J. Stiles, dean of the University of Wisconsin's School of Education before the Senate Subcommittee on Education. In his statement, Dean Stiles presciently called for a "program of evaluation . . . designed to measure the increments of educational gain achieved by individual pupils, school systems, and States that have support under Title I" and argued that "federal assistance without

educational accountability . . . is sheer educational and fiscal irresponsibility." U.S. Senate Subcommittee on Education of the Committee on Labor and Public Welfare, *Hearings on a Bill to Strengthen and Improve Educational Quality and Educational Opportunities*, 3076–91.

32. As quoted in Manning, "The Measurement of Intellectual Capacity," 261.

33. Coleman, *Equality of Educational Opportunity*, 22.

34. Coleman later noted that he thought that the use of achievement test scores could be a useful means of evaluating programs targeted toward disadvantaged children, but that the current system schools used was unlikely to succeed in this since "the school is trapped by its own organizational weight." He suggested that private contractors could be compensated and incentivized through their ability to raise the test scores of poor children. U.S. Senate Subcommittee on Education of the Committee on Labor and Public Welfare, *First Session on S. 2218*, 1255.

35. Cohen and Moffitt, *The Ordeal of Equality*, 252n13.

36. Mosbaek, *Analysis of Compensatory Education in Five School Districts*, 2–3.

37. Jeffrey, *Education for Children of the Poor*, 17; Hutt, "'Seeing Like a State,'" 622–24.

38. In fact, as Julie Roy Jeffrey notes, "the whole idea of compensatory education implied teaching the deprived student separately in his own lower-class school, not integrating him with more advanced students." Jeffrey, *Education for Children of the Poor*, 17.

39. As quoted in Hutt, "'Seeing Like a State,'" 624.

40. McLaughlin, *Evaluation and Reform*, 36. For example, at the time health programs were largely assessed on terms of distribution and delivery rather than impact. McLaughlin, *Evaluation and Reform*, 46n28. Jeffrey suggests the decision to embrace test scores as the metric of success might also have been due to the fact that it would have been more difficult for school districts to collect and evaluate broader metrics of success such as college attendance and school attendance rates. Jeffrey, *Education for Children of the Poor*, 160.

41. Martin and McClure, *Is It Helping Poor Children?* 29.

42. Martin and McClure, iii–iv.

43. Martin and McClure, iii–iv.

44. Kantor and Lowe, "Introduction: What Difference Did the Coleman Report Make?" 572; see also Jeffrey, *Education for Children of the Poor*, 160.

45. For example, in his 1969 testimony, DHEW Secretary Robert Finch told Congress that ESEA could not be seen as an unqualified success since some reports indicated that only 2 percent of programs had been able to show measurable improvements in math or English scores. Jeffrey, *Education for Children of the Poor*, 130.

46. Jeffrey, *Education for Children of the Poor*, 227.

47. As quoted in Cohen and Moffitt, *The Ordeal of Equality*, 73.

48. Martin and McClure, *Is It Helping Poor Children?* 54.

49. Martin and McClure, 58.

50. For example, in a letter to Senator Claiborne Pell (D-RI), Walter McCann of the Center for Law and Education and David Cohen of the Center for Education Policy Research expressed concern that the "existing legislation calls for some evaluation, but it is too narrowly conceived" and called for the evaluation metrics outside of the "objective measures of educational achievement" that had become the standard. U.S. Senate Subcommittee on Education of the Committee on Labor and Public Welfare, *First Session on S. 2218*, 1250–51.

51. U.S. Senate Committee on Labor and Public Welfare, *Elementary and Secondary Education Amendments of 1969, Report of the Committee*, 8–9.

52. U.S. Senate Committee on Labor and Public Welfare, *Elementary and Secondary Education Amendments of 1969, Report of the Committee*, 15.

53. U.S. House of Representatives Committee on Education and Labor, *Elementary and Secondary Education Amendments of 1969, Conference Report*, 88.

54. U.S. House of Representatives Committee on Education and Labor, *Elementary and Secondary Education Amendments of 1969, Conference Report*, 65.

55. Halperin, "ESEA: Ten Years Later," 8.

56. U.S. Senate Committee on Labor and Public Welfare, *Elementary and Secondary Education Amendments of 1969, Report of the Committee*, 9.

57. U.S. Senate Committee on Labor and Public Welfare, *Elementary and Secondary Education Amendments of 1969, Report of the Committee*, 10. See also Cohen and Moffitt, *The Ordeal of Equality*, 60–61.

58. "USOE Orders States to Repay Title I Funds Improperly Spent," 199.

59. National Institute of Education, *Administration of Compensatory Education*.

60. Halperin, "ESEA: Ten Years Later," 8.

61. Halperin, 8.

62. For example, Robert Kennedy blamed schools for condemning some children to poor outcomes during congressional hearings. U.S. Senate Subcommittee on Education of the Committee on Labor and Public Welfare, *Hearings on a Bill to Strengthen and Improve Educational Quality and Educational Opportunities*, 3014.

63. Todd-Breland, *A Political Education*, 51–55, 193.

64. Dantley, "The Ineffectiveness of Effective Schools," 589–90.

65. Todd-Breland, *A Political Education*, 191–93.

66. Mace-Matluck, *The Effective Schools Movement*, 9. See also Weber, *Inner City Children Can Be Taught*.

67. Todd-Breland, *A Political Education*, 193.

68. Todd-Breland, 193–96.

69. Carmichael beat the more moderate John Lewis in the election. Goldstein, *The Teacher Wars*, 141; see also Johnson, *Revolutionaries to Race Leaders*, xxi.

70. As quoted in Teodori, *The New Left*, 257.

71. Hamilton, "Race and Education," 671.

72. Hamilton, 684.

73. For an account of how the Coleman Report helped fuel backlash against integration among Black northerners, see Burkholder, "The Perils of Integration."

74. McKissick wrote, "Public education, instead of combatting racism, feeds upon and perpetuates racism." McKissick, "Negro Voices," 46.

75. McKissick, "Negro Voices," 46.

76. McKissick, 46.

77. Rickford, *We Are an African People*, 6–17.

78. Rickford, 262.

79. As quoted in Rickford, 257.

80. Rickford, 263, 258.

81. Rickford notes that there were some exceptions despite these broader trends. He points to the Oakland Community School and the Black and Proud Liberation School of Jackson, Mississippi, as examples of independent Black educational institutions that were able to maintain independent bastions of institutional authority characterized by democratic education techniques and progressive ethics well into the 1970s. Rickford, *We Are an African People*, 263–67.

82. Robinson, *Black Nationalism in American Politics*, 88–103; Reed, *Toward Freedom*, 69–74.

83. Johnson, "The Panthers Can't Save Us Now," 64.

84. Ferguson, *Top Down*, 89. For more on foundations' attempt to direct "Black power" in a pro-capitalist direction, see Roelofs, *Foundations and Public Policy*, 95.

85. Ferguson, *Top Down*, 73.

86. Goldstein, *The Teacher Wars*, 144–45.

87. As James Forman notes, earlier examples such as the Mississippi Freedom Schools and the Free Schools movement were also based on dissatisfaction with public schools. However, these movements tended to support a progressive pedagogical vision that was closer to that of the social reconstructionists. The Mississippi Freedom Schools viewed students and teachers as agents of social change, and the Free School advocated for an overtly political pedagogy that focused on the social issues of the day, including the Vietnam War, the Civil Rights Movement, and women's liberation. Both at times also called for a different vision of the classroom itself, including changes in the relationship between student and teacher, and many were opposed to testing and grades. Forman, "The Secret History of School Choice," 1298–303.

88. Clark, "Social Dynamics of the Ghetto," 51.

89. Clark, 51.

90. Clark, 51; see also Clark, "Alternative Public School Systems," 101.

91. Clark, "Alternative Public School Systems," 110. Clark also placed education at the center of Black advancement in an article the following year, arguing "A massive program for the upgrading of the quality of education for Negro youth is now imperative if there is to be any meaningful change in the economic and ghetto status of the Negro in America." Clark, "Social Dynamics of the Ghetto," 52.

92. Clark, "Answer for 'Disadvantaged' Is Effective Teaching," 63.

93. Clark, "Clash of Cultures in the Classroom." Clark's critiques of the "well-intentioned" teachers that hold lower standards reads like an early version of what then-presidential candidate George W. Bush would later call "the soft bigotry of low expectations" as he pushed for increased accountability in a campaign speech before the NAACP. Bush, "Speech at the NAACP's 91st Annual Convention."

94. Clark, "Alternative Public School Systems," 112.

95. Clark, "Answer for 'Disadvantaged' Is Effective Teaching," 63.

96. Clark, "Alternative Public School Systems," 111.

97. Clark, 110; see also Clark, "Efficiency as a Prod to Social Action," 55.

98. Clark, "Alternative Public School Systems," 113.

99. Clark, "Answer for 'Disadvantaged' Is Effective Teaching," 63.

100. U.S. House of Representatives Special Select Subcommittee on District of Columbia of the Committee on the District of Columbia, *Problems in D.C. Public Schools*, 77.

101. Clark, *A Possible Reality*, 14.

102. According to the proposed plan, "sociological and other dimensions of social injustices are critical determinants of academic retardation only when they are permitted to intrude into, and dominate, the atmosphere of schools. They need not." Clark, *A Possible Reality*, 14.

103. Clark, *A Possible Reality*, 23.

104. Clark, 49.

105. Clark, 43. Although the MARC researchers ultimately rejected direct cash payments as a means of tapping into student competitiveness, they ultimately rejected this approach "more for moral and esthetic than for scientific or practical reasons." Clark, *A Possible Reality*, 43. As Lester Spence points out, a later generation of Black social scientists would not feel the same hesitancy. Spence, *Knocking the Hustle.*

106. Clark, *A Possible Reality*, 32.

107. Cuban, "Reform by Fiat," 18.

108. As quoted in Cuban, "Reform by Fiat," 16.

109. Williams, "At the Center of the School Strike."

110. As quoted in Cuban, "Reform by Fiat," 20.

111. Cuban, "Reform by Fiat," 23.

112. "Kenneth Clark's Revolutionary Slogan."

113. "Kenneth Clark's Revolutionary Slogan."

114. For more on Rustin's general criticism of Black Power, see Reed, *Toward Freedom*, 69–75.

115. Rustin, "The Mind of the Black Militant," 211.

116. As Rustin argued, "Pressure tactics will not solve unemployment or eradicate slums, but they can give the local board of education a hard time—a substitute satisfaction. It may be impossible to get at those in the Pentagon who are sending the boys to Vietnam, but it is relatively easy to strike back at those who run the schools." Rustin, "The Mind of the Black Militant," 211.

117. Rustin, "Integration Within Decentralization," 215, 221.

118. Rustin, "The Mind of the Black Militant," 212.

119. Gordon, "If Opportunity Is Not Enough," 613–14.

120. Todd-Breland, *A Political Education*, 13. See also pages 178–218.

121. Lessinger, "Engineering Accountability," 217. See also Lessinger, "Educational Engineering," 277–81.

122. Lessinger, "Engineering Accountability," 217.

123. Lessinger, 217.

124. Ascher, "Performance Contracting," 616.

125. Page, "How We All Failed," 115.

126. Carpenter, "An Evaluation of Performance Contracting," 44, 56.

127. Lessinger and Allen, "Performance Proposals for Educational Funding," 136.

128. Lessinger, "Engineering Accountability," 221–24.

129. Ascher, "Performance Contracting," 616. Dorsett set up trailers outside of the school that contained machines with filmstrips, sound, and buttons. When students answered a question correctly, the machines would move to the next question.

130. Ascher, "Performance Contracting," 616.

131. Carpenter, "An Evaluation of Performance Contracting," 53.

132. Gramlich and Koshel, *Educational Performance Contracting*, 13n16.

133. In fact, the interest in performance contracting was so great that Dorsett had 700 requests for information and 800 visitors to their Texarkana site, including educational personnel from every state. Ascher, "Performance Contracting," 616; Gramlich and Koshel, *Educational Performance Contracting*, 7. The principal and project director of the Texarkana experiment also traveled across the country to discuss the performance contract. Ascher, "Performance Contracting," 616.

134. Ascher, "Performance Contracting," 617; "Evaluation of the Office of Economic Opportunity's Performance Contracting Experiment," 1.

135. Like Dorsett in Texarkana, Ascher notes that all of the OEO performance contracts used teaching machines, filmstrips, and audiovisual equipment in their instructional plans. Ascher, "Performance Contracting," 617.

136. Gramlich and Koshel, *Educational Performance Contracting*, 17.

137. Gramlich and Koshel, 17.

138. Hall and Rapp, *Case Studies in Educational Performance Contracting*, 11.

139. Hall and Rapp, 12–13.

140. Hall and Rapp, 1.

141. Ascher, "Performance Contracting," 619.

142. Carpenter, "An Evaluation of Performance Contracting," 52.

143. Ascher, "Performance Contracting," 619; see also Hall and Rapp, *Case Studies in Educational Performance Contracting*, 29.

144. Ascher, "Performance Contracting," 619. For more on the "bubble students," see Booher-Jennings, "Below the Bubble"; McNeil, *Contradictions of School Reform*; Madaus, "The Influence of Testing on Teaching"; and Amrein and Berliner, "An Analysis of Unintended and Negative Consequences."

145. Hall and Rapp, *Case Studies in Educational Performance Contracting*, 23.

146. Hall and Rapp, 37–38. Unsurprisingly, both the NEA and the AFT had opposed performance contracting from the start. Gramlich and Koshel, *Educational Performance Contracting*, 8–9.

147. Hall and Rapp, *Case Studies in Educational Performance Contracting*, 33.

148. Ascher, "Performance Contracting," 620.

149. As quoted in "Evaluation of the Office of Economic Opportunity's Performance Contracting Experiment," 1–2.

150. Carpenter, "An Evaluation of Performance Contracting," 56.

151. Ascher, "Performance Contracting," 618.

152. Gramlich and Koshel, *Educational Performance Contracting*, 50.

153. "Evaluation of the Office of Economic Opportunity's Performance Contracting Experiment," 4.

154. The report notes that all but one of the firms had failed to secure indemnification bonds and instead offered corporate assets as collateral to cover their potential debt to the federal government in case of failure, and two of the firms did not have enough assets to cover their liability. "Evaluation of the Office of Economic Opportunity's Performance Contracting Experiment," 49.

155. Gramlich and Koshel, *Educational Performance Contracting*, 62.

156. Ascher, "Performance Contracting," 621.

157. U.S. House of Representatives General Subcommittee on Education of the Committee on Education and Labor, *Hearings on the Elementary and Secondary Education Amendments of 1973*, 180.

158. U.S. House of Representatives General Subcommittee on Education of the Committee on Education and Labor, *Hearings on the Elementary and Secondary Education Amendments of 1973*, 178.

159. U.S. House of Representatives General Subcommittee on Education of the Committee on Education and Labor, *Hearings on the Elementary and Secondary Education Amendments of 1973*, 200.

160. U.S. House of Representatives General Subcommittee on Education of the Committee on Education and Labor, *Hearings on the Elementary and Secondary Education Amendments of 1973*, 200.

161. U.S. House of Representatives General Subcommittee on Education of the Committee on Education and Labor, *Hearings on the Elementary and Secondary Education Amendments of 1973*, 179, 184. In fact, in 1972 teachers at one school were forced to return $600 because their students did not meet the established benchmarks in math.

162. U.S. House of Representatives General Subcommittee on Education of the Committee on Education and Labor, *Hearings on the Elementary and Secondary Education Amendments of 1973*, 195–96. Congressman Lehman advocated for the broad introduction of market-based accountability policies in public education, arguing, "I think it is just as simple as trying to run any other kind of business that the proper line is the profit line and performance line. You are going to be paid off in dividends on the way you perform. This is the way you are going to have to direct this whole thing." U.S. House of Representatives General Subcommittee on Education of the Committee on Education and Labor, *Hearings on the Elementary and Secondary Education Amendments of 1973*, 195–96.

163. According to Superintendent Porter's testimony, Michigan specifically authorized performance contracting as a means of ensuring accountability. U.S. House of Representatives General Subcommittee on Education of the Committee on Education and Labor, *Hearings on the Elementary and Secondary Education Amendments of 1973*, 208. Several other examples of local authorities pushing similar accountability schemes were discussed in congressional testimony, including a project in Woodland, California, where the entire school building was under a bonus-penalty arrangement based on student performance and attitude arrangements. U.S. House of Representatives General Subcommittee on Education of the Committee on Education and Labor, *Hearings on the Elementary and Secondary Education Amendments of 1973*, 180.

164. Friedman, "The Role of Government in Education," 124–44.

165. Molnar, *School Vouchers*.

166. In 1966, Friedman wrote a short comment in *Public Interest* where he proclaimed, "I am delighted to welcome Christopher Jencks to the company of those who favor the voucher system for distributing governmental funds to finance schooling. The welcome is all the warmer because Mr. Jencks is of the still smaller company of those who recognize that market competition would be far more effective than governmental operation in fostering diversity, experimentation, and improvement in the quality of schooling." Friedman, "A Free Market in Education," 107.

167. Jencks, "Is the Public School Obsolete?" 27.

168. Jencks, 22–23.

169. Jencks, 26.

170. Jencks, 27.

171. Coleman, "Toward Open Schools," 25.

172. Coleman, 25.

173. Coleman, 26.

174. Sizer, "The Case for a Free Market," 42. See also Sizer and Whitten, "A Proposal."

175. Sizer, "The Case for a Free Market," 42.

176. Sizer, 42.

177. Sizer, 93.

178. Sizer, 36.

179. Jencks, "An Alternative to Endless School Crisis."

180. Jencks.

181. Campbell, *Voucher Payments and the Public Schools*, 1.

182. Campbell, 23.

183. Nixon, "Special Message to the Congress on Education Reform."

184. Nixon.

185. Nixon.

186. Campbell, *Voucher Payments and the Public Schools*, 20.

187. Coleman and Areen, *Education Vouchers*, ix–xi.

188. The report was released in two parts: a preliminary report was released in March 1970 and the final report was released in December 1970.

189. Coleman and Areen, *Education Vouchers*, viii.

190. Coleman and Areen, 10.

191. Coleman and Areen, 8–11.

192. Coleman and Areen, 2.

193. Coleman and Areen, 59–128, 151–299.

194. *Education Vouchers: The Experience at Alum Rock*, 3.

195. Levinson, *The Alum Rock Voucher Demonstration*, 6.

196. *Education Vouchers: The Experience at Alum Rock*, 4–5.

197. *Education Vouchers: The Experience at Alum Rock*, 6.

198. In 1973, the base value of the voucher was $904, and those that met the Title I threshold were given an additional compensatory voucher worth $275. Reinhold, "Few Using Vouchers," 1; *Education Vouchers: The Experience at Alum Rock*, 7.

199. *Education Vouchers: The Experience at Alum Rock*, 6.

200. Levinson, *The Alum Rock Voucher Demonstration*, 18, 24.

201. Levinson, 16.

202. Levinson, 24. The same RAND study reported that "the belief that public education should operate as a free market was not congruent with existing beliefs about education in Alum Rock." Levinson, *The Alum Rock Voucher Demonstration*, 34.

203. *Education Vouchers: The Experience at Alum Rock*, 14.

204. Wortman, Reichardt, and St. Pierre, "The First Year of the Education Voucher Demonstration."

205. Reinhold, "Few Using Vouchers."

206. Reinhold, "Few Using Vouchers."

207. See California Assembly, Assembly Bill No. 2118; Coleman and Areen, *Education Vouchers*, 330–31.

208. California Assembly, Assembly Bill No. 2118.

209. Meltsner, *Political Feasibility of Reform in School Financing*, 243.

210. California Assembly, Assembly Bill No. 2471.

211. U.S. Senate Subcommittee on Intergovernmental Relations of the Committee on Governmental Affairs, *Hearings on State and Local Innovations in Educations Choice*, 29.

212. See Doyle, Munro, and DeShryver, "Reforming the Schools."

213. As cited in Meltsner, *Political Feasibility of Reform in School Financing*, 244.

214. Reagan, "Text of the State Message to a Joint Session of the California State Legislature, 1971," 2–3.

215. Reagan, "Text of State-of-the-State Message to a Joint Session of the California State Legislature, 1972," 6–7.

216. Rickford, *We Are an African People*, 258–62.

217. Baker, "Desegregation, Minimum Competency Testing, and the Origins of Accountability," 37–38.

218. Baker, 36.

219. Baker, 35, 49.

220. Baker, 46–49.

221. Republican National Convention, "Platform of the Republican Party, 1980."

Conclusion

1. Obama, "Remarks to the United States Hispanic Chamber of Commerce."

2. Trump, "Remarks at the Cleveland Arts and Social Sciences Academy." Some moves by the Trump administration suggested a return to an earlier era of the Republican Party's general skepticism of federal authority in education, for example, the repeal of Obama-era educational requirements regarding teacher training and accountability rules for ESSA. Brown, "Trump Signs Bills Overturning." However, the Trump administration also sought to use the governing power of that same federal education apparatus to extend market-based solutions, and frequently justified these moves by arguing that they would lead to better outcomes for poor and minority students trapped in a failing public education system. Whether sincerely or not, President Trump maintained the liberal incorporationist tendency to point to education as the best way to address the issue of racial inequality and other social problems. In a remarkable example, in his final year in office during a Rose Garden address, President Trump announced an executive order to encourage police reform in the wake of widespread protest after the murder of George Floyd by a police officer. After noting that his administration had been "fighting for equal justice and delivering results," President Trump veered off the subject of policing to note, "We're fighting for school choice, which really is the civil rights of all time in this country. Frankly school choice is the civil rights statement of the year, of the decade and probably beyond because all children have to have access to quality education. A child's zip code in America should never determine their future and that's what was happening." Trump, "Remarks on Signing an Executive Order on Safe Policing."

3. For example, the vote approving the 2015 Every Students Succeed Act was 359–64 in the House of Representatives and 85–12 in the Senate. The vote approving the 2001 No Child Left Behind Act was 381–41 in the House of Representatives and 87–10 in the Senate. The vote approving the 1994 Improving America's Schools Act was 262–132 in the House of Representatives and 77–20 in the Senate.

4. For examples of scholarship pointing to the 1980s as the critical period for explaining current education policies, see Rhodes, *An Education in Politics*; Manna, *School's In*; McGuinn, "Education Policy from the Great Society to 1980"; McGuinn, *No Child Left Behind*; Henig, "Education Policy from 1980 to the Present"; Debray, *Politics, Ideology, and Education*; Cohen and Moffitt, *The Ordeal of Equality*.

5. Goddard, *Human Efficiency*, 99.

6. Patterson, "Colleges for Negro Youth," 114.

7. Jones, *Masters of the Universe*; Rodgers, *Age of Fracture*; Lipman, *The New Political Economy*; Spence, "The Neoliberal Turn."

8. Soss, Fording, and Schram, *Disciplining the Poor*; Ball, "Education, Governance and the Tyranny of Numbers."

9. Darling-Hammond, "Race, Inequality and Educational Accountability." For more on NCLB, see Rhodes, *An Education in Politics*; McGuinn, *No Child Left Behind*; and Debray, *Politics, Ideology and Education*.

10. Korte, "The Every Student Succeeds Act vs. No Child Left Behind"; and Burnette, "States, Districts to Call Shots."

11. Neill, Scionti, Baker, and Guisbond, *State ESSA Plans*, 2.

12. Saultz, Schneider, and McGovern, "Why ESSA Has Been Reform Without Repair," 19. For a similar analysis, see Ravitch, *Slaying Goliath*, 13–26. Not all scholars agree, with some arguing that ESSA represented a significant reduction in federal authority in education. For example, see McGuinn, "From No Child Left Behind to the Every Student Succeeds Act."

13. U.S. Department of Education, "Race to the Top Executive Summary," 2.

14. In the three rounds of RTT grants funding, forty-five states and the District of Columbia submitted applications, and eighteen states and the District of Columbia eventually received funding.

15. Howell, "Results of President Obama's Race to the Top."

16. A number of former Gates Foundation officials took senior roles in the Department of Education under Secretary Arne Duncan and were influential in drafting teacher evaluation reforms promoted by RTT. See Reckhow and Tompkins-Stange, "Financing the Education Policy Discourse," 275.

17. Strauss, "Everything You Need to Know"; see also "Bill Gates' Latest Mission."

18. "Bill Gates' Latest Mission"; "The Reformer"; see also "Michelle Rhee: 'I Don't Think There Is a Need for Tenure.'"

19. Klein, "Will Teacher Evaluations Through Test Scores Outlast Obama?"

20. Not only has the number of states employing student achievement test scores in teacher evaluation increased, but their weight of importance in teacher evaluation has increased as well. The number of states where these test scores are the biggest factor in teacher evaluation increased from four in 2009 to seventeen by 2015, and the number of states including student test scores in teacher tenure decisions went from zero in 2009 to twenty-three just six years later. See Doherty and Jacobs, *State of States 2015*. There is evi-

dence of a recent pushback at the state level to this approach, as nine states got rid of the direct connection between student test scores and teacher evaluation between 2015 and 2019. However, thirty-four states still require test scores to be used as part of teacher evaluations. Barnum, "No Thanks, Obama."

21. Reckhow, "More Than Patrons," 449.

22. Reckhow and Tompkins-Strange, "Financing the Education Policy," 277.

23. The more extreme version of tracking, where the entire educational program of students differed on the basis of intelligence test scores or perceptions of ability, was widely popular in the mid-twentieth century, when a majority of high schools used some form of this tracking. See Hallinan, "The Detracking Movement." This form of wholesale college and vocational tracking died out in the 1970s. See Loveless, *The Resurgence of Ability Grouping*.

24. The growth in AP (Advanced Placement) classes is indicative of the continued influence of tracking in high school. In many subjects, there are three groupings (basic, regular, and advanced) for core subjects, such as math and English. The three-group division is the same recommendation that many of the social efficiency progressives made in the 1920s and 1930s.

25. Yee, "Grouping Students by Ability"; Mathews, "My Bluebird Group Is Back"; Loveless, *The Resurgence of Ability Grouping*; and Hallinan, "The Detracking Movement."

26. Eisenhart and Towne, "Contestation and Change."

27. Much like the social efficiency of progressives' importation of the scientific methods of industrial organization to the schools, the term and definition of *scientifically based research* originates in the medical field and is seen as a way of rationalizing and improving a disorganized education system.

28. Eisenhart and Towne, "Contestation and Change," 34.

29. Lagemann, *An Elusive Science*, 235–38.

30. Franco, "Time to Reconsider the Scientifically Based Research Requirement."

31. Sparks, "What Role Will Research Play in ESSA?"

32. Layton, "How Bill Gates Pulled Off." See also Strauss, "Everything You Need to Know."

33. U.S. Department of Education, "Race to the Top Executive Summary," 8. The application process for Race to the Top funds is expensive and complex, and the Gates Foundation has provided several states with financial and logistical help in putting together their applications, most of which have included the adoption of the Common Core standards. Layton, "How Bill Gates Pulled Off."

34. "Read the Standards."

35. "Frequently Asked Questions."

36. Although there has been pushback against Common Core and several states repealed the standards, the subsequent reforms frequently implement nearly identical standards, suggesting the recent changes have been more about the branding rather than the substance. Goldstein, "After 10 Years of Hopes."

37. Layton, "How Bill Gates Pulled Off."

38. Reckhow, "More Than Patrons," 449.

39. Layton, "How Bill Gates Pulled Off."

40. Strauss, "Everything You Need to Know."

41. Contreras, "Bill Gates: Poverty Not Excuse." The presence of large philanthropic foundations pushing a top-down educational agenda for poor students to better prepare them for the labor market bears more than a passing similarity to the dynamic between large foundations and Black education in the early twentieth century identified by James Anderson. Anderson, *The Education of Blacks*.

42. In 2014, Microsoft—the corporate source of the Gates fortune—announced that it had partnered with the world's largest education publisher to load its Common Core materials on Microsoft's tablet. This move would allow Microsoft to compete with Apple for lucrative contracts with local and state education agencies. Layton, "How Bill Gates Pulled Off."

43. Secretary of Education Arne Duncan warned, "States that do not have public charter laws or put artificial caps on the growth of charter schools will jeopardize their applications under the Race to the Top Fund." U.S. Department of Education, "States Open to Charters."

44. Layton, "Charter Love."

45. Layton, Petrilli, "State ESSA Plans."

46. Barnum, "Charter Networks."

47. U.S. Department of Education, "The U.S. Department of Education's Charter Schools Program Overview 2019."

48. Webber, "'The Magic of Philanthropy.'"

49. Dowdall and Warner, *Shuttered Public Schools*.

50. Journey for Justice Alliance, *Death By a Thousand Cuts*, 3.

51. Rotberg, "Charter Schools."

52. Journey for Justice Alliance, *Death By a Thousand Cuts*.

53. Rotberg, "Charter Schools."

54. Burris, Cimarusti, and Kilfoyle, *Still Asleep at the Wheel*.

55. Samuels, "'They've Shifted the Burden to Us.'"

56. See Whitehorne, "Social Justice Slate Sweeps"; Winslow, "L.A. Teachers Run on a Bigger Vision"; Winslow, "Activist Coalition Wins Control"; Lasden and Edminster, "San Francisco Teachers Elect Reformers." On the larger strategy of social justice unionism, which captures much of the programmatic and strategic approach of the more activist unions, see Weiner, *The Future of Our Schools*.

57. Lewis, "Karen Lewis, CTU President-Elect Acceptance Speech."

58. Lewis pushed for greater teacher autonomy at the expense of business influence, noting that "inside the classroom, the only people who can improve our schools are professional educators. Corporate heads and politicians do not have a clue about teaching and learning." Lewis, "Karen Lewis, CTU President-Elect Acceptance Speech."

59. Lewis argued that standardized tests, which were costing the district roughly $60 million a year, did little more than label "students, families and educators failures" and measure the district's "slow death by starvation." Lewis, "Karen Lewis, CTU President-Elect Acceptance Speech."

60. Lewis, "Karen Lewis, CTU President-Elect Acceptance Speech."

61. Uetricht, *Strike for America*.

62. Lewis, "Karen Lewis Speech to City Club Today." In the same speech Lewis argued forcefully that attacking teachers through accountability discourse distracts from those that

truly needed to be held accountable. Lewis asked, "who holds the venture capitalist accountable? Who has been held responsible for the foreclosure crisis that saw the greatest reduction of wealth among the middle class in our nation's history? Who has been held accountable for the rampant pension thefts? For the destruction of American jobs?"

63. Chicago Teachers Union Research Department, *A Just Chicago*, 22.

64. Chicago Teachers Union Research Department, 13. Significantly, the CTU report positioned their proposals as a corrective to "current CPS policies of closing schools, attacking teachers, and giving more tests," arguing that instead of this approach, "students need policies that acknowledge the existence of and work to eradicate poverty and segregation." Chicago Teachers Union Research Department, *A Just Chicago*, 13.

65. In one of its most damning passages, the report critiqued the economic system by noting that "inequitable justice policies, healthcare, housing, education, and job availability is the expected outcome of a system designed to maintain two distinct Chicagos: one for those with access to income . . . and one for those left to navigate whatever is left over." Chicago Teachers Union Research Department, *A Just Chicago*, 29.

66. Pearce, "West Virginia Teachers Win."

67. DenHoed, "Striking Oklahoma Teachers Win."

68. Blanc, *Red State Revolt*, 8.

69. Blanc, 100–101.

70. Gym, "Commentary: You're Not Speaking to Me."

71. Strauss, "NAACP Ratifies Controversial Resolution."

72. Journey for Justice Alliance, *Death By a Thousand Cuts*, 18.

73. Journey for Justice Alliance, 27.

74. Rotherham, "Fenty's Loss in D.C." Although President Obama did not endorse either candidate in the election, his secretary of education Arne Duncan made it quite clear that he supported Rhee's education agenda. Aarons, "Updated: Fate of Fenty."

75. Aarons, "Updated: Fate of Fenty."

76. Blume, "Walton Foundation Gives $8 Million"; Baye, "Why Michelle Rhee."

77. The final bill passed by a vote of 359–64 in the House, and 85–12 in the Senate. In both chambers, Democrats supported the bill unanimously.

78. Obama, "Remarks on Signing the Every Student Succeeds Act." President Obama went on to frame the ESSA as carrying on the spirit that animated the original ESEA, noting, "this bill upholds the core value that animated the original Elementary and Secondary Education Act signed by President Lyndon Johnson—the value that says education, the key to economic opportunity, is a civil right."

79. Obama, "Remarks on Signing the Every Student Succeeds Act," emphasis added.

80. Trump, "Remarks at a Roundtable Discussion on Empowering Families."

81. Biden, Democratic Primary Debate on "Special Edition: This Week."

82. In his earlier run for the presidency, Biden argued, "We should go to school longer. We should have a minimum 16 years of education. We should be focusing on the socioeconomic disadvantaged, mostly minorities in inner cities." Biden, Democratic Debate at Drexel University.

83. Biden, 2020 South Carolina Town Hall.

84. Biden, "Speech at National Education Association Assembly."

Bibliography

Aarons, Dakarai. "Updated: Fate of Fenty, Rhee Before Voters Today." *Education Week,* September 14, 2010. https://www.edweek.org/policy-politics/updated-fate-of-fenty -rhee-before-voters-today/2010/09.

"Accused Educator Blasts Reds, Refutes Charges." *Pittsburg Post-Gazette,* March 14, 1952.

Adler, Les K., and Thomas G. Patterson. "Red Fascism: The Merger of Nazi Germany and Soviet Russia in the American Image of Totalitarianism, 1930's–1950's." *American Historical Review* 75, no. 4 (April 1970): 1046–64.

Allen, Quaylan, and Kimberly A. White-Smith. "'Just as Bad as Prisons': The Challenge of Dismantling the School-to-Prison Pipeline Through Teacher and Community Education." *Equity & Excellence in Education* 47, no. 4 (2014): 445–60.

Almond, Lindsay. "Argument on behalf of the Attorney General of Virginia by Mr. Lindsay Almond." In Landmark Briefs and Arguments of the Supreme Court of the United States, vol. 49, *Constitutional Law: Brown v. Board of Education,* edited by Gerhard Casper and Philip B. Kurland, 119. Arlington, VA: University Publications of America, 1975.

American Historical Association. *Conclusions and Recommendations of the Commission: Report of the Commission on the Social Studies.* New York: Charles Scribner's Sons, 1934.

Amerman, Helen E. "Perspective for Evaluating Intergroup Relations in a Public School System." *Journal of Negro Education* 26, no. 2 (1957): 108–20.

"Amicus Curiae Brief of the Attorney General of Florida." In Landmark Briefs and Arguments of the Supreme Court of the United States, vol. 49, *Constitutional Law: Brown v. Board of Education,* edited by Gerhard Casper and Philip B. Kurland, 883. Arlington, VA: University Publications of America, 1975.

Amrein, Aubrey L., and David C. Berliner. *An Analysis of Some Unintended and Negative Consequences of High-Stakes Testing.* Tempe, AZ: Education Policy Lab, 2002.

Anderson, Carol. "Bleached Souls and Red Negroes: The NAACP and Black Communists in the Early Cold War, 1948–1952." In *Window on Freedom: Race, Civil Rights, and Foreign Affairs, 1945–1988,* edited by Brenda Gayle Plummer, 93–114. Chapel Hill: University of North Carolina Press, 2003.

Anderson, Gary L., and Kathryn G. Herr. *Encyclopedia of Activism and Social Justice.* Vol. 1. Thousand Oaks, CA: Sage Publications, 2007.

Anderson, James D. *The Education of Blacks in the South, 1860–1935.* Chapel Hill: University of North Carolina Press, 2010.

Anderson, Nick. "Education Secretary Duncan Calls Hurricane Katrina Good for New Orleans Schools." *Washington Post,* January 30, 2010.

Anderson, Noel S., and Haroon Kharem. *Education as Freedom: African American Educational Thought and Activism.* Lanham, MD: Lexington Books, 2010.

Ansell, Ben W. *From the Ballot to the Blackboard: The Redistributive Political Economy of Education.* New York: Cambridge University Press, 2010.

"Anti-Red Speaker Hit as Pro-Red." *Pittsburgh Post-Gazette*, March 13, 1952.

Apple, Michael W. *Educating the "Right" Way: Markets, Standards, God, and Inequality.* New York: Routledge, 2006.

Apple, Michael W., and Thomas C. Pedroni. "Conservative Alliance Building and African American Support of Vouchers: The End of Brown's Promise or a New Beginning?" *Teachers College Record* 107, no. 9 (September 2005): 2068–2105.

Aptheker, Herbert. "Literacy, the Negro and World War II." *Journal of Negro Education* 15, no. 4 (1946): 595–602.

Armfield, Felix L. *Eugene Kinckle Jones: The National Urban League and Black Social Work, 1910–1940.* Urbana: University of Illinois Press, 2014.

Arnesen, Eric. "No 'Graver Danger': Black Anticommunism, the Communist Party, and the Race Question." *Labor: Studies in Working-Class History of the Americas* 3, no. 4 (December 21, 2006): 13–52.

Ascher, Carol. "Performance Contracting: A Forgotten Experiment in School Privatization." *Phi Delta Kappan* 77, no. 9 (May 1996): 615–21.

Associated Press. "Text of the Platform as Approved for Adoption Today by the Progressive Party: Text of the Wallace Party." *New York Times*, July 25, 1948.

Au, Wayne. *Unequal By Design: High-Stakes Testing and the Standardization of Inequality.* New York: Routledge, 2009.

Bailer, Lloyd H. "The Negro in the Labor Force of the United States." *Journal of Negro Education* 22, no. 3 (1953): 297–306.

Baker, Scott. "Desegregation, Minimum Competency Testing, and the Origins of Accountability: North Carolina and the Nation." *History of Education Quarterly* 55, no. 1 (2015): 33–57.

———. "Testing Equality: The National Teacher Examination and the NAACP's Legal Campaign to Equalize Teachers' Salaries in the South, 1936–63." *History of Education Quarterly* 35, no. 1 (1995): 49–64.

Ball, Stephen J. "Education, Governance and the Tyranny of Numbers." *Journal of Education Policy* 30, no. 3 (March 23, 2015): 299–301.

Banks, Waldo R. "Changing Attitudes Towards the Negro in the United States: The Primary Causes." *Journal of Negro Education* 30, no. 2 (1961): 87–93.

Barnum, Matt. "Charter Networks KIPP and IDEA Win Big Federal Grants to Fuel Expansion." *Chalkbeat*, April 22, 2019. https://www.chalkbeat.org/2019/4/18/21107967 /charter-networks-kipp-and-idea-win-big-federal-grants-to-fund-ambitious-growth-plans.

———. "No Thanks, Obama: 9 States No Longer Require Test Scores Be Used to Judge Teachers." *Chalkbeat*, October 8, 2019. https://www.chalkbeat.org/2019/10/8/21108964 /no-thanks-obama-9-states-no-longer-require-test-scores-be-used-to-judge-teachers.

Barrett, Nathan, and Douglas Harris. *Significant Changes in the New Orleans Teacher Workforce Policy Brief.* New Orleans: Education Research Alliance of New Orleans, 2015.

Baye, Rachel. "Why Michelle Rhee Is Giving Millions to Conservatives in Dozens of States." *Slate Magazine*, March 7, 2014.

Beadie, Nancy. *Education and the Creation of Capital in the Early American Republic.* New York: Cambridge University Press, 2010.

Becker, Gary S., and Barry R. Chiswick. "Education and the Distribution of Earnings." *American Economic Review* 56, no. 1/2 (March 1966): 358–69.

Beittel, A. D. "Some Effects of the 'Separate but Equal' Doctrine of Education." *Journal of Negro Education* 20, no. 2 (1951): 140–47.

Bell, Derrick A. "Serving Two Masters: Integration Ideals and Client Interests in School Desegregation Litigation." *Yale Law Journal* 85, no. 4 (1976): 470–516.

Bell, Howard M., and Charles H. Judd. "Occupational Adjustments of Young Adults." *Journal of Adult Education* 12, no. 4 (October 1940): 525.

Ben-Porath, Sigal. "Deferring Virtue: The New Management of Students and the Civic Role of Schools." *Theory and Research in Education* 11, no. 2 (July 2013): 111–28.

Berliner, David. "Rational Responses to High Stakes Testing: The Case of Curriculum Narrowing and the Harm That Follows." *Cambridge Journal of Education* 41, no. 3 (October 2011): 287–302.

Berliner, David C., and Bruce J. Biddle. *The Manufactured Crisis: Myths, Fraud, and the Attack on America's Public Schools.* New York: Basic Books, 1995.

Bertram, Eva. *The Workfare State: Public Assistance Politics from the New Deal to the New Democrats.* Philadelphia: University of Pennsylvania Press, 2015.

Betts, Julian R., and Tom Loveless. *Getting Choice Right: Ensuring Equity and Efficiency in Education Policy.* Washington, DC: Brookings Institution Press, 2005.

Biden, Joseph R. Democratic Debate at Drexel University. October 30, 2007. https://www.ontheissues.org/2020/Joe_Biden_Education.htm.

———. Democratic Primary Debate on "Special Edition: This Week." August 19, 2007. https://www.ontheissues.org/Archive/2007_Stephanopoulos_Dems_Joe_Biden.htm.

———. "Speech at National Education Association Assembly." National Education Association. July 3, 2020. https://educationvotes.nea.org/2020/07/03/joe-biden-to-educators-you-are-the-most-important-profession-in-the-united-states/.

———. 2020 South Carolina Town Hall, *CNN.* February 26, 2020. https://www.ontheissues.org/Archive/2020_CNN_SC_Education.htm.

"Bill Gates' Latest Mission: Fixing America's Schools." NBCNews.com, July 17, 2010. https://www.nbcnews.com/id/wbna38282806.

Blalock, H. M. "Educational Achievement and Job Opportunities: A Vicious Circle." *Journal of Negro Education* 27, no. 4 (1958): 544–48.

Blanc, Eric. *Red State Revolt: The Teachers' Strike Wave and Working-Class Politics.* Brooklyn, NY: Verso, 2019.

Blume, Howard. "Walton Foundation Gives $8 Million to StudentsFirst." *Los Angeles Times*, April 30, 2013. https://www.latimes.com/local/lanow/la-me-ln-walton-8-million-studentsfirst-20130429-story.html.

Bobbitt, John Franklin. "The Supervision of City Schools: Some General Principles of Management Applied to the Problems of City-School Systems." In *Yearbook of the National Society for the Science of Education.* Chicago: University of Chicago Press, 1913.

Bond, Horace Mann. *The Education of the Negro in the American Social Order.* New York: Octagon Books, 1966.

———. *Negro Education in Alabama: A Study in Cotton and Steel.* Tuscaloosa: University of Alabama Press, 1994.

Booher-Jennings, Jennifer. "Below the Bubble: 'Educational Triage' and the Texas Accountability System." *American Educational Research Journal* 42, no. 2 (2005): 231–68.

Borstelmann, Thomas. *The Cold War and the Color Line: American Race Relations in the Global Arena*. Cambridge, MA: Harvard University Press, 2003.

Bousfield, Maudelle B. "Redirection of the Education of Negroes in Terms of Social Needs." *Journal of Negro Education* 5, no. 3 (July 1936): 412–19.

Bowers, C. A. *The Progressive Educator and the Depression, The Radical Years*. New York: Random House, 1969.

Bowles, Samuel, and Herbert Gintis. *Schooling in Capitalist America*. New York: Basic Books, 1976.

Boykin, Leander L. "The Vocational Education and Guidance of Negro Youth in a Changing Social Order." *Journal of Negro Education* 17, no. 1 (1948): 42–49.

Boyles, Deron. *American Education and Corporations: The Free Market Goes to School*. New York: Falmer Press, 2000.

Breen, Jennifer Stepp. "Capitalizing Labor: What Work Is Worth and Why, from the New Deal to the New Economy." Ph.D. dissertation, University of Pennsylvania, 2011. http://search.proquest.com/docview/888151857/abstract/E3F9793C82654833PQ/1.

"Brief for the United States as Amicus Curiae," Shelley v. Kraemer, 334 U.S. 1, (1948).

"Brief of Harry McMullan, Attorney General of North Carolina, Amicus Curiae." In *Landmark Briefs and Arguments of the Supreme Court of the United States*, vol. 49, *Constitutional Law: Brown v. Board of Education*, edited by Gerhard Casper and Philip B. Kurland, 1015–17. Arlington, VA: University Publications of America, 1975.

Brown, Aaron. *Ladders to Improvement: Report of a Project for the Improvement of Instruction in Secondary Schools*. New York: Phelps-Stokes Fund, 1960.

———. "The Phelps-Stokes Fund and Its Projects." *Journal of Negro Education* 25, no. 4 (1956): 456–62.

Brown, Emma. "Trump Signs Bills Overturning Obama-Era Education Regulations." *Washington Post*, March 27, 2017.

Brown, Ina Corrinne. *Problems of Race and Culture in American Education*. Vol. 5. Race Relations in a Democracy. New York: Harper, 1949.

Brown, William O. "Race Prejudice as a Factor in the Status of the American Negro." *Journal of Negro Education* 8, no. 3 (July 1939): 349–58.

Brownlee, Fred L. "Educational Programs for the Improvement of Race Relations: Philanthropic Foundations." *Journal of Negro Education* 13, no. 3 (1944): 329–39.

Bunche, Ralph J. "A Critical Analysis of the Tactics and Programs of Minority Groups." *Journal of Negro Education* 4, no. 3 (July 1935): 308–20.

———. "Education in Black and White." *Journal of Negro Education* 5, no. 3 (1936): 351–58.

———. "The Negro in the Political Life of the United States." *Journal of Negro Education* 10, no. 3 (July 1941): 567–84.

———. "The Programs of Organizations Devoted to the Improvement of the Status of the American Negro." *Journal of Negro Education* 8, no. 3 (July 1939): 539–50.

———. "The Role of the University in the Political Orientation of Negro Youth." *Journal of Negro Education* 9, no. 4 (October 1940): 571–79.

Buras, Kristen L. *Rightist Multiculturalism: Core Lessons on Neoconservative School Reform*. New York: Routledge, 2008.

Burkholder, Zoë. "The Perils of Integration: Conflicting Northern Black Responses to the Coleman Report in the Black Power Era, 1966–1974." *History of Education Quarterly* 57, no. 4 (2017): 579–90.

Burnette, Daarel. "States, Districts to Call Shots on Turnarounds Under ESSA." *Education Week*, January 5, 2016. https://www.edweek.org/policy-politics/states-districts-to-call -shots-on-turnarounds-under-essa/2016/01.

Burris, Carol, and Jeff Bryant. *Asleep at the Wheel: How the Federal Charter Schools Program Recklessly Takes Taxpayers and Students for a Ride.* Network for Public Education, 2019.

Burris, Carol, Darcie Cimarusti, and Marla Kilfoyle. *Still Asleep at the Wheel: How the Federal Charter Schools Program Results in a Pileup of Fraud and Waste.* Network for Public Education, January 2020. https://networkforpubliceducation.org/wp-content /uploads/2020/02/Still-Asleep-at-the-Wheel.pdf.

Bush, George W. "Speech at the NAACP's 91st Annual Convention." *Washington Post: On Politics.*

Butchart, Ronald E. *Northern Schools, Southern Blacks, and Reconstruction: Freedmen's Education, 1862–1875.* Westport, CT: Greenwood Press, 1980.

Cahill, Jerry. "No Room for Commie Teacher, Says Educator." *Milwaukee Sentinel*, November 6, 1954.

California Assembly. Assembly Bill No. 2118: The Self-Determination in Education Act of 1969. Assembly Bills, Original and Amended, Vol. 22, California Legislature, 1969.

California Assembly. Assembly Bill No. 2471: The Education Demonstration Scholarship Act of 1970. Assembly Bills, Original and Amended, Vol. 23, California Legislature, 1970.

Callahan, Raymond E. *Education and the Cult of Efficiency: A Study of the Social Forces That Have Shaped the Administration of the Public Schools.* Chicago: University of Chicago Press, 1962.

Campbell, Colleen. *Voucher Payments and the Public Schools.* Washington, DC: Congressional Research Service, 1970.

Canady, Herman G. "The Social Psychology of Youth." *Journal of Negro Education* 17, no. 2 (1948): 120–23.

Carpenter, Polly. "An Evaluation of Performance Contracting for HEW." In *The National Conference on Performance Contracting in Education: Final Report*, edited by Donald M. Levine, 44–61. Washington, DC: Department of Health, Education, and Welfare, Office of Education, National Center for Educational Research and Development, 1972.

Carson, John. "Army Alpha, Army Brass, and the Search for Army Intelligence." *Isis* 84, no. 2 (1993): 278–309.

Carter, Robert L. "The Effects of Segregation and the Consequences of Desegregation: A Social Science Statement." *Journal of Negro Education* 22, no. 1 (1953): 68–76.

———. "Opening Argument of Robert L. Carter, Esq., on Behalf of the Appellants." In Landmark Briefs and Arguments of the Supreme Court of the United States, vol. 49, *Constitutional Law: Brown v. Board of Education*, edited by Gerhard Casper and Philip B. Kurland, 284. Arlington, VA: University Publications of America, 1975.

Carter, Robert L., and Thurgood Marshall. "The Meaning and Significance of the Supreme Court Decree." *Journal of Negro Education* 24, no. 3 (1955): 397–404.

Chaffee, Mary Law. "William E. B. Dubois' Concept of the Racial Problem in the United States: The Early Negro Educational Movement." *Journal of Negro History* 41, no. 3 (July 1956): 241–58.

"Charter Presented to Teachers' Unit." *Reading Eagle*, December 28, 1938.

Chen, Anthony S. *The Fifth Freedom: Jobs, Politics, and Civil Rights in the United States, 1941–1972.* Princeton, NJ: Princeton University Press, 2009.

Chicago Teachers Union Research Department. *A Just Chicago: Fighting for the City Our Students Deserve.* Chicago Teachers Union, February 2015. https://news.wttw.com/sites /default/files/article/file-attachments/A%20Just%20Chicago-CTU%20Report.pdf.

Chu, Jeff. "Obama and McCain Fight Over a Woman." *Fast Company*, October 20, 2008.

Church, Robert L., and Michael W. Sedlack. *Education in the United States: An Interpretive History.* New York: Free Press, 1976.

"Claim Reds Make Poor Instructors." *Schenectady Gazette*, June 2, 1954.

Clark, Kenneth B. "Alternative Public School Systems." *Harvard Educational Review* 38, no. 1 (1968): 100–113.

———. "American Education Today." *Integrated Education* 3, no. 6 (December 1965): 51–53.

———. "Answer for 'Disadvantaged' Is Effective Teaching." *New York Times*, January 12, 1970.

———. "Clash of Cultures in the Classroom." *Integrated Education* 1, no. 4 (1963): 7–14.

———. "Color, Class, Personality and Juvenile Delinquency." *Journal of Negro Education* 28, no. 3 (1959): 240–51.

———. *Dark Ghetto: Dilemmas of Social Power*, 2nd ed. Middletown, CT: Wesleyan University Press, 1965.

———. "Efficiency as a Prod to Social Action." *Monthly Labor Review* 92, no. 8 (August 1969): 54–56.

———. *A Possible Reality: A Design for the Attainment of High Academic Achievement for Inner-City Students.* New York: MARC Corporation, 1972.

———. "Social Dynamics of the Ghetto." In *Annual National Vocational-Technical Teacher Education Seminar Proceedings, Teaching Disadvantaged Youth*, 47–57. Washington, DC: Department of Health, Education and Welfare, Office of Education, Bureau of Research, 1969.

Clark, Kenneth B., Isidor Chein, and Stuart W. Cook. "The Effects of Segregation and the Consequences of Desegregation: A (September 1952) Social Science Statement in the *Brown v. Board of Education of Topeka* Supreme Court Case." *American Psychologist* 59, no. 6 (2004): 495–501.

Clark, Kenneth B., and Mamie K. Clark. "The Development of Consciousness of Self and the Emergence of Racial Identification in Negro Preschool Children." *Journal of Social Psychology* 10, no. 4 (November 1939): 591–99.

———. "Emotional Factors in Racial Identification and Preference in Negro Children." *Journal of Negro Education* 19, no. 3 (1950): 341–50.

———. "Segregation as a Factor in the Racial Identification of Negro Pre-School Children." *Journal of Experimental Education* 8, no. 2 (December 1939): 161–63.

Clark, Leroy D. "The Lawyer in the Civil Rights Movement—Catalytic Agent or Counter-Revolutionary?" *University of Kansas Law Review* 19, no. 3 (1970): 459–74.

Clarke, Daniel P. "The Role of Psychology in Race Survival." *Journal of Negro Education* 10, no. 1 (January 1941): 51–53.

Clement, Rufus E. "Educational Programs for the Improvement of Race Relations: Interracial Committees." *Journal of Negro Education* 13, no. 3 (1944): 316–28.

Cloward, Richard A., and Lloyd E. Ohlin. *Delinquency and Opportunity: A Theory of Delinquent Gangs*. Glencoe: Free Press, 1960.

Cockerham, Sean. "We Knew Michelle Rhee Was Meeting with Trump. But Why Kevin Johnson?" *McClatchy DC*, November 19, 2016.

Cohen, David K., and Susan L. Moffitt. *The Ordeal of Equality: Did Federal Regulation Fix the Schools?* Cambridge, MA: Harvard University Press, 2009.

Cohen, Miriam. "Reconsidering Schools and the American Welfare State." *History of Education Quarterly* 45, no. 4 (2005): 511–37.

Coleman, James S. *Equality of Educational Opportunity*. Washington, DC: U.S. Department of Health, Education, and Welfare, Office of Education, 1966.

———. "Toward Open Schools." *Public Interest* 9 (1967): 20–27.

Coleman, James S., and Judith Areen. *Education Vouchers: A Report on Financing Elementary Education by Grants to Parents*. Cambridge: Center for the Study of Public Policy, 1970.

Collins, Robert M. *The Business Response to Keynes, 1929–1964*. New York: Columbia University Press, 1981.

Contreras, Russell. "Bill Gates: Poverty Not Excuse for No Education." MPR News, July 28, 2011. https://www.mprnews.org/story/2011/07/28/bill-gates-poverty-race.

Council of Economic Advisers: Oral History Interview. John F. Kennedy Presidential Library, August 1, 1964. https://www.jfklibrary.org/Asset-Viewer/Archives/JFKOH-CEA-01 .aspx.

Counts, George S. *Dare the Schools Build a New Social Order?* New York: John Day, 1932.

Cox, Oliver C. "An American Dilemma: A Mystical Approach to the Study of Race Relations." *Journal of Negro Education* 14, no. 2 (1945): 132–48.

———. "Modern Democracy and the Class Struggle." *Journal of Negro Education* 16, no. 2 (1947): 155–64.

———. "The New Crisis in Leadership Among Negroes." *Journal of Negro Education* 19, no. 4 (1950): 459–65.

———. "Vested Interests Involved in the Integration of Schools for Negroes." *Journal of Negro Education* 20, no. 1 (1951): 112–14.

Cremin, Lawrence A. "John Dewey and the Progressive-Education Movement, 1915–1952." *School Review* 67, no. 2 (1959): 160–73.

———. *The Transformation of the School: Progressivism in American Education*. New York: Vintage Books, 1964.

Crocco, Margaret S., and Arthur T. Costigan. "The Narrowing of Curriculum and Pedagogy in the Age of Accountability Urban Educators Speak Out." *Urban Education* 42, no. 6 (November 2007): 512–35.

Crooks, Kenneth B. "Is Negro Education Failing?" *Journal of Negro Education* 8, no. 1 (January 1939): 19–25.

Cuban, Larry. *The Blackboard and the Bottom Line: Why Schools Can't Be Businesses*. Cambridge, MA: Harvard University Press, 2005.

———. "Reform by Fiat: The Clark Plan in Washington, 1970–1972." *Urban Education* 9, no. 1 (1974): 8–34.

Cubberley, Ellwood P. *Public School Administration: A Statement of the Fundamental Principles Underlying the Organization and Administration of Public Education.* Cambridge, MA: Riverside Press, 1916.

Dancy, T. Elon. "(Un)Doing Hegemony in Education: Disrupting School-to-Prison Pipelines for Black Males." *Equity & Excellence in Education* 47, no. 4 (2014): 476–93.

Daniel, Walter G. "The Responsibility of Education for the Preparation of Children and Youth to Live in a Multi-Racial Society." *Journal of Negro Education* 19, no. 3 (1950): 388–98.

Daniel, Walter G., and Marion T. Wright. "The Role of Educational Agencies in Maintaining Morale Among Negroes." *Journal of Negro Education* 12, no. 3 (1943): 490–501.

Dantley, Michael E. "The Ineffectiveness of Effective Schools Leadership: An Analysis of the Effective Schools Movement from a Critical Perspective." *Journal of Negro Education* 59, no. 4 (1990): 585–98.

Darling-Hammond, Linda. "Race, Inequality and Educational Accountability: The Irony of 'No Child Left Behind.'" *Race Ethnicity and Education* 10, no. 3 (September 2007): 245–60.

Davenport, Charles B. "Science Replies to Secretary Wallace's Article: 'The Scientist in an Unscientific Society.'" *Scientific American* 151, no. 2 (August 1934): 77–78.

Davenport, Roy K. "Implications of Military Selection and Classification in Relation to Universal Military Training." *Journal of Negro Education* 15, no. 4 (1946): 585–94.

Davis, Allison. "The Socialization of the American Negro Child and Adolescent." *Journal of Negro Education* 8, no. 3 (July 1939): 264–74.

Davis, John A. "Educational Programs for the Improvement of Race Relations: Organized Labor and Industrial Organizations." *Journal of Negro Education* 13, no. 3 (1944): 340–48.

Davis, John P. "A Survey of the Problems of the Negro Under the New Deal." *Journal of Negro Education* 5, no. 1 (January 1936): 3–12.

Debray, Elizabeth H. *Politics, Ideology and Education: Federal Policy During the Clinton and Bush Administrations.* New York: Teachers College, 2006.

DeCosta, Frank A. "The Use and Results of Standardized Tests." In *Ladders to Improvement: Report of a Project for the Improvement of Instruction in Secondary Schools,* edited by Aaron Brown, C-1–C-41. New York: Phelps-Stokes Fund, 1960.

DenHoed, Andrea. "Striking Oklahoma Teachers Win Historic School-Funding Increase and Keep On Marching." *New Yorker,* April 4, 2018.

Democratic National Convention. Platform of the Democratic Party, 2012. Online by Gerhard Peters and John T. Woolley, The American Presidency Project, https://www.presidency.ucsb.edu.

Deutsch, Monroe E. "Equality in Life as Well as in Death." *Journal of Negro Education* 23, no. 4 (1954): 496–501.

Dewey, John. "Can Education Share in Social Reconstruction?" *Social Frontier* 1, no. 1 (1934): 11–12.

———. "Education and Social Change." *Social Frontier* 3, no. 26 (May 1937): 235–38.

———. "The Meaning of Liberalism." *Social Frontier* 2, no. 3 (1935): 74–75.

———. "The Social Significance of Academic Freedom." *Social Frontier* 2, no. 6 (1926): 165–66.

———. "The Teacher and His World." *Social Frontier* 1, no. 4 (1935): 7.

DiSanto, Lauren. "17K Students Will Be Moved in Philly Schools Overhaul." NBC 10 Philadelphia, December 13, 2012.

Doherty, Kathryn M., and Sandi Jacobs. *State of States 2015: Evaluating Teaching, Leading and Learning.* The National Council on Teacher Quality, November 2015. https://www.nctq.org/dmsView/StateofStates2015.

Donovan, H. L. "Teacher Training for the New Age." In *Proceedings of the Seventy-First Annual Meeting Held at Chicago, Illinois, July 1–7, 1933,* 71, 71:96–100. Washington, DC: National Education Association, 1933.

Dorsey, Emmett E. "The Negro and Social Planning." *Journal of Negro Education* 5, no. 1 (January 1936): 105–9.

Dowdall, Emily, and Susan Warner. *Shuttered Public Schools: The Struggle to Bring Old Buildings to New Life.* Pew Charitable Trust, February 11, 2013. https://www.pewtrusts.org/~/media/assets/2013/02/11/philadelphia_school_closings_report.pdf?la=en.

Doyle, Denis P., Douglas P. Munro, and David A. DeShryver. "Reforming the Schools to Save the City, Part 1." Calvert Institute. Calvert Institute for Policy Research, August 1, 1997. http://www.calvertinstitute.org/?p=517.

Drake, St. Clair. "The International Implications of Race and Race Relations." *Journal of Negro Education* 20, no. 3 (1951): 261–78.

Dreilinger, Danielle. "Most Katrina Laid-off Teachers Never Came Back, Study Confirms." *New Orleans Times-Picayune,* May 31, 2017.

Du Bois, W. E. Burghardt, ed. *An Appeal to the World: A Statement on the Denial of Human Rights to Minorities in the Case of Citizens of Negro Descent in the United States of America and an Appeal to the United Nations for Redress.* National Association for the Advancement of Colored People, 1947.

———. "Does the Negro Need Separate Schools?" *Journal of Negro Education* 4, no. 3 (July 1935): 328–35.

Dudziak, Mary L. *Cold War Civil Rights: Race and the Image of American Democracy.* Princeton, NJ: Princeton University Press, 2011.

———. "Desegregation as a Cold War Imperative." *Stanford Law Review* 41, no. 1 (1988): 61–120.

Editorial Board. "'Class' and Social Purpose." *Social Frontier* 2, no. 5 (1936): 134–35.

———. "Orientation." *Social Frontier* 1, no. 1 (1934): 3–5.

———. "The Social Order Desired by Society." *Social Frontier* 2, no. 5 (1936): 133–34.

"Editorial Comment: Investing in Negro Brains." *Journal of Negro Education* 4, no. 2 (1935): 153 55.

"Editorial Comments on *The Social Frontier.*" *Social Frontier* 1, no. 2 (1934): 22.

Education Vouchers: The Experience at Alum Rock. Washington, DC: Department of Health, Education, and Welfare, National Institute of Education, 1973.

Eells, Walter Crosby. "The Higher Education of Negroes in the United States." *Journal of Negro Education* 24, no. 4 (1955): 426–34.

Eisenhart, Margaret, and Lisa Towne. "Contestation and Change in National Policy on 'Scientifically Based' Education Research." *Educational Researcher* 32, no. 7 (October 1, 2003): 31–38.

Embree, Edwin R. "The Status of Minorities as a Test of Democracy." *Journal of Negro Education* 10, no. 3 (July 1941): 453–58.

Ethridge, Samuel. "Impact of the 1954 *Brown vs. Board of Education* Decision on Black Educators." *Negro Educational Review* 30, no. 4 (1979): 224–30.

Evaluation of the Office of Economic Opportunity's Performance Contracting Experiment. Washington, DC: General Accounting Office, 1973.

"An Exhibit." *Milwaukee Sentinel*, March 25, 1941.

Ezzell, Bill. "Laws of Racial Identification and Racial Purity in Nazi Germany and the United States: Did Jim Crow Write the Laws That Spawned the Holocaust." *Southern University Law Review* 30 (2002): 1–13.

Fabricant, Michael, and Michelle Fine. *Charter Schools and the Corporate Makeover of Public Education: What's at Stake?* New York: Teachers College Press, 2012.

Fallace, Thomas Daniel. *Race and the Origins of Progressive Education, 1880–1929.* New York: Teachers College Press, 2015.

Fasching-Varner, Kenneth J., Roland W. Mitchell, Lori L. Martin, and Karen P. Bennett-Haron. "Beyond School-to-Prison Pipeline and Toward an Educational and Penal Realism." *Equity & Excellence in Education* 47, no. 4 (2014): 410–29.

Fass, Paula. "Without Design: Education Policy in the New Deal." *American Journal of Education* 91, no. 1 (1982): 36–64.

Ferguson, Karen. *Top Down: The Ford Foundation, Black Power, and the Reinvention of Racial Liberalism.* Philadelphia: University of Pennsylvania Press, 2013.

Forbath, William. "Civil Rights and Economic Citizenship: Notes on the Past and Future of the Civil Rights and Labor Movements." *University of Pennsylvania Journal of Business Law* 2, no. 4 (July 1, 2000): 697–718.

Ford, James W. "The Communist's Way Out for the Negro." *Journal of Negro Education* 5, no. 1 (January 1936): 88–95.

Forman, James. "The Secret History of School Choice: How Progressives Got There First." *Georgetown Law Journal* 93, no. 4 (April 2005): 1287–1319.

Foster, Stuart J. *Red Alert! Educators Confront the Red Scare in American Public Schools, 1947–1954.* New York: Peter Lang, 2000.

Franco, Suzanne. "Time to Reconsider the Scientifically Based Research Requirement." *Nonpartisan Education Review* 3, no. 6 (2007). http://nonpartisaneducation.org /Review/Essays/v3n6.htm.

Frazier, E. Franklin. "The Present Status of the Negro Family in the United States." *Journal of Negro Education* 8, no. 3 (July 1939): 376–82.

———. "Problems and Needs of Negro Children and Youth Resulting from Family Disorganization." *Journal of Negro Education* 19, no. 3 (1950): 269–77.

"Frequently Asked Questions." Common Core State Standards Initiative. National Governors Association and Council of Chief State School Officers. Accessed August 7, 2017. http://www.corestandards.org/wp-content/uploads/FAQs.pdf.

Freyre, Gilberto. "Brazil and the International Crisis." *Journal of Negro Education* 10, no. 3 (July 1941): 510–14.

Friedman, Milton. "A Free Market in Education." *Public Interest* 3 (1966): 107.

———. "The Role of Government in Education." In *Economics and the Public Interest,* edited by Robert A. Solo, 124–44. New Brunswick, NJ: Rutgers University Press, 1955.

Full Employment Act of 1945. Bill (1945). Section 2, c.

Fultz, Michael. "The Displacement of Black Educators Post-Brown: An Overview and Analysis." *History of Education Quarterly* 44, no. 1 (March 2004): 11–45.

Gallagher, Buell Gordon. "Reorganize the College to Discharge Its Social Function." *Journal of Negro Education* 5, no. 3 (July 1936): 464–73.

Garfinkel, Irwin, Lee Rainwater, and Timothy M. Smeeding. *Wealth and Welfare States: Is America a Laggard or Leader?* Oxford: Oxford University Press, 2010.

"Georgia School Board Meeting Has 'Red Row': Author of Textbook Accused of Having Communistic Leanings." *Florence Times*, September 18, 1940.

Gerson, Jack. "The Neoliberal Agenda and the Response of Teachers Unions." In *The Assault on Public Education: Confronting the Politics of Corporate School Reform*, edited by William H. Watkins, 97–124. New York: Teachers College Press, 2012.

Goddard, Henry H. "Anniversary Address." In *Twenty-Five Years: The Vineland Laboratory, 1906–1931*, edited by Edgar A. Doll, 59. Vineland: The Smith Printing House, 1931.

———. "The Bearing of Heredity Upon Educational Problems." *Journal of Educational Psychology* 2, no. 9 (November 1911): 491–97.

———. "The Gifted Child." *Journal of Educational Sociology* 6, no. 6 (February 1933): 354–61.

———. *Human Efficiency and Levels of Intelligence.* Princeton, NJ: Princeton University Press, 1920.

———. "A Scientific Program of Child Welfare." *Annals of the American Academy of Political and Social Science* 105, no. 1 (January 1923): 256–66.

Goff, Regina M. "Problems and Emotional Difficulties of Negro Children Due to Race." *Journal of Negro Education* 19, no. 2 (1950): 152–58.

Goldin, Claudia Dale, and Lawrence F. Katz. *The Race Between Education and Technology.* Cambridge, MA: Harvard University Press, 2008.

Goldstein, Dana. "After 10 Years of Hopes and Setbacks, What Happened to the Common Core?" *New York Times*, December 6, 2019.

———. *The Teacher Wars: A History of America's Most Embattled Profession.* New York: Anchor Books, 2015.

Goluboff, Risa L. "'Let Economic Equality Take Care of Itself': The NAACP, Labor Litigation, and the Making of Civil Rights in the 1940s." *UCLA Law Review* 52, no. 5 (June 2005): 1393–1486.

———. *The Lost Promise of Civil Rights.* Cambridge, MA: Harvard University Press, 2010.

Good, Carter V. "The Social Crisis and Reconstruction in Higher Education." *Journal of Negro Education* 11, no. 3 (July 1942): 267–73.

Goodman, Mary Ellen. "The Education of Children and Youth to Live in a Multi-Racial Society." *Journal of Negro Education* 19, no. 3 (1950): 399–407.

Gordon, Leah N. *From Power to Prejudice: The Rise of Racial Individualism in Midcentury America.* Chicago: University of Chicago Press, 2015.

———. "If Opportunity Is Not Enough: Coleman and His Critics in the Era of Equality of Results." *History of Education Quarterly* 57, no. 4 (2017): 601–15.

———. "The Question of Prejudice: Social Science, Education, and the Struggle to Define 'the Race Problem' in Mid-Century America, 1935–1965," Ph.D. diss., University of Pennsylvania, 2008.

Gottschalk, Marie. *The Shadow Welfare State: Labor, Business, and the Politics of Health Care in the United States*. Ithaca, NY: Cornell University Press, 2000.

Graham, Hugh Davis. *The Uncertain Triumph: Federal Education Policy in the Kennedy and Johnson Years*. Chapel Hill: University of North Carolina Press, 1984.

Gramlich, Edward M., and Patricia P. Koshel. *Educational Performance Contracting: An Evaluation of an Experiment*. Washington, DC: Brookings Institution, 1975.

Grossman, Mary Foley. "Redefining the Relationship of the Federal Government to the Education of Racial and Other Minority Groups." *Journal of Negro Education* 7, no. 3 (July 1938): 450–53.

Grubb, W. Norton, and Marvin Lazerson. *The Education Gospel: The Economic Power of Schooling*. Cambridge, MA: Harvard University Press, 2004.

Guinier, Lani. "From Racial Liberalism to Racial Literacy: *Brown v. Board of Education* and the Interest-Divergence Dilemma." *Journal of American History* 91, no. 1 (2004): 92–118.

Gutman, Herbert. "Schools for Freedom: The Post-Emancipation Origins of Afro-American Education." In *Power and Culture: Essays on the American Working Class*, edited by Ira Berlin, 260–97. New York: New Press, 1987.

Gym, Helen. "Commentary: You're Not Speaking to Me, Mr. Knudsen." *Philadelphia Public School Notebook*, April 24, 2012. http://thenotebook.org/articles/2012/04/24 /commentary-you-re-not-speaking-to-me-mr-knudsen.

Hall, George R., and Marjorie L. Rapp. *Case Studies in Educational Performance Contracting. Part 4. Gary, Indiana*. Santa Monica, CA: RAND Corporation, 1971.

Hallinan, Maureen T. "The Detracking Movement: Why Children Are Still Grouped by Ability." *Education Next*, 2004. http://educationnext.org/the-detracking-movement.

Halperin, Samuel. "ESEA: Five Years Later." *Congressional Record* (1970): 8492–94.

———. "ESEA Ten Years Later." *Educational Researcher* 4, no. 8 (1975): 5–9.

Hamilton, Charles. "Race and Education: A Search for Legitimacy." *Harvard Educational Review* 38, no. 4 (1968): 669–84.

Haney, James E. "The Effects of the *Brown* Decision on Black Educators." *Journal of Negro Education* 47, no. 1 (1978): 88–95.

Harlem Youth Opportunities Unlimited. *Youth in the Ghetto: A Study of the Consequences of Powerlessness and a Blueprint for Change*. New York, 1964.

Hartley, Eugene L. "Psychological Investigations and the Modification of Racial Attitudes." *Journal of Negro Education* 13, no. 3 (1944): 287–94.

Hartman, Andrew. *Education and the Cold War: The Battle for the American School*. New York: Palgrave Macmillan, 2008.

Hauptmann, Emily. "The Ford Foundation and the Rise of Behavioralism in Political Science." *Journal of the History of the Behavioral Sciences* 48, no. 2 (2012): 154–73.

Heilig, Julian Vasquez, and Linda Darling-Hammond. "Accountability Texas-Style: The Progress and Learning of Urban Minority Students in a High-Stakes Testing Context." *Educational Evaluation and Policy Analysis* 30, no. 2 (June 2008): 75–110.

Heitzeg, Nancy A. "Education or Incarceration: Zero Tolerance Policies and the School to Prison Pipeline." *Forum on Public Policy Online* 2009, no. 2 (2009).

Henig, Jeffrey. "Education Policy from 1980 to the Present: The Politics of Privatization." In *Conservatism in American Political Development*, edited by Brian J. Glenn and Steven Michael Teles, 291–323. New York: Oxford University Press, 2009.

Herbert, Bob. "Education, Education, Education." *New York Times*, March 5, 2007.

Hess, Frederick M., and Patrick J. McGuinn. "Seeking the Mantle of Opportunity: Presidential Politics and the Educational Metaphor, 1964–2000." *Educational Policy* 16, no. 1 (January 2002): 72–95.

Hill, T. Arnold. "Educating and Guiding Negro Youth for Occupational Efficiency." *Journal of Negro Education* 4, no. 1 (January 1935): 23–31.

"Hillman Elected Party Chairman." *Milwaukee Journal*, April 9, 1944.

Hinton, Elizabeth Kai. *From the War on Poverty to the War on Crime: The Making of Mass Incarceration in America*. Cambridge, MA: Harvard University Press, 2016.

Hochschild, Jennifer L., and Nathan B. Scovronick. *The American Dream and the Public Schools*. New York: Oxford University Press, 2003.

Holles, Everett. "Wirt's Warning." *Berkeley Daily Gazette*, January 16, 1935.

Holloway, Jonathan Scott. *Confronting the Veil: Abram Harris Jr., E. Franklin Frazier, and Ralph Bunche, 1919–1941*. Chapel Hill: University of North Carolina Press, 2002.

———. "Ralph Bunche and the Responsibilities of the Public Intellectual." *Journal of Negro Education* 73, no. 2 (2004): 125–36.

Hooker, Robert W. Rep. *Displacement of Black Teachers in the Eleven Southern States*. Nashville: Race Relations Information Center, 1970.

Hopkinson, Natalie. "Why Michelle Rhee's Education 'Brand' Failed in D.C." *Atlantic*, September 15, 2010.

Horne, Gerald. *Black and Red: W. E. B. Du Bois and the Afro-American Response to the Cold War, 1944–1963*. Albany: State University of New York Press, 1986.

———. "Race from Power: U.S. Foreign Policy and the General Crisis of 'White Supremacy.'" *Diplomatic History* 23, no. 3 (July 1999): 437–61.

Horowitz, Ruth E. "Racial Aspects of Self-Identification in Nursery School Children." *Journal of Psychology* 7, no. 1 (1939): 91–99.

Horton, James Oliver, and Lois E. Horton. *In Hope of Liberty: Culture, Community and Protest among Northern Free Blacks, 1700–1860*. New York: Oxford University Press, 1997.

"How to Fix America's Schools." *Time*, December 8, 2008.

Howell, William G. "Results of President Obama's Race to the Top: Win or Lose, States Enacted Education Reforms." *Education Next*, 2015. http://educationnext.org/results-president-obama-race-to-the-top-reform/.

Hughes, Marian I. *Refusing Ignorance: The Struggle to Educate Black Children in Albany, New York, 1816–1873*. Albany, NY: Mount Ida Press, 1998.

Hughes, W. Hardin. "What About Human Equality?" *Journal of Negro Education* 16, no. 1 (1947): 57–60.

Hutt, Ethan L. "'Seeing Like a State' in the Postwar Era: The Coleman Report, Longitudinal Datasets, and the Measurement of Human Capital." *History of Education Quarterly* 57, no. 4 (2017): 615–25.

Imbroscio, David. "Urban Policy as Meritocracy: A Critique." *Journal of Urban Affairs* 38, no. 1 (2016): 79–104.

"Intellectual 'Hot Potato' Stirs Row." *Miami Daily News*, September 19, 1940.

Jamison, Peter. "A Short Guide to the D.C. Public Schools Scandals." *Washington Post*, March 8, 2018.

Janken, Kenneth R. "From Colonial Liberation to Cold War Liberalism: Walter White, the NAACP, and Foreign Affairs, 1941–1955." *Ethnic and Racial Studies* 21, no. 6 (November 1998): 1074–95.

Jeffrey, Julie Roy. *Education for Children of the Poor: A Study of the Origins and Implementation of the Elementary and Secondary Education Act of 1965.* Columbus: Ohio State University Press, 1978.

Jencks, Christopher. "An Alternative to Endless School Crisis: Private Schools for Black Children." *New York Times Magazine*, November 3, 1968, 30.

———. "Is the Public School Obsolete." *Public Interest* 2 (1966): 18–27.

Jenkins, Martin D. *The Black and White of Rejections for Military Service: A Study of Rejections of Selective Service Registrants, by Race, on Account of Educational and Mental Deficiencies.* Montgomery, AL: American Teachers Association, 1944.

———. "Editorial Comment: Education for Racial Understanding." *Journal of Negro Education* 13, no. 3 (1944): 265–69.

Johnson, Cedric. "The Panthers Can't Save Us Now." *Catalyst* 1, no. 1 (2017): 56–85.

———. *Revolutionaries to Race Leaders: Black Power and the Making of African American Politics.* Minneapolis: University of Minnesota Press, 2007.

Johnson, Charles S. "The Negro and the Present Crisis." *Journal of Negro Education* 10, no. 3 (July 1941): 585–95.

———. "The Next Decade in Race Relations." *Journal of Negro Education* 13, no. 3 (1944): 441–46.

———. "On the Need of Realism in Negro Education." *Journal of Negro Education* 5, no. 3 (July 1936): 375–82.

———. "Some Significant Social and Educational Implications of the U.S. Supreme Court's Decision." *Journal of Negro Education* 23, no. 3 (1954): 364–71.

Johnson, Doug. "Sacramento High School Students Hold Walk-Out in Protest of School's Recent Changes." Fox 40, September 7, 2018.

Johnson, George M., and Jane Marshall Lucas. "The Present Legal Status of the Negro Separate School." *Journal of Negro Education* 16, no. 3 (1947): 280–89.

Johnson, Guion Griffis. "The Impact of War Upon the Negro." *Journal of Negro Education* 10, no. 3 (July 1941): 596–611.

Johnson, Lyndon B. "Annual Message to the Congress on the State of the Union." State of the Union Address, January 8, 1964. https://www.presidency.ucsb.edu/node/242292.

———. "Commencement Address at Howard University: 'To Fulfill These Rights,' June 4, 1965." Public Papers of the Presidents, Lyndon B. Johnson 1965 (1965): 635–640.

———. *Economic Report of the President Together with* The Annual Report of the Council of Economic Advisers. Washington: United States Government Printing Office, January 1964.

———. "Presidential Policy Paper No. 1: Education." November 1, 1964. Online by Gerhard Peters and John T. Woolley, The American Presidency Project. http://www.presidency.ucsb.edu.

———. *The Vantage Point: Perspectives of the Presidency, 1963–1969.* New York: Holt, Rinehart, and Winston, 1971.

Jonas, Gilbert. *Freedom's Sword: The NAACP and the Struggle Against Racism in America, 1909–1969.* New York: Routledge, 2004.

Jones, Daniel Stedman. *Masters of the Universe: Hayek, Friedman, and the Birth of Neoliberal Politics*. Princeton, NJ: Princeton University Press, 2014.

Jones, Jacqueline. *Soldiers of Light and Love: Northern Teachers and Georgia Blacks, 1865–1873*. Athens: University of Georgia Press, 1980.

Journal of Political Economy 70, no. 5 (October 1962): 1–157.

Journey for Justice Alliance. *Death by a Thousand Cuts: Racism, School Closures, and Public School Sabotage*. Washington, DC: Journey for Justice Alliance, 2014.

Judd, Charles H. "Is Contact with Logically Organized Subject Matter Sufficient for the Education of Children?" *Elementary School Journal* 36, no. 9 (May 1936): 657–64.

——. "New Standards for Secondary Schools." *Yearbook of the National Association of Secondary-School Principals* 18, no. 50 (1934): 7–15.

——. "Programs of Social Studies for the Schools of the United States." *Elementary School Journal* 33, no. 1 (September 1932): 17–24.

——. "This Era of Uncertainty in Education." *School and Society* 44 (September 19, 1936): 353–60.

——. "The Training of Teachers for a Progressive Educational Program." *Elementary School Journal* 31, no. 8 (April 1931): 576–84.

Kaestle, Carl F. *Pillars of the Republic: Common Schools and American Society: 1780–1860*. New York: Hill and Wang, 1983.

Kalb, Loretta. "St. Hope Taps Michelle Rhee as Board Chair, Removes Superindendent." *Sacramento Bee*, August 1, 2014.

Kantor, Harvey. "Education, Social Reform, and the State: ESEA and Federal Education Policy in the 1960s." *American Journal of Education* 100, no. 1 (1991): 47–83.

Kantor, Harvey, and Barbara Brenzel. "Urban Education and the 'Truly Disadvantaged': The Historical Roots of Contemporary Crisis." *Teachers College Record* 94, no. 2 (1992): 278–314.

Kantor, Harvey, and Robert Lowe. "Class, Race, and the Emergence of Federal Education Policy: From the New Deal to the Great Society." *Educational Researcher* 24, no. 3 (1995): 4–21.

——. "Educationalizing the Welfare State and Privatizing Education." In *Learning from the Federal Market-Based Reforms: Lessons for ESSA*, edited by William J. Mathis and Tina M. Trujillo, 37–60. Charlotte, NC: Information Age Publishing, Inc., 2016.

——. "From New Deal to No Deal: No Child Left Behind and the Devolution of Responsibility for Equal Opportunity." *Harvard Educational Review* 76, no. 4 (2006): 474–502.

——. "Introduction: What Difference Did the Coleman Report Make?" *History of Education Quarterly* 57, no. 4 (2017): 570–78.

——. "The Price of Human Capital: Educational Reform and the Illusion of Equal Opportunity." *Dissent* 58, no. 3 (2011): 15–20.

Karier, Clarence J. "Testing for Order and Control in the Corporate Liberal State." *Educational Theory* 22, no. 2 (April 1972): 154–80.

Karier, Clarence J., Paul C. Violas, and Joel H. Spring. *Roots of Crisis: American Education in the Twentieth Century*. Chicago: Rand McNally, 1972.

Katz, Michael B. *The Irony of Early School Reform: Educational Innovation in Mid-Nineteenth Century Massachusetts*. New York: Teachers College Press, 1968.

———. "Public Education as Welfare." *Dissent* 57, no. 3 (2010): 52–56.

———. *Reconstructing American Education.* Cambridge, MA: Harvard University Press, 1987.

———. *The Undeserving Poor: America's Enduring Confrontation with Poverty: Fully Updated and Revised.* Oxford: Oxford University Press, 2013.

Katznelson, Ira. "Was the Great Society a Lost Opportunity?" In *The Rise and Fall of the New Deal Order, 1930–1980,* edited by Steve Fraser and Gary Gerstle, 185–211. Princeton, NJ: Princeton University Press, 1989.

Katznelson, Ira, and Margaret Weir. *Schooling for All: Class, Race, and the Decline of the Democratic Ideal.* Berkeley: University of California Press, 1985.

Kazin, Michael. *American Dreamers: How the Left Changed a Nation.* New York: Vintage Books, 2012.

"Kenneth Clark's Revolutionary Slogan: Just Teach Them to Read!" *New York Times,* March 18, 1973.

Keyserling, Leon. "Economic Progress and the Great Society." In *The Great Society Reader: The Failure of American Liberalism,* edited by Marvin E. Gettleman and David Mermelstein, 85–96. New York: Random House, 1967.

Kilpatrick, William H. "Launching *The Social Frontier.*" *Social Frontier* 1, no. 1 (1934): 2.

———. "Speech Before Annual Meeting." In *Proceedings of the Seventy-First Annual Meeting Held at Chicago, Illinois, July 1–7, 1933,* 71, 71:58. Washington, DC: National Education Association, 1933.

Kimeldorf, Howard, and Judith Stepan-Norris. "Historical Studies of Labor Movements in the United States." *Annual Review of Sociology* 18, no. 1 (1992): 495–517.

Klare, Karl E. "Judicial Deradicalization of the Wagner Act and the Origins of Modern Legal Consciousness, 1937–1941." *Minnesota Law Review* 65 (1977): 265–339.

Klein, Alyson. "Will Teacher Evaluations Through Test Scores Outlast Obama?" *Education Week,* November 4, 2015. http://blogs.edweek.org/edweek/campaign-k-12/2015/11/will_teacher_evaluations_throu.html?cmp=SOC-SHR-FB.

Klein, Joel I. *Lessons of Hope: How to Fix Our Schools.* New York: Harper, 2014.

Kliebard, Herbert M. *The Struggle for the American Curriculum, 1893–1958,* 3rd ed. New York: Routledge, 2005.

Klinkner, Philip A., and Rogers M. Smith. *The Unsteady March: The Rise and Decline of Racial Equality in America.* Chicago: University of Chicago Press, 2002.

Korstad, Robert, and Nelson Lichtenstein. "Opportunities Found and Lost: Labor, Radicals, and the Early Civil Rights Movement." *Journal of American History* 75, no. 3 (1988): 786–811.

Korte, Gregory. "The Every Student Succeeds Act vs. No Child Left Behind: What's Changed?" *USA Today,* December 10, 2015. http://www.usatoday.com/story/news/politics/2015/12/10/every-student-succeeds-act-vs-no-child-left-behind-whats-changed/77088780/.

Kozol, Jonathan. *Savage Inequalities: Children in America's Schools.* New York: Broadway, 1991.

Kristof, Nicholas. "Democrats and Schools." *New York Times,* October 15, 2009.

Kuhl, Stefan. *The Nazi Connection Eugenics, American Racism, and German National Socialism.* New York: Oxford University Press, 2002.

Laats, Adam. *The Other School Reformers: Conservative Activism in American Education.* Cambridge, MA: Harvard University Press, 2015.

Labaree, David F. "The Ed School's Romance with Progressivism." *Brookings Papers on Education Policy* 7 (2004): 89–129.

———. *Someone Has to Fail: The Zero-Sum Game of Public Schoolings.* Cambridge, MA: Harvard University Press, 2010.

———. "The Winning Ways of a Losing Strategy: Educationalizing Social Problems in the United States." *Educational Theory* 58, no. 4 (2008): 447–60.

Lagemann, Ellen Condliffe. *An Elusive Science: The Troubling History of Education Research.* Chicago: University of Chicago Press, 2002.

———. "The Plural Worlds of Educational Research." *History of Education Quarterly* 29, no. 2 (1989): 185–214.

Lal, Shafali. "1930s Multiculturalism: Rachel Davis DuBois and the Bureau for Intercultural Education." *Radical Teacher* 69 (May 2004): 18–22.

Lane, Layle. "Report of the Committee on Cultural Minorities of the American Federation of Teachers." *Journal of Negro Education* 14, no. 1 (1945): 109–12.

Lang, Clarence. "Freedom Train Derailed: The National Negro Labor Council and the Nadir of Black Radicalism." In *Anticommunism and the African American Freedom Movement: "Another Side of the Story,"* edited by Robbie Lieberman and Clarence Lang, 161–88. New York: Palgrave Macmillan, 2011.

Lasden, Cynthia, and Tom Edminster. "San Francisco Teachers Elect Reformers to Lead Union." *Labor Notes*, June 10, 2015. http://www.labornotes.org/2015/06/san-francisco -teachers-elect-reformers-lead-union.

Laski, Harold J. "A New Education Needs a New World." *Social Frontier* 2, no. 5 (1936): 144–47.

Layton, Lyndsey. "Charter Love: Feds Give $157 Million to Expand Charter Schools," *Washington Post*, September 28, 2015.

———. "How Bill Gates Pulled Off the Swift Common Core Revolution." *Washington Post*, June 7, 2014.

Lemann, Nicholas. *The Big Test: The Secret History of the American Meritocracy.* New York: Farrar, Straus and Giroux, 2000.

Lessinger, Leon M. "Educational Engineering: Managing Change to Secure Stipulated Results for Disadvantaged Children." *Journal of Negro Education* 40, no. 3 (1971): 277–81.

———. "Engineering Accountability for Results in Public Education." *Phi Delta Kappan* 52, no. 4 (December 1970): 217–25.

Lessinger, Leon M., and Dwight H. Allen. "Performance Proposals for Educational Funding: A New Approach to Federal Resource Allocation." *Phi Delta Kappan* 51, no. 3 (November 1969): 136–37.

Levinson, Eliot. *The Alum Rock Voucher Demonstration: Three Years of Implementation.* Santa Monica, CA: RAND Corporation, 1976.

Lewin, Tamar. "School Chancellor Fires 241 Teachers in Washington." *New York Times*, July 24, 2010.

Lewis, E. E. "The Economic Position of the American Negro: A Brief Summary." *Journal of Negro Education* 8, no. 3 (July 1939): 446–48.

Lewis, Karen. "Karen Lewis Speech to City Club Today." Chicago Teachers Union. February 2, 2015. https://www.ctulocal1.org/posts/karen-lewis-speech-to-city-club-today/.

———. "Karen Lewis, CTU President-Elect Acceptance Speech." CORE: The Caucus of Rank and File Educators, June 12, 2010. https://www.coreteachers.org/karen-lewis-ctu -president-elect-acceptance-speech-2/.

Lewis, Roscoe E. "The Role of Pressure Groups in Maintaining Morale Among Negroes." *Journal of Negro Education* 12, no. 3 (1943): 464–73.

Lichtenstein, Nelson. "Taft-Hartley: A Slave-Labor Law." *Catholic University Law Review* 47 (1997): 763–89.

Lieberman, Robbie, and Clarence Lang. "Introduction." In *Anticommunism and the African American Freedom Movement: "Another Side of the Story,"* 1–15. New York: Palgrave Macmillan, 2009.

Lieberman, Robert C. "Ideas, Institutions, and Political Order: Explaining Political Change." *American Political Science Review* 96, no. 4 (2002): 697–712.

———. *Shifting the Color Line: Race and the American Welfare State.* Cambridge, MA: Harvard University Press, 1998.

Lipman, Pauline. *The New Political Economy of Urban Education: Neoliberalism, Race and the Right to the City.* New York: Routledge, 2011.

Lips, Dan, Jennifer A. Marshall, and Lindsey Burke. *A Parent's Guide to Education Reform.* Washington, DC: Heritage Foundation, 2008.

Locke, Alain. "Whither Race Relations? A Critical Commentary." *Journal of Negro Education* 13, no. 3 (1944): 398–406.

Long, Heather. "Hidden Crisis: D.C.-Area Students Owe Nearly Half a Million in K–12 School Lunch Debt." *Washington Post*, December 28, 2018.

Long, Herman H. "On the Emergence of New Hope and Challenge in the Current Revolution." In *Second National NEA-PR and R Conference on Civil and Human Rights in Education.* Washington, DC: National Education Association, May 1965, 13.

Long, Howard Hale. "Cultural and Racial Tension." *Journal of Negro Education* 21, no. 1 (1952): 8–19.

———. "The Position of the Negro in the American Social Order: A Forecast." *Journal of Negro Education* 8, no. 3 (1939): 603–16.

———. "The Relative Learning Capacities of Negroes and Whites." *Journal of Negro Education* 26, no. 2 (1957): 121–34.

———. "Some Psychogenic Hazards of Segregated Education of Negroes." *Journal of Negro Education* 4, no. 3 (July 1935): 336–50.

Loveless, Tom. *The Resurgence of Ability Grouping and Persistence of Tracking.* Brookings Institute, March 18, 2013. https://www.brookings.edu/research/the-resurgence-of -ability-grouping-and-persistence-of-tracking/.

Mace-Matluck, Betty. *The Effective Schools Movement: Its History and Context. An SEDL Monograph.* Austin, TX: Southwest Educational Development Lab, 1987.

Madaus, George F. *The Influence of Testing on Teaching Math and Science in Grades 4–12.* Chestnut Hill, MA: Center for the Study of Testing, Evaluation, and Educational Policy, 1992.

Madaus, George, and Michael Russell. "Paradoxes of High-Stakes Testing." *Journal of Education* 190, no. 1–2 (2010): 21–30.

Manna, Paul. *School's In: Federalism and the National Education Agenda.* Washington, DC: Georgetown University Press, 2006.

Manning, Winton H. "The Measurement of Intellectual Capacity and Performance." *Journal of Negro Education* 37, no. 3 (1968): 258–67.

Marable, Manning. *Race, Reform, and Rebellion: The Second Reconstruction and Beyond in Black America,* 3rd ed. Jackson: University Press of Mississippi, 2007.

Marsh, John. *Class Dismissed: Why We Cannot Teach or Learn Our Way Out of Inequality.* New York: NYU Press, 2011.

Marshall, Thurgood. "Argument of Thurgood Marshall, Esq., on Behalf of Harry Briggs, et al., and Dorothy Davis, et al." In Landmark Briefs and Arguments of the Supreme Court of the United States, vol. 49, *Constitutional Law: Brown v. Board of Education,* edited by Gerhard Casper and Philip B. Kurland, 1154. Arlington, VA: University Publications of America, 1975.

———. "An Evaluation of Recent Efforts to Achieve Racial Integration in Education Through Resort to the Courts." *Journal of Negro Education* 21, no. 3 (1952): 316–27.

———. "Marshall to George Beaver, Jr." In *Marshalling Justice: The Early Civil Rights Letters of Thurgood Marshall,* edited by Michael G. Long, 236. New York: HarperCollins, 2011.

———. "Opening Argument of Thurgood Marshall, Esq., on Behalf of the Appellants." In Landmark Briefs and Arguments of the Supreme Court of the United States, vol. 49, *Constitutional Law: Brown v. Board of Education,* edited by Gerhard Casper and Philip B. Kurland, 310. Arlington, VA: University Publications of America, 1975.

Martin, Ruby, and Phyllis McClure. *Is It Helping Poor Children? Title I of ESEA.* Washington, DC: Washington Research Project of the Southern Center for Studies in Public Policy and the NAACP Legal Defense and Education Fund, 1969.

Mason, Lucy Randolph. "The CIO and the Negro in the South." *Journal of Negro Education* 14, no. 4 (1945): 552–61.

Mathews, Jay. "My Bluebird Group Is Back despite Scholarly Qualms." *Washington Post,* March 17, 2013.

McCulloch, Margaret C. "Educational Programs for the Improvement of Race Relations: Seven Religious Agencies." *Journal of Negro Education* 13, no. 3 (1944): 303–15.

———. "What Should the American Negro Reasonably Expect as the Outcome of a Real Peace?" *Journal of Negro Education* 12, no. 3 (1943): 557–67.

McGill, Kevin. "Jindal Sings Education Reforms into Law." *Houma Today,* April 18, 2012.

McGuinn, Henry J. "Equal Protection of the Law and Fair Trials in Maryland." *Journal of Negro History* 24, no. 2 (April 1939): 143–66.

McGuinn, Patrick J. "Education Policy from the Great Society to 1980: The Expansion and Institutionalization of the Federal Role in Schools." In *Conservatism and American Political Development,* edited by Brian J. Glenn and Steven Michael Teles, 188–219. New York: Oxford University Press, 2009.

———. "From No Child Left Behind to the Every Student Succeeds Act: Federalism and the Education Legacy of the Obama Administration." *Publius: The Journal of Federalism* 46, no. 3 (2016): 392–415.

———. *No Child Left Behind and the Transformation of Federal Education Policy: 1965–2005.* Lawrence: University Press of Kansas, 2006.

McKinney, Ernest Rice. "The Workers Party's Way Out for the Negro." *Journal of Negro Education* 5, no. 1 (January 1936): 96–99.

McKissick, Floyd B. "Negro Voices: The Failure to Educate Children." *New York Times*, November 13, 1967.

McLaughlin, Milbrey Wallin. *Evaluation and Reform: The Elementary and Secondary Education Act of 1965, Title 1*. Cambridge: Ballinger Publishing, 1975.

McMillan, Lewis K. "Light Which Two World Wars Throw Upon the Plight of the American Negro." *Journal of Negro Education* 12, no. 3 (1943): 429–37.

McNeil, Linda M. *Contradictions of School Reform: Educational Costs of Standardized Teaching*. New York: Routledge, 2000.

———. "Faking Equity: High-Stakes Testing and the Education of Latino Youth." In *Leaving Children Behind: How "Texas-Style" Accountability Fails Latino Youth*, edited by Angela Valenzuela, 57–112. Albany: State University of New York Press, 2005.

Mehrens, William A. "Consequences of Assessment: What Is the Evidence?" *Education Policy Analysis Archives* 6, no. 13 (July 1998): 1–30.

Meltsner, Arnold J. *Political Feasibility of Reform in School Financing: The Case of California*. New York: Praeger Publishers, 1973.

"Michelle Rhee: 'I Don't Think There Is a Need for Tenure.'" *New Jersey Star-Ledger*, December 19, 2010. https://www.nj.com/njvoices/2010/12/ask_michelle_rhee_there_is_no.html.

Miller, Carroll L. "The Price of Educational Inequality." *Journal of Negro Education* 24, no. 2 (1955): 129–30.

Miller, Eben. *Born along the Color Line: The 1933 Amenia Conference and the Rise of a National Civil Rights Movement*. New York: Oxford University Press, 2012.

Mirel, Jeffrey. "Old Educational Ideas, New American Schools: Progressivism and the Rhetoric of Educational Revolution." *Paedagogica Historica* 39, no. 4 (2003): 477–97.

Moak, Daniel S. "Thurgood Marshall: The Legacy and Limits of Equality Under the Law." In *African American Political Thought: A Collected History*, edited by Melvin L. Rogers and Jack Turner, 386–412. Chicago: University of Chicago Press, 2021.

Molnar, Alex. *School Commercialism: From Democratic Ideal to Market Commodity*. New York: Routledge, 2005.

———. *School Vouchers: The Law, the Research, and Public Policy Implications*. Tucson, AZ: Education Policy Studies Laboratory, 2001.

Moore, Robert. "Applying Ethics to Economics." In *Proceedings of the Seventy-First Annual Meeting Held at Chicago, Illinois, July 1–7, 1933*, 71, 71:158–59. Washington, DC: National Education Association, 1933.

Morgan, Kimberly J., and Andrea Louise Campbell. *The Delegated Welfare State: Medicare, Markets, and the Governance of Social Policy*. New York: Oxford University Press, 2011.

Morris, Robert Charles. *Reading, 'Riting, and Reconstruction: The Education of Freedmen in the South, 1861–1870*. Chicago: University of Chicago Press, 1976.

Mosbaek, E. J. *Analysis of Compensatory Education in Five School Districts. Volume I Summary*. Washington, DC: U.S. Department of Health, Education, and Welfare, Office of Education, Bureau of Research, 1968.

Moss, Hilary J. *Schooling Citizens: The Struggle for African American Education in Antebellum America*. Chicago: University of Chicago Press, 2013.

Moynihan, Daniel Patrick. *The Negro Family: The Case for National Action.* Washington, DC: US Government Printing Office, 1965.

Mucciaroni, Gary. *The Political Failure of Employment Policy, 1945–1982.* Pittsburgh, PA: University of Pittsburgh Press, 1990.

Muhammad, Khalil Gibran. *The Condemnation of Blackness: Race, Crime, and the Making of Modern Urban America.* Cambridge, MA: Harvard University Press, 2011.

Murakawa, Naomi. *The First Civil Right: How Liberals Built Prison America.* New York: Oxford University Press, 2014.

Myrdal, Gunnar. *An American Dilemma: The Negro Problem and Modern Democracy,* 9th ed. New York: Harper & Brothers Publishers, 1944.

NAACP (National Association for the Advancement of Colored People). *Affirming America's Promise: 2011 Annual Report.* Baltimore: National Association for the Advancement of Colored People, 2011.

———. "A Letter to President Woodrow Wilson on Federal Race Discrimination," August 15, 1913. http://www.loc.gov/exhibits/naacp/founding-and-early-years.html#obj20.

Nasaw, David. *Schooled to Order: A Social History of Public Schooling in the United States.* New York: Oxford University Press, 1979.

National Conference on Life Adjustment Education. *Life Adjustment Education for Every Youth.* Washington, DC: Federal Security Agency, Office of Education, 1948.

National Education Association. "ESEA Reauthorization: NEA's Message to Congress," March 2011. http://educationvotes.nea.org/wp-content/uploads/2011/03/ESEAReauthorization.pdf.

National Education Association. *School Desegregation: Louisiana and Mississippi.* Report of NEA Task Force III. Washington, DC: National Education Association, November 12, 1970.

National Education Association of the United States and National Commission on Professional Rights and Responsibilities. *Report of Task Force Survey of Teacher Displacement in Seventeen States.* Washington, DC: December 1965.

National Institute of Education. *Administration of Compensatory Education: A Report from the National Institute of Education.* Washington, DC: U.S. Department of Health, Education, and Welfare, 1977.

National Negro Committee. "Platform Adopted by the National Negro Committee, 1909," 1909. http://www.loc.gov/exhibits/naacp/founding-and-early-years.html#obj10.

Neal, Ernest E. "Two Negro Problems Instead of One: A Challenge to Negro Colleges." *Journal of Negro Education* 21, no. 2 (1952): 161–66.

Neill, Monty, Julianna Scionti, Evan Baker, and Lisa Guisbond. *State ESSA Plans: Uneven Progress toward Better Assessment and Accountability.* FairTest: The National Center for Fair & Open Testing, February 4, 2018. http://fairtest.org/sites/default/files/State-ESSA-Plans-Report.pdf.

Nelson, Murry R., and H. Wells Singleton. *Governmental Surveillance of Three Progressive Educators.* Toronto: American Educational Research Association, 1978.

"New Group Fights Any Freedom Curb: 96 Scholars and Artists Led by John Dewey Revolt Against Failure to Denounce Reds." *New York Times,* May 15, 1939.

Nicholson, Lawrence E. "The Urban League and the Vocational Guidance and Adjustment of Negro Youth." *Journal of Negro Education* 21, no. 4 (1952): 448–58.

Nixon, Richard. "Special Message to the Congress on Education Reform." Online by Gerhard Peters and John T. Woolley, The American Presidency Project. March 3, 1970. https://www.presidency.ucsb.edu/node/240940.

Noble, Jeanne L. "Future Educational Emphasis: Psychological or Sociological." *Journal of Negro Education* 25, no. 4 (1956): 402–9.

Obama, Barack H. "Remarks by the President on Education Reform at the National Urban League Centennial Conference." Speech presented at the National Urban League Centennial Conference, July 29, 2010.

———. "Remarks on Signing the Every Student Succeeds Act." Speech, December 10, 2015. https://www.presidency.ucsb.edu/documents/remarks-signing-the-every-student-succeeds-act.

O'Connor, Alice. *Poverty Knowledge: Social Science, Social Policy, and the Poor in Twentieth-Century U.S. History.* Princeton, NJ: Princeton University Press, 2002.

Ohles, John F. *Biographical Dictionary of American Educators.* Westport, CT: Greenwood Press, 1978.

Orfield, Gary, and Johanna Wald. "Testing, Testing." *Nation* 270, no. 22 (June 5, 2000): 38–40.

Orren, Karen, and Stephen Skowronek. *The Search for American Political Development.* New York: Cambridge University Press, 2004.

Osbourne, David. *A Tale of Two Systems: Education Reform in Washington D.C.* Washington, DC: Progressive Policy Institute, 2015.

Padden, Joe. "Correspondence: Prodding the Educational Worm." *Social Frontier* 1, no. 4 (1934): 34.

Page, Ellis B. "How We All Failed at Performance Contracting." *Phi Delta Kappan* 54, no. 2 (October 1972): 115–17.

Patterson, F. D. "Colleges for Negro Youth and the Future." *Journal of Negro Education* 27, no. 2 (1958): 107–14.

Patterson, William L. *We Charge Genocide: The Crime of Government Against the Negro People.* New York: International Publishers, 1951.

Pearce, Matt. "West Virginia Teachers Win 5% Pay Raise as Massive Strike Comes to an End." *Los Angeles Times*, March 7, 2018.

Pedroni, Thomas C. *Market Movements: African American Involvement in School Voucher Reform.* New York: Routledge, 2007.

Petrilli, Michael J. "State ESSA Plans May Use Federal Funds to Start New Charter Schools." *Education Next*, March 26, 2020. https://www.educationnext.org/state-essa-plans-may-use-federal-funds-start-new-charter-schools/.

Petrovich, Janice, and Amy Stuart Wells. *Bringing Equity Back: Research for a New Era in American Educational Policy.* New York: Teachers College Press, 2005.

Piven, Frances Fox, and Richard A. Cloward. *Regulating the Poor: The Functions of Public Welfare.* New York: Pantheon, 1971.

Plaut, Richard. *Blueprint for Talent Searching: America's Hidden Manpower.* New York: National Scholarship Service and Fund for Negro Students, 1957.

———. *Southern Project Report, 1953–55.* New York: National Scholarship Service and Fund for Negro Students, 1956.

Pope, James Gray. "Labor and the Constitution: From Abolition to Deindustrialization." *Texas Law Review* 65, no. 6 (May 1987): 1071–1136.

Powdermaker, Hortense. "The Anthropological Approach to the Problem of Modifying Race Attitudes." *Journal of Negro Education* 13, no. 3 (1944): 295–302.

Powdermaker, Hortense, and Helen Frances Storen. *Probing Our Prejudices: A Unit for High School Students*. New York: Harper, 1944.

Puzzanghera, Jim. "A Decade After the Financial Crisis, Many Americans Are Still Struggling to Recover." *Los Angeles Times*, September 9, 2018.

Randolph, A. Philip. "The Trade Union Movement and the Negro." *Journal of Negro Education* 5, no. 1 (January 1936): 54–58.

Ravitch, Diane. *Reign of Error: The Hoax of the Privatization Movement and the Danger to America's Public Schools*. New York: Vintage Books, 2014.

———. *The Revisionists Revised: A Critique of the Radical Attack on the Schools*. New York: Basic Books, 1978.

———. *Slaying Goliath: The Passionate Resistance to Privatization and the Fight to Save America's Public Schools*. New York: Vintage Books, 2020.

———. *The Troubled Crusade: American Education, 1945–1980*. New York: Basic Books, 1983.

"Read the Standards." Common Core State Standards Initiative. National Governors Association and Council of Chief State School Officers. Accessed August 7, 2017.

Reagan, Ronald. "Text of the State Message to a Joint Session of the California State Legislature." Ronald Reagan Presidential Library Digital Library Collection, January 12, 1971. https://www.reaganlibrary.gov/public/digitallibrary/gubernatorial/pressunit /p18/40-840-7408624-p18-007-2017.pdf.

———. "Text of State-of-the-State Message to a Joint Session of the California State Legislature." Ronald Reagan Presidential Library Digital Library Collection, January 6, 1972. https://www.reaganlibrary.gov/public/digitallibrary/gubernatorial/pressunit /p18/40-840-7408624-p18-010-2017.pdf.

Reckhow, Sarah. "More Than Patrons: How Foundations Fuel Policy Change and Backlash." *Political Science & Politics* 49, no. 3 (July 2016): 449–54.

Reckhow, Sarah, and Megan Tompkins-Stange. "Financing the Education Policy Discourse: Philanthropic Funders as Entrepreneurs in Policy Networks." *Interest Groups & Advocacy* 7, no. 3 (2018): 258–88.

Redd, George N. "The Educational and Cultural Level of the American Negro." *Journal of Negro Education* 19, no. 3 (1950): 244–52.

Reddick, L. D. "Educational Programs for the Improvement of Race Relations: Motion Pictures Radio, the Press, and Libraries." *Journal of Negro Education* 13, no. 3 (1944): 367–89.

———. "What Should the American Negro Reasonably Expect as the Outcome of a Real Peace?" *Journal of Negro Education* 12, no. 3 (1943): 568–78.

Redding, Arthur. *Turncoats, Traitors, and Fellow Travelers: Culture and Politics of the Early Cold War*. Jackson: University Press of Mississippi, 2012.

Reed, Adolph L. *Stirrings in the Jug: Black Politics in the Post-Segregation Era*. Minneapolis: University of Minnesota Press, 1999.

Reed Touré F. *Not Alms but Opportunity: The Urban League and the Politics of Racial Uplift, 1910–1950*. Chapel Hill: University of North Carolina Press, 2008.

———. *Toward Freedom: The Case Against Race Reductionism*. Brooklyn, NY: Verso Books, 2020.

"The Reformer." *San Diego Union-Tribune*, March 24, 2013.

Reinhold, Robert. "Few Using Vouchers to Pay for School." *New York Times*, May 25, 1975.

Republican National Convention. Platform of the Republican Party, 1980. Online by Gerhard Peters and John T. Woolley, The American Presidency Project, https://www.presidency.ucsb.edu.

Republican National Convention. Platform of the Republican Party, 2012. Online by Gerhard Peters and John T. Woolley, The American Presidency Project, https://www.presidency.ucsb.edu.

Rhee, Michelle. *Radical: Fighting to Put Students First*. New York: Harper, 2013.

Rhodes, Jesse H. *An Education in Politics: The Origins and Evolution of No Child Left Behind*. Ithaca, NY: Cornell University Press, 2012.

Rickford, Russell. *We Are an African People: Independent Education, Black Power, and the Radical Imagination*. New York: Oxford University Press, 2016.

"Rightists Bolt N.Y. Labor Party, Charge Browder Now Has Control of A.L.P." *Chicago Tribune*, March 30, 1944.

Rippa, S. Alexander. "The Textbook Controversy and the Free Enterprise Campaign, 1940–1941." *History of Education Journal* 9, no. 3 (1958): 49–58.

Roberts, Thomas N. "The Negro in Government War Agencies." *Journal of Negro Education* 12, no. 3 (1943): 367–75.

Robey, Ralph West. *Abstracts of Social Science Textbooks*. New York: National Association of Manufacturers, 1941.

Robinson, Dean E. *Black Nationalism in American Politics and Thought*. Cambridge: Cambridge University Press, 2006.

Robinson, Malila N., and Catherine A. Lugg. "The Role of the Religious Right in Restructuring Education." In *The Assault on Public Education: Confronting the Politics of Corporate School Reform*, edited by William H. Watkins, 125–42. New York: Teachers College Press, 2012.

Rodgers, Daniel T. *Age of Fracture*. Cambridge, MA: Harvard University Press, 2012.

Roelofs, Joan. *Foundations and Public Policy: The Mask of Pluralism*. Albany: State University of New York Press, 2003.

Rossinow, Doug. *Visions of Progress: The Left-Liberal Tradition in America*. Philadelphia: University of Pennsylvania Press, 2009.

Rotberg, Iris C. "Charter Schools and the Risk of Increased Segregation." *Phi Delta Kappan* 95, no. 5 (February 1, 2014): 26–31.

Rotherham, Andrew J. "Fenty's Loss in D.C.: A Blow to Education Reform?" *Time*, September 16, 2010. http://content.time.com/time/nation/article/0,8599,2019395,00.html.

Rudwick, Elliott M. "Du Bois' Last Year as Crisis Editor." *Journal of Negro Education* 27, no. 4 (1958): 526–33.

Rugg, Harold. "Social Reconstruction Through Education." *Progressive Education* 9, no. 12 (1932): 11–18.

Russell, Judith. *Economics, Bureaucracy, and Race: How Keynesians Misguided the War on Poverty*. New York: Columbia University Press, 2004.

Rustin, Bayard. "From Protest to Politics." In *The Great Society Reader: The Failure of American Liberalism*, edited by Marvin E. Gettleman and David Mermelstein, 261–77. New York: Random House, 1967.

———. "Integration Within Decentralization." In *Down the Line: The Collected Writings of Bayard Rustin*, 213–21. Chicago: Quadrangle Books, 1971.

———. "The Mind of the Black Militant." In *Down the Line: The Collected Writings of Bayard Rustin*, 206–12. Chicago: Quadrangle Books, 1971.

Saltman, Kenneth J. *Capitalizing on Disaster: Taking and Breaking Public Schools*. Boulder, CO: Paradigm Publishers, 2007.

———. *The Failure of Corporate School Reform*. New York: Routledge, 2015.

———. "The Rise of Venture Philanthropy and the Ongoing Neoliberal Assault on Public Education: The Eli and Edith Broad Foundation." In *The Assault on Public Education: Confronting the Politics of Corporate School Reform*, edited by William H. Watkins, 55–78. New York: Teachers College Press, 2004.

Samuels, Robert. "'They've Shifted the Burden to Us': A Food Pantry Struggles to Feed an Increasingly Hungry Ohio Community." *Washington Post*, November 1, 2018. https://www.washingtonpost.com/politics/theyve-shifted-the-burden-to-us-a-food-pantry-struggles-to-feed-an-increasingly-hungry-ohio-community/2018/11/01/b70c1402-cb0c-11e8-a3e6-44daa3d35ede_story.html.

Saultz, Andrew, Jack Schneider, and Karalyn McGovern. "Why ESSA Has Been Reform Without Repair." *Phi Delta Kappan* 101, no. 2 (2019): 18–21.

Schlink, F. J. "Correspondence." *Social Frontier* 1, no. 3 (1934): 28.

Schmidt, Vivien A. "Taking Ideas and Discourse Seriously: Explaining Change through Discursive Institutionalism as the Fourth 'New Institutionalism.'" *European Political Science Review* 2, no. 01 (2010): 1–25.

Schmitt, Edward R. *President of the Other America: Robert Kennedy and the Politics of Poverty*. Amherst: University of Massachusetts Press, 2010.

Schoedel, Alan F. "OSU Speaker Controversy Still Hot Issue After 5 Months." *Toledo Blade*, December 9, 1951.

Schrecker, Ellen. *The Age of McCarthyism: A Brief History with Documents*. Boston: St. Martin's Press, 1994.

———. *The Lost Soul of Higher Education: Corporatization, the Assault on Academic Freedom, and the End of the American University*. New York: New Press, 2010.

———. *Many Are the Crimes: McCarthyism in America*. Princeton, NJ: Princeton University Press, 1999.

———, ed. "Resolution on Expulsion of the United Electrical, Radio, and Machine Workers of America and Withdrawal of Certificate of Affiliation." In *The Age of McCarthyism: A Brief History with Documents*, 197. Boston: St. Martin's Press, 1994.

Schultz, Theodore W. "Investment in Human Capital." *American Economic Review* 51, no. 1 (1961): 1–17.

Scott, Daryl Michael. *Contempt and Pity: Social Policy and the Image of the Damaged Black Psyche, 1880–1996*. Chapel Hill: University of North Carolina Press, 1997.

"Second National Conference on Intergroup Relations." *Journal of Negro Education* 18, no. 2 (1949): 186–91.

Selective Service System. *Special Monograph No. 10: Special Groups.* Washington, DC: Government Printing Office, 1953.

Sheldon, Kennon M., and Bruce J. Biddle. "Standards, Accountability, and School Reform: Perils and Pitfalls." *Teachers College Record* 100, no. 1 (1998): 164–80.

Sizer, Theodore R. "The Case for a Free Market." *Saturday Review*, January 11, 1969, 34–93.

Sizer, Theodore R., and Phillip Whitten. "A Proposal for a Poor Children's Bill of Rights." *Pyschology Today*, August 1968, 59–63.

Smith, Alfred Edgar. "Educational Programs for the Improvement of Race Relations: Government Agencies." *Journal of Negro Education* 13, no. 3 (1944): 361–66.

Smith, Darrell, Hector Amezcua, and Michael McGough. "Sac High Boss Resigns, Blasts St. Hope Leaders for 'History of Neglect.'" *Sacramento Bee*, September 12, 2018.

Smith, Mary Lee, Linda Miller-Kahn, Walter Heinecke, and Patricia F. Jarvis. *Political Spectacle and the Fate of American Schools: Symbolic Politics and Educational Policies.* New York: RoutledgeFalmer, 2004.

Smith, Preston H. "The Quest for Racial Democracy: Black Civic Ideology and Housing Interests in Postwar Chicago." *Journal of Urban History* 26, no. 2 (2000): 131–57.

——. *Racial Democracy and the Black Metropolis: Housing Policy in Postwar Chicago.* Minneapolis: University of Minnesota Press, 2012.

Smith, Rogers M. "Ideas and the Spiral of Politics: The Place of American Political Thought in American Political Development." *American Political Thought* 3, no. 1 (2014): 126–36.

——. *Political Peoplehood: The Roles of Values, Interests, and Identities.* Chicago: University of Chicago Press, 2015.

——. "Which Comes First, the Ideas or the Institutions?" In *Rethinking Political Institutions: The Art of the State*, edited by Ian Shapiro, Stephen Skowronek, and Daniel Galvin, 91–113. New York: New York University Press, 2006.

Smuts, Robert W. "The Negro Community and the Development of Negro Potential." *Journal of Negro Education* 26, no. 4 (1957): 456–65.

Snedden, David. "Seeking Realistic Objectives." *California Journal of Secondary Education* 25 (January 1950): 455–59.

Snowden, Frank M. "The Italian Press Views America's Attitude Toward Civil Rights and the Negro." *Journal of Negro Education* 21, no. 1 (1952): 20–26.

Social Frontier 1, no. 5 (1935).

Soss, Joe, Richard C. Fording, and Sanford Schram. *Disciplining the Poor: Neoliberal Paternalism and the Persistent Power of Race.* Chicago: University of Chicago Press, 2011.

Sparks, Sarah D. "What Role Will Research Play in ESSA?" *Education Week*, December 4, 2015. https://www.edweek.org/teaching-learning/what-role-will-research-play-in-essa /2015/12.

Spence, Lester K. *Knocking the Hustle: Against the Neoliberal Turn in Black Politics.* Brooklyn, NY: Punctum Books, 2016.

——. "The Neoliberal Turn in Black Politics." *Souls* 14, no. 3–4 (2012): 139–59.

Spring, Joel. *The Sorting Machine: National Educational Policy Since 1945.* New York: McKay, 1976.

"Squabble over Accused Red's Appearance Grows Hot." *Pittsburg Press*, March 13, 1952.

Stamm, Dan. "23 Philly Schools Slated to Close." NBC 10 Philadelphia, March 7, 2013.

Steffes, Tracy L. *School, Society, and State: A New Education to Govern Modern America, 1890–1940*. Chicago: University of Chicago Press, 2012.

Stein, Judith. *Pivotal Decade: How the United States Traded Factories for Finance in the Seventies*. New Haven, CT: Yale University Press, 2010.

Stein, Perry. "'It's Absolutely Terrible': When a Charter School Closes, What Happens to the Kids?" *Washington Post*, February 1, 2019.

———. "'I've Been a Hostage for Nine Years': Fired Teacher Wins Battle with D.C. Schools." *Washington Post*, July 22, 2018.

Stokes, Anson Phelps. "American Race Relations in War Time." *Journal of Negro Education* 14, no. 4 (1945): 535–51.

Storrs, Landon R. Y. *The Second Red Scare and the Unmaking of the New Deal Left*. Princeton, NJ: Princeton University Press, 2012.

Stovall, David. "Schools Suck, But They're Supposed To: Schooling, Incarceration and the Future of Education." *Journal of Curriculum and Pedagogy* 13, no. 1 (2016): 20–22.

Strauss, Valerie. "Everything You Need to Know about Common Core—Ravitch." *Washington Post*, June 18, 2014.

———. "NAACP Ratifies Controversial Resolution for a Moratorium on Charter Schools." *Washington Post*, October 15, 2016.

———. "What Michelle Rhee Has Been Up To." *Washington Post*, June 7, 2011.

Sugrue, Thomas J. "Reassessing the History of Postwar America." *Prospects* 20 (October 1995): 493–509.

Superfine, Benjamin Michael. *Equality in Educational Law and Policy, 1954–2010*. New York: Cambridge University Press, 2013.

Task Force on Economic Growth and Opportunity. *The Disadvantaged Poor: Education and Employment*. Washington, DC: Chamber of Commerce of the United States, 1966.

Taylor, Clarence. *Reds at the Blackboard: Communism, Civil Rights, and the New York City Teachers Union*. New York: Columbia University Press, 2013.

Taylor, Frederick Winslow. *The Principles of Scientific Management*. New York: Harper & Brothers, 1919.

"Teacher's Union Holds Convention." *Reading Eagle*, December 27, 1938.

Teodori, Massimo. *The New Left: A Documentary History*. Indianapolis: Bobbs-Merrill, 1969.

Thomas, Norman. "The Socialist's Way Out for the Negro." *Journal of Negro Education* 5, no. 1 (January 1936): 100–104.

Thompson, Chas. H. "The Basis of Negro Morale in World War II." *Journal of Negro Education* 11, no. 4 (October 1942): 454–64.

———. "Editorial Comment: FEPC Hearings Reduce Race Problem to Lowest Terms—Equal Economic Opportunity." *Journal of Negro Education* 12, no. 4 (1943): 585–88.

———. "Editorial Comment: How Imminent Is the Outlawing of Segregation." *Journal of Negro Education* 20, no. 4 (1951): 495–98.

Thompson, Daniel C. "Evaluation as a Factor in Planning Programs for the Culturally Disadvantaged." *Journal of Negro Education* 33, no. 3 (1964): 333–40.

Thorndike, Edward L. "The Distribution of Education." *School Review* 40, no. 5 (May 1932): 335–45.

———. "The Goal of the Social Effort." *Educational Record* 17, no. 2 (April 1, 1936): 153–68.

———. "The Influence of Disparity of Incomes on Welfare." *American Journal of Sociology* 44, no. 1 (1938): 25–35.

———. "Intelligence and Its Uses." *Harper's Magazine* 140 (1920): 227–35.

———. "Racial Inequalities." *Educational Forum* 10, no. 2 (January 1946): 133–37.

———. "Scales and Tests Supersede Old-Fashioned School Marks." *Journal of Education* 94, no. 15 (October 27, 1921): 395–97.

Thorndike, Edward L., and S. A. Courtis. "The Nature, Purposes, and General Methods of Measurement of Educational Products." In *Seventeenth Yearbook of the National Society for the Study of Education* 2, 2:16–24. Bloomington, 1918.

Tomlinson, Stephen. "Edward Lee Thorndike and John Dewey on the Science of Education." *Oxford Review of Education* 23, no. 3 (1997): 365–83.

Todd-Breland, Elizabeth. *A Political Education: Black Politics and Education Reform in Chicago since the 1960s.* Chapel Hill: University of North Carolina Press, 2018.

Townsend, Willard S. "Full Employment and the Negro Worker." *Journal of Negro Education* 14, no. 1 (1945): 6–10.

Truman, Harry S. Executive Order 9835: Prescribing Procedures for the Administration of an Employees Loyalty Program in the Executive Branch of the Government. President's Temporary Commission on Employee Loyalty, 1947.

———. Executive Order 9980: Regulations Governing Fair Employment Practices Within the Federal Establishment, 1948.

———. Executive Order 9981: Establishing the President's Committee on Equality of Treatment and Opportunity in the Armed Services. *Federal Register* 13 (1948): 4313.

———. "Special Message to the Congress on Civil Rights." American Presidency Project, 2, (1948).

Trump, Donald J. "Remarks at a Roundtable Discussion on Empowering Families with Education Choice and an Exchange with Reporters." December 9, 2019. https://www.presidency.ucsb.edu/node/335090.

———. "Remarks on Signing an Executive Order on Safe Policing for Safe Communities." June 16, 2020. https://www.presidency.ucsb.edu/node/342038.

Turque, Bill. "Foundations Reserve the Right to Pull Funding If D.C. School Chief Rhee Leaves." *Washington Post*, April 28, 2010.

Tyack, David B. *The One Best System: A History of American Urban Education.* Cambridge, MA: Harvard University Press, 1974.

Tyack, David, and Larry Cuban. *Tinkering Toward Utopia: A Century of Public School Reform.* Cambridge, MA: Harvard University Press, 1995.

United Press. "Books Criticized by Legionnaires Reported Stolen: Prof. Rugg's History Texts Missing at Sunbury." *Pittsburg Press*, January 2, 1941.

U.S. Department of Education. "States Open to Charters Start Fast in 'Race to Top.'" June 8, 2009.

———. "The U.S. Department of Education's Charter Schools Program Overview 2019." July 2019. https://oese.ed.gov/files/2019/12/CSP-Data-Overview-WestEd-7.22.2019.pdf.

U.S. Department of Justice. "Abe Fortas, Special Inquiry," November 9, 1964. File WFO 161–2419, Abe Fortas part 02 of 03. Federal Bureau of Investigation, https://vault.fbi.gov/.

U.S. House of Representatives. *Departments of Labor, and Health, Education, and Welfare and Related Agencies Appropriations Bills 1966.* 89th Cong., 1st sess., 1965 H. Rep. 272. Washington, DC: Government Printing Office, 1965.

———. *Special Report on Subversive Activities Aimed at Destroying our Representative Form of Government, Report No. 2277.* 77th Cong. 2nd sess., 1942. Washington, DC: Government Printing Office, 1942.

U.S. House of Representatives Committee on Education. *Hearings on Federal Aid to the States for the Support of Public Schools.* 75th Cong., 1st sess., 1937. Washington, DC: Government Printing Office, 1937.

U.S. House of Representatives Committee on Education and Labor. *Elementary and Secondary Education Amendments of 1969, Conference Report to Accompany H.R. 514.* 91st Cong., 2nd sess., 1970. Washington, DC: Government Printing Office, 1970.

———. *House Document 45: Message from the President of the United States Transmitting Educational Program.* 89th Cong., 1st sess., 1965. Washington, DC: Government Printing Office, 1965.

U.S. House of Representatives Committee on Labor. *Proposed Amendments to the National Labor Relations Act.* 76th Cong., 2nd sess., 1948. Washington, DC: Government Printing Office, 1948.

U.S. House of Representatives Committee on Un-American Activities. *Investigation of Communist Activities in Philadelphia Area: Hearing before the Committee on Un-American Activities. Part 4.* 83rd Cong., 2nd sess., 1954. Washington, DC: Government Printing Office, 1954.

———. *Investigation of Un-American Propaganda Activities in the United States.* 80th Cong. 1st sess., 1947. Washington, DC: Government Printing Office, 1947.

U.S. House of Representatives Committee to Investigate Campaign Expenditures. *Hearings on Campaign Expenditures. Part 3: Union for Democratic Action; James Loeb Jr., Executive Secretary, Witness.* 78th Cong. 2nd sess., 1944. Washington, DC: Government Printing Office, 1944.

U.S. House of Representatives General Subcommittee on Education. *Hearings on Bills to Strengthen and Improve Educational Quality and Educational Opportunity in the Nation's Elementary and Secondary Schools. Part 2.* 89th Cong., 1st sess., 1965. Washington, DC: Government Printing Office, 1965.

U.S. House of Representatives General Subcommittee on Education of the Committee on Education and Labor. *Hearings on the Elementary and Secondary Education Amendments of 1973.* 93rd Cong., 1st sess., 1973. Washington, DC: Government Printing Office, 1973.

U.S. House of Representatives Special Committee on Un-American Activities. *Investigation of Un-American Propaganda Activities in the United States.* 78th Cong. 2nd sess., 1944. Washington, DC: Government Printing Office, 1944.

———. *Investigation of Un-American Propaganda Activities in U.S.* Volume 10. 76th Cong. 1st sess., 1939. Washington, DC: Government Printing Office, 1939.

U.S. House of Representatives Special Select Subcommittee on District of Columbia of the Committee on the District of Columbia. *Problems in D.C. Public Schools.* 91st Cong., 2nd sess., 1970. Washington, DC: Government Printing Office, 1970.

U.S. House of Representatives Special Subcommittee of the Committee on Appropriation. *Hearings on the Fitness for Continuance in Federal Employment of Goodwin B. Watson,*

William E. Dodd, Jr., Employees of the Federal Communications Commission, and Robert Morss Lovett, and Employee of the Department of the Interior. 78th Cong. 1st sess., 1943. Washington, DC: Government Printing Office, 1943.

U.S. House of Representatives Special Subcommittee of the Committee on Education and Labor. *Hearings on Public School Assistance Act of 1949.* 81st Cong., 1st sess., 1949. Washington, DC: Government Printing Office, 1949.

U.S. National Commission on Excellence in Education. *A Nation at Risk: The Imperative for Educational Reform: A Report to the Nation and the Secretary of Education, United States Department of Education.* National Commission on Excellence in Education, 1983.

U.S. Office of Education, Division of Secondary Education. *Life Adjustment Education for Every Youth.* Washington, DC: Office of Education, Federal Security Agency, 1948.

U.S. President's Commission on Higher Education. *Higher Education for American Democracy: A Report of the President's Commission on Higher Education.* Washington, DC: U.S. Government Printing Office, 1947.

U.S. President's Committee on Civil Rights. *To Secure These Rights. The Report of the President's Committee on Civil Rights.* U.S. Government Printing Office, 1947.

U.S. Senate Committee on Education and Labor. *Federal Aid for Education: Hearings Before the Committee on Education and Labor.* 79th Cong., 1st sess., 1945. Washington, DC: Government Printing Office, 1945.

U.S. Senate Committee on Labor and Public Welfare. *Elementary and Secondary Education Amendments of 1969, Report of the Committee on Labor and Public Welfare, United States Senate, on H.R. 514, To Extend Programs of Assistance for Elementary and Secondary Education, and for Other Purposes.* 91st Cong., 2nd sess., 1970. Washington, DC: Government Printing Office, 1970.

———. *Report on Elementary and Secondary Education Act of 1965.* 89th Cong., 1st sess., 1965. Washington, DC: United States Senate, April 6, 1965.

U.S. Senate Committee on Military Affairs. *Lowering the Draft Age to 18 Years.* 77th Cong., 2nd sess., 1942. Washington, DC: Government Printing Office, 1942.

U.S. Senate Committee on the Judiciary. *Hearing on the Confirmation of the Nomination of Honorable William Henry Hastie of the Virgin Islands to be Judge of the United States Court of Appeals of the Third Circuit.* 81st Cong., 2nd sess., 1950. Washington, DC: Government Printing Office, 1950.

———. *Hearing on the Nomination of George M. Johnson, of California, to be a Member of the Commission on Civil Rights.* 86th Cong., 1st sess., 1959. Washington, DC: Government Printing Office, 1959.

U.S. Senate Permanent Subcommittee on Investigations of the Committee on Government Operations. *Hearings on Communist Infiltration Among Army Civilian Workers.* 83rd Cong., 1st sess., 1953. Washington, DC: Government Printing Office, 1953.

U.S. Senate Subcommittee of the Committee on Education and Labor. *Hearing on American Youth Act.* 75th Cong., 2nd sess., 1938. Washington, DC: Government Printing Office, 1938.

———. *Hearing on Federal Aid to Education Act of 1939.* 76th Cong., 1st sess., 1939. Washington, DC: Government Printing Office, 1939.

U.S. Senate Subcommittee of the Committee on the Judiciary. *Hearing on the Nomination of Thurgood Marshall.* 87th Cong., 2nd sess., 1962. Washington, DC: Government Printing Office, 1962.

U.S. Senate Subcommittee on Education. *Hearings on Bills to Improve Educational Quality and Opportunity*. 88th Cong., 1st. sess., 1963. Washington DC: Government Printing Office, 1963.

U.S. Senate Subcommittee on Education of the Committee on Labor and Public Welfare. *First Session on S. 2218 to Amend the Elementary and Secondary Youth Act of 1965 and Related Acts, and for Other Purposes*. 91st Cong., 1st sess., 1969. Washington, DC: Government Printing Office, 1969.

———. *Hearings on a Bill to Strengthen and Improve Educational Quality and Educational Opportunities in the Nation's Elementary and Secondary Schools*. 89th Cong., 1st. sess., 1965. Washington DC: Government Printing Office, 1965.

U.S. Senate Subcommittee on Employment and Manpower of the Committee on Labor and Public Welfare. *Hearing Relating to the Training and Utilization of the Manpower Resources of the Nation*. 88th Cong., 1st sess., 1963. Washington, DC: Government Printing Office, 1963.

U.S. Senate Subcommittee on Intergovernmental Relations of the Committee on Governmental Affairs. *Hearing on State and Local Innovations in Education Choice*. 99th Cong., 1st sess., 1985. Washington, DC: Government Printing Office, 1985.

U.S. Senate Subcommittee to Investigate the Administration of the Internal Security Act and Other Internal Security Laws. *Subversive Influence in the Educational Process: Hearings Before the Subcommittee to Investigate the Administration of the Internal Security Act and Other Internal Security Laws of the Committee on the Judiciary*. 82nd Cong., 2nd sess., 1952. Washington, DC: Government Printing Office, 1952.

———. *Subversive Influence in the Educational Process: Hearings Before the Subcommittee to Investigate the Administration of the Internal Security Act and Other Internal Security Laws of the Committee on the Judiciary*. 83rd Cong., 1st sess., 1953. Washington, D.C.: Government Printing Office, 1953.

U.S. Senate Temporary National Economic Committee. *Investigation of Concentration of Economic Power. Part 30: Technology and Concentration of Economic Power*. 76th Cong., 3rd sess., 1940. Washington, DC: United States Senate, 1940.

Uetricht, Micah. *Strike for America: Chicago Teachers Against Austerity*. Brooklyn, NY: Verso, 2014.

Urban, Wayne J., and Jennings L. Wagoner. *American Education: A History*, 4th ed. New York: Routledge, 2008.

"USOE Orders States to Repay Title I Funds Improperly Spent." *Phi Delta Kappan* 53 (November 1971): 199.

Varel, David A. *The Scholar and the Struggle: Lawrence Reddick's Crusade for Black History and Black Power*. Chapel Hill: University of North Carolina Press, 2020.

Vickery, William E., and Steward G. Cole. *Intercultural Education in American Schools, Proposed Objectives and Methods*. New York: Harper & Brothers Publishers, 1943.

Wacquant, Loïc. *Punishing the Poor: The Neoliberal Government of Social Insecurity*. Durham, NC: Duke University Press, 2009.

Wall, Wendy. *Inventing the "American Way": The Politics of Consensus from the New Deal to the Civil Rights Movement*. New York: Oxford University Press, 2008.

Wallace, Henry A. "The Scientist in an Unscientific Society." *Scientific American* 150, no. 6 (August 1934): 285–87.

Walker, Vanessa Siddle. *The Lost Education of Horace Tate: Uncovering the Hidden Heroes Who Fought for Justice in Schools*. New York: New Press, 2018.

Washington, Booker T. "Atlanta Exposition Address, September 18, 1895." *Booker T. Washington Papers* (1895): 584–87.

———. "My View of Segregation Laws." *New Republic*, December 4, 1915.

———. "The Rights and Duties of the Negro." National Afro-American Council. July 2, 1903. https://openlibrary.org.

Ware, Caroline F. "The Role of the Schools in Education for Racial Understanding." *Journal of Negro Education* 13, no. 3 (1944): 421–31.

Watkins, William H. "The New Social Order: An Educator Looks at Economics, Politics, and Race." In *The Assault on Public Education: Confronting the Politics of Corporate School Reform*, 7–32. New York: Teachers College Press, 2012.

Weaver, George L-P. "The Role of Organized Labor in Education for Racial Understanding." *Journal of Negro Education* 13, no. 3 (1944): 414–20.

Weaver, Timothy Paul Ryan. *Blazing the Neoliberal Trail: Urban Political Development in the United States and the United Kingdom*. Philadelphia: University of Pennsylvania Press, 2016.

Webber, Jim. "'The Magic of Philanthropy': The Gates Foundation's Reframing of Education Reform Debate." *Rhetoric and Public Affairs* 23, no. 2 (2020): 293–330.

Weber, George. *Inner-City Children Can Be Taught to Read: Four Successful Schools*. CBE Occasional Papers, Number 18. Washington, DC: Council for Basic Education, 1971.

Weiner, Lois. *The Future of Our Schools: Teachers Unions and Social Justice*. Chicago: Haymarket Books, 2012.

Weir, Margaret. *Politics and Jobs: The Boundaries of Employment Policy in the United States*. Princeton, NJ: Princeton University Press, 1992.

Wesley, Charles H. "Education for Citizenship in a Democracy." *Journal of Negro Education* 10, no. 1 (January 1941): 68–78.

White, Walter. "Memorandum from Mr. White to Mr. Wilkins," November 23, 1951, Group II, Series A, General Office File, United Nations, Papers of the NAACP, Part 14: Race Relations in the International Arena, 1940–1955, http://congressional.proquest.com/histvault?q=001439-016-0001.

———. "Statement by Walter White Made Upon Request of the U.S. State Department," November 20, 1951, Group II, Series A, General Office File, United Nations, Papers of the NAACP, Part 14: Race Relations in the International Arena, 1940–1955, http://congressional.proquest.com/histvault?q=001439-016-0001.

———. "Time for a Progress Report." *Saturday Review of Literature*, September 22, 1951.

Whitehorne, Ron. "Social Justice Slate Sweeps to Victory in the Chicago Teachers Union." *Chalkbeat Philadelphia*, June 14, 2010. https://philadelphia.chalkbeat.org/2010/6/14/22182153/social-justice-slate-sweeps-to-victory-in-the-chicago-teachers-union.

Wilkerson, Doxey A. "Russia's Proposed New World Order of Socialism." *Journal of Negro Education* 10, no. 3 (July 1941): 387–419.

———. *Special Problems of Negro Education*. Washington, DC: U.S. Government Printing Office, 1939.

———. "The Vocational Education and Guidance of Negroes." *Journal of Negro Education* 7, no. 1 (January 1938): 104–8.

———. "The Vocational Education and Guidance of Negroes: A Measure of the Economic Value of Vocational Education." *Journal of Negro Education* 8, no. 1 (January 1939): 118–20.

———. "The Vocational Education and Guidance of Negroes: The Negro and the Battle of Production." *Journal of Negro Education* 11, no. 2 (April 1942): 228–39.

———. "The Vocational Education, Guidance and Placement of Negroes in the United States." *Journal of Negro Education* 8, no. 3 (July 1939): 462–88.

Wilkins, Roy. "Memorandum to Mr. White from Mr. Wilkins," November 21, 1951, Group II, Series A, General Office File, United Nations, Papers of the NAACP, Part 14: Race Relations in the International Arena, 1940–1955, http://congressional.proquest.com /histvault?q=001439-016-0001.

———. "Next Steps in Education for Racial Understanding." *Journal of Negro Education* 13, no. 3 (1944): 432–40.

Williams, Heather Andrea. *Self-Taught: African American Education in Slavery and Freedom.* Chapel Hill: University of North Carolina Press, 2009.

Williams, Juan. "At the Center of the School Strike." *Washington Post*, March 12, 1979.

Williams, Lorraine A. "The Interracial Conference of the National Council of Negro Women." *Journal of Negro Education* 26, no. 2 (1957): 204–6.

Winfield, Ann G. "Resuscitating Bad Science: Eugenics Past and Present." In *The Assault on Public Education: Confronting the Politics of Corporate School Reform*, edited by William H. Watkins, 143–59. New York: Teachers College Press, 2012.

Winslow, Samantha. "Activist Coalition Wins Control of L.A. Teachers Union." *In These Times*, March 25, 2014. https://inthesetimes.com/article/activist-coalition-wins-control -of-l-a-teachers-union.

———. "L.A. Teachers Run on a Bigger Vision." *Labor Notes*, June 26, 2015. https:// labornotes.org/2014/01/la-teachers-run-bigger-vision.

Woodson, Carter Godwin. *The Education of the Negro Prior to 1861: A History of the Education of the Colored People of the United States from the Beginning of Slavery to the Civil War.* Washington, DC: Associated Publishers, 1919.

Wortman, Paul M., Charles S. Reichardt, and Robert G. St. Pierre. "The First Year of the Education Voucher Demonstration." *Evaluation Quarterly* 2, no. 2 (1978): 193–214.

Wright, Guy. "Once Pro-Russian But Not Now, Speaker at Pitt and Tech Claims." *Pittsburg Press*, March 14, 1952.

Wright, Marion T. "Educational Programs for the Improvement of Race Relations: Negro Advancement Organizations." *Journal of Negro Education* 13, no. 3 (1944): 349–60.

———. "Some Educational and Cultural Problems and Needs of Negro Children and Youth." *Journal of Negro Education* 19, no. 3 (1950): 310–21.

Wright, Richard. *The God That Failed.* Reprinted. Salem: AYER Company, 1984.

Yee, Vivian. "Grouping Students by Ability Regains Favor With Educators." *New York Times*, June 9, 2013.

Yerkes, Robert M. "News Items and Communications." *Journal of Educational Research* 1, no. 4 (April 1920): 321–24.

Yoakum, Clarence Stone, and Robert Mearns Yerkes. *Army Mental Tests.* New York: Holt, 1920.

Zeligs, Rose. "Children Explain Their Intergroup Attitudes." *Journal of Negro Education* 22, no. 4 (1953): 534–48.

———. "Growth in Intergroup Attitudes During Brotherhood Week." *Journal of Negro Education* 19, no. 1 (1950): 94–102.

Zimring, Fred, Barrows Dunham, and John Dewey. "Notes and Documents: Cold War Compromises: Albert Barnes, John Dewey, and the Federal Bureau of Investigation." *Pennsylvania Magazine of History and Biography* 108, no. 1 (January 1984): 87–100.

Index

Hunt, James, 194
Hurricane Katrina, 215n7, 215n9

IDEA, 207
illiteracy in U.S. military, 81–82
imperialism, 38, 96, 98, 243n9, 244n32;
    anti-, 101, 116, 174, 242n6
Improving America's Schools Act, 270n3
incorporationism, 3, 171
individualism, individuals, 12, 20, 23, 31, 36,
    42, 60, 148, 156, 206; criticisms of, 38, 53;
    full employment and, 143, 144; liberal
    incorporationist education order and, 4,
    19, 91, 137; responsibility of, 13, 150; social
    reconstructionists on, 9, 35, 39
industrial democracy, 229n25, 229n32
industrialization, 5, 22, 23, 221n10
inequality, 3, 5, 20, 33, 38, 53, 228n14; human
    capital theory and, 145–49
inflation, 12, 141, 143
integration, 3, 11, 52, 66, 68, 173; disagree-
    ment of Black people on, 51–52, 174
intelligence, 30–32, 34, 224n58; differentia-
    tion by, 25, 43
intelligence testing, tests, 22, 79, 85,
    239n204, 271n23; scientific efficiency
    progressives and, 10, 43; World War I
    and, 27–28; World War II and, 82, 131,
    238n198, 240n215
intercultural education, 231n67, 232n81,
    232n83, 232n85
International Labor Defense, 113
international relations, 91–95
Interracial Conference, 127
interracial education, 61, 232n83, 232n86,
    233–34n106, 234n131; racial democrats
    and, 64–70
Iowa Tests of Educational Development,
    241n232
IQ, 56, 79
isolationism, 93, 242n6
Italy, 93, 243n11

J4J (Journey for Justice), 211
Jeffrey, Julie Roy, 262n38, 262n40

Jencks, Christopher, 187–89, 195, 267n166
Jenkins, Martin, 66–67, 82, 93, 244n20
Jennings, John F., 168
Jim Crow, 11, 60, 94, 99, 101, 117–21, 228n14,
    243n18; material consequences of,
    126–28
Jindall, Bobby, 2, 215n7
JNE (Journal of Negro Education), 8, 51, 57,
    60, 63, 65, 72, 83, 97, 106, 124, 232n79,
    253n185; Black personality in, 74–75;
    contributors to, 54, 85, 87, 121, 126,
    241n229, 244–45n32; economic
    democracy and, 55, 88–89, 228n13; editor
    of, 82, 243n15; interracial education in,
    65–68, 70; racial democracy in, 58–59,
    127; testing in, 79–80; Wilkerson
    publishes in, 112, 116, 242n6, 243n9
JNH (Journal of Negro History), 51
Johnson, Cedric, 175
Johnson, Charles, 63, 72, 78, 116, 122, 231n75,
    232n76, 235n136; Bureau for Intercultural
    Education and, 66, 99
Johnson, George, 114, 121
Johnson, Lyndon B., 12, 114, 136, 145, 149,
    167, 213, 219n49, 257n51; CEA and, 142,
    155; Clark and, 153, 154; education and,
    135, 156, 161; ESEA and, 13, 144, 273n78;
    speeches and addresses by, 143, 152.
    See also Great Society; War on Poverty
Journal of Educational Method, 38
Journal of Negro Education. See JNE
Journal of Negro History. See JNH
Journal of Political Economy, "Investment in
    Human Beings" issue of, 147
Journey for Justice. See J4J
Judd, Charles H., 22, 26, 44, 226n123,
    227n124
juvenile delinquency, 150–51, 156, 258n73

K–12 schools, 3, 157, 161, 197
Kantor, Harvey, 139–40, 157
Kazin, Michael, 95
Kelly, Fred J., 39
Kennedy, John F., 12, 145, 149–50; CEA
    and, 142–43, 155

U.S. Hispanic Chamber of Commerce, 196

U.S. House of Representatives, 33, 135, 140, 147–48, 168, 257n53, 270n3

U.S. Navy, 82

USOE (U.S. Office of Education), 139, 163–64, 168–70, 181–82, 261n21

U.S. OEO (Office of Economic Opportunity), 182–85, 189, 190, 207, 266n135

U.S. Office of Education. *See* USOE

U.S. Secretary of Agriculture, 224n66, 243n11

U.S. Secretary of Education, 215n7, 272n43

U.S. Secretary of Health, Education, and Welfare, 135

U.S. Secretary of Housing and Urban Development, 122

U.S. Secretary of Labor, 219n49

U.S. Secretary of State, 244n25

U.S. Secretary of the Interior, 243n11

U.S. Senate, 33, 114, 135, 140, 143, 163, 270n3; committees of, 113, 147, 164, 169

U.S. State Department, 99, 245n47, 246n49

U.S. Supreme Court, 91, 114, 121, 129, 252n154; *Brown v. Board of Education* (1954) and, 11, 49, 124–28, 152, 176; changing doctrines of, 117–28, 198; NAACP and, 119–28, 128

Venn, Grant, 144

Vickery, William, 68, 69

Vietnam War, 264n87

Virginia State University, 112

vocational education, 10, 23, 30, 43, 78

voting rights, 97, 99

vouchers and voucher programs, 2, 14, 160, 171, 186–91, 212, 268n198; Reagan and, 191–94

Wagner, Robert, 118

Wagner Act, 111

Wall, Wendy, 104

Wallace, Henry, 97, 224n66, 243n11, 245n39

Walton Foundation, 1, 212

Ware, Caroline, 70–71, 234n131

War on Poverty, 143, 151, 156, 161, 217n37, 218n38

Warren, Earl, 253n191

Washington, Booker T., 51, 228n14

Washington, D.C., 204, 215n15, 219n49; Board of Education of, 177, 178; education reform in, 1, 2, 212; public school system of, 60, 177–81, 215n9

Washington Committee for Democratic Action, 114

Washington Research Project, 167

Washington Teachers' Union. *See* WTU

Watson, Goodwin, 42

Weaver, George L. P., 55

Weaver, Robert, 122

Weaver, R. P., 99

We Charge Genocide petition, 98, 100, 246n52

Weir, Margaret, 217n37, 221n9, 256n12

West Virginia, 211

White, Walter, 98, 99, 245n46, 246n53; NAACP and, 100, 245n47

white supremacy, 67–68, 94

Whittington, Will, 141

Wieler, Daniel, 191

Wilkerson, Doxey, 9, 11, 92, 242n6, 251n144; in AFT, 93, 106; persecution of, 103, 112–16

Wilkins, Roy, 67–68, 96, 100, 233n104, 245n46

Winfield, Ann, 6

Wirt, William, 105

Workers Party, 52

working class, workers, 12, 54, 57, 92, 117; educated, 19, 49, 220n5; interracial coalition of, 101, 116; solidarity of, 4, 55

Works Progress Administration. *See* WPA

World Book Company, 28

World War I, 223n37; intelligence testing and, 27–28; psychologists in, 27, 29

www.ingramcontent.com/pod-product-compliance
Lightning Source LLC
Chambersburg PA
CBHW021120270326
41929CB00009B/977